PRINCIPLES OF CATHOLIC THEOLOGY

JOSEPH CARDINAL RATZINGER

PRINCIPLES OF CATHOLIC THEOLOGY

Building Stones for a Fundamental Theology

Translated by
Sister Mary Frances McCarthy, S.N.D.

IGNATIUS PRESS   SAN FRANCISCO

Title of German original:
Theologische Prinzipienlehre
© 1982 Erich Wewel Verlag, Munich

Cover by Victoria Hoke Lane

© 1987 Ignatius Press, San Francisco
Second printing 1989
All rights reserved
ISBN 0–89870–133–3
Library of Congress catalogue number 86–83133
Printed in the United States of America

CONTENTS

Preface   9

PART ONE

FORMAL PRINCIPLES OF CHRISTIANITY—
CATHOLIC VIEW

1. On the Relationship of Structure and Content in Christian Faith

   Section 1: The We-Structure of Faith as Key to its Content

   A. What Constitutes Christian Faith Today?   15
   B. Baptism, Faith and Membership in the Church—
       the Unity of Structure and Content   27
   C. The Church as the Sacrament of Salvation   44

   Section 2: Structure, Content, Attitudes

   A. Faith as Conversion—Metanoia   55
   B. Faith as Knowledge and as Praxis—the
       Fundamental Option of the Christian Credo   67
   C. Faith as Trust and Joy—Evangelium   75

2. Formal Principles of Catholicism

   Section 1: Scripture and Tradition

   A. Anthropological Foundation of the Concept of
       Tradition   85
   B. Baptism and the Formulation of the Content of
       Faith—Liturgy and the Development of Tradition   101
   C. The Creeds of Nicaea and Constantinople: History,
       Structure, Content   112
   D. Short Formulas of Faith? On the Relationship
       between Formula and Interpretation   122
   E. Importance of the Fathers for the Structure of Faith   133

   Section 2: Faith and History

   A. Salvation and History   153
   B. Salvation History, Metaphysics and Eschatology   171

PART TWO

FORMAL PRINCIPLES OF CHRISTIANITY IN ECUMENICAL DISPUTE

1. General Orientation with Regard to the Ecumenical Dispute about the Formal Principles of Faith

    A. The Ecumenical Situation—Orthodoxy, Catholicism and Protestantism   193

    B. Rome and the Churches of the East after the Removal of the Ban of Excommunication of 1054   203

    C. Elucidations of the Question of a "Recognition" of the *Confessio Augustana* by the Catholic Church   218

    D. Ecumenism at a Standstill? Explanatory Comments on *Mysterium Ecclesiae*   228

2. The Key Question in the Catholic-Protestant Dispute: Tradition and *Successio Apostolica*

    A. Holy Orders (Ordo) as the Sacramental Expression of the Principle of Tradition   239

    B. Sacrifice, Sacrament and Priesthood in the Development of the Church   250

    C. The Priest as Mediator and Minister of Christ in the Light of the Message of the New Testament   267

3. Catholicity as the Formal Structure of Christianity

    A. The Community's Right to the Eucharist? The "Community" and the Catholicity of the Church   285

    B. Local Ecumenism   299

PART THREE

THE FORMAL PRINCIPLES OF CHRISTIANITY AND THE METHOD OF THEOLOGY

1. Questions about the Structure of Theology

    A. What Is Theology?   315

    B. The Church and Scientific Theology   322

2. The Anthropological Element in Theology

A. Faith and Education   333
B. Faith and Experience   343
C. The Gift of Wisdom   355

EPILOGUE

ON THE STATUS OF CHURCH
AND THEOLOGY TODAY

A. Review of the Postconciliar Era—Failures,
     Tasks, Hopes   367
B. Church and World: An Inquiry into the Reception
     of Vatican Council II   378

Acknowledgments   395

PREFACE

One of the most significant results of Vatican Council II for theology is the now pervasive accommodation of its thought and language to the ecumenical dimension. While it draws primarily on the inner core of Church tradition, theology cannot ultimately ignore the fact that there are other ways of interpreting the Christian inheritance with which it must come to terms. For theology, this means that, despite the ever-increasing multiplicity of its themes, questions about structure, about the principles on which the whole is based, are pressing more and more urgently to the fore.

A frequently recurring problem in the intellectual climate of our age is that of reconciling history with the present—of transforming the events and words of a time now past into the realities and needs of the present. When theology is engaged in the service of ecumenism, the question arises about the relationship between Scripture and tradition; or, when several traditions are involved, about the very nature of tradition itself. Practically speaking, this resolves itself into a question of which interpretation of our biblical heritage is the valid one; of whence, in the face of so many possible interpretations, one is to derive that certainty with which one can live and for which one is willing to suffer and die. In such a case, the certainty of having found the best hypothesis will not suffice: where there is question of life itself, which is not a hypothesis but something unique and unrepeatable, another kind of certainty is needed. The question of whether a court of binding interpretation exists is, in consequence, inseparable from the question about the relationship between Scripture and tradition.

This leads inevitably to a second focal point in an ecumenical discussion of the principles of theology: the objective problem of the relationship between Bible and tradition has a personal aspect in the question of apostolic succession. We are speaking, of course, not of the formal ritual of an unbroken laying-on of hands, but of the problem of personal responsibility for the witness that has been given, of the obligation this witness imposes on the community that stands for the whole as well as of the obligation devolving upon this community as the sacramental expression of the inadequacy of one's own efforts, of the dependence of all faith on prayer and, at the same time, as the embodiment of those signs that guarantee to the Church the unity of her history and the continuing nearness of the revelation that was heard in the beginning. "Apostolic

9

succession", then, is but the personal and sacramental aspect of the problem of tradition, of the interpretation and realization of the gospel that has been given once and for all. In the search for the structure of what is Christian, it thus becomes a question of principles—a question that, not by chance, becomes again and again the hard core and the real test of ecumenical dialogue.

We come here to the third focal point of our inquiry—a point that, in conjunction with the problem of aspostolic succession, has emerged more and more clearly in recent years, that is, the question of whether Catholicity is the structural form of belief. The world of today bears ever more plainly the mark of those anonymous mega-organizations that are inevitably patterned on the megastructures of technology that circumscribe the world in a kind of spectral noosphere that has no relationship to Teilhardian optimism. Man's malaise increases proportionately as his dependence is extended with regard to even the most ordinary things of life—light, water, food, warmth; the mounting cry for anarchy is a reaction against the oppressive feeling of total dependence that is capable of creating, in the very midst of man's bourgeois freedoms, a new kind of total unfreedom. In this context, there is increasingly evident among Christians the temptation to understand the megachurches also as superorganizations that cannot be done away with, although they are more conducive to malaise than to salvation. But because man's very belief in the malaise of the "world" leads him to hope for a counterworld in which salvation will be revealed, there is today a more and more universal flight to "community". Only in community does what is genuinely Christian— a world of nearness and humanity—seem able to exist. But if this is the case, the community must be sufficient unto itself in both word and sacrament; the megachurch, as carrier-organization, must provide all that is needed for the achieving of her own ends. But such a community is not ipso facto a Christian one. For the concept of apostolic succession as the essence of the principle of Catholicity (and apostolicity) is thereby rendered meaningless, and the problem of correct interpretation is transferred from the Church as a whole to the individual community. Yet further: Does community thus become a guarantee that extends even beyond death? And if not, can it really be a guarantee for *this* life? It becomes clear at this point that the question about Catholicity is not just a corollary of the principle of community, which is seen as the only properly sufficient one, but reaches into the fundamental act of faith itself and must be numbered among the formal principles of Christianity.

When I began, last fall, to review my writings of the past decade, it became apparent that, despite the variety of their subject matter and of the events that occasioned them, they were bound together by and could be classified in terms of the network of problems engendered by our present situation and could thus provide "Building Stones for a Fundamental Theology" to which recourse could be had in the debate about theological principles. Admittedly, they are but building stones, not a finished structure. Since this is so, the title *Principles of Catholic Theology* would indeed be presumptuous were it not for this subtitle, from which it is not to be separated. What a collection of these works can offer is but a tentative sketch, a preliminary draft, of a great theme which it approaches from a variety of angles. I am well aware of the fragmentary and unfinished nature of these efforts; I hope that, despite their insufficiencies, these "building stones" will, nevertheless, be of assistance in the search for an ecumenically oriented fundamental theology, of which we are so much in need.

JOSEPH RATZINGER

Holy Saturday, 1982

PART ONE

FORMAL PRINCIPLES OF CHRISTIANITY—CATHOLIC VIEW

CHAPTER I

ON THE RELATIONSHIP OF STRUCTURE AND CONTENT IN CHRISTIAN FAITH

Section I

The We-Structure of Faith as Key to Its Content

A. What Constitutes Christian Faith Today?

The problem

The question of what constitutes Christian faith *today* was not first raised by the author; it was assigned to him as a question that is always and everywhere being asked.[1] Upon closer reflection one may, nevertheless, conclude that it has not been precisely formulated, for only that can be constitutive that is not just of today. The more precise and accurate formulation would be: With the passing of yesterday, what continues to constitute Christian faith even today? It is not by chance, however, that the question is usually raised in its imprecise form—and for that reason and in just that form it is of considerable heuristic significance. For there is apparent in it a consciousness of the incomparable newness of the present situation, of a change in the world and mankind that cannot be measured by the usual norms of historical change as they have always existed but rather signifies an epochal transformation for which there is no adequate comparison. This fact—that something wholly new is happening to man and to the world in a culture in which scientific and technical self-determination is becoming ever more total—is the reason for the crisis that is occurring in a tradition that has no compunction about explaining itself, if need be, in terms of the scientifically proven behavioral patterns of higher animals but can discover no binding force in human history as such and, in consequence, raises afresh the whole question of validity even with

[1] The remarks that follow were prepared originally as a lecture for the meeting in Schwerte on April 9–10, 1973, of the ecumenical discussion group founded by Cardinal Jaeger and (the Protestant) Bishop Stählin. The topic was assigned beforehand and was treated from the Protestant perspective by Professor E. Schlink of Heidelberg.

respect to tradition-bound institutions like the Catholic Church which seem to be unequivocally characterized by clearly defined norms.[2]

This awareness of change, which is thus the real force behind our question, is in part just a reflection of particular experiences, but it is also in part a product of philosophical movements that have appropriated these experiences and made them the whole structure of reality. The old problem of being and time, which the Eleatic School, and later Plato and Aristotle, solved almost exclusively in favor of being, raises its head anew. The decisive turning point lies with Hegel, since which being and time have been more and more intertwined in philosophical thinking. Being itself is now regarded as time; the logos becomes itself in history. It cannot be assigned, therefore, to any particular point in history or be viewed as something existing in itself outside of history; all its historical objectifications are but movements in the whole of which they are parts. This view gives rise to two opposing positions. On the one hand, the philosophy of the history of ideas seeks to bring about a universal reconciliation: all that has hitherto been thought has meaning as a moment of the whole; it can be understood and classified as a moment in the self-evolution of the logos. In such a view, both the Catholic and the Protestant interpretation of Christianity have meaning, each in its own way; they are true in their historical moment, but they can remain true only by being abandoned when their hour has come and assimilated into the newly developing whole. Truth becomes a function of time; the true is not that which simply *is* true, for truth is not simply that which *is*; it is true for a time because it is part of the becoming of truth, which *is* by becoming. This means that, of their very nature, the contours between true and untrue are less sharply defined; it means above all that man's basic attitude toward reality and toward himself must be altered. In such a view, fidelity to yesterday's truth consists precisely in abandoning it, in assimilating it into today's truth; assimilation becomes the form of preservation. What was constitutive yesterday is constitutive today only as that which has been assimilated. In the realm of Marxist thought, on the other hand, this ideology of reconciliation (as it might be called) is converted into an ideology of revolution; assimilation becomes transformation. The concept of the continuity of being in the changeableness of time is now understood as

---

[2] On the subject of continuity and the break with tradition, see below, Part One, Chapter 2, 1A: "Anthropological Foundation of the Concept of Tradition". For an attempt to derive new norms from the realm of instincts, cf. Konrad Lorenz, "Zivilisationspathologie und Kulturfreiheit", in Ansgar Paus, ed., *Freiheit des Menschen* (Graz: Styria, 1974), 147–85; cf. also the well-known book by Konrad Lorenz, *Die acht Todsünden der zivilisierten Menschheit* (Munich: Piper, 1973).

an ideological superstructure conditioned by the interests of those who are favored by things as they are. It is thus a response that runs counter to the logic of history, which demands progress and forbids lingering in the status quo. The notion of truth comes to be regarded as an expression of the vested interests of a particular historical moment; it gives place to the notion of progress: the "true" is whatever serves progress, that is, whatever serves the logic of history. Vested interest on the one hand and progress on the other lay claim to the legacy of truth; the "true", that is, what is in accord with the logic of history, must be sought at every step of history because anything that is designated as enduring truth is in direct contradiction with the logic of history, is but the static vested interest of a given moment.[3]

Although these two viewpoints seldom manifest themselves in the schematic purity with which they are here described, the basic orientation with regard to the relationship of being and time that is at the root of both of them is nonetheless firmly entrenched. The ultimate decision about the question we have raised lies, not in the material dispute about individual Christian teachings, but here, in the realm of their philosophical presuppositions. Discussions about content remain isolated and losing skirmishes if no consideration is given to the question: Is there, in the course of historical time, a recognizable identity of man with himself? Is there a human "nature"? Is there a truth that *remains* true in every historical time because it *is* true? The question of hermeneutics is, in the last analysis, the ontological one, the question of the oneness of truth in the multiplicity of its historical manifestations.[4]

The testimony of the primitive Church as to what constitutes Christianity

Let us pause at this point in our considerations, which have attempted only to establish the scope of the problem and its proper situs, in order to ask—quite simply—what was considered constitutive of Christianity in its *very beginning*. The early Church expressed the central core of her belief in the form of confessions. Heinrich Schlier has pointed out that there were, from the start, two kinds of confessions of faith, differing from one

---

[3] Incorporation into the historical process as the standard of good and evil, true and untrue, is powerfully portrayed in Aleksandr Solzhenitsyn's novel, *The First Circle,* trans. Thomas P. Whitney (New York: Harper & Row, 1968), in the conversations with Lev Rubin that run through the whole book, especially section 33, 193–98.

[4] Cf. Emerich Coreth, *Grundfragen der Hermeneutik. Ein philosophischer Beitrag* (Freiburg: Herder, 1969).

another in language but in actuality very closely related: the nominal and the verbal.[5] Both are reflected in the classic passage in Romans 10:9–10: "If your lips confess that Jesus is Lord and if you believe in your heart that God has raised him from the dead, then you will be saved. By believing from the heart you are made righteous; by confessing with your lips you are saved."

Alongside the *confession* of faith: Jesus is Lord, stands, then, the *content* of faith, which is formulated in the sentence: God raised him from the dead. The *confession* occurs in the form of an *acclamation*, which, as an affirmation inspired by the Holy Spirit and officially binding, exemplifies a linguistic genre proper to the age:[6] "Jesus is Lord." This *nominal* acclamation, which states who and what Jesus *is*, combines with the *verbal* statement of faith, which formulates what God has *done* in, to and through Jesus to form the "word of faith", the gospel.

An important development is to be observed in both types of confession before they eventually fuse to form the later credal formulas. In the case of the nominal confession, there were two such developments. The *Kyrios* (Lord)-formula, as an official acclamation of the Lord in the Holy Spirit, became, at the same time, a standard against which to judge those "things called gods" (1 Cor 8:5), those powers of the surrounding world, who called themselves "lords" and had themselves honored as lords. It expanded—in this case, too, in reliance on an acclamation already existing in antiquity—into the confession: Εἷς κύριος ("There is but *one* Lord"), that is, into an affirmation of the oneness, the uniqueness, of Jesus' lordship. In doing so, it drew close to the basic confession of Israel: Εἷς θεός ("There is but *one* God"), with which it soon combined to form a single affirmation: there is but one God and but one Lord (cf. 1 Cor 8:6). The oneness of Jesus is not in opposition to the oneness of God; it is to be understood in terms of this oneness, of which it is the expression, the form, the concrete fulfillment. The *Kyrios*-confession forms a whole with Israel's confession of the one God. It becomes the expression of the Church's fidelity to the central and definitive credo of the Old Testament.[7]

---

[5] Heinrich Schlier, "Die Anfänge des christologischen Credo", in Bernhard Welte, ed., *Zur Frühgeschichte der Christologie* (Freiburg: Herder, 1970), 13–58. On the subject of the formation of the creed, see also Karl Lehmann, *Auferweckt am dritten Tag nach der Schrift* [henceforth *Auferweckt*] (Freiburg: Herder, 1968), esp. 27–67; Hans von Campenhausen, "Das Bekenntnis im Urchristentum", in *Zeitschrift für neutestamentliche Wissenschaft* 63 (1972): 210–53.

[6] Schlier, 14; Theodor Klauser, "Akklamation", in *Reallexikon für Antike und Christentum* [henceforth RAC], 10 vols. to date (Stuttgart: Hiersemann, 1950–), vol. 1, ed. Theodor Klauser (1950): 216–33.

[7] In addition to 1 Cor 8:6, see also Eph 4:5–6 (εἷς κύριος . . . εἷς θεός); 1 Tim 2:5 (εἷς γὰρ θεός, εἷς καὶ μεσίτης) and 1 Cor 12:4–7 (. . . τὸ δὲ αὐτὸ . . . πνεῦμα . . . ὁ αὐτὸς κύριος . . .

The second development reflects a process of sifting and concentration. Of the many titles by which Jesus was originally named in acclamations, there soon remained only three: Christ (Messiah)—Lord—Son of God (Χριστός—κύριος—υἱὸς τοῦ θεοῦ). Each of these titles has its own semantic content. "Christ" is used without exception in sentences that speak of the death of Jesus. In the end, it came to be simply a reference to the human fate of Jesus and thus, more and more, a proper name with which this fate was identified.[8] But that meant that the title afforded no further potential for theological development. In becoming a name, it ceased to exist as a *title*. "Lord" designates Jesus as Ruler of the Universe and, in particular, as the Lord who gathers his Church about him. It therefore draws attention also to his cultic and eschatological manifestation. But it cannot answer the all-important question of how the two εἰς-formulas are to be reconciled. The expression "Son of God" thus becomes the true axis around which the nominal confession of faith continues to develop and which eventually subsumes the other two titles. At this point, the second development fuses with the first: the result is the union [of the title "Son of God"] with Israel's credo, with its theocentrism, and, thus, the clarification of Christianity's claim to both of them. At the same time, this title demonstrates its ability to assimilate the basic content of the *verbal* confession of faith: Jesus *is* the Son of God, but what this means is revealed precisely in what he is for us, in his history.

Let us turn now from the nominal confession of faith, which states who and what Jesus is, to the verbal—or, as we would say today, the salvation-historical—one. It is, as we saw, a confession of the Resurrection. As the Risen One, Jesus is Lord, and he is Lord because he has risen. But confession of the Resurrection is inseparable from confession of the Cross. Developments proceed by a kind of inner necessity from both these confes-

---

ὁ δὲ αὐτὸς θεός). The εἰς-θεός-formula alone (i.e., without direct reference to Christ) appears also in Rom 3:30 and Gal 3:20. Hence Campenhausen is mistaken when he says (215): "It would seem, then, that until after the turn of the first century primitive Christianity, so far as we can tell, never required an explicit 'confession' per se of the one God." Even though it is generally recognized that the primitive Church was hardly aware of a relationship between this text and the development of the creed, it is surely not without significance that, in this otherwise scholarly work, Mt 28:19 has been entirely omitted from the history of the development of the creed. In this connection, the conclusions reached by Isidor Frank in *Der Sinn der Kanonbildung* (Freiburg: Herder, 1971) seem to me to be worthy of note: that for Irenaeus the gospel of the one true God was "the proper object of the preaching of Jesus and the apostles"; that Irenaeus was at pains to prove "that the gospel of the one true God is, properly speaking, the essential core of Holy Scripture in both the Old and New Testaments. . . . The one God and the true service of him are, then, the ultimately definitive object of the Christology and ecclesiology that prevailed in the formation of the canon" (211–12).

[8] Schlier: on "Kyrios", 38–40; on "Son", 40–43.

sions. Granted, what we acknowledge when we acknowledge the Resurrection is primarily and essentially an event that has already taken place. But this event is, nevertheless, noteworthy precisely because it reveals what is here and now valid: Jesus is the Risen One, God's power present in a man, or, as Origen expresses it: "Even to the end of the world, the day of reconciliation is now."[9] In other words, the world stands henceforth under the aegis of reconciliation; or, as Origen also says, what is poured out for us is not corporeal blood but the "Blood of the Word" (αἶμα τοῦ Λόγου), the reconciling and unifying power of the Spirit of God that issues from the death of Jesus. Confession of the Resurrection is, of its very nature, confession of Jesus' exaltation, confession of the Spirit, confession of the unifying power of God—which is God himself—that is bestowed on us by the Lord.

Conversely, where the Cross is acknowledged, there the earthly Jesus is acknowledged. At this point in their development, the verbal and nominal confessions converge. Knowledge about the preexistence of Jesus, who as Son is always with the Father, is just as decisive for the nominal confession as is the title Son of God. In like manner, the Incarnation, which is recognized as a salvation event from God, is ultimately interpreted in Hebrews 10:5–10 as an event that takes place, as it were, in dialogue [Wortgeschehen], in prayer [Gebetsgeschehen], between Father and Son and is thus linked with the theology of the Cross: "You who wanted no sacrifice or oblation prepared a body for me" (Heb 10:5)—Incarnation is acceptance by Father and Son in word—in a dialogue in the Spirit—of the body "prepared" for the Cross. The extension of the verbal—salvation-historical—confession backward from the Cross into the life of Jesus and the extension of the nominal substantive confession into the statement of Jesus' Sonship meet here and coalesce.

With this we have the answer to the question debated by Pierre Benoit and Oscar Cullmann concerning the original structure of the creed and the original orientation of Christian belief.[10] Cullmann regards the diversity between creeds relating to salvation history and those relating to the Trinity as a parting of the ways in credal history; the latter embody for him

---

[9] Origen, "Homiliae in Leviticum", in Patrologiae Cursus Completus, Series Graeca [henceforth PG], ed. J. P. Migne, 161 vols. (Paris, 1857–1866), Homilia 9:5, in PG 12:515; Homilia 9:10, in PG 12:523. In reliance on Ignatius of Antioch, Campenhausen (243–53) gives an excellent presentation of the course of the salvation-historical development of the creed. The material published by Schlier (21–33) demonstrates, however, that the process can be traced even farther back under a variety of key words.

[10] Oscar Cullmann, Die ersten christlichen Glaubensbekenntnisse (Zurich: Evangelischer Verlag, 1943); Pierre Benoît. "Les Origines du symbole des apôtres dans le Nouveau Testament", in Lumière et vie (February 1952), 39–60.

a metaphysical type that no longer understands faith as entrance into a history rooted in Jesus Christ but as devotion to the trinitarian God in a way that is essentially unhistorical. In the transition to a trinitarian credo, Cullmann perceives a fundamental shift in the Christian structure; by contrast, he looks upon the salvation-historical/christological credo as the only legitimate expression of what is Christian. Benoit (and after him Henri de Lubac),[11] on the other hand, emphatically uphold the trinitarian credo that is found in Matthew 28:19—for both of them it is the mature conclusion of developments within the New Testament itself and, at the same time, an acknowledgement of the oneness of the two Testaments: the confession of Christianity continues to be, like that of Israel, a confession of the one God, but it is concretized in the encounter with him who became man and with the Holy Spirit who was sent by him; this encounter achieves its full meaning, however, only in the realization that it is an encounter with God himself. De Lubac maintains further that the trinitarian structure bestows on the credo the unique concentration of a unified, simple act of *"credere in . . ."* (believing in . . .), of committing one's own existence to the trinitarian God; where this trinitarian structure is forgotten, the credo deteriorates into a "catalogue" of the contents of faith, such as was formulated in the Middle Ages.[12] But where confession becomes a listing of things that must be believed, where faith appears quantitative, the question of diminution necessarily arises. On the other hand, if the trinitarian structure is kept in mind, the act of faith is quite different: "Whether it is a question of the object of faith or of the totality of believing subjects—faith, in this case, is one faith, just as the triune God is one God. And if the dogma is developed and actualized, if the mystery is intensified and deepened, this happens always within the closed circle of the credo. The characteristic form of faith, 'I believe in . . . ,' is one of those Christian 'barbarisms' that occurred necessarily and spontaneously prior to any explicit reflection to express the newness inherent in Christianity."[13] It should be clear from what has been said that, far from nullifying salvation history, it is precisely this "believing in" which shapes the inner oneness of faith, that confers on it its true meaning.

It seems to me that a further conclusion might be drawn here from the baptismal and catechumenal context of the trinitarian credo: to confess as

[11] Henri de Lubac, S. J., *La Foi chrétienne, Essai sur la structure du Symbole des Apôtres,* 2d ed. (Paris: Aubier-Montaigne, 1970), 61–98. [English trans.: *The Christian Faith, an Essay on the Structure of the Apostles' Creed* (San Francisco: Ignatius Press, 1986). (Trans.)]

[12] De Lubac, *La Foi chrétienne,* 62. De Lubac refers, in particular, to the terminology of Robert of Melun, who calls the credo a "compendiosa collectio" and a "singulorum brevis comprehensio".

[13] Ibid., 22.

Israel does means "to take up the yoke of God's dominion".[14] One cannot fail to observe how directly and inseparably, in the Old Testament, God's statement "I am the Lord" is linked with ethical obligation.[15] The revelation of God's name is embedded in a passage developed around the words: "I know your groanings" (Ex 6:5). It is inseparably linked to the fact that God has heard the cry of Israel; it is the expression of this hearing. Confession of the one God is confession of the God who protects the rights of widows, orphans and strangers. It is confession of him who continues to be the power of justice even there where earthly power and justice go their separate or opposing ways. The liberation of Jewish belief in God from the national law and traditions of Israel, which Paul accomplished, is certainly not a liberation from the fundamental demand for justice, which is inherent in Israel's concept of God, but rather the intensified affirmation of this context, which had been obscured by the particularization of the Jewish God as a God of justice. Obviously there is no intention here of reducing Christianity to orthopraxis, but the notion is even less acceptable that Christianity can make no moral statement of its own but must, at every historical moment, borrow from its milieu: the holiness of the God of Israel and of the God of Jesus Christ includes a very precise ethic which, in the affirmations and renunciations of the baptismal rite, is correctly and closely interwoven with the dialogue of faith—is, indeed, even its precondition.

The structural precondition of the testimony: communio

After this glance at questions associated with the content of Christian faith, let us return to the philosophical problem with which we began. De Lubac's sentence about the oneness of the trinitarian credo, which I have quoted above, seems to me to contain a valuable cue for the solving of this problem. De Lubac speaks of the closed circle of the credo, which confesses but one faith whether it refers to the object or the subject of that faith. In the case of the "object", this oneness lies in the fact that everything is referred to the triune God, who, though triune in what he is and does, is, nevertheless, but one God. De Lubac clarifies this thought by adding that, for such a view of faith, God does not exemplify loneliness but ec-stasy, a complete going-out-from himself. This means that "the mystery of the Trinity has opened to us a totally new perspective: the

---

[14] Cf. Arnold Goldberg, "Schema", in Herbert Haag, *Bibel-Lexikon,* 2d ed. (Einsiedeln: Benziger, 1968), 1536–37.

[15] Theodor Schneider called special attention to this aspect of the question in *Plädoyer für eine wirkliche Kirche* (Stuttgart, 1972), 24–31.

ground of being is *communio*."[16] From this perspective, we can now understand how the unity of the object can include that of the subject: belief in the Trinity is *communio*; to believe in the Trinity means to become *communio*. Historically, this means that the "I" of the credo-formulas is a collective "I", the "I" of the believing Church, to which the individual "I" belongs as long as it believes. In other words, the "I" of the credo embraces the transition from the individual "I" to the ecclesial "I". In the case of the subject, the "I" of the Church is a structural precondition of the creed: this "I" utters itself only in the *communio* of the Church; the oneness of the believing subject is the necessary counterpart and consequence of the known "object", of that "Other" who is known by faith and who thereby ceases to be merely the "Other".[17]

If there really is such a thing as this "I" of the credo, called forth and made possible by the trinitarian God, then the hermeneutic question is thereby basically answered. For in that case this transtemporal subject, the *communio Ecclesiae*, is the mediator between being and time. In his philosophy of memory, St. Augustine had begun to reflect philosophically on this insight with the help of both his Platonic and his biblical heritage. He recognized memory as the mediator between being and time; in view of this, one can readily see what it means when he interprets the Father as *memoria*, as "memory". God is memory per se, that is, all-embracing being, in whom, however, being is embraced *as* time. Christian faith, by its very nature, includes the act of remembering; in this way, it brings about the unity of history and the unity of man before God, or rather: it can bring about the unity of history because God has given it memory.[18]

The seat of all faith is, then, the *memoria Ecclesiae*, the memory of the Church, the Church as memory. It exists through all ages, waxing and waning but never ceasing to be the common situs of faith. This sheds light once again on the question about the content of faith: without this [believing] subject, which unifies the whole, the content of faith is neither more nor less than a long catalogue of things to be believed; within and by

[16] De Lubac, *La Foi chrétienne*, 14. Cf. 13: "À l'intérieur même de l'Être, c'est l'exstase, la sortie de soi."

[17] I have enlarged on these observations of de Lubac's in Internationale Theologenkommission [henceforth ITK], *Die Einheit des Glaubens und der theologische Pluralismus* (Einsiedeln: Johannes Verlag, 1973), commentary on thesis 6, 36–42.

[18] For a further discussion of Augustine's thought, cf. Erich Lampey, *Das Zeitproblem nach den Bekenntnissen Augustins* (Regensburg: J. Habbel, 1960); B. Schmidt, *Der Geist als Grund der Zeit. Die Zeitauslegung des Aurelius Augustinus,* typed dissertation (Freiburg, 1967). For a further discussion of the subject of memory, cf. Hans Urs von Balthasar, *Theologie der Geschichte* (Einsiedeln: Johannes Verlag, 1959); Johannes Baptist Metz, "Erinnerung", in Hermann Krings, Hans Michael Baumgartner, Christoph Wild, *Handbuch philosophischer Grundbegriffe* 1 (Munich: Kösel, 1973): 385–96.

the Church, they are made one. The Church is the locus that gives unity to the content of faith. At the same time, the question about history is also, to some extent, elucidated: there can be a waxing or waning, a forgetting or remembering, but no recasting of truth in time. The question of what constitutes Christian faith today is thus a question of whether or not the subject has sufficient vitality to remain in existence. If not, there will come into existence a new subject—a subject with which elements of the old one may perhaps be intermingled, just as elements of the Roman Empire and elements of the theocracy of the Old Testament were intermingled with the medieval Imperium, but, nonetheless, a new historical subject. No arbitrary selection of constants can ensure continued existence. Properly phrased, then, the decisive question for today is whether that memory can continue to exist through which the Church becomes Church and without which she sinks into nothingness.

This raises the question of the concrete form the identity of the Church takes in history. It may, indeed, be impossible to reduce this form to a formula; the eucharistic celebration, the administration of the sacraments and the proclamation of the word are all elements of it. It must be added, too, that, since the confrontation with *gnosis,* the *successio apostolica* has consistently been regarded as the basic form of this identity—therein lies the specific meaning of this theme for Catholic theology, a meaning which does not permit us to reduce the question to the status of one problem among many others.[19] But it is not my intention to deal with this problem here. Something else seems important to me: to work out anew the biblical basis of a Christian doctrine of *memoria.* I believe John's Gospel in particular can offer significant assistance in this regard. I have only two brief comments to make. The first clear declaration of the basic mystery of death and Resurrection as the core of Christian belief, which forms the con- clusion of the pericope that describes the cleansing of the temple, offers as it were, a cognitive reflection on precisely this belief when it states that, after the Resurrection, the disciples remembered Jesus' words "and they believed the Scripture and the words he said" (Jn 2:22). According to this passage, Christian belief and knowledge subsist in the framework of belief in Scripture and in the word of Jesus (Old + New Testament) as the disciples remembered them in the Spirit. The fact that remembrance in the Spirit is the situs of the growth and identity of faith seems to me to be actually the basic formula of the Johannine interpretation of faith in contradistinction to *gnosis.* John explains this formula even more exactly with respect to its concrete demand and practical fulfillment in his

---

[19] On this subject, cf. ITK, "L'Apostolicité de l'Église et la succession apostolique", in *Esprit et vie* 84 (1974): 433–40. The German text has been published in *Internationale katholische Zeitschrift* [henceforth IKZ] 4 (1975): 112–24.

description of the Paraclete, who brings remembrance: it is his nature not to take from what is his own or to speak in his own name (just as it was characteristic of Jesus, too, not to speak in his own name). The basic characteristic of speech in the Spirit is, then, that it is not speech in one's own name but speech out of what has been remembered. The true meaning of this touchstone of speech in the Spirit is probably clearer in the first epistle of John than in his Gospel. And it is surely not by chance that the author of 2 John 9 berates him who would go beyond (προάγων) what Jesus taught and advises him to "keep within the teachings of Christ".[20]

The task for today

But what is the object of this whole inquiry? To what answer is it leading? The positive aspect is, I think, most readily elucidated by way of contrast with an effort I believe cannot succeed. The question everywhere being raised about what constitutes Christian faith today has unleashed a hectic search for answers that has caused "short formulas" of faith to spring up, as it were, out of the woodwork. But the purposes for which such texts are prepared reflect a considerable variety: they extend from harmless catechetical aids, and perhaps even less pretentious efforts to develop devotional forms with a contemporary look, to the demand that the old creeds be abolished and that the Christianity of the past be "replaced" by a Christianity of and for today—that, in place of yesterday's truth, a truth be constructed for today on that spiritual background that was spoken of in the beginning. Between the two extremities is the effort of those who do not seek to abolish the old creeds but only to make the essential elements of faith "marketable" in new ones.

Surely no one will deny that many benefits can accrue from such an effort; so, too, the many discoveries that are the side-effects of space travel may be more beneficial to the human race than the goals actually intended. Nevertheless, the effort is doomed to failure. I have discussed elsewhere the anthropological, linguistic and ecclesiological misapprehensions that are at the root of this effort and will not repeat them here.[21] But even

[20] Cf. especially 1 Jn 2:20–27. For a further discussion of "speech in the Spirit", cf. Joseph Ratzinger, "Der Heilige Geist als communio. Zum Verhältnis von Pneumatologie und Spiritualität bei Augustinus", in Claus Heitmann und Heribert Mühlen, *Erfahrung und Theologie des Heiligen Geistes* (Munich: Kösel, 1974), 223–38.

[21] Cf. below, Part One, Chapter 2, Section 1D: "Short Formulas of Faith?" There the positive task that confronts theology in this connection is likewise more closely examined. Cf. also the carefully considered study by Wolfgang Beinert, "Kurzformeln des Glaubens— Reduktion oder Konzentration?", in *Theologisch-praktische Quartalschrift* 122 (1974): 105–17, which suggests further literature on the subject.

without exhaustive analysis it should be abundantly clear that anyone who would construct Christianity from formulas—from the drawing board—is on the wrong track. The malady from which the Church suffers today is, to a large extent, the attempt to achieve her renewal by this and similar means. Nothing living comes into existence in this way, least of all, of course, the Church herself. She came into existence because someone lived and suffered his word; by reason of his death, his word is understood as word par excellence, as the meaning of all being, as logos. Even the primitive Church did not shrewdly devise formulas of faith and then promulgate them—had she done so, they would soon have gathered dust in their manuscripts as so many formulas do today in books that become obsolete almost as soon as they are published. The Church's creed has been developed, above all, from the existential context of the catechumenate, and it was in this context that it was promulgated. The life embraced the word, and the word formed the life. Indeed, it is only to one who has entered into the community of faith that the word of faith reveals itself. Our principal need today is not primarily new formulas; on the contrary, we must confess to a superfluity of unheeded words. Our principal need is for a reconstruction of the existential context of catechumenal training in the faith as the source of a common experience of the Spirit that can thus become also the foundation of realistic reflection. Undoubtedly, this will give rise to new formulations in which the central truths of the Christian faith will be expressed in a way that is both easily remembered and easily understood. Even more important than the brief answers that can be found in any catechism will be a cohesive logic of faith in which even partial answers have their place. Formulas live by the logic that supports them; but logic lives by the logos, the meaning, which does not reveal itself without the cooperation of life—it is bound to the "circle" of *communio* that can be penetrated only by the union of thought and life.

Let us pause here for a summary. What, then, is constitutive of Christian faith "today"? What else but that which actually constitutes it: confession of the triune God in the *communio* of the Church, in whose solemn remembrance the means of salvation history—the death and Resurrection of the Lord—is truly present. This means is not, as we can see, merely a "timeless truth"—an eternal idea hovering independently over a realm of changing facts. This means, which is inseparably bound to the act of "faith in", introduces us into the dynamic circle of trinitarian love that not only unites subject and object but even brings individual subjects together without depriving them of their individuality. Because this creative love is neither blind will nor pure feeling but love as meaning and meaning as love, because it is the creative reason of all reality, it cannot be reciprocated without logic, without thought and word. But because true reason makes itself known, not in the abstraction of thought, but in the purification of the heart, it is linked to a way, to the way followed by him of whom it may be said: He is the Logos. This way is death and Resurrection; to the trinitarian *communio* there corresponds the sacramentally real *communio* of a life lived in faith, for which we are purified in the death and resurrection of conversion. If we understand this, then the scope and nature of the present task become clear to us: drawing-board theology, however useful its products, is certainly not adequate to the task. Christian doctrine arose initially in the context of the catechumenate; only from there can it be renewed. For this reason, as we have indicated above, the development of a contemporary form of catechumenate is one of the pressing tasks confronting the Church and theology today.

B. Baptism, Faith and Membership in the Church— the Unity of Structure and Content

1. Preliminary reflection on the meaning and structure of the sacraments

Although baptism is the sacrament of entrance into the community of faith, it has, despite many significant studies, remained more or less on the sidelines in the renewal of liturgical and theological awareness that has taken place in the last decades.[22] Nevertheless, one cannot rightly comprehend either the nature of the Church or the structure of the act of

[22] Basic for the history of the baptismal liturgy: Alois Stenzel, *Die Taufe* (Innsbruck: Rauch, 1958); also important: Georg Kretschmar, "Die Geschichte des Taufgottesdienstes in der alten Kirche", in *Leiturgia. Handbuch des evangelischen Gottesdienstes,* 5 (Kassel, 1964): esp. 145–273; a practical survey (with special attention to elements of magic and superstition): Carl Andresen, *Die Kirchen der alten Christenheit* (Stuttgart: Kohlhammer, 1971), 470–82. For the whole scope of the dogmatic history of baptism, the articles in *Dictionnaire de théologie catholique* [henceforth DTC], 2:1 (Paris: Letouzey et Ané, 1923): 167–378, and in *Dictionnaire d'archéologie chrétienne et de liturgie* [henceforth DACL], 2:1 (Paris: Letouzey et Ané, 1925): 251–346, are indispensable; a good survey is also to be found in Aimé Georges Martimort, Roger Béraudy et al., eds., *L'Église en prière. Introduction à la liturgie,* pt. 3, chap. 2: Roger Béraudy, "L'Initiation chrétienne", 514–51. [Ratzinger quotes from the German translation of this work: *Handbuch der Liturgiewissenschaft,* 2 (Freiburg: Herder and Herder, 1964–1965): 45–84. For an English translation of part of the original French text, see *The Church at Prayer,* vol. 1: *Introduction to the Liturgy;* vol. 2: *The Eucharist,* Austin Flannery, O. P., and Vincent Ryan, O. P., eds. (New York: Herder and Herder, 1968 and 1973). (Trans.)] For an evaluation from systematic and pastoral perspectives, see Hansjörg auf der Maur and Bruno Kleinheyer, eds., *Zeichen des Glaubens. Studien zu Taufe und Firmung* (Einsiedeln-Freiburg: Benziger, 1972); Günter Biemer, Josef Müller, Rolf Zerfass, *Eiungliederung in die Kirche* (Mainz: Matthias Grünewald, 1972); August Croegaert, *Baptême, confirmation, eucharistie, sacrements de l'initiation chrétienne,* 4th ed. (Bruges: St. André, 1946); Pierre Paris, *L'Initiation*

faith if one leaves baptism out of the reckoning; on the other hand, one cannot really properly understand baptism if one considers it only from the liturgical point of view or in the context of original sin. What follows is intended neither as a comprehensive theology of baptism nor as a treatise on faith or on membership in the Church but rather as a reflection that touches upon all these themes and, in doing so, attempts to make evident something about them that is apparent only when they are contemplated together.

To avoid digressions and to come to as full an understanding as possible of both the nature of baptism and the depth of its meaning, our method will be to examine only the fundamental act of administering baptism, that is, the dynamism of the conferral of the sacrament. It is, in any event, generally to be recommended that a theology of the sacraments avoid abstraction and remain as close as possible to the liturgical event itself. Admittedly, an obstacle of a very fundamental kind arises here and demands a short preliminary reflection, namely, the inner alienation with respect to this sacrament in particular, an alienation that has its source in the modern attitude to life.[23] What have a few drops of water to do with an individual's relationship to God, with the meaning of his life, with his spiritual journey—this is the question that is proving a stumbling block to more and more people today. Pastoral theologians have recently expressed the opinion that baptism and the imposition of hands [as in confirmation and holy orders] came into common usage because most Christians were, at the time, unable to write; that records would have been kept, as they are today, if that had been possible. This leads immediately to the suggestion that we introduce a new and long overdue phase of "liturgical history" by doing now what it was impossible to do then. The sacrament as a preliminary stage of bureaucracy? Such suggestions let us see how foreign the concept of "sacrament" has become today even among theologians. In the discussion that follows, we must keep constantly in mind the question of the replaceability or irreplaceability of baptism. But first, let us make some preliminary remarks about fundamentals.

---

chrétienne (Paris: Beauchesne et ses fils, 1944); Thomas Camelot, Spiritualité du baptême (Paris: Éditions du Cerf, 1960); Jean Daniélou, Bible et liturgie (Paris: Éditions du Cerf, 1951). [For an English translation of the latter work, see Jean Daniélou, The Bible and Liturgy (Notre Dame, Indiana: Notre Dame University Press, 1956). (Trans.)]. De Lubac, La Foi chrétienne; Johann Auer, Die Sakramente der Kirche, Kleine katholische Dogmatik, 7 (Regensburg: Pustet, 1972): 21–78. This subject will be treated again in Part One, Chapter 2, Section 1B below: "Baptism and the Formulation of the Content of Faith—Liturgy and the Development of Tradition".

[23] For a further discussion of what follows, see my short study: Die sakramentale Begründung christlicher Existenz, 2d ed. (Freising, 1967), and my more recent work: Zum Begriff des Sakraments, Eichstätter Hochschulreden 15 (Munich: Minerva, 1979).

The ceremony of baptism consists of the sacramental word and the act of pouring or of immersing or submerging in water. But why—apart from the (admittedly central) positivistic argument that Jesus himself was baptized with water? One who looks more closely will observe that the two-in-oneness of word and matter is characteristic of the Christian liturgy, of the structure of the Christian relationship with God in general. It involves, on the one hand, the inclusion of the cosmos, of matter: Christian belief knows no absolute separation between spirit and matter, between God and matter. The separation of *res extensa* and *res cogitans* that Descartes has so deeply implanted in the consciousness of the modern age does not exist in this way when the whole world is looked upon as creation. The assumption of the cosmos, of matter, into the relationship with God is thus a confession of the Creator God and of the world as creation, of the oneness bestowed on all reality by the *Creator Spiritus*. It also forms a link between the Christian faith and the religions of the nations, which, as cosmic religions, seek God in the elements of the world and are actually on his trail, albeit at a distance. It is, at the same time, an expression of hope for the transformation of the cosmos. These considerations should help us in our efforts to understand once more the basic meaning of the sacrament. Despite the rediscovery of the body, despite the glorification of matter, we are, even now, deeply influenced by the Cartesian division of reality: we do not want matter to have any part in our relationship with God. We do not consider it capable of becoming the expression of our relationship with God or *a fortiori* the medium through which God touches us. We are tempted as much as ever to restrict religion to spirit and mind, but, by the very fact that we thereby give God only half of reality, we evoke a crass materialism, which, in its turn, is no longer able to discover in matter any capacity for change.

In the sacrament, on the other hand, matter and word belong together, and precisely this is the source of its uniqueness. If the material sign expresses the unity of creation, the assumption of the cosmos into religion, the word, for its part, signifies the assumption of the cosmos into history. Even in Israel there was no such thing as a purely cosmic sign, as, for instance, the wordless cosmic dance or the purely natural sacrifice that existed in many so-called natural religions. Hand in hand with the sign there was always the instruction, the word, that gave the sign its place in the history of Israel's covenant with its God.[24] The relationship with God proceeded not simply from the cosmos and its eternal symbols but from a common history in which God brought the people together and became

---

[24] Cf. T. Maertens, *Heidnisch-jüdische Wurzeln der christlichen Feste* (Mainz, 1965); Alfons Deissler, "Das Priestertum im Alten Testament", in Alfons Deissler, Heinrich Schlier, Jean-Paul Audet, *Der priesterliche Dienst,* 2 vols. (Freiburg: Herder, 1970), 1:9–80.

their way.[25] In the sacrament, the word expresses the historical character of faith; faith does not come to the human individual as an isolated "I"; he receives it from the community of those who have believed before him and who tell him of God as an accepted reality of their history. The historicity of faith signifies at the same time its communality and its power to transcend time: to unite yesterday, today and tomorrow by trust in one and the same God. Hence it can also be said that the word introduces the factor of time into our relationship with God just as the material element introduces the cosmic sphere. And, with time, it also brings in other persons who, in this word, express their common faith and experience the nearness of God. Here, too, the sacramental structure corrects an attitude that is typical of the modern age: the tendency to confine religion not just to the purely spiritual but also to the purely individual. As though we ourselves had invented God, we erect a contradiction that is ultimately fatal between tradition and reason, between tradition and truth. Without tradition, without the context of a living history, the human individual is without roots, is striving for an autonomy that is in conflict with his nature.[26]

Let us summarize. The sacrament, as the fundamental form of the Christian liturgy, embraces both matter and word, that is, it gives religion both a cosmic and a historical dimension and points to cosmos and history as the place of our encounter with God. In this fact lies the related insight that Christian faith does not simply abolish the early forms and stages of religion but rather purifies them and absorbs them into itself, thus bringing them for the first time to their full fruition. The sacrament's double structure of word and matter, which it derives from the Old Testament with its belief in creation and in history, receives its ultimate deepening and grounding in Christology, in the Word made flesh, in the Redeemer, who is, at the same time, the Mediator of creation. The materiality and historicity of the sacramental liturgy is thus always at the same time a christological confession: a reference to the one God who did not shrink from taking on our flesh and, by doing so, has drawn to his heart, in the historical turmoil of man's life on earth, the burden and the hope of history as well as the burden and the hope of the cosmos.

---

[25] Cf. especially Jean Daniélou, *Essai sur le mystère de l'histoire* (Paris: Éditions du Seuil, 1953), in particular his critique of René Guéron, 120–26. [For an English translation, see Jean Daniélou, S. J., *The Lord of History*, trans. Nigel Abercrombie (London: Longmans, 1958). (Trans.)]

[26] Cf. Josef Pieper, *Überlieferung. Begriff und Anspruch* [henceforth *Über-lieferung*] (Munich: Kösel, 1970) and Part One, Chapter 2, Section 1A below: "Anthropological Foundation of the Concept of Tradition".

2. The word in baptism: the invocation of the Trinity

Let us return, after these preliminary observations, to the subject of baptism. In analyzing its central event, it is advisable to begin with what is more understandable, that is, with the word that serves as the formula for administering it. In its present form, that word reads: "I baptize you in the name of the Father and of the Son and of the Holy Spirit." Although this is, as we shall see below, an abbreviation of an originally richer text, a certain definitive element is, nevertheless, discernible in it: baptism establishes a communion of name with the Father, Son and Holy Spirit. It is, in this respect, somewhat analogous to the act of marriage, which establishes between two individuals a communion of name that is, in turn, an expression of the fact that, from now on, they form a new unity by virtue of which they abandon their former mode of existence and are no longer to be met separately but always together. Baptism brings about a communion of name between the human individual and the Father, Son and Holy Spirit. The situation of the newly baptized is, in this respect, analogous to that of a woman in a patriarchal society: in baptism, he has taken a new name and is henceforth to be associated with the existential sphere of that name. What this means seems to me to be especially clear in Jesus' dispute with the Sadducees on the subject of the resurrection (Mk 12:18–27). The Sadducees did not recognize the later books of the canon, hence Jesus had to argue the question on the basis of the Torah. He did so by pointing out that God designates himself to Moses as the God of Abraham, Isaac and Jacob. God has linked himself to a man in such a way that, by referring to this man, it is possible to say of God, in contradistinction to all other gods, who he is. He names himself by reference to men; men have become, as it were, his own name. Abraham, Isaac and Jacob are thus, one might say, attributes of God. And Jesus bases his argument on this perception. These men make God nameable; they belong to the concept of God; they are his name. But God is the living God—if anyone is associated with God in such a way that he is, as it were, God's identification before the world, then such a one must himself belong to God, and God is the God of the living, not of the dead.

"The Son" belongs even more closely to God than do these "fathers"; he is God's real name, his identification in the world. He is truly the attribute of God. No: he belongs to God as God himself, as his true name. Henceforth God will be definitively named by reference to Jesus Christ. Being baptized means entering into a communion of name with him who is the Name and thus becoming, more truly than Abraham, Isaac and Jacob, the attribute of God. From this perspective it is now obvious that baptism is the inception of resurrection, inclusion in the name of God and, by the same token, in the indestructible aliveness of God.

This insight is deepened when we inquire more closely into the "name" of God. God is named here as Father, Son and Holy Spirit. This means, to begin with, that God himself exists in the relationship of Father and Son as well as in the unity of the Spirit. It means also that we ourselves are destined to be sons, to enter into the Son's relationship with God and so to be transported into the unity of the Spirit with the Father. Being baptized would thus be the call to share in Jesus' relationship with God. At this point, we begin to understand why baptism can take place only passively, as *being* baptized, for no one can make himself a son. He must *be* made. He must receive sonship before he can make himself a son. Anyone who denies this, who recognizes only what is makable, destroys his own roots. How profoundly this applies to all of us in this technological age! What astute ideological criticism is to be found here! But let us return to our subject. To share in the Son's relationship: How is this to be done? What did it mean for Jesus himself? It manifests itself in the Gospels primarily in the prayer of Jesus. The fact that he is Son means, above all, that he prays. That, in the ground of his being, whether he works among men or takes his rest, he is always open to the living God, always has his place in him, always regards his existence as an exchange with him and so always lives from this innermost depth. The exchange can become a struggle: Let this chalice pass from me; yet not my will but thine be done. He is always one who receives. The Son does not simply design his own existence; he receives it in a most profound dialogue with God. It is this dialogue that makes him free to walk among men and makes him free to serve. It is this dialogue that teaches him, without school or teacher, to know Scripture more deeply than anyone else—to know it truly from God himself.[27]

If being baptized in the name of the triune God means man's entrance into the Son's existence, we know from what has been said that this demands an existence centered around a prayerful communion with the Father. And, in that case, praying means not just the occasional recitation of formal prayers but that inner openness to God that causes a man to be attentive to God in every decision he makes—even wrestling with him, should that be necessary, as Jacob wrestled with the angel. But that is not all. Whoever becomes the son of this Father no longer stands alone. Entrance into this sonship is entrance into the great family of those who are sons along with us. It creates a relationship. To draw near to Christ

---

[27] On this subject, see the more exhaustive treatment in Part One, Chapter 2, Section 1A.

means always to draw near to all those of whom he wants to make a single body. The ecclesial dimension of baptism is already apparent, then, in the trinitarian formula. It is not just an afterthought but has been introduced into the concept of God by Christ. To be born of God means to be born into the whole Christ, Head and members.

There is another viewpoint from which we can examine what has thus far been said. We have already determined that, by his entrance into a communion of name with God, man is drawn into a new existence, that he is, as it were, one who has been born anew, who has already been resurrected. But this mystery of life embraces also a mystery of death. Let us look once more at the example of marriage. In adopting her husband's name, the wife at the same time surrenders her own name. She leaves behind what is hers and belongs henceforth no longer to herself. And this surrender of the old is, for both spouses, the condition of the new that is opening to them. Behind this more external act of renouncing one's name, of losing one's independence, is the deeper mystery of life and death that is love itself. The Yes of love for another involves a far-reaching renunciation of self. Only if one risks this giving of oneself to the other, only if existence is, as it were, first given away can a great love ensue. Other examples could be suggested. It will always be hard for man to speak the truth and to abide by the truth. That is why he takes refuge in the lie that will make life easier for him. Truth and witness, witness and martyrdom, are very closely associated in this world. Truth, if it is consistently maintained, is always perilous. But only in the measure in which man risks the passion of truth does he become a man. And in the measure in which he holds fast to himself, in which he withdraws into the safety of a lie, he loses himself. "Anyone who finds his life will lose it, anyone who loses his life . . . will find it" (Mt 10:39). Only the grain of wheat that dies will bear fruit (cf. Jn 12:24–25).

It is precisely of this mystery of death in life that we are speaking here. Being baptized means assuming the name of Christ, means becoming a son with and in him. The demand made by the name into which one here enters is more radical than the demand of any earthly name can be. It attacks the roots of our autonomy more deeply than the deepest earthly bond can do. For it demands that our existence become "sonlike", that we belong so totally to God that we become an "attribute" of God. And as sons we are to acknowledge so totally that we belong to Christ that we know ourselves to be one flesh, "one body", with all his brethren. Baptism means, then, that we lose ourselves as a separate, independent "I" and find ourselves again in a new "I". It is the sacrament of death and—by that fact, but also *only* by that fact—the sacrament of resurrection.

3. The background of the trinitarian formula: the interrogatory confession

All this can be learned from the formula of baptism, and it would be logical to proceed from here directly to a consideration of the matter of baptism, the water, in which the life-and-death aspect of the sacrament becomes even clearer. But it will be rewarding first to inquire briefly into the historical context of the baptismal formula. In recent times, it has become no more than a formula recited over the one to be baptized by the priest who administers the sacrament. But this was not always the case. In the early Church it had, even into the fourth or fifth century, the form of a dialogue.[28] According to the *Traditio apostolica* of Hippolytus of Rome, which dates from the third century but is, nevertheless, to a large extent representative also of the earlier form of baptism, the officiating priest asked first: "Do you believe in God the Father, the Lord of all?" To this, the catechumen responded: "I do believe." Thereupon he was immersed in water. There followed a question about the Son, which was similar in content to the christological articles of our Apostles' Creed, and a question about the Holy Spirit, after each of which the catechumen was again immersed in water. He was then anointed with the baptismal oil. It is clear from what has been said that the baptismal formula was, in its oldest form, a confession of faith. But the reverse is also true: the confession of faith was, in its oldest form, a part of the sacrament, a concrete expression of the act of conversion, of the new orientation of the catechumen's whole existence to the faith of the Church. For that reason, the confession of faith could not be simply and exclusively an "I"-formula, nor could the administration of baptism be restricted to a strictly priestly formula—it was the dialogue of faith, a confession necessarily couched in the language of "I" and "thou". One does not simply confer faith upon oneself. By its very nature, faith is always the establishment of fellowship with all the brethren of Jesus in his holy Church, from which alone it can be received. That is why it consists of question and answer, of a call and the acceptance of what is offered. On the other hand, one's conversion cannot be simply ordained from on high; one must make it one's own. Hence, a simple act of conferral is not enough; it must be joined to the answer of an "I" that includes also a "thou" and a "we".

It seems to me that this original dialogical form of administering the sacrament also contained essential insights into the relationship of priest and

---

[28] Cf. Stenzel (see n. 22), 55–98. A thorough study of the development of the baptismal credo and its relationship to the *regula fidei* can be found in Hans-Jochen Jaschke, *Der Heilige Geist im Bekenntnis der Kirche. Eine Studie zur Pneumatologie des Irenaeus von Lyon in Ausgang vom altchristlichen Glaubensbekenntnis* (Münster: Aschendroff, 1976).

layman, of Church and individual. Later, those elements that originally belonged together drifted noticeably apart: the baptismal formula became just a formula, a solemn act required for the administration of the sacrament and decreed once and for all with no clear expectation of an I-thou relationship. The creed became a pure "I"-formula to be recited—as though faith were the result of a philosophical study, a pure doctrine that one could appropriate to oneself and so possess independently of others. The original dialogical form held these two elements together: faith as a gift; the Church as an essential prerequisite without which I cannot believe and, at the same time, as the active involvement of him who, as son, attains his majority in the Church and, with his brethren, dares to say "Our Father". Finally, it is clear from what has been said that the creed has meaning only as the verbal expression of the act of conversion. The recent demand for short formulas of the creed that will be comprehensible as propaganda slogans reflects a serious misunderstanding of the creed. For, in its structure, it is the exact opposite of a propaganda text. Such a text overpowers the subject and seeks to impress itself upon him even against his will. The creed, on the other hand, can be spoken only by one who gives himself wholly to the crucified Son of God, accepting in him both the passion and the promise of truth. Thus everything that has been said above about the existence of the Son, about the Church, about death and resurrection, is applicable here as well.

4. *The prerequisite of dialogical confession: the catechumenate*

At this point, our attention is drawn to another aspect of the question. The baptismal formula, which is, properly speaking, a dialogical creed, presupposes a long learning process. It is not enough to study and understand it as a text: it must also be put into practice as the expression of a definite existential orientation. The two aspects interact with one another: the word reveals its full meaning only to the extent that one follows the way to which it points; on the other hand, the way makes itself known only through the word. This means that the whole catechumenate is ordered to baptism through the baptismal confession of faith. If this confession is essential for baptism, then the catechumenate itself is a part of baptism. In later times, an effort was made to preserve this insight by integrating the essential stages of the catechumenate into the rite of infant baptism: the administration of salt during the opening ceremony—salt as a symbol of hospitality and thus, as it were, a foreshadowing of the Eucharist, an admittance into Christian hospitality; the various exorcisms; the *traditio* and *redditio* of the confession of faith and the Our Father, that is, the proclaiming and subsequent repetition of the basic formulas of Christianity as central elements in the instruction of catechumens. It is thus made clear that the administration of baptism points always to something beyond itself and requires the larger context of the catechumenate, which is itself a part of the sacrament.

This insight is of great importance. On the one hand, it reveals the catechumenate as something quite different from religious instruction as it is generally understood, as part of a sacrament—not a preliminary course of instruction, but an integral part of the sacrament itself. On the other hand, the sacrament is not just a liturgical act but a process, a long road that demands an individual's whole strength, mind, will and heart. Here, too, the separation has had disastrous consequences. It has led to a ritualization of the sacrament and a doctrinalization of the word and, in doing so, has obscured a unity that is one of the central components of Christianity.

But what precisely do we mean when we speak of the sacramental character of the catechumenate? We have already indicated one meaning: in the dialogical creed (which is technically called the interrogatory, as opposed to the declaratory, creed), the essential content of the cate-chumenate enters directly into the *forma sacramenti* (into the central act of the administration of the sacrament). It is possible to distinguish in the requisite catechumenate three components that are thereby brought together in unity. First, an integral part of the catechumenate is the factor of instruction, a process of learning, in which one reflects upon and appropriates to oneself the essential contents of the Christian faith. That is why there was developed within the context of the catechumenate a teaching ministry with the obligation to reflect upon the faith and repeatedly make the word of faith comprehensible as the answer to human questioning. There is, however, a significant area of instruction in which the teaching ceases to be purely doctrinal: Christian faith is also an ethos. Later, this fact was expressed in the form of the Ten Commandments; the early Church did not abandon the form she had inherited from Judaism— the doctrine of the two ways, which describes human existence as a choosing between two ways. The effort to adapt oneself to the Christian way is proper to the catechumenate. Only he who has adapted himself to the hospitality of Christians, which was made accessible to him by the gift of salt, can come to know their fraternal community as, at the same time, the abode of truth. Only he who knows Jesus as the way can also know him as the truth. And perhaps we should recall here that salt has also been interpreted as a symbol of wisdom—wisdom, *sapientia*, but always in association with *sapere*, with tasting: one must learn to discover the taste of truth, to acquire a taste for truth. As Thomas Aquinas observes: He is wise for whom things *sapiunt,* for whom things, as they are, are pleasing to the taste. Nor should it be forgotten that salt served in the Old Testament as a sacrificial offering: only by salt were such offerings made pleasing to the taste of the Godhead. But this sacrificial symbolism must be reinterpreted now in terms of Christ: man must be salted if he is to be pleasing to God and if he himself is to acquire a taste for God.[29] The salt of the Passion is necessary for him if he is to walk the way of truth. Christian hospitality leads to the communion of the Cross and, only by doing so, to a taste for truth.

A further experience discloses itself here. As the making of a decision that will affect one's whole life and as a training for what that decision entails, the catechumenate requires more than the candidate's own efforts. For such a decision means the embracing of an already existing life form, the life form of the Church of Jesus Christ. Consequently, it is not an isolated and autonomous decision of the subject but essentially a reception: a sharing in the already existing decision of the believing community. The very fact that one is able to turn in this direction is due to the radiance that emanates from it. One is incorporated, as it were, into the already existing decision of the Church. One's own decision is an accepting of and a letting oneself be accepted into the decision that has already been made. As a result, the community of catechumens enjoys, throughout the catechumenate, the continual support of the ecclesial community. What was said previously about the active-passive character of the baptismal dialogue is even more relevant here: baptism is, from the beginning, a being-baptized, a being-presented-with the gift of faith. And the moral path down which it leads is always, at one and the same time, a being-led and a being-carried.

But from whom does one receive this gift? Proximately, of course, from the Church. But even the Church does not possess it of herself. It is bestowed on her by the Lord—and not just in the distant past. On the contrary, the Church is able to live the faith both now and forever because she receives it as a gift. For the Church is not a club that makes her own statutes and rules and whose activities are limited to the sum of the activities of her individual members. She receives herself again and again from without: she lives from the word that is given her; she lives from the sacraments that she cannot institute but can only receive. If faith is directly a gift of the Church, it is nevertheless also true that the Church herself exists at all times only as the Lord's gift. In the preliminaries of the baptismal rite, this is expressed above all in the exorcisms; the catechumenate does not consist solely of instruction and decision; the Lord

---

[29] Cf. Friedrich Hauck, "ἄλας", in *Theologisches Wörterbuch zum Neuen Testament* [henceforth ThWNT], 10 vols. (Stuttgart: Kohlhammer, 1953–1979), 1 (1953): 229. On the significance of salt in the catechumenate, see Stenzel, 171–75.

himself is at work there. Only he can break the resistance of hostile forces, only he can inspire the decision to believe. Along with instruction and decision, the exorcisms give expression to the third—or, in reality, the first—dimension of the catechumenate: conversion as a gift that only the Lord can bestow and make effective against our own arbitrariness and the powers that would enslave us.

5. The symbolism of water

The rite of exorcism, finally, receives its central and comprehensive form in the symbol of water. Immersion in this element of death is the radical exorcism in which the baptismal rite achieves its goal. Our analysis of the word of baptism brings us, thus, to a consideration of the "matter" of the sacrament. We shall attempt to do no more here than indicate the many levels of symbolism associated with this element. In conjunction with the process of immersion, water is, as we have said, primarily a symbol of death. Rescue from the waters of the deep is as much a part of this imagery of the Bible as is the understanding of the sea as the abode of Leviathan, the enemy of God, and hence as an expression of chaos, of hostility to God, of death. Building on this symbolism, the Apocalypse says that there will be no sea in the new heaven or on the new earth (Rev 21:1)—God will reign alone, and death will have been conquered forever. Consequently, it is possible for the water of baptism not only to represent the mystery of the Cross of Jesus Christ but, at the same time, to serve as a reminder of the great experiences of death and rescue in the Old Testament, especially of the miracle of the Red Sea, which thus become types and foreshadowings of the Cross of Christ and point to it as the mystical center of the whole of salvation history.[30]

That conversion is a death-event, that the way to truth and the hazard of love lead through the Red Sea, that the Promised Land can be reached only through the mortal passion of truth—all this becomes evident here. For this reason, baptism is more than a washing, more than a cleansing, although this concept, too, is inherent in the symbolism of water. But baptism in the name of Jesus, the Crucified One, demands more than can be accomplished by a mere washing. The only begotten Son of God has died. Only the mysterious power of the sea, only the abyss of its depths, can begin to suggest the greatness of what has happened here.

The symbolism of water suggests, then, the radicality of what takes place in baptism. What takes place there touches the roots of human

---

[30] Cf. Daniélou, Bible et liturgie, 60–69.

existence in a way that extends into the very realm of death; it cannot be otherwise. For it is only thus that baptism, that becoming a Christian and the resultant state of being a Christian, can touch the roots of human questioning. For human life, death is the only real question. It is only by arriving at death that one arrives at life. Christianity goes beyond the level for which records are sufficient; it goes beyond the level of washing, of peripheral embellishment. It is grounded in the sacrament of death; and in this fact lies the greatness of its claim. One who would keep it at the level of a club into which one is inducted and from which one receives a formal attestation of membership has no understanding at all of the true meaning of being a Christian or of the Church.

But let us continue our discussion of the symbolism of water. On the evidence of the sacrament of baptism, that symbolism is twofold. Insofar as it represents the sea, it symbolizes the adversary of life, which is death; but insofar as it reminds us of its source, it is at the same time the symbol of life itself. Along with the representation of death, there is also this other symbolism: water is life. Water fructifies the earth. Water is creative. Man lives by water. The Church very early adopted the life symbol of the source in the rubric requiring that the water of baptism be living, that is, flowing water.[31] Death and life are here uniquely combined: that sacrifice alone leads to life, that only the giving of oneself in the mystery of death leads to the land of the living—this becomes wonderfully clear in the twofold symbolism of water in which the unity of death and resurrection proclaims itself in a single symbolic action.

6. Baptism, faith and Church

From what has been said thus far, it may seem that the topic proposed at the beginning has somehow been forgotten, since our remarks have been confined almost exclusively to baptism. It may be helpful, therefore, to state more plainly, by way of conclusion, how this strict concentration on the theo-logical means of baptism—the invocation of the triune God—actually opened for us an understanding of the necessary ecclesiality of faith, of the very state of being a Christian, and how, on the other hand, the nature of the Church herself was clarified from this viewpoint. We saw that being a Christian means becoming a son with the Son and thus, precisely by reason of one's belief in God, being incorporated also into the communion of saints, the Body of Christ. We saw that the Church,

---

[31] *Teaching of the Twelve Apostles* [early second century], edited with a translation, introduction and notes by Boswell D. Hitchcock and Francis Brown (New York: Charles Scribner's Sons, 1884), chap. 7, 15. Cf. also, Stenzel, 46 and 108.

properly speaking, is not a bureaucratic institution, an association of believers, as it were; rather, she is a gift from him who holds the key to death. We saw that baptism is the necessary form of entrance into the company of believers if faith is not to be essentially a product of one's own invention and milieu.

We must examine this aspect of the question more closely now, for with it we have arrived at the point where modern theology reaches a dead end because it does not sufficiently understand the problem that engages us— the relationship of baptism, faith and membership in the Church.

What is the problem here? In the New Testament, there is, as we know, a series of texts that establish a link between man's justification and faith: ". . . as we see it, a man is justified by faith and not by doing something the law tells him to do" (Rom 3:28; cf. 5:1; Gal 2:16; 3:8). But these texts are balanced by others, in the same Pauline epistles, that link man's justification to baptism: "When a man dies, of course, he has finished with sin" (Rom 6:7; cf. Gal 3:26–29). The less the underlying synthesis is understood, the more the question will be raised as to the relationship between the two sets of texts. How is one justified? By faith alone, by baptism alone or by faith and baptism? Bultmann reflects to some extent the more recent interpretation when he suggests that two concepts of faith are juxtaposed in Paul,[32] who "can hardly be said" to have freed himself completely from the concept of the mystery religions—that is, the concept that the sacrament has a magical effect—even though he "certainly does not unconditionally ascribe a magical effect to baptism".[33]

But such statements are obviously far from solving the problem. From

---

[32] Rudolf Bultmann, *Theologie des Neuen Testaments*, 3d ed. (Tübingen: Mohr, 1958). [For an English translation, see Rudolf Bultmann, *Theology of the New Testament*, trans. Kendrick Grobel, 2 vols. (New York: Charles Scribner's Sons, 1951 and 1955). The reference in the text will be found in 1:300 of the English translation. (Trans.)]

[33] Ibid., 1:311–12 (in English translation). The "strong relationship" between faith and baptism is emphatically stated by Hans Conzelmann, *Grundriss der Theologie des Neuen Testaments* (Munich: Kaiser, 1968), 297–300, but the "how" of this relationship remains essentially unexplained. The lengthy digressions on "Der Glaube" (131–54) and "Die Taufe" (307–19) in Otto Kuss' *Der Römerbrief*, 2 vols., 2d ed. (Regensburg: Pustet, 1963), are especially helpful: "But just what is 'faith' . . . ? If one surveys the numerous references, one uncovers for closer scrutiny the fact that what we are talking about here is something complex; faith is an abbreviated formula, the epitome of something that permeates the whole being of one who believes" (132); "The fact that in Paul, too, acceptance of the good news of faith, the act of becoming a believer, faith itself, are all oriented toward baptism; that the incorporation of this faith into the community of the Church through baptism is part of the process that was initiated with the decision to accept the content of the good news can scarcely be doubted. . . . Nowhere, however, is there the slightest indication that any significance for salvation was attributed to faith alone, that is, without baptism" (146); cf. esp. also 113. Ernst Käsemann's *An die Römer* (Tübingen: Mohr, 1973), 151–61, is not pertinent to our discussion.

our earlier observations, it is clear that the two formulas, which, however, form but *one* statement, possess an inner unity. For there is no such thing as a faith that is the decision of an isolated individual. Faith that is not a concrete being-accepted-into the Church is not Christian faith. Acceptance into the believing community is a part of faith itself, not just a subsequent juridical act. This believing community, for its part, is a sacramental community, that is, it lives from that which it does not itself give; it lives from the worship of God in which it receives itself. But if faith involves a being-accepted-into this community, it must mean at the same time a being-accepted-into the sacrament. Thus the act of baptism expresses the twofold transcendence of the act of faith. Faith is a gift received through the community, which is itself given. Without this twofold transcendence, that is, without this sacramental concreteness, faith is not Christian faith. Justification through faith demands a faith that is ecclesial—and that means sacramental—a faith that is received and made one's own in the sacrament. But baptism is none other than the concrete ecclesial realization of the decision of the creed that an individual has both dared to make and let be bestowed upon him.

Faith flows from the Church and leads back to the Church. The gift of God, which is faith, lays claim both to man's own will and to the activity and existence of the Church. No one can represent himself alone, however much he may believe. Faith is a process of death and birth—an active passivity and a passive activity that need other persons: the divine worship of the Church, in which the liturgy of the Cross and Resurrection of Jesus Christ is celebrated. Baptism is the sacrament of faith just as the Church is the sacrament of faith. Consequently, only one who understands baptism can understand what it means to belong to the Church, and only one who looks to faith, which, in turn, points to the divine worship of the family of Jesus Christ, can understand baptism.

Appendix: On the question of infant baptism

The close connection we have discovered between baptism and catechumenate cannot fail to raise the question of whether there is room in such a view for the baptism of infants. Let us examine this question step by step. We can say, to begin with, that baptism, as we have viewed it, has two components: the activity of God, on the one hand, and, on the other, the cooperation of man, who finds his true freedom under the quiet guidance of God. The notion that becoming a Christian depends on man's own decision runs the certain risk of diminishing the awareness of what is properly the first component, the initiative of God, which awakens and calls me. The fact that something objective takes place in baptism, that something happens to me that is over and above my own decision and capacity, is impressively demonstrated in infant baptism. But does not the other component, man's own contribution, then become an empty formula that is contrary to the facts? Are not decisions then anticipated and imposed upon the infant which he is not able to make? The question must be asked even though it shows, in the urgency it has acquired today, that we ourselves have become uncertain about our Christian faith: we obviously construe it more as a burden than as a grace. For a grace can be received; a burden one must lay upon oneself.

We shall return to this point. But first let us confirm that the catechumenate belongs to baptism; that the Church did not alter her stand when infant baptism became common procedure. It need only be pointed out that catechesis can be "prebaptismal" or "postbaptismal". In the latter case, it must, however, be initiated in the course of the baptismal rite. Beginning with the parents and godparents, who represent the infant, the catechumenal rites of the sacrament of baptism serve as an anticipation of the catechumenate. By thus acting for the child, parents and friends hold in their hands not only its biological life but also its spiritual life. The spiritual life of the child unfolds *within* the spiritual life of its parents and teachers. In a birth process that is much longer than the biological one, the child's spiritual existence grows in the bosom of parental thinking and willing until the child is eventually able to assume responsibility for itself. The "I" of the child is hidden in the "I" of the parents. Such representation is not just a theological fiction; it is man's fundamental destiny.

This representation, which bears the weight of the parental love or neglect that will determine the child's life, is, of its very nature, the beginning by anticipation of the course the child will take. Like representation, like the beginning of life in the life of another, anticipation is man's ineluctable destiny.[34] Life itself is an anticipation; it is given us without our asking. With the collapse of former certainties, this is the question that most concerns us: Is human life really worth living? Can the anticipatory (the unasked) gift of life be vindicated when we do not even

---

[34] It touches the heart of the matter, therefore, that, in the new rite of baptism, the idea of representation is now hardly recognizable because parents are no longer allowed to profess the faith of the child by anticipation but are called upon instead to make a confession of faith in memory of their own baptism. Although the formulas remain unchanged, the meaning of the ritual is profoundly altered by this; the statements now designated as acts of remembrance have no inner relationship with the baptism of the child that is presently taking place. This is true also of the resolute reduction of the former catechumenal rites. When the concept of representation is allowed to become discernible, as is the case here, the whole *raison d'être* for the baptism of children has been nullified; there is no longer any justification for it. Granted, the rite in its new form has gained in immediate comprehensibility—but at what a price!

know what fearful destiny may await this individual? Indeed, if we pursue the question to this point, we must say that, in the last analysis, such a gift of life can be defended only if the individual has more to offer than life has; if he is able to plead a meaning that is stronger than death, than the unknown horrors that await him and are able to turn his life from a blessing into a curse.

But let us postpone this ultimate and admittedly crucial question until we have considered the following point: anticipatory (unasked) gifts are inevitable; they present themselves in one form or another along with the gift of life, which, from the outset, bears the stamp of both heredity and milieu. Even the rejection of anticipatory spiritual gifts would be an anticipatory gift of serious import. The question cannot be, then, whether there is any justification for anticipatory gifts. Given their inevitability, the question can only be: Which anticipatory gifts are defensible in view of the freedom, the dignity and the inalienable right of the human person? To all intents and purposes, the answer is already contained in the question: those anticipatory gifts are justifiable that are least likely to treat the future life as something foreign, that are most likely to open it to its own freedom, to make man human. The believing Christian is convinced that optimal and, consequently, inwardly binding anticipation is precisely the way of faith for him. The Church of God is acknowledged to be that historical context, that "milieu", in which we meet the history of God with man that, in the God-man Christ Jesus, truly makes man free. In the gift of self to him who, as the Crucified and Risen One, holds the key of death in his hands, is revealed that anticipation of meaning that is alone capable of withstanding the fate of an unknown future. The conflict over infant baptism shows the extent to which we have lost sight of the true nature of faith, baptism and membership in the Church. Once we begin to understand again, it will be clear to us that baptism is neither the imposition of burdens about which we should have been allowed to make our own decision nor acceptance by a society into which we have been forced without being consulted in advance but rather the grace of that meaning which, in the crisis of self-doubting mankind, can alone enable us to rejoice in being human. It is obvious also that the meaning of baptism is destroyed wherever it is no longer understood as an anticipatory gift but only as a self-contained rite. Wherever it is severed from the catechumenate, baptism loses its *raison d'être*.[35]

---

[35] On the question of the baptism of children and its theological context, cf. the basic observations of Karl Lehmann, *Gegenwart des Glaubens* (Mainz: Matthias Grünewald, 1974), 201–28, which also suggests further literature on the subject.

C. The Church as the Sacrament of Salvation

Origin of this formula in Vatican Council II

When the word *sacramentum* as a designation for the Church first made its appearance in March 1963 in a schema presented by the Theological Commission of Vatican Council II, it aroused consternation in some Council Fathers. This schema was the third in a series of so-called drafts. The word had not appeared in the first draft of the Theological Commission, which had been prepared by Sebastian Tromp, S. J., the principal author of Pius XII's encyclical on the Mystical Body. Nor had it occurred in the first alternative draft offered by the Belgian theologian Gérard Philips on November 22, 1962. Toward the end of 1962, Philips revised his text and distributed it in photocopies. On March 6, 1963, the Commission accepted as the basis of further discussion this revision, which contained the words that survived all further alterations: *Cum vero Ecclesia sit in Christo signum et instrumentum seu veluti sacramentum intimae totius generis humani unitatis eiusque in Deum unionis. . .:* ". . . the Church is, in Christ, a sacrament, as it were, a sign and instrument of the most intimate union with God as well as of the unity of all mankind. . . ."[36] Philips may have adopted this formula from a draft that was composed by German theologians, approved at a meeting in Munich on December 28–30, 1962, and also distributed to the Council Fathers in photocopies. There is, however, a small but significant difference between Philips' text, which is the one finally adopted, and the German one. The German theologians state plainly and without more ado that the Church is the

[36] For a textual history, see Gérard Philips, "Die Geschichte der dogmatischen Konstitution über die Kirche 'Lumen Gentium' ", in *Das Zweite Vatikanische Konzil. Die Dokumente und Kommentare, Lexikon für Theologie und Kirche* [henceforth LTK], *Supplement,* vol. 1, ed. Heinrich Suso Brechter et al. (Freiburg: Herder, 1966): 138–55; Gérard Philips, *L'Église et son mystère au IIe Concile du Vatican* [henceforth L'Église] (Paris: Desclée, 1967). The texts are now available in clearly arranged synoptical order in Giuseppe Alberigo and Franca Magistretti, *Constitutionis Dogmaticae Lumen gentium Synopsis historica* (Bologna: Instituto per le Scienze Religiose, 1975), which also provides a chronological table in appendix A (XXIII–XXV). For a history of the designation of the Church as "sacrament", see Matthäus Bernards, "Zur Lehre von der Kirche als Sakrament. Beobachtungen aus der Theologie des 19. und 20. Jahrhunderts", in *Münchener Theologische Zeitung* 20 (1969): 29–54. Werner Löser (*Im Geiste des Origenes* [Frankfurt: Knecht, 1976], 94–99) points out that, as early as 1936, Hans Urs von Balthasar had explored the significance of Origen's use of the term "sacrament" as a designation for the Church. A thorough study of the question is also found in H. Schnackers, *Kirche als Sakrament und Mutter. Zur Ekklesiologie von H. de Lubac* [henceforth *Kirche als Sakrament*] (Frankfurt, 1979), esp. 76–85.

sacrament of the union of men among themselves and with God.[37] The Belgian text is more cautious in its approach. It begins by defining *sacramentum* as "a sign and an instrument" but even then introduces the word itself with circumspection and a qualifying *veluti* ("as it were"), thus characterizing the usage as figurative by comparison with the usual use of the term and explaining it at the outset. It is obvious in Philips' draft that a new terminology is being carefully introduced, whereas the German theologians simply assumed the term was familiar and would pose no problem. In this, they showed themselves less aware of the psychological mood of the world episcopacy than did the experienced canonist from Louvain. The word *sacramentum* is used twice more[38] in reference to the Church in the Council's final text—in both instances without constraint and without clarification, the earlier explanation being deemed sufficient.

More than ten years after the promulgation of the text, it must be admitted that the concept of the Church as a sacrament is not yet deeply entrenched either in the consciousness of the Church or in theology. While the expression "people of God" spread with the speed of wind and today is equally at home in the vocabularies of bishops, parish councils, professors and ordinary believers, the word "sacrament" as a designation for the Church is in no one's mouth. Yet the Council intended the two expressions to be mutually complementary and explanatory; only against the background provided by the concept "sacrament" can the concept "people of God" become meaningful. We shall have more to say later about these two expressions with such different fates. First, however, it is important to ask what is really meant when the Church is spoken of as a sacrament. The ordinary believer will doubtless raise here the same objection that was raised by some of the Council Fathers. Since the Council of Trent, the designation "sacraments" has been reserved for those unique and strictly defined liturgical actions of the Church of which there are precisely seven, no more and no less. Is the reference here to a real sacrament?[39] or is it intended that one and the same word be used with two essentially different meanings? Neither explanation seems to be the correct one.

[37] The text is to be found in Alberigo-Magistretti. "Adumbratio schematis constitutionis dogmaticae De Ecclesia a quibusdam Patribus et Peritis linguae Germanicae proposita", 381, lines 13–14: "Cum vero sese ut sacramentum unionis totius generis humani in se et cum Deo . . . cognoscat".

[38] "Dogmatic Constitution on the Church [*Lumen gentium*]", chap. 2:9 and chap. 7:48, in *Vatican Council II. The Conciliar and Post Conciliar Documents,* Austin Flannery, O. P., gen. ed. (Northport, N. Y.: Costello Publishing Co., 1975). [Henceforth cited as *Lumen gentium.*] Cf. *Indices verborum et locutionum decretorum Concilii Vaticani* 2:3: *Constitutio dogmatica de Ecclesia Lumen gentium* (Florence: Valecchi, 1968–).

[39] Cf. Alberigo-Magistretti, 436, line 90–437, line 92.

The first and seemingly irrefutable response of those who favor the new terminology is far from satisfactory: they point out that even the Fathers of the Church understood the concept of sacrament in a broad sense and designated the Church as a sacrament.[40] To this, one might object that history cannot be reversed. If, after a particular concept has made its appearance and language has been accommodated to it, I again use this language in its former sense, I no longer think as its original users thought. For it is one thing to act, with regard to a past insight, as though it did not exist and quite another, in the time *before* this insight has occurred, to be ready for it and perhaps even, by my own thinking and acting, to prepare the way for its eventual emergence. That is the fundamental objection that must be opposed to biblicism as well as to all linguistic and intellectual archaeologisms. Nevertheless, it may be useful to cite Cyprian's text, which is the one most frequently adduced: "The Church is the indissoluble sacrament of unity. Whoever introduces a schism, abandons his bishop and appoints for himself a pseudobishop outside the Church is without hope and brings upon himself a great perdition from God's displeasure."[41] It is obvious that the notion of sacrament is here clearly related to the notion of unity and that the individual sacraments do not exist for themselves alone but refer to the sacrament of unity, to which they are bound. Only in unity can they be effective; unity is an integral part of the sacrament itself; it is not something outside it, but the ground on which it rests, the very means that support the sacrament.

The relationship that here emerges from the at first purely historical reference to the Fathers of the Church is deepened when we turn our

---

[40] Cf. Joseph de Ghellinck et al., *Pour l'histoire du mot "Sacramentum"* (Louvain: Spicilegium, 1924).

[41] [Cyprian's text has been slightly paraphrased here but without changing its meaning. In speaking of Novatianus, a Novatian admitted to the priesthood and later consecrated bishop without having been confirmed, Cyprian states: "si Novatianus huic pani dominico adunatus est, si Christi poculo et ipse conmixtus est, poterit uideri et unici ecclesiastici baptismi habere gratiam posse, *si eum constiterit ecclesiae unitatem tenere*" (italics added). He continues: "Denique quam sit inseparabili *unitatis sacramentum*" (undoubtedly a reference to the "ecclesiae unitatem" of the preceding sentence; italics added) and, in the remainder of the passage quoted in the text, describes the fate of those who appoint false bishops *outside the Church*. For the full text of Cyprian's letter, see S. Thasci Caecili Cypriani, *Opera omnia*, ed. Guilelmus Hartel, *Epistulae*, 69, 5–6, in *Corpus scriptorum ecclesiasticorum latinorum* (henceforth CSEL) (Vindobonae: apud C. Geroldi filium bibliopolam academiae, 1871), vol. 3, pars 2, col. 754. For an English translation of Cyprian's letter, see Saint Cyprian, *Letters* (1–81), trans. Sr. Rose Bernard Donna, C. S. J., in *The Fathers of the Church* 51 (Washington: Catholic University Press, 1964): 244–57. A new translation, *The Letters of St. Cyprian of Carthage*, trans. G. W. Clarke, is being published in *Ancient Christian Writers* (New York: Newman Press). Volumes 1 and 2 (Letters 1–54) have appeared to date (1984). (Trans.)] Cf. Philips, *L'Église*, 72–74.

attention to the second of the patristic texts that is relevant here: "The sacrament [*mysterium*] of God is nothing and no one but Christ", St. Augustine wrote in one of his letters.[42] All sacraments, that is, all the fundamental liturgical acts of the Church, have a christological structure; they are the communications of him who, because he is God's visible Word, is truly the founder of the Christian sacrament.

Theological content of the formula

We are now in a position to ask why it is meaningful to supplement current theological language in this way by borrowing from an older terminology. If we begin our answer with a simple reference to the wording of the Tridentine concept of sacrament, we shall see that this wording actually points beyond itself to the usage of Vatican Council II. The Roman Catechism, commissioned by the Council of Trent, defines a sacrament in this way: "A sacrament is a visible sign of invisible grace instituted for our justification."[43] Clearly observable here are three elements that are to be found, in somewhat simplified form, in all popular catechisms since that time: to the sacrament belongs, on the one hand, a visible sign that, on the other hand, must point beyond itself to an inner reality that is here identified as "grace" or "justification", for either of which we might substitute "salvation", which is the word used by Vatican Council II.[44] But if the sign is actually to effect such mediation from external to internal, from earthly to heavenly, from temporal to eternal, it must have behind it the full power of authority—and this is indicated by the word "instituted". Let us attempt now to examine these individual elements more closely. The first is the sign. In keeping with tradition, Vatican Council II juxtaposes two concepts here: "sign" and "instrument". The two are not identical, but neither are they to be separated. For the word "sign" expresses a relationship. A sign becomes what it is by pointing beyond itself; as a sign it does not rest in itself but is always on the way to something else. Consequently, I understand it as a sign only if I enter into its referential context, if I enter upon the way that it is. But if a

[42] St. Augustine, "Epistolae", ep. 187, chap. 11, sec. 34, in *Patrologiae Cursus Completus*, Series Latina [henceforth PL], ed. J. P. Migne, 221 vols. (Paris: 1844–1864), 33:845. [For an English translation of all the letters, see St. Augustine, *Letters*, trans. Sister Wilfrid Parsons, 5 vols., in *The Fathers of the Church* (New York: Fathers of the Church, Inc., vols. 12 [1951], 18 [1953], 20 [1953], 30 [1955], 32 [1956]). (Trans.)] See also, Philips, *L'Eglise*, 73.

[43] *Catechismus Concilii Tridentini Pii V, Pontif. Max. . . . .* (Paris: Via Sancti Sulpicii, 38, 1853), pars II, caput I, v, 118.

[44] *Lumen gentium*, chap. 7, 48.

sign, a visible reality, points to what is invisible, what is divine, it is eminently clear that I can discover its referential context only by identifying
myself with it, by allowing myself to be incorporated into the relationship
that makes the sign a sign. Or, as Origen says: We discover the spiritual
meaning of a *mysterium*, of a *holy* sign, only when we live the mystery.
Accordingly, the occurrence of the insight that reveals the sign as sign is
simultaneous with conversion. For conversion is the movement of our
visible life toward a relationship with God. Or, more exactly: it has as its
point of reference God's plan for mankind and means directing one's life in
conformity with that plan.[45]

If we examine this insight more closely, we become immediately aware
of the inner relationship between sign and instrument. The sign is an *actio*,
an event, a token—it is an effective tool [*ein Werk-zeug*]. But if the sign is an
event, an action, then it is not simply something that is there, something I
can acknowledge or ignore at will. It is not just present; it must be realized.
But, as we saw above, this realization must be accomplished by a fullness
of power that, for its part, cannot simply proceed from things in
themselves or from persons as individuals. A holy sign, in other words,
requires liturgical action, and liturgical action requires a community in
which to exist and which embodies the fullness of power for such liturgical
action. We might add that even grace is not just the most intimate
inwardness of a single individual in which all other persons have no place:
when it is called justification, this points to a justice that abounds not only
before God but even before men, that is a genuine opening of the
individual to the demands of existence with others and as a whole. We can
say, then, that the seven sacraments are unthinkable and impossible
without the one sacrament that is the Church; they are understandable at
all only as practical realizations of what the Church is as such and as a
whole. The Church is the sacrament in the sacraments; sacraments are the
means by which the sacramentality of the Church is realized. Church and
sacraments explain each other.

Relation to the basic questions of humanity

It is time now to ask what is the purpose of all that has been said? What is
being expressed here? Is it not, in the last analysis, a mere play on words?

[45] Schnackers makes this point in *Kirche als Sakrament*, 74: "The spiritual meaning of a
mysterium [sacrament] reveals itself only, as Origen says, when one lives the mystery.
According to Origen, the moment of spiritual insight coincides with conversion."
Schnackers bases his comment on de Lubac's *Méditation sur l'Église* (Paris: Aubier, 1953), 12,
and *Histoire et Esprit. L'Intelligence de l'Écriture d'après Origène* (Paris: Aubier, 1950), 332,
391ff.

Already at work behind such a question is the theme of salvation, which is the main topic of our reflections, for the question about purpose is always ultimately concerned with whatever is happening anywhere to mankind and is hence open to the question about salvation. What is being expressed here is, first of all, a collective view of Christianity to replace the individual or purely institutional manner of thinking. It was in this framework that Henri de Lubac's designation of the Church as a sacrament made its appearance in the 1930s. De Lubac was deeply affected by the lapse of faith that occurred no longer under the aegis of an agnostic philosophy but in the name of humanism, in the name of suffering humanity, in the name of a humanity that is a community and demands the service of all. At the beginning of his book *Catholicisme; les aspects sociaux du dogme,* he placed a quotation from Jean Giono that he regarded as a most pungent criticism of the Christian way: "Am I supposed to have found joy? Alas, no. . . . Only *my* joy! And that is something terribly different. The joy of Jesus can be personal. It can belong to one man alone, and he is saved. He is at peace; he is joyful, but he is not alone. . . . When affliction lays siege to my gates, I can no longer quiet myself with the blandishments of genius. Only then will my joy be lasting when it is the joy of all. I don't want to pass through the battlefields with a rose in my hand."[46] The concept of a Christianity concerned only with *my* soul, in which I seek only *my* justification before God, *my* saving grace, *my* entrance into heaven, is for de Lubac that caricature of Christianity that, in the nineteenth and twentieth centuries, made possible the rise of atheism. The concept of sacraments as the means of a grace that I receive like a supernatural medicine in order, as it were, to ensure only my own private eternal health is *the* supreme misunderstanding of what a sacrament truly is. De Lubac, for his part, is convinced that Christianity is, by its very nature, a mystery of union. The essence of original sin is the split into individuality, which knows only itself. The essence of redemption is the mending of the shattered image of God, the union of the human race through and in the One who stands for all and in whom, as Paul says (Gal 3:28), all are one: Jesus Christ. On this premise, the word *Catholic* became for de Lubac the main theme of all his theological speculation: to be a Christian means to be Catholic, means to be on one's way to an all-embracing unity. Union is redemption, for it is the realization of our likeness to God, the Three-in-One. But union with him is, accordingly,

---

[46] Henri de Lubac, *Catholicisme; les aspects sociaux du dogme* [henceforth *Catholicisme*], 3d ed. (Paris: Éditions du Cerf, 1941). [For an English translation, see Henri de Lubac, S. J., *Catholicism: A Study of Dogma in Relation to the Corporate Destiny of Mankind,* trans. Lancelot C. Sheppard (London: Burns, Oates & Washbourne, 1950). The quotation in the text will be found on p. viii of the English translation. (Trans.)] For a further discussion of the matter treated here, cf. the above-mentioned dissertation by Schnackers as well as Hans Urs von Balthasar, *Henri de Lubac. Sein organisches Lebenswerk* (Einsiedeln: Johannes Verlag, 1976).

inseparable from and a consequence of our own unity. The concentration on what is Catholic, which seems at first glance to be directed exclusively inward, thus is revealed in its original impulse to be an emphatic orientation toward those today who are searching; only when the most inward aspect of Christianity is proclaimed and lived does it reveal itself as both the answer to and a·force equivalent to the dynamism of humanistic atheism—to that humanism that seeks the unification of mankind. Only when we see this clearly can we rightly understand the purpose of Vatican Council II, which, in all its comments about the Church, was moving precisely in the direction of de Lubac's thought. The Council was not primarily concerned with how the Church envisaged herself, with the view from within, but with the discovery of the Church as sacrament, as the sign and instrument of unity, and consequently with the answer to the question that no one in our century can regard as unimportant. Perhaps it will be useful to repeat here the sentence with which de Lubac opened the door to a new perspective in 1938: "If Christ can be called the 'sacrament of God', then the Church is for us the sacrament of Christ. In the full original sense of the word, it represents him; it bestows on us his real presence. . . . The Catholic is not merely the subject of a power; he is also the member of a body. His juridical dependence on the former has as its goal his living incorporation into the latter. Consequently, . . . his duty is not only to obey its commands and follow its counsels but, even more, to share in its life, to be of one mind."[47]

We are ready now to formulate a threefold conclusion:

1. The designation of the Church as a sacrament is opposed to an individualistic understanding of the sacraments as a means of grace; it teaches us to understand the sacraments as the fulfillment of the life of the Church; in doing so, it enriches the teaching about grace: grace is always the beginning of union. As a liturgical event, a sacrament is always the work of a community; it is, as it were, the Christian way of celebrating, the warranty of a joy that issues from the community and from the fullness of power that is vested in it.

2. The designation of the Church as a sacrament thus deepens and clarifies the concept of Church and offers a response to contemporary man's search for the unity of mankind: the Church is not merely an external society of believers; by her nature, she is a liturgical community; she is most truly Church when she celebrates the Eucharist and makes present the redemptive love of Jesus Christ, which, as love, frees men from their loneliness and leads them to one another by leading them to God.

3. The positive element common to both of these statements is to be

[47] De Lubac, *Catholicisme,* 50–51.

found in the concept of *unio* and *unitas*: union with God is the content of grace, but such a union has as its consequence the unity of men with one another.

The problem of realization

Here we meet with another objection. For it can be asked: Is this not extremely unrealistic? How is it relevant to man's actual lack of unity? It was, in fact, from reflections such as these that the new generation after the Council transformed de Lubac's theology of Catholicity into a political theology that sought to put Christianity to practical use as a catalyst for achieving political unity.[48] From that perspective, his position, which was adopted and developed by the Council, could not be regarded as anything but a first step in Christianity's confrontation with atheistic humanism—a step that was necessary if the problem was to be addressed at all but that should then lead logically to the more realistic model of political theology. Hence, fidelity to the concept advanced by Vatican Council II could be understood only as the cutting short of the logical development because of an inability to recognize its ultimate goal. It would lack, so to speak, that second impetus that could alone bring it to completion. Toward the end of the sixties, this logic seemed to have become irrefutable. Since then, its effects have led many to question it. Nevertheless, we must ask ourselves why it was inevitable that this path should lead in the wrong direction.

The first indication of the answer lies in the words already quoted from Origen: A mystery can be seen only by one who lives it; here the moment of spiritual insight coincides of necessity with the moment of conversion. The fact that so many regard as total loss whatever does not fall within the parameters of politics and economics and that, in consequence, all genuinely theological discussion is giving way more and more frequently to political discussion should not be too readily explained by the allegation that Christianity is out of touch with reality; it may also be the outcome of our blindness, which is incapable of perceiving one whole dimension of reality because we have fallen prey to a progressive barbarization of our spiritual vision. Even from a purely human standpoint, it seems to me, there is abundant evidence for the thesis that without conversion, without a radical inner change in our thinking and being, we cannot draw closer to one another. For even the simplest intelligence must realize that barbarization cannot be the path to

[48] Cf. M. J. Guillou, Olivier Clément, Jean Bosc, *Évangile et révolution. Au coeur de notre crise spirituelle* (Paris, 1968). Cf. also Part Four, Chapter 2 of the present work: "Church and World: An Inquiry into the Reception of Vatican Council II".

humanization. But where man is barred from every path that leads within, from every means of purification, where, instead, only his envy and his greed are being rekindled, there barbarism becomes method. And we come here upon something unexpected: rightly understood, the path that leads men within and the path that draws them together are not in conflict; on the contrary, they need and support one another. For it is only when men are united inwardly that they can really be united outwardly. But if they are inwardly impenetrable to one another, their outward encounters will serve only to increase their potential for aggressiveness. The Bible portrays this graphically in the story of the tower of Babel: the most advanced union in terms of technical skill turns suddenly into a total incapacity for human communication. Even from the inner structure of the episode, that is the logical outcome: where each person wants to be a god, that is, to be so adult and independent that he owes himself to no one but determines his own destiny simply and solely for himself, then every other person becomes for him an antigod, and communication between them becomes a contradiction in itself.

But we might also approach the question from the opposite direction and ask: In what does man's wretchedness actually consist? Above all, in his insecurity; in the uncertainties with which he is burdened; in the limitations that oppress him; in the lack of freedom that binds him; in the pain that makes his life hateful to him. Ultimately there is, behind all this, the meaninglessness of his existence that offers satisfaction neither to himself nor to anyone else for whom it might have been necessary, irreplaceable, consequential. We can say, then, that the root of man's wretchedness is loneliness, is the absence of love—is the fact that my existence is not embraced by a love that makes it necessary, that is strong enough to justify it despite all the pain and limitations it imposes. What this means will perhaps be made clearer by a passage from Solzhenitsyn's *The Cancer Ward*: ". . . all our lives we've kept telling a man: 'You're a member of the collective! A member of the collective!' And so he is! But that's only while he's alive. When his hour of death comes we release him from the collective. He may be a member, but he'll have to die by himself. His tumor will fasten itself on him alone, not on the whole collective. 'You, you!' His finger jabbed rudely at Rusanov. 'Tell me, what are you most afraid of in the world right now? Of dying! What are you most afraid of talking about? About death! What is the word for this? Hypocrisy!' "[49]

We referred above to the allegation that one does not follow de Lubac's

---

[49] Aleksandr I. Solzhenitsyn, *The Cancer Ward*, trans. Rebecca Frank (New York: Dell, 1968), 160; cf. H. W. Krumwiese, "Absolute Normen und die Individualisierung der Ethik in der Moderne", in Willi Oelmüller, ed., *Fortschritt wohin?* (Düsseldorf, 1972), 42–62, esp. 56.

thought to its logical conclusion, does not advance from theory to practice, if one fails to take the further step from his concept of Catholicism to the concept of class struggle. Now we must say that one does not pursue the question of community to its logical conclusion and is, therefore, not really practical if one does not pursue it even to the question of suffering and death, to the very limits of the collective, to the point where community would have its ultimate significance and its true beginning—where it is no longer a question of doing but of being, where I myself am the issue. This does not mean a return to individualism; on the contrary, it means discovering the conditions without which the collective is a mere hypocrisy, an externally established dictatorship, rather than a true union of mankind. What man needs is a communion that goes beyond that of the collective; a unity that reaches deep into the heart of man and endures even in death. The human unity that man requires by nature must know how to answer the problem of death in which it must find its truest confirmation. For this reason, man seeks to go beyond the boundaries of love of fellowman and to make his life truly a promise by identifying himself with the power of history itself; the liberation movements of today have no lesser goal. But can man identify himself with this power that we need not hesitate to call God? No. That is why even the best of these movements are but well-meaning attempts that succeed only in miring man more deeply in his tragic situation. Man cannot identify himself with God, but God has identified himself with man—that is the content of the communion that is offered us in the Eucharist. A *communio* that offers less offers too little.[50]

Now at last we have reached the inmost core of the concept "Church" and the deepest meaning of the designation "sacrament of unity". The Church is *communio*; she is God's communing with men in Christ and hence the communing of men with one another—and, in consequence, sacrament, sign, instrument of salvation. The Church is the celebration of the Eucharist; the Eucharist is the Church; they do not simply stand side by side; they are one and the same. The Eucharist is the *sacramentum Christi* and, because the Church is *Eucharistia,* she is therefore also *sacramentum*—the sacrament to which all the other sacraments are ordered.

With this in mind, it is now both possible and necessary to address ourselves to individual questions. I would like, however, to make one further point. In his commentary, G. Philips, the principal author of the Second Vatican Council's text on the Church, rightly spoke as follows: "The Church is, then, the sacrament of union with God and, for that reason, of the mutual union of the faithful in a single movement of love for

---

[50] Cf. Karl Lehmann and Joseph Ratzinger, *Mit der Kirche leben* (Freiburg: Herder, 1977), 29–35.

him. She serves, therefore, as a sign for the whole human race. Granted, it
is not her task to exert herself directly for the purpose of establishing world
peace. The task of building an order of peace on our planet lies with the
people. But for the realization of this ideal the unity of the Church . . . is a
constant incentive."[51] "If, then, a unified temporal order on the worldly
level and the building of the universal kingdom of God by Jesus Christ
must continue to be quite separate realities, man would, nevertheless,
have to be blind indeed if he denied the interaction that links the two
together."[52]

Two things are important here: the sacrament we call Church does not
directly establish man's secular, political unity; the sacrament does not
replace politics; and theocracy, whatever its form, is a misunderstanding.
Nevertheless, the unity of faith operates in the most routine and ordinary
matters and has significant power even in the temporal sphere. In this
context, St. John's Gospel seems to me to have an important contribution
to make. Interestingly enough, John has very little to say about the
Christian's universal love of all mankind. He thinks, rather, primarily of
brotherhood and interprets Christian love in terms of fraternal
structures.[53] This has been called a closed ethic and has been criticized as a
forfeiture of universality. Doubtless there is a danger here for which
correctives like the parable of the Good Samaritan are clearly needed. But
John's perspective also has its realistic meaning: universal love can be
realized only in the concrete form of brotherly love. Perhaps it is precisely
here that we see most clearly the practical task concealed in the expression
"sacrament of unity": to build up units of brotherhood that have their
source in the Eucharist, thus allowing the Church to become concrete,
and, in the freedom of faith, to take steps toward unity that can challenge
the claim of a tyrannically imposed external unity to have a monopoly on
practicality.

That concludes my remarks. At the outset, we came to the realization
that of the two new ecclesiological keywords introduced by Vatican
Council II—people of God and sacrament—only the first has found public
resonance in the Church. Perhaps the word "sacrament" as a designation
for the Church will, for many reasons, continue to be confined to the
lingua docta, the professional language, of the theologians. But if the
meaning it was intended to convey also remains esoteric, the isolated
concept of "people of God" could become a caricature of conciliar

---

[51] Philips, *L'Église,* 74.

[52] Ibid., 76.

[53] In opposition to the theses of Anders Nygren, *Eros und Agape* I (Lund, 1930): 132ff.,
Rudolf Schnackenburg demonstrates clearly in *Die Johannesbriefe* (Freiburg: Herder, 1953),
105–6, that John was also aware of the universal dimension of brotherly love.

ecclesiology. Norbert Lohfink has shown that, even in the Old Testament, the designation "people of God" referred to the people of Israel not simply in their empirical setting but only at the moment in which they were addressed by God and answered his call.[54] This is even more true in the New Testament: of herself, the Church is not a people but an exteriorly very heterogeneous society. This nonpeople can become a people only through him who unites them from above and from within: through communion with Christ. Without this christological mediation it would be presumptuous, if not actually blasphemous, for the Church to designate herself the "people of God". One of the most crucial tasks in the study of the conciliar legacy today, then, will be to reveal anew the sacramental character of the Church and, in so doing, to call attention once again to what this really means: that union with God which is the condition of man's unity and freedom.

Section 2
Structure, Content, Attitudes

A. Faith as Conversion—Metanoia

Any attempt to translate the word "metanoia" runs immediately into difficulty: repudiation, change of mind, repentance, atonement, conversion, reformation—all these suggest themselves, but none of them exhausts the word's full meaning. "Conversion" and "reformation" [of one's whole life: Be-kehrung], however, perhaps best reveal its radical character, what it really is: a process that affects one's entire existence—and one's existence entirely, that is, to the full extent of its temporal span—and that requires far more than just a single or even a repeated act of thinking, feeling or willing. Perhaps the difficulty of linguistic interpretation is linked to the fact that the whole concept has become strange to us, that we know it only in isolated bits and pieces and no longer as a comprehensive whole. And there is a strangeness even about the pieces that remain. Probably no one today would echo Nietzsche's comment: " 'Sin' . . . is a Jewish feeling, a Jewish invention, and, in view of this background, . . . Christianity has

---

[54] Norbert Lohfink, "Beobachtungen zur Geschichte des Ausdrucks 'Am Jahwe' ", in Hans Walter Wolff, ed., Probleme historischer Theologie, Gerhard von Rad zum 70. Geburtstag (Munich: Kaiser, 1971), 275–305.

actually attempted to 'judaize' the whole world. How far it has succeeded in Europe is best seen in the degree of strangeness that Greek antiquity—a world without the feeling of sin—still has for our sensibilities. . . . 'Only when thou *repentest* is God gracious to thee'—for a Greek, such a concept would be both laughable and shocking. . . .''[55]

But if the notion of sin and repentance is, understandably enough, no longer ridiculed as Jewish, the basic statement itself still stands with unabated force even today. A second comment of Nietzsche's, which I should like to quote in this context, might well have been spoken by any modern theologian: "The concept of guilt and punishment is lacking in the whole psychology of the 'gospel'. . . ; 'sin', indeed every distance between God and man, has been done away with—precisely that is the 'glad tidings'."[56]

The attempt to give Christianity a new publicity value by putting it in an unqualifiedly positive relationship to the world—by actually picturing it as a conversion to the world—corresponds to our feeling about life and hence continues to thrive. Many a false anxiety about sin, created by a narrow-minded moral theology and all too often nourished and encouraged by spiritual advisers, avenges itself today by leading people to regard the Christianity of the past as a kind of harassment that kept man constantly in opposition to himself instead of freeing him for open and anxiety-free cooperation with all men of good will. One might almost say that the words sin–repentance–penance belong to the new taboos with which the modern consciousness protects itself against the powers of those dark questions that could be dangerous to its self-assured pragmatism.

Even here, however, the scene has changed again in the last three or four years. That all-too-guileless progressivism of the first postconciliar years, which happily proclaimed its solidarity with everything modern, with everything that promised progress, and strove with the self-conscious zeal of a model schoolboy to prove the compatibility of what is Christian with all that is modern, to demonstrate the loyalty of Christians to the trends of contemporary life—that progressivism has today come under suspicion of being merely the apotheosis of the late-capitalistic bourgeoisie, on which, instead of attacking it critically, it sheds a kind of religious glow. Granted, a relatively harmless little demon has thereby been surreptitiously replaced by seven increasingly harmful ones, but the disillusionment can be salutary. For it becomes more and more clear, in the harsh lightning of the

[55] Friedrich Nietzsche, *Die fröhliche Wissenschaft* 3:135, in *Nietzsche's Werke* 5 (Leipzig: Naumann, 1908): 169–70. [For an English translation, see Friedrich Nietzsche, *The Gay Science*, trans. Walter Kaufmann (New York: Random House, 1974). (Trans.)]

[56] Friedrich Nietzsche, *Der Antichrist*, in *Werke in zwei Bänden* 2 (Munich: Carl Hanser,

storm aroused by such criticism, that man's existence and his world are not so pleasantly peaceful in their pursuit of progress that one would readily choose to be converted to such a world—if one is to serve it, one must criticize it, one must change it. A Christianity that believes it has no other function than to be completely in tune with the spirit of the times has nothing to say and no meaning to offer. It can abdicate without more ado. Those who live vigilantly in the world of today, who recognize its contradictions and its destructive tendencies—from the self-destruction of technology by the destruction of the environment to the self-destruction of society by racial and class struggles—such people do not look to Christianity for approbation but for the prophetic salt that burns, consumes, accuses and changes. Nevertheless, a basic aspect of metanoia comes thereby into view—for it demands that man change if he is to be saved. It is not the ideology of adaptation that will rescue Christianity, although adaptation is still operative wherever, with sycophantic zeal or tardy courage, those institutions are criticized which, in any event, have become the powerless butt of world publicity (and in so doing, incidentally, have entered once again into the apostolic tradition [1 Cor 4:13]);[57] nothing can rescue it but the prophetic courage to make its voice heard decisively and unmistakably at this very hour.

If the social and public components of metanoia come once again to the fore, there is, nevertheless, no lack of signs to remind us of the inevitability of conversion, of reformation and of its visible marks in the individual. Like Protestant Christianity, Frank Buchmann has discovered anew, for the movement of moral rearmament that he founded, the necessity of the confession [of faith] as an act of liberation, of renewal, of surrendering the past and the destructive concealment of one's own guilt; in the secular sphere, psychology has come, in its fashion, to the realization that guilt, if unmastered, divides a man, destroys him physically and eventually also corporally, but that it can be mastered only by a confrontation that releases into the consciousness what has been suppressed and is festering within for an outlet: the increasing number of such secular confessors should show even a blind man that sin is not a Jewish invention but the burden of all mankind. The true burden from which, above all, man must be freed if he wants and is to be free.

1967), sec. 33, 511. [For an English translation, see "The Antichrist", in *The Portable Nietzsche*, ed. Walter Kaufmann (New York: Viking Press, 1954), 565–656. (Trans.)]

[57] Cf. Hans Urs von Balthasar, *Klarstellungen* (Freiburg: Herder, 1971), 94–99. [For an English translation, see Hans Urs von Balthasar, *Elucidations* (London: SPCK, 1975). (Trans.)]

On the basic biblical meaning of metanoia

Because secular components of the fundamental state of metanoia are so much in evidence today, the question of the real meaning of a properly Christian metanoia acquires, for the first time, a degree of urgency. Nietzsche, as we saw, represented sin and repentance as something typically Jewish, in contrast to which he ascribed to the Greeks the noble virtue of finding even crime beautiful and of regarding repentance as something to be scorned. For the close observer, Greek tragedy, which he offered as evidence, reveals exactly the opposite tendency: dread in the face of a curse that not even the gods can ward off.[58] Anyone who looks, however briefly, at the history of religion will learn to what extent it is dominated by the theme of guilt and atonement, with what abstruse and often strange efforts man has attempted to free himself from the burdensome feeling of guilt without being able actually to do so. To demonstrate the special nature of biblical metanoia, I shall limit myself here to two brief observations. The word metanoia has no special significance in classical or Hellenistic Greek. The verb μετανοιεῖν means "to perceive afterward, to change one's mind, to regret, to experience remorse, to repent"; correspondingly, the noun means "change of mind, regret, repentance". "For the Greek, μετάνοια does not suggest a transformation of one's whole moral attitude, an effectual change in the whole direction of one's life, a conversion that determines the whole course of one's subsequent behavior. Before himself as well as before the gods, the Greek is able to repent, μετανοιεῖν, a sin *in actu* . . . , but μετάνοια as penance or conversion in the sense of the Old and New Testaments . . . is unknown to him."[59] Individual acts of metanoia remain separate acts of repentance or regret; they never combine into a single whole—a single permanent and total turning of one's whole existence into a new way; metanoia continues to be just repentance; it does not become conversion. The notion never suggests itself that one's whole existence, precisely *as* a whole, has need of a total conversion in order to become itself. One might perhaps say that the difference between polytheism and monotheism is silently at work here: an existence that is oriented toward many divine powers, that seeks to affirm itself in their confusion and rivalries, is never more than a many-sided gamble with the powers that be,

---

[58] Cf., for example, Gilbert Murray's searching analyses in *Euripides and His Age* (London: Oxford University Press, 1965); Hans Urs von Balthasar, *Herrlichkeit. Eine theologische Ästhetik* 3:1: "Im Raum der Metaphysik" (Einsiedeln: Johannes Verlag, 1965), 94–142.

[59] Johannes Behm, "μετανοέω, μετάνοια", in ThWNT 4:972–1004. For the passage quoted in the text, see 975–76; on the meaning of the word, see esp. 972–75.

whereas the one God becomes the one way that places man before the Yes or No of acceptance or rejection, that unifies his existence around a single call.

An objection arises at this point that will, at the same time, help to clarify our meaning. For it might be said that the arguments thus far adduced are relevant only as long as they are applied exclusively to the words μετάνοια and μετανοεῖν; they become untenable if they are applied to the Greek word for conversion, namely, ἐπιστροφή-ἐπιστρέφειν (the word generally used in this sense in the Septuagint to translate the Hebrew šūb).[60] Plato uses the word στρέφειν to designate circular movement, that is, the perfect movement that is proper to the gods, the heavens and the world. The circle, at first a cosmic sign, becomes also an existential symbol: a sign for the return of existence to itself. From this origin, ἐπιστροφή—a return to the oneness of reality, incorporation into the circular form of the world— becomes for the Stoa and for Neoplatonism the central ethical postulate.[61] Then follows the realization that, to be truly himself, man, as a whole, has need of the comprehensive movement of conversion [Umkehr: turning away] and self-communion [Einkehr: turning within], which, as the never-ending task of metanoia, requires that he turn his life away from dissipation in external matters and direct it within, where truth dwells. In my opinion, there is no need to deny, out of false anxiety about the originality of the Bible or naive counterpoising of biblical and Greek thought, that philosophical thought is here close to Christian belief and offers a formula by which the Fathers of the Church were able to express the ontological depths of the historical process of Christian conversion. Let us not hesitate to say that advance has been made here. But we must add that with this reference to man's communion with himself we have not encompassed the whole range of the conversion demanded by the Bible. The Greek ἐπιστροφή is a turning within to that innermost depth of man that is at once one and all. It is idealistic: if man penetrates deeply enough, he reaches the divine in himself. Biblical belief is more critical, more radical. Its criticism is directed not just to the outer man. It knows that danger lurks precisely in man's arrogance of spirit, in the most inward depths of

---

[60] ThWNT 4:985–94. Granted, Behm does not see the significance of this fact. His whole presentation is based on the antithetical relationships: biblical-Greek, legal-prophetic, cultic-religious (personal), and is consequently open to question despite the comprehensive body of material in the evaluations and the ordering of the matter under consideration. P. Hoffmann ("Umkehr", in Heinrich Fries, ed., Handbuch theologischer Grundbegriffe 2 [Munich: Kösel, 1963]: 719–24) has simply appropriated the plan of Behm's article.

[61] Cf. "Conversio", the careful presentation by Pierre Hadot, in Joachim Ritter, Historisches Wörterbuch der Philosophie 1 (Darmstadt: Wissenschaftliche Buchgesellschaft, 1971): 1033–36.

his being. It criticizes not just half but all of man. Salvation comes not just from inwardness, for this very inwardness can be rigid, tyrannical, egoistical, evil: "It is what comes out of a man that makes him unclean" (Mk 7:20). It is not just the turning to oneself that saves but rather the turning away from oneself and toward the God who calls. Man is oriented, not to the innermost depths of his own being, but to the God who comes to him from without, to the Thou who reveals himself to him and, in doing so, redeems him. Thus metanoia is synonomous with obedience and faith; that is why it belongs in the framework of the reality of the Covenant; that is why it refers to the community of those who are called to the same way: where there is belief in a personal God, there horizontality and verticality, inwardness and service, are ultimately not opposites. From this fact, it is immediately clear that metanoia is not just any Christian attitude but the fundamental Christian act per se, understood admittedly from a very definite perspective: that of transformation, conversion, renewal and change. To be a Christian, one must change not just in some particular area but without reservation even to the innermost depths of one's being.

Change and constancy

We have arrived now at a point that is very important especially for the modern consciousness, for which notions of "change" and "progress" are surrounded by an almost religious aura. Salvation comes only through change; labeling a person conservative is practically synonomous with social excommunication, for it means, in today's language, that such a one is opposed to progress, closed to what is new and, consequently, a defender of the old, the obscure, the enslaving; that he is an enemy of the salvation that change is expected to bring about. Does metanoia have something of the same meaning? At its entrance into history, was Christianity, which is based on the fundamental act of metanoia, also no more than a total struggle for change that only later became solidified, as lava solidifies from a molten mass into hard stone? What is the relationship between the Christian readiness to change that is metanoia and the contemporary will to change? In an early work written before World War II, Dietrich von Hildebrand, who is unfortunately best remembered today for his "Trojan Horse",[62] wrote a noteworthy treatise on Christian

---

[62] Dietrich von Hildebrand, *Das trojanische Pferd in der Stadt Gottes,* 4th ed. (Regensburg: Habbel, 1968). [For the English text, see *Trojan Horse in the City of God* (Chicago: Franciscan Herald Press, 1967). (Trans.)]

readiness to change[63] that reads, in part, like a reasoned justification of his conversion to the Catholic faith, like an apologia for that great change in his life which many refused to understand, which was condemned as infidelity, as apostasy from the faith of his fathers. In the passionate plea for a readiness for radical change that he uttered then, there can also be clearly heard the No to every glorification of that movement whose seizure of power compelled him first to let his work be published under a pseudonym and then to flee the continent of Europe. I believe that the inner oneness of radical transformation and radical constancy, which is what metanoia really is, has seldom been so accurately diagnosed as in this work that was written both as an apologia for total and radical transformation and as a condemnation of that "movement" whose revolution promised salvation but ended in a terror and destruction that are unparalleled in history.

I propose, therefore, to offer a brief summary of von Hildebrand's principal comments on the subject that here concerns us and to trace them somewhat more clearly than he does to their biblical origin. Above all, von Hildebrand regards as the chief characteristic of Christian readiness to change its boundlessness, its utter radicality. In this, it differs from the attitude of the ethical idealist, who wants to change only in certain respects but without letting the whole of his nature become involved. Granted, even Christians remain all too easily rooted in such a limited readiness to change, in those innumerable reservations by which they often withhold from change precisely what is most in need of it: "With untroubled conscience, they remain fixed in their self-assertion; for instance, they do not feel obliged to love their enemies, and they believe they have a perfect right to ward off humiliations by giving vent to their natural reactions. They regard as self-evident their claim to be respected by the world; they do not want to be looked upon as 'fools of Christ'—they make concessions, in certain circumstances, to human respect; they also want to amount to something in the eyes of the world. They are not ready for a total break with the world and its standards. They cling to many conventions and have no qualms about letting themselves go within well-defined limits."[64] Metanoia is an ethical concept; it is not specifically Christian. But when we consider that becoming a Christian depends on one's experiencing genuinely *Christian* metanoia as it was preached by the prophets or by Jesus, then it is clear that this circumscription of the scope

---

[63] Dietrich von Hildebrand, *Die Umgestaltung in Christus* [henceforth *Umgestaltung*], 3d ed. (Einsiedeln: Benziger, 1950), 11–29. [For the English text, see Dietrich von Hildebrand, *Transformation in Christ* (New York: Longmans, Green and Co., 1948). (Trans.)]

[64] *Umgestaltung*, 14.

of metanoia is the real cause of the crisis of Christianity today: "They want to amount to something in the eyes of the world. They are not ready for a total break with the world . . ."—this catering to human respect corrupts the Church today as it has done in the past, but perhaps even more today because human respect has at its disposal more means than formerly for exerting pressure. Unfortunately it cannot be denied that even members of the Church do not make their decisions today simply on the basis of what faith in Jesus Christ requires of them but very strongly on the basis of what other people will say, of whether they can save face; indeed, many a one who has earned the reputation of being a man of progress becomes all too quickly a prisoner of that reputation, which may seem to be oriented to freedom but in truth serves only to make him a slave to vanity and to counteract metanoia. The humorously ironic words of Wilhelm Busch should give Christians somewhat more courage than they usually display against the pressures of contemporary mores: "Once your good name's undermined, / That's one worry off your mind. . . ." Freedom comes, and comes only, to one who has the courage to change—the courage that the Bible calls metanoia; but it is precisely this courage that is wanting to us: "*Unreserved* readiness to change is the indispensable prerequisite for the reception of Christ in our soul"[65]—a statement that should startle us, for it is exactly what the precursor of Christ demanded, and it is only along the way he preached that we are led to Christ.

Thus, the fluidity of existence that is required of the Christian is, at the same time, "the exact opposite . . . of the cult of constant activity. . . ."[66] Readiness to be changed by Christ has nothing to do with the lack of direction of a reed shaken by the wind; it has nothing to do with that indecisiveness about existence, that facile conformity, that can be pushed in any direction. It is, rather, a standing-firm in Christ, a "standing-firm against all tendencies to change that come from below and a sensitive receptivity to every change that would mold us from above."[67] In other words, Christian metanoia is, to all intents and purposes, identical with *pistis* (faith, constancy), a change that does not exclude constancy but makes it possible. The New Testament speaks, with a sternness that may well make us uncomfortable, of the immutability of the basic decision in favor of Christianity: "As for those people who were once brought into the light and tasted the gift from heaven and received a share of the Holy Spirit and appreciated the good message of God and the powers of the world to come and yet in spite of this have fallen away—it is impossible for them to be renewed a second time. They cannot be repentant if they have

[65] *Umgestaltung*, 28.
[66] *Umgestaltung*, 17–18. [The reference is to the Youth Movement under Hitler. (Trans.)]
[67] *Umgestaltung*, 17.

willfully crucified the Son of God and openly mocked him" (Heb 6:4–6). One who reverses his conversion goes backward, not forward. Once the true way, that is, the way of truth, has been found, it never ceases to be a way, a path; it never ceases to be a goal and to demand movement toward it. But as a way it is no longer changeable, because turning aside or turning back will always be a turning away from truth. Von Hildebrand rightly calls attention to the fact that this constancy in the way of discovered truth is something entirely different and must always be a "formal conservatism": its permanence is grounded in the enduring validity of truth. "The same motive that induces one endowed with continuity to cling imperturbably to truth will compel him also to be open to every new truth."[68] This has a twofold meaning. It means, first of all, that after his conversion the Christian cannot simply jettison his readiness to change, his metanoia, as a burden belonging to the past. For there will remain in him the conflict of two opposing forces of gravity: the gravitational pull of interest, of egoism, and the gravitational pull of truth, of love. The first is always the one most "natural" to him; it points, as it were, to the more plausible way of acting. The second, on the other hand, will continue to exist in him only if he repeatedly rejects the gravitational pull of self-interest in favor of that of truth, if he is ready for the change this will require of him and prepared to let himself be transformed and molded in the image of Christ. In this sense, the malleability of his existence must not decrease but increase. This means that truth remains always a way, a goal—that it never becomes something wholly one's own. Christ, who is the truth, is in this world also the way, precisely because he is the truth.

An etymological observation will not be out of place here. To the best of my knowledge, it is only in Christianity, but there relatively early, that the words *proficere-profectus: to make progress-progress* acquire positive meaning and clear semantic content.[69] The prayers of the Roman Missal ask as a matter of course for the grace to *proficere*: to make progress; Vincent of Lérins speaks of progress in the knowledge of the truth of God; Bonaventure, in turn, coins the striking phrase: *Christi opera non deficiunt, sed proficiunt* (the works of Christ do not regress but progress) by which he justifies against the conservatism of the secular priesthood the emergence

---

[68] *Umgestaltung*, 22.

[69] On the slow development of the semantic content of *progressus*, cf. M. Seckler, "Der Fortschrittsgedanke in der Theologie", in *Theologie im Wandel*, edited by the Catholic theology department of Tübingen under the direction of Joseph Ratzinger and J. Neumann (Munich: Wewel, 1967), 41–67, esp. 42–43. For a thorough and discriminating presentation of the question (though without additional etymological investigation), see Klaus Thraede, "Fortschritt", in RAC 8 (1972): 141–82. Cf. also E. von Ivánka, "Die Wurzeln des Fortschrittsglaubens in Antike und Mittelalter", in U. Schöndorfer, *Der Fortschritt. Sinn und Gefahren* (Graz, 1966), 13–23.

of the new mendicant orders: the seed of apostolicity waxes through the ages unto the fullness of Christ.[70] Whereas antiquity is stamped with the circular schema *status-progressio-regressio*,[71] there can now be "progress" wherever a new direction reveals itself—indeed, without such new direction, there can be no progress. "Progress" and "constancy" condition each other. I may, perhaps, be permitted a comparison from the realm of human relationships: Who really grows, strides ahead, makes progress as a human being?—the playboy, who slips from one fleeting encounter to another, who never has time really to know a "thou"? or the person who is truly constant in his Yes to another man, who goes forward with this other, whose Yes never lapses into apathy but who learns slowly and ever more deeply from his Yes to give himself to this "thou" and, in doing so, to find freedom, truth and love? The ability to remain constant in the Yes once given requires an unremitting readiness to change—a readiness in which one grows to maturity. In contrasting the two modes of change, von Hildebrand, I think, has made abundantly clear the true nature of the Christian readiness to change as opposed to that of the [Nazi] "cult of activity".

Inwardness and community

If one wishes to describe the essential and fundamental characteristics of Christian metanoia, two further attitudes must be pointed out in addition to and similar to the interrelationship of inwardness and social orientation: the interrelationship of gift and obligation. I shall limit myself to a few words about each. Behm, I think, is clearly mistaken in his otherwise excellent article on μετάνοια in the *Theologisches Wörterbuch zum Neuen Testament* when, of the four possible meanings of this word, that is, "feel remorse", "change one's mind", "do penance", "turn away, be converted", he accepts only the last as the true meaning of Jesus' command and rejects the others as a lapse into legalism.[72] It seems more likely to me

[70] *S. Bonaventurae opera omnia* 8 (Florence: Ad claras aquas [Quaracchi]: 1898), opusculum 12, "Epistola de Tribus Quaestionibus", 13, 336. On St. Bonaventure's total writings, see Joseph Ratzinger, *Die Geschichtstheologie des hl. Bonaventura* (Munich, 1959).

[71] This is the formula proposed by Marius Victorinus: "Hymnus [Tertius] de Trinitate", lines 71–73, *Marii Victorini opera*, pars I, *Opera theologica*, in CSEL (Vindobonae: Hoelder, Pichler, Tempsky, 1971), 295. It is offered here as a trinitarian theological interpretation of the neoplatonic formula for being. Cf. Hadot (n. 61 above), 1034–35. It is clear that the encounter between Christianity and antiquity—which, from the beginning, was also an interrelationship—cannot be reduced to the simple antithesis: cyclic-linear; cf. Thraede (n. 69 above), esp. 161–62.

[72] ThWNT 4:994–95, and elsewhere.

that Jesus' command included the whole spectrum of meanings—
admittedly, with conversion as the central concept. The radicality of
Christian conversion requires its concrete manifestation as an incarnate
and social event: this explains why the sacrament of penance, with the focal points of genuine penance (fasting-prayer-alms)[73] and profession of
faith, is the public and ecclesial form of renewed conversion. . . .

Gift and obligation: the little way

The interrelationship of gift and obligation is eminently clear in Jesus'
words: "I tell you solemnly, unless you change and become like little
children you will never enter the kingdom of heaven" (Mt 18:3). Behm
comments on this passage: "To be a child . . . means to be small, to need
help and to be receptive to it. One who is converted becomes small before
God . . ., ready to let God have his way with him. The children of the
heavenly Father whom Jesus made known to us . . . are completely
receptive to him. He gives them what they cannot give themselves. . . .
That is true also of μετάνοια. It is God's gift, but it does not, for that
reason, cease to be a binding obligation."[74] Toward the end of the last
century, this simple means of metanoia, based, not on heroic
extravagances, but on our daily patience with God and his with us, was
charmingly demonstrated in the life of St. Thérèse of Lisieux: instead of a
saintly model that relied on heroic virtues and failed to recognize the truly
Christian way, she offered her "little way"—the daily reception of and
meeting with God. Ida Friederike Görres observed in her diary that she
was becoming more and more convinced that Thérèse was by no means
unique; she was but the prototype of a whole chain of "little" saints who,
without knowing one another, grew up unnoticed in the Church at about
the turn of the last century and, as if by silent command, went their little
way. She quotes then these striking words of the Irish Jesuit William
Doyle, who was born in the same year as Thérèse and fell at Ypres in 1917:
"I do not believe I could ever find food for vainglory or pride in anything I
do—any more than an organ grinder can take pride in the beautiful music

[73] This ancient Christian triad should be put into effect more strongly in the Church as a
concrete evidence of penance.

[74] ThWNT 4:998. Joachim Jeremias' interpretation of Mt 13:3 is beautiful (but somewhat
one-sided): " 'To become a child again' means: to learn to say Abba again. With that we are at
the center of what penance means. To be converted means to learn to say Abba, to cast one's
whole confidence on the heavenly Father, to return to one's Father's house and arms. . . . In
the last analysis, penance is nothing other than reliance on the grace of God"
(*Neutestamentliche Theologie* 1 [Gütersloh: Mohn, 1971]: 154–55).

he produces when he turns the handle. . . . I feel ashamed when people praise me . . . just as a piano might feel ashamed if someone were to compliment it on the beautiful music that flows from its keys."[75] I. F. Görres comments: "The hidden holiness that exists in the Church is a story in its own right. There are probably dozens of people like this . . ., but no one pays them much attention."[76] Why, she asks, with some irritation, do people make "such a fuss"[77] about "little Thérèse", who is but one among many? "But, of course, people accept such things more readily from a lovely young girl with her smile, her roses and her veil. We might ask ourselves if Thérèse would have been so enthusiastically received if she had been hopelessly ugly—hunchbacked, say, or squint-eyed—or if she had been very old."[78]

Today, I believe, we can offer a kind of answer—and a very surprising one—to this question. For it seems to me that we are all, once again, witnesses of a saint of this "movement": John XXIII. One who reads his diary is disappointed at first and cannot believe that the man who practices this old-fashioned, seminary asceticism and the great Pope of the renewal can be one and the same person. But it is only when one sees the interrelationship of the two that one sees him properly, that one sees the whole person. This diary, begun at a time when Thérèse was still alive, is in truth a "little way"—not a pretentious one.[79] It reflects, in the beginning, the average spirituality to be found during those years in an Italian seminary for priests—somewhat ordinary, somewhat narrow, and yet wide open to what is essential. And it is precisely in pursuit of this way, of this simplicity and this patience with the daily routine, which can succeed only if one lets oneself be changed daily—it is precisely in pursuit of this way that that spiritual simplicity finally grows to maturity which enables one to see and which can make a short, fat, elderly man beautiful by reason of the light that radiates from within. Here everything is gift, and yet everything is conversion, is metanoia, which forms Christians and

---

[75] Ida Friederike Görres, *Zwischen den Zeiten: aus meinen Tagebüchern* (Olten–Freiburg: Walter, 1960), 271. [For an English translation, see Ida Friederike Görres, *Broken Lights, Diaries and Letters: 1951–1959,* trans. Barbara Waldstein-Wartenberg [Westminster, Md.: Newman, 1964], (Trans.)]

[76] Görres, 273.

[77] Görres, 270.

[78] Görres, 270.

[79] The diary begins, significantly enough, with one of the first personal resolutions of the "little rule" given by the spiritual director at Bergamo to the seminarian Roncalli. The editor (Don Loris Capovilla) comments: "He kept them always by him and constantly observed them, even when he was pope." Giovanni XXIII, *Il Giornale dell' Anima* (Rome: Edizioni di Storia e Letteratura, 1904). [For an English translation, see Pope John XXIII, *Journal of a Soul,* trans. Dorothy White (New York: McGraw-Hill, 1965). The above quotation will be found on 4, n. 1, of the English translation. (Trans.)]

creates saints. "There are probably dozens of people like that", says I. F. Görres—actually, we should all try to be of their number. For only then are we Christians.

B. Faith as Knowledge and as Praxis—the Fundamental Option of the Christian Credo

What does it really mean when a person decides to believe in God, the Father Almighty, Creator of heaven and earth? The content of such a decision will, perhaps, be best understood if we look first at two current misunderstandings that fail to take into account the essential meaning of such a faith. The first misunderstanding consists in regarding the question of God as a purely theoretical one that, in the last analysis, has no impact on the course of the world or of one's own life. According to positivistic philosophy, it is impossible to prove such propositions either true or false; that is, there is no possibility of showing clearly that they are false, but this very fact testifies to their lack of importance. For if something that is, to all intents and purposes, unprovable as true can also not be rejected as false, it is clear that nothing in man's life will be altered by it whether it is true or false; it can, therefore, be comfortably ignored.[80] Theoretical irrefutability becomes thus a sign of practical negligibility; what has no impact has also no meaning. Anyone who is aware of the contradictory situations in which Christianity is involved today, of how, by reason of its monarchical and nationalistic structures, it has come to be regarded as an appurtenance of Marxist thought, might indeed be tempted to consider the faith of Christians as a useless placebo that can be used as one will because it has no content of its own.

But there also exists a diametrically opposed view. Its proponents maintain that belief in God is but the expedient of a particular social group, in terms of which it can be fully explained and with the disappearance of which it, too, will disappear. It was invented to ensure domination and to keep man subservient to existing powers. And if there are some who see in the God of Israel a revolutionary principle, they, too, are basically in accord with this view: they are merely equating the notion of God with the praxis that seems right to them.

One who reads the Bible will have no doubt as to the practical character of the profession of faith in God, the Almighty. The Bible makes it

---

[80] On the subject of positivism, cf. Bernhard Casper, "Die Unfähigkeit zur Gottesfrage in positivistischen Bewusstsein", in Joseph Ratzinger, *Die Frage nach Gott* (Freiburg: Herder, 1972), 27–42; Norbert Schiffers, "Die Welt als Tatsache", in Johannes Hüttenbügel, *Gott-Mensch-Universum* (Graz: Styria, 1974), 31–69.

abundantly clear that a world under God's sway is quite different from a world without God—that nothing, in fact, remains the same if God is taken away and that, by the same token, everything changes when one turns to God. Husbands, for instance, are told almost, as it were, parenthetically, in Paul's first epistle to the Thessalonians (4:3–5), that their relationship to their wives is to be marked by a holy respect, "not giving way to selfish lust like the pagans who do not know God." The change that takes place when God enters the context of human life reaches to the most personal and intimate level of human relationships; ignorance of God, atheism, finds its concrete expression in a lack of respect for one's fellowmen, whereas knowledge of God means seeing them in a new way.

This same fact is affirmed in the other texts in which Paul speaks of atheism. In the epistle to the Galatians (4:8–9), he designates as the characteristic effect of ignorance of God enslavement to the "elemental principles of this world", with which one enters into a kind of worshipful relationship that soon turns to slavery because it rests on untruth; the Christian can ridicule these elemental principles as "pitiable" and "despicable" because he knows the truth and is thereby free of their tyranny. In the epistle to the Romans (1:18–32), Paul develops this thought further. In speaking of the philosophy of the heathens and its relationship to existing religions, he notes that the Mediterranean nations have reduced the knowledge of God to mere theory and, by reason of this perversion, have themselves fallen into perversity; by excluding from their way of life the foundation of all things, whom they very well know, they have distorted reality and have become disoriented, without norms and incapable of distinguishing what is base from what is noble, what is great from what is ordinary, and are thus, in practice, susceptible to every perversity—a train of thought to which we cannot deny a certain validity for the present as well.

If we turn our attention, finally, to the central Old Testament text about belief in God, it, too, affirms what has been said. In it, the revelation of God's name (Ex 3) is, at the same time, the revelation of God's will; it changes everything not only in the life of Moses but also in the lives of the people and hence in the history of the world. Significantly, it is not a concept of God that is propounded here but a name that is revealed. We are not offered a series of theological deliberations leading to a certain conclusion but a relationship that is comparable to the relationship between persons, yet superior to it because it alters the foundation of life itself, or, more accurately, it exposes to the light the foundation of life that has hitherto been hidden and turns it into a summons, a call. That is why the Israelite regards the daily repetition of the act by which he professes his belief in God as the acceptance of the yoke of God's dominion; praying the credo is the act by which he lays claim to his place in reality.

One more fact must be noted here—a fact that is assuredly most repugnant to a mind that would remain neutral. My thought is well expressed in the above-mentioned passage from the epistle to the Galatians in which Paul, having recalled the atheistic past of those to whom he is writing, adds the comment: But now you have acknowledged God—and immediately corrects himself: or rather, you have been acknowledged by God (Gal 4:9). A universal experience finds expression here: knowing and believing in God is an active-passive process, not a philosophical structure, whether theoretical or practical; it is an act in which one is first touched by God and then responds in thought and deed but which one is, however, free to reject. It is only from this perspective that we can understand what it means to call God a "Person" or to speak of "revelation": in our knowledge of God there occurs also—and, indeed, first—something from God's side. God is not a resting object but the ground of our being, who establishes his own credentials, who makes his presence known at the very center of our being and who can, precisely for this reason, be ignored because we are so easily inclined to live far from the center of our being, far from ourselves. By revealing the passive element in our knowledge of God, we have also touched the roots of the two misunderstandings of which we spoke at the beginning. Both of them presume a knowledge in which the individual is himself active. They know man only as an active subject in the world and see the whole of reality as but a system of lifeless objects manipulated by man. It is precisely at this point, however, that faith offers a different perspective. Only here can we begin to understand what faith really is.

But let us not move too quickly. Before going on, let us first review what has already been said. We have seen that the sentence "I believe in God, the Father Almighty" is not just a theoretical formula with no implications of further meaning. Its validity or lack of validity alters the very foundations of the world. The next step is to turn our attention to Werner Heisenberg's formulation of this thought in his conversations about science and religion. His account of what the physicist Wolfgang Pauli said to him in 1927 has an unmistakably prophetic ring. Pauli was afraid that the collapse of religious convictions would be followed all too shortly by the collapse of the existing ethical code, ". . . and there will happen things so terrible that we cannot even conceive of them now."[81] At

[81] Werner Heisenberg, *Der Teil und das Ganze. Gespräche im Umkreis der Atomphysik* (Munich: Piper, 1969), 118. A comment from the year 1952 reechoes this thought: "Once the

the time, no one could have known how soon thereafter mockery of the God of Jesus Christ as a Jewish invention would turn into fact what had hitherto been unthinkable.

In the same discussion, Heisenberg attacked with great energy the question that has thus far gone unanswered in our deliberations: Is it perhaps correct to say that "God" is merely the function of a particular praxis? Heisenberg reports that he asked the great Danish physicist Niels Bohr if God should not be relegated to the same level of reality as certain imaginary numbers in the field of mathematics that do not exist as natural numbers but on which whole branches of mathematics have been built, so that "there are such numbers, after all. . . . Would it not be possible in religion, too, . . . to regard the expression 'there is' as the ascent to a higher level of abstraction? This ascent would have the function of facilitating our understanding of cosmic connections, nothing more."[82] Is God a kind of moral fiction in terms of which it is possible to present spiritual contexts in an abstract and synoptical way? That is the question that is raised here.

In the same conversation, Heisenberg approaches another aspect of the problem—the concept of religion proposed by Max Planck. On the model of nineteenth-century thought, this great scholar differentiated strictly between the objective and subjective aspects of the world. The objective aspect can be investigated with exact scientific procedures; but the subjective aspect rests on personal decisions that are beyond the categories of true and false. To these subjective decisions, which each must make for himself alone, he assigned the realm of religion, which can therefore be lived with personal conviction without impinging on the objective world of science. Heisenberg reports that it became clear to him during a conversation with Wolfgang Pauli that such a total rift between knowing and believing would "hardly be more than an emergency measure adopted for a limited period of time."[83] To separate religion, belief in God, from objective truth is to fail to recognize its innermost nature. "Religion is concerned with objective truth." This, says Heisenberg, was Niels Bohr's answer to the question. Heisenberg added: "But it seems to me that the

magnetic force that guides this compass has been completely eliminated, . . . I am afraid very terrible things will happen—worse things even than concentration camps and atom bombs" (195). [For an English translation of this work, see Werner Heisenberg, *Physics and Beyond: Encounters and Conversations,* trans. Arnold J. Pomerans (New York: Harper & Row, 1971). (Trans.)]

[82] Heisenberg, 126.
[83] Heisenberg, 117–18.

whole division into objective and subjective aspects of the world is carried too far here."[84]

It is not necessary for our purpose to examine how Bohr, in his conversation with Heisenberg, overemphasized the scientific aspect of the distinction between objective and subjective and searched for a central order behind the two. Even without this, the point at issue is clear: belief in God does not claim to offer a fictitious and abstract union of different modes of action; it claims to be more than a subjective conviction inexplicably juxtaposed to a godless objectivity. It claims to reveal the essence, the root, of the objective, to bring into sharper focus the demands of objective reality. It does so by leading to that source which unites object and subject and offers the only true explanation of their relationship. Einstein pointed out that the relationship of subject and object is, ultimately, the greatest of all puzzles, or, more exactly, that our thinking, our mathematical worlds conceived solely in our consciousness, correspond to reality, that our consciousness has the same structure as reality and vice versa.[85] That is the principal ground on which all science rests. It acts as though this were a matter of course, whereas, in fact, nothing is less so. For it means that all being has the same nature as consciousness; that there is present in human thought, in human subjectivity, that which objectively moves the world. The world itself has the same nature as consciousness. The subjective is not something alien to objective reality; rather, this reality is itself like a subject. The subjective is objective, and vice versa. This affects even the language of natural science, which here, under the pressure of objects, often reveals more than its users are aware.

An example from an entirely different sphere suggests itself: even the most obstinate neo-Darwinists, who want to exclude from evolution every final, goal-directed cause so as not to be suspected of metaphysics or of belief in God, nevertheless speak with total artlessness of how nature contrives to profit by the best chances of survival. One who studies their customary linguistic usage cannot fail to conclude that nature is here consistently endowed with the attributes of God, or, more exactly perhaps: it has appropriated the very place ascribed in the Old Testament to wisdom. It is a conscious power acting with utmost intelligence. Without doubt, these scientists would explain, if asked, that the word nature is here only an abstract schematization of many individual

[84] Heisenberg, 123ff.; 126–30.

[85] Quoted here from Josef Pieper, "Kreatürlichkeit. Bemerkungen über die Elemente eines Grundbegriffs", in Ludger Oeing-Hanhoff, *Thomas von Aquin 1274–1974* (Munich: Kösel, 1974), 47–70. Quotation is on 50.

elements—somewhat in the nature of an imaginary number that serves to facilitate the construction of theories and make them more comprehensible. But we must seriously ask ourselves whether any part of this whole theory would survive were we strictly to prohibit this latter fiction and insist on its elimination. We know for a fact that no logical context would remain.

Josef Pieper has shed light on our subject from yet another perspective. He reminds us that, according to Sartre, human beings and things cannot have a nature. If they did, Sartre argues, there would have to be a God. If reality itself does not proceed from a creative consciousness, if it is not the realization of a design, of an idea, then it will always be a structure without firm contours, to be used as one will; but if there are meaningful forms in it that are antecedent to man, then there must also be a meaning that is responsible for their existence. For Sartre, the one unchanging certainty was that there is no God; therefore, there can be no nature. This means that man is condemned to a monstrous freedom; he must discover for himself with no norm to guide him what he will make of himself and of the world.[86] At this point, the nature of the alternative with which we are confronted in the first article of the Creed should be growing gradually clear. The question is whether we accept reality as pure matter or as the expression of a meaning that refers to us; whether we invent values or must find them. On our answer depends the kind of freedom of which we must speak, for two completely different freedoms, two completely different fundamental attitudes toward life, are involved here.

Many, perhaps, will feel compelled to object to these considerations on the grounds that what has been said thus far is just fruitless speculation about the God of the philosophers; it has no relevance to the living God of Abraham, Isaac and Jacob, the Father of Jesus Christ. The Bible, they will protest, does not speak about a central order (as Heisenberg does)[87] or about nature and being (as the early philosophers did); to do so would be to dilute faith, which is concerned with the Father, with Jesus Christ, with I and thou, with a personal relationship with the living God through prayer. Such objections may sound pious, but they miss the point and conceal the greatness of the real object of faith. Granted, God cannot be measured as we might measure some measurable object. Granted, too, there is no measuring without the intellectual context that links the measurer with the measured. But, for that very reason, this foundation cannot itself be measured; it is antecedent to all measuring. Greek philosophy expressed

---

[86] Pieper has referred repeatedly and with increasing emphasis to this question, most recently in the above-mentioned publication, esp. 50.

[87] Heisenberg, 118. The central concept is the one contained in the conversation, "Positivism, Metaphysics and Religion" (1952), 291ff.

the thought in this way: The ultimate foundations of all proof, on which thought rests, are never measured; they are only perceived. But everyone knows that perception is something unique. It is not to be separated from the intellectual stance an individual has adopted during his lifetime. The deepest perceptions of man require the whole man. It is clear, then, that such knowledge has its own mode of existence. We cannot verify God as we would verify some measurable object. There is question here *also* of an act of humility; the acceptance of the fact that one's own intellect has been called by the eternal intellect. Counter to this is the desire for an autonomy that first invents the world and then opposes to the Christian humility of acknowledgement of being that other strange humility which despises being: in himself, man is nothing, an unfinished animal, but perhaps we can still make something of him. . . .

If we distinguish too closely between the God of faith and the God of the philosophers, we deprive faith of its objectivity and again split object and subject into two different worlds. Granted, there can be many different approaches to the one God. Heisenberg's conversations with friends show how a mind that is sincerely seeking can penetrate through the spirit in nature to a central order that not only exists but makes demands upon us and, by its demands, becomes present to us, becomes like the soul: the central order can be present to us just as the center of a human being can be present to another human being. It can meet us.[88] For one who has grown up in the Christian tradition, the way begins in the "thou" of prayer: such a one knows that he can address the Lord; that this Jesus is not just a historical personage of the past but is the same in all ages. And he knows, too, that in, with and through the Lord he can address him to whom Jesus says "Father". In Jesus, he sees likewise the Father. For he sees that this Jesus does not have his life from himself, that his whole existence is an exchange with the Other, a coming from him and a returning to him. He sees that this Jesus is truly "Son" in his whole existence, is one who receives his inmost being from another, that his life is a receiving. In him is to be found the hidden foundation; in the actions, words, life, suffering of him who is truly Son it is possible to see, hear and touch him who is unknown. The unknown ground of being reveals itself as Father.[89] Omnipotence is like a Father. God no longer appears as Supreme Being in the process of becoming, or as Being per se, but as Person. And yet: the

---

[88] Heisenberg, 293.

[89] This thought is developed at greater length in Part One, Chapter 2, Section 1A of the present work: "Anthropological Foundation of the Concept of Tradition". On what follows, see my *Einführung in das Christentum*, 11th ed. (Munich: Kösel, 1974), 48–53. [For an English translation, see Joseph Ratzinger, *Introduction to Christianity*, trans. J. R. Foster (New York: Herder and Herder, 1970). (Trans.)]

personal relationship that exists here is not to be equated with purely human relationships—to that extent, it is an oversimplification to speak of our relationship with God in terms of an I-thou relationship. Speaking to God does not mean speaking with just anyone who happens to stand before me as another "thou"; on the contrary, it touches the ground of my own being, without which I would not be, and this ground of my being is identical with the ground of being per se; indeed, it is that being without which nothing is. What is so striking here is, of course, the fact that this whole ground of being is, at the same time, a relationship; not less than I, who know, think, feel and love, but rather more than I, so that I can know only because I am known, love only because I am already loved. The first article of the Creed signifies, then, a highly personal and, at the same time, a highly objective knowledge. A highly personal knowledge: the finding of a "thou" who gives me meaning, to whom I can entrust myself absolutely. That is why this first article is formulated, not as a neutral sentence, but as a prayer, an address: I believe in God—I believe in thee, I entrust myself to thee. Where God is truly known, he is not something we can discuss as we would discuss imaginary or natural numbers, but a "thou" to whom we can speak because he speaks to us. I can entrust myself absolutely to him because he *is* absolute, because his person is the objective ground of all reality. Confidence and trust as firmly based realities are possible in this world only because the ground of being is trustworthy—if this were not so, all the trust of individuals would be, in the last analysis, but an empty farce or a tragic irony.

Is it necessary, after these reflections, to turn again to the questions raised at the beginning, in which there lurks the objection so frequently raised by Marxism today—that God is but the imaginary number by which the ruling class makes its power visible; that a view of life contained in the concepts "Father" and "omnipotence" and requiring worship of this Father and this omnipotence is revealed to be a credo of oppression; that only the radical emancipation of Father and omnipotence can restore freedom? To do so, we would have to retrace our whole train of thought from this one perspective; but perhaps, after all that has been said, it will suffice if, instead, I recall a scene from Solzhenitsyn's *August 1914* that has a direct bearing on these questions. In the extraordinary circumstances created by the patriotic upsurge at the beginning of the war in 1914, two Russian students, enthusiastic as are nearly all their generation about revolutionary social ideas, engage in conversation with an unusual wise man to whom they have given the nickname "the astrologist". He attempts very cautiously to woo them from the specter of a scientifically conceived social order and to show them how illusory is the hope that the world can be changed by a revolutionary intellect: "Who would be so presumptuous as to claim he has the ability to *invent* ideal conditions? . . .

Presumption is the mark of limited intellectual development. A person whose intellectual development is limited is presumptuous; one whose intellect is highly developed is humble." In the end, after much back and forth, the young men ask: "But isn't justice a sufficient principle on which to found a social order?" And the answer: "By all means! But not our own justice as we imagine it for ourselves in some comfortable earthly paradise. Rather, that justice that is before us, that exists without us and for its own sake. And we must *conform* to it."[90] Solzhenitsyn has been at pains to stress the antithetical concepts invent / conform in various ways in the printed text: "invent" in boastful capitals, "conform" in humble italics. Nevertheless, the key issue is not "invent" but "conform". Without mentioning the word God, and with the hesitancy of one who must lead to the center those who have gone far astray (". . . he spoke; he looked at both of them; had he not perhaps gone too far?"), the author describes very precisely what worship is, what the first article of the Creed is all about. For man, the key issue is not invention but conformity, attention to the justice of the Creator, to the truth of creation itself. That is the only guarantee of freedom; it alone ensures that inviolable respect of person for person, for God's creature, that, according to Paul, is the mark of one who knows God. Conformity of this kind, acceptance of the truth of the Creator in his creatures, is worship. That is what is at issue when we say: I believe in God, the Father Almighty, Creator of heaven and earth.

C. Faith as Trust and Joy—Evangelium

The history of Christianity begins with the word χαῖϱε: Rejoice! According to Luke, it is the first word spoken by the angel who announced to Mary the birth of Jesus (Lk 1:28).[91] For Luke, this word, which inaugurates the history of Jesus and, with it, the history of Christianity, is a comprehensive programmatic designation of what Christianity is by nature. In narrating the birth of Jesus, he repeats this introduction with variations and more expansively in the words the angel addresses to the shepherds: "I bring you news of great joy": χαϱὰν μεγάλην. In the Greek text, the accent on joy, on rejoicing, on good tidings, is present in a very special way in the words "I bring you news", for the expression used there is the momentous one that eventually became both the designation par excellence for the whole Christian message and its central literary

[90] Aleksandr Solzhenitsyn, *August 1914*, trans. Michael Glenny (New York: Farrar, Straus and Giroux, 1972), 409 and 412. See also, all of chap. 42, 395–412.

[91] Cf. R. Laurentin, *Struktur und Theologie der lukanischen Kindheitsgeschichte* (Stuttgart, 1967), 75–76. Important works by Stanislas Lyonnet are also named there.

expression: εὐαγγελίζομαι: I bring you an eu-angelion—glad, happy tidings. The whole text is saturated, as it were, with a feeling of joy, of a fresh beginning that will make all things new.

That the word *evangelium* means "glad tidings" is one of those bits of information that remains in nearly everyone's memory from religious instruction or from a sermon. All too often, however, we compare this attractive designation—with melancholy, if not with bitterness—with our own daily experience of Christianity and the impression made on us by Christians, with the joylessness, the cramped scrupulosity, the narrowness of spirit that seems to us to be the most telling refutation of what Christianity claims to be. This feeling that Christianity is opposed to joy, this impression of punctiliousness and unhappiness, is surely a more likely explanation of why people leave the Church than are any of the theoretical problems the faith may pose today. Friedrich Nietzsche has given this revolt of sentiment its most stirring and striking formulation: "The whole absurd residue of Christian fable, cobwebbery of concepts and theology matters little to us; if it were a thousand times more absurd, I wouldn't raise a finger against it." "Until now, we have always attacked Christianity in a false, not just a timid, way. So long as we do not regard Christian morality as a capital crime against life, its defenders will have an easy time of it. The problem of the simple 'truth' of Christianity . . . is a quite secondary matter so long as we do not question the value of Christian morality."[92] And what of the revolt against the Christian concept of value? Two passages may make clear to us the change with which Nietzsche was concerned. "What has been until now the greatest sin here on earth? Was it not the word of him who said: 'Woe unto those who laugh here'?" The second passage reads: " 'To be sure, unless you become like little children, you shall not enter the kingdom of heaven.' (And Zarathustra pointed upward with his hands.) But we do not want to enter the kingdom of heaven. We have become men—and so we want the kingdom of earth."[93] The young Albert Camus sounded the same note when, in his matriculation thesis for the University of Algiers, he parried the words of Christ: "My kingdom is not of this world" with the statement: "*Notre royaume est de ce monde*—our kingdom is of this world."[94]

[92] Quoted in Henri de Lubac, S. J., *Le Drame de l'humanisme athée* (Paris: Éditions Spes, 1950), 118 and 119. [For an English translation, see Henri de Lubac, *The Drama of Atheist Humanism,* trans. Edith M. Riley (New York: World, 1963). (Trans.)] See also, Friedrich Nietzsche, "Der Wille zur Macht", in *Werke* (Leipzig, 1899ff.), 15:328 and 327 (from the year 1888).

[93] Quoted in de Lubac, *Le Drame,* 313 and 313–14; see also Friedrich Nietzsche, "Also Sprach Zarathustra", in *Werke,* 6:386 and 459.

[94] Albert Camus, *Essais* (Bibl. de la Pléiade, 1965), 1225; cf. Gisela Linde, *Das Problem der Gottesvorstellungen im Werk von Albert Camus* (Münster: Aschendorff, 1975), 20ff.

We have come now to the heart of the problem: Did not Christianity forbid us the tree in the middle of the garden and, in doing so, really forbid us everything? Toward the end of the nineteenth century, French psychiatrists coined the phrase "*maladie catholique*", by which they meant that special neurosis that is the product of a warped pedagogy so exclusively concentrated on the fourth and sixth commandments that the resultant complex with regard to authority and purity renders the individual so incapable of free self-development that his selflessness degenerates into a loss of self and a denial of love, and his faith leads, not to freedom, but to rigidity and an absence of freedom.

But now we must, in all justice, consider the arguments of the other side. Nietzsche's notion of contrasting the Crucified and his virtues of the weak, the "morality of resentment", with Dionysius and the morality of the strong, the fearless, led him to create, in contrast to the "virtuous average animal" (as he expressed it), the "ideal of a mind that makes sport ingenuously, that is to say, unintentionally and with overwhelming inventiveness and power, of everything that has hitherto been called holy, good, untouchable, divine."[95] What he anticipated and designed in details that are uncannily prophetic is the morality of the later concentration-camp guards; a world peopled by the inhuman and violent who are a mystery even to themselves. I find the way of Albert Camus more practical and impressive: My kingdom is of this world. The light and sun of his African homeland were, for him, the embodiment of this world which it must have been a joy to enter, to embrace, to possess. But even the early work *L'Envers et l'endroit,* which he wrote at about the same time as the enthusiastic depiction of bathing in early morning light and water in the essay "Les noces", depicts also the opposite experience: the author in Prague, in a city where he understands no one and whose beauty becomes for him a dark prison. The city of the foreign language, the city of total loneliness and meaninglessness, becomes the symbol of man's life in this world; encaged in a city with whose language he is unacquainted; immured in deadly solitude; in the end, its beauty becomes a mockery, and the prisoner drowns in the abyss of the absurd.[96] Let us look, finally, at our own experience, at the trite everyday world that surrounds us. A glance at any magazine stand will show us that mankind has completely freed itself of what the French called the "Catholic sickness". There are no longer any

[95] De Lubac, *Le Drame,* 120 and 122; Friedrich Nietzsche, "Ecce Homo", in *Werke,* 15:154; also, 71 and 122. For an important study of the aspects of Nietzsche's work that are discussed here, see P. Köster, *Der sterbliche Gott. Nietzsches Entwurf übermenschlicher Grösse* (Meisenheim am Glan, 1972), esp. 27–68.

[96] Fusion with the cosmos: "Les noces", in Albert Camus, *Essais;* "L'Envers et l'endroit", in ibid., 15–20 (Prag = La mort dans l'âme, 31–39); see also, Linde, 4–28.

forbidden trees. But has mankind become healthier? Has it become free? As we can read in a variety of commentaries, even the avant-garde of libertinism would deny that it has: disgust and boredom consume them—lack of freedom has increased.

What is wrong with man? Whatever it is, the notion of joy seems not to be the simple matter that many of the Fathers of Vatican Council II apparently thought it was. Wherever we look, the way of escape seems barred to us on all sides. Morality and immorality seem to enslave man, to make him joyless and empty. Is there, in the last analysis, no hope for him? Was Camus right? Have we no recourse but to admit that, seen in the light, man is an absurd creature whose only hope is to accept the absurd; to roll the rock of Sisyphus uphill again and again, knowing full well that it will roll back down again?

Before accepting such a harrowing and devastating diagnosis, we must begin again to study it, to examine it from all sides—for we can surely not accept the premise that man is absurd; we are so constructed that we must find meaning if we are to live at all. One who can no longer project meaning knows he is also no longer justified in passing on human life. The refusal to accept the future, which we experience more and more frequently today, is the logical product of the crisis of meaning in which we find ourselves; it must be obvious, then, that what we are discussing here is not some incidental spice of life but that the tree of "meaning", which, to say the least, is closely related to the shrub of "joy", is identical with the tree of life itself.[97] Let us inquire once more, then, about the proclamation of joy that is the rubric over Christendom. What is it like? What is its true form? Let us begin again, very cautiously at first, with a linguistic statement. The word *evangelium* means "glad tidings", we said. But it did not have, originally, the neat and somewhat ineffectual ring that it has today even when it is translated more comprehensively—and, admittedly, with a concomitant poverty of meaning—as "good news". In Jesus' time, the word had found its way into the language of contemporary political theology: the decrees of the emperor, all his proclamations, were called *evangelium*, even when, for the recipients, they were far from being good news. *Evangelium* meant "a message from the emperor". There was nothing trivial or sentimental about it but rather something majestic. Even though such messages were not always manifestly joyful, they were called joyful because they came from him who held the world together.[98] Granted, it would be presumptuous for just any individual—even an emperor—to claim to be God and, for that reason, to call his messages

[97] On this subject, cf. Part One, Chapter Two, Section 1B in this volume: "Baptism and the Formulation of the Content of Faith—Liturgy and the Development of Tradition".
[98] G. Friedrich, "εὐαγγέλιον", in ThWNT, 705–34, esp. 721–22.

"glad tidings", for it would be an expression of man's glorification of self. But when the carpenter's son of Nazareth uses this manner of speech, then all that has gone before is absorbed and surpassed: Jesus' message is *evangelium,* not because it is immediately pleasing to us or comfortable or attractive, but because it comes from him who has the key to true joy. Truth is not always comfortable for man, but it is only truth that makes him free and only freedom that brings him joy. Now, however, we must ask more precisely: What makes a man joyful? What robs him of joy? What puts him at odds with himself? What opens him to himself and to others? When we want to describe the most extreme form of being at odds with existence, we often say of an individual that he does not like himself. But whom or what is he to like who does not like himself? Something very important makes its appearance here: egoism, certainly, is natural to man and needs no encouragement; but this is not true of self-acceptance. The former must be overcome; the latter must be discovered, and it is assuredly one of the most dangerous errors of Christian teachers and moralists that they have all too often confused the two and, by exorcizing the affirmation of self, have enabled egoism to avenge such a betrayal by becoming all the more rampant—this, ultimately, is the root of what the French have labeled the *maladie catholique*: one who wants to live only on the supernatural level and to the exclusion of self will be, in the end, without a self but not, for that reason, selfless. The last entry Bernanos has his country priest enter into his diary reads: "It is easier than one thinks to hate oneself. Grace consists in forgetting oneself. But if pride were completely dead in us, then the grace of graces would be to love oneself humbly as just one, however unessential, part of the suffering members of Christ." This word sheds a deep peace over the diary that is otherwise so pensive. At the end, a breath of the *evangelium,* of the joy that comes from glad tidings, is felt. For that man is truly redeemed who can love himself as a part of the suffering members of Christ, who can be simultaneously forgetful of self, free and so in harmony with himself.

Let us express the same thought more simply and more practically: the root of man's joy is the harmony he enjoys with himself. He lives in this affirmation. And only one who can accept himself can also accept the *thou,* can accept the world. The reason why an individual cannot accept the *thou,* cannot come to terms with him, is that he does not like his own *I* and, for that reason, cannot accept a *thou.*

Something strange happens here. We have seen that the inability to accept one's *I* leads to the inability to accept a *thou.* But how does one go about affirming, assenting to, one's *I*? The answer may perhaps be unexpected: We cannot do so by our own efforts alone. Of ourselves, we cannot come to terms with ourselves. Our *I* becomes acceptable to us only if it has first become acceptable to another *I*. We can love ourselves only if we have first been loved by someone else. The life a mother gives to her child is not just physical life; she gives total life when she takes the child's tears and turns them into smiles. It is only when life has been accepted and is perceived as accepted that it becomes also acceptable. Man is that strange creature that needs not just physical birth but also appreciation if he is to subsist. This is the root of the phenomenon known as hospitalism. When the initial harmony of our existence has been rejected, when that psycho-physical oneness has been ruptured by which the "Yes, it is good that you are alive" sinks, with life itself, deep into the core of the unconscious—then birth itself is interrupted; existence itself is not completely established.[99] However, it is not just hospitalism but also the violent disturbances of our generation that have their roots here: the charism of revolution has been for a long time not just remonstrance against reparable injustices but protestation against existence itself, which has not experienced its acceptance and hence does not know that it is acceptable. If an individual is to accept himself, someone must say to him: "It is good that you exist"—must say it, not with words, but with that act of the entire being that we call love. For it is the way of love to will the other's existence and, at the same time, to bring that existence forth again. The key to the *I* lies with the *thou*; the way to the *thou* leads through the *I*.

We come now to the all-important question: Is it true, then, when someone says to me: "It is good that you exist"? Is it really good? Is it not possible that that person's love, which wills my existence, is just a tragic error? If the love that gives me courage to exist is not based on truth, then I must, in the end, come to curse the love that deceives me, that maintains in existence something that were better destroyed. This dilemma could be strikingly illustrated by reference to the interpretations of the contemporary experience of life in Sartre or Camus or in the attitudes of the new Left. Even without such evidence, it is obvious, however, that the apparently so simple act of liking myself, of being at one with myself, actually raises the question of the whole universe. It raises the question of truth: Is it good that I exist? Is it good that anything at all exists? Is the world good? How many persons today would dare to affirm this question from the heart—to believe it is good that they exist? That is the source of the anxiety and despair that incessantly affect mankind. Love alone is of no avail. It serves no purpose if truth is not on its side. Only when truth and love are in harmony can man know joy. For it is truth that makes man free.[100]

[99] I base this thought on the penetrating analyses of Josef Pieper, *Über die Liebe* (Munich: Kösel, 1972), esp. 38–66.

[100] I have tried to develop this context somewhat more fully in "Vorfragen zu einer

The content of the Christian *evangelium* reads: God finds man so important that he himself has suffered for man. The Cross, which was for Nietzsche the most detestable expression of the negative character of the Christian religion, is in truth the center of the *evangelium*, the glad tidings: "It is good that you exist"—no, "It is necessary that you exist." The Cross is the approbation of our existence, not in words, but in an act so completely radical that it caused God to become flesh and pierced this flesh to the quick; that, to God, it was worth the death of his incarnate Son. One who is so loved that the other identifies his life with this love and no longer desires to live if he is deprived of it; one who is loved even unto death—such a one knows that he is truly loved. But if God so loves us, then we are loved in truth. Then love is truth, and truth is love. Then life is worth living. This is the *evangelium*. This is why, even as the message of the Cross, it is glad tidings for one who believes; the only glad tidings that destroy the ambiguity of all other joys and make them worthy to be joy. Christianity is, by its very nature, joy—the ability to be joyful. The χαῖρε: "Rejoice!" with which it begins expresses its whole nature.

By its very essence, by its very nature, Christian belief is "glad tidings" But we have still to ask: How can it bestow on us today its power to liberate, to make us joyful? One thing above all should be clear: the joyous character of Christian faith does not depend on the effectiveness of ecclesiastical events. The Church is not a society for the promotion of good cheer, whose value rises and falls with the success of its activities. If the events of such a society are boring and without humour, it has become superfluous. The joy it gives depends on its activities. But the strength of the Christian message lies deeper. The promise of love that makes our own life worthwhile remains firm even if the messengers are themselves unprepossessing, even if the priest is far from being an entertaining speaker—although it is not a bad thing if he is one, because deep joy of the heart is also the true prerequisite for a sense of humor, and thus humor is, in a certain sense, the measure of faith. The value of human love does not cease when those who love are separated from one another. A prisoner in Russia, for instance, may come to realize for the first time what it means to be sure that someone at home is waiting for him and loving him. The *evangelium* is like that: its joy reaches the roots of our existence and proves its strength not least in the fact that it sustains us when all else about us is darkness. Christian joy is intended precisely also for those who labor and

---

Theologie der Erlösung", in Leo Scheffczyk, ed., *Erlösung und Emanzipation* (Freiburg: Herder, 1973), 141–55.

[101] Cf. Josef Pieper, *Zustimmung zur Welt: Eine Theorie des Festes*, 2d ed. (Munich: Kösel, 1964).

are heavy-burdened; those who have no reason to laugh here—this word of Jesus, in which Nietzsche saw "the greatest sin", is in reality a sign that the joy of the *evangelium* extends to the very foundation and, consequently, reaches also to that region where the manifold entertainers of mankind founder and their words become dull.

Granted all this, the question still remains: What can the Church do, what ought she to do, that we may truly experience the joy of the *evangelium*? Obviously, we cannot offer a catalogue of the pastoral opportunities that are open to individuals. Free scope must be left here for the Christian's unprogrammed creativity. It may well be that, by so limiting ourselves, we renounce what is, in many respects, most important, for the Christian sense of humor, which springs from the liberating certainty of being ultimately accepted, should really be the way in which the joy of the *evangelium* shines unobserved in the routine of daily life, in the humorless harshness of the technological world. With respect to the official ministry, I have two comments to make.

The holy day, which is something quite different from the holiday,[101] is the Church's gift to man. The mere not-having-to-work does not constitute a holy day. This is one of the problems of contemporary society: that it is, on the one hand, thoroughly sated with the worship of work but, on the other hand, cannot find the alternative—which would be freedom, a break with routine—and hence comes gradually to find freedom more threatening and more uncomfortable than work. But what makes a day a holy day? Precisely the fact that it is not dependent on our own decision; that it is, as it were, not homemade but ordained; that it is based on a precept we have not decreed. There is nothing arbitrary about a holy day. We do not make it; we receive it. Even more: a holy day possesses a reality that is lasting and by reason of which it is transformed from a pause in our occupations into a reality of another kind. A third fact must be mentioned here: a holiday can become a holy day, in the true sense of the word, only if it stems from a precept that it be celebrated as such. The holy day, on the other hand, is an expression of the fact that we receive our time not just from the movement of the stars but from those who have lived, loved and suffered before us—in other words, that man's time is human time. Even more significantly, it is an expression of the fact that we receive our time from him who sustains the universe. It is the invasion of the quite Other into our lives—the sign that we are not alone in this world.

For its part, the holy day has engendered art, beauty for its own sake, which we find so endlessly comforting precisely because it has no compulsion to be useful, because it does not owe its existence to a leisure we have devised for ourselves. We might begin here to reach into history and to ask: What would a world be life if the prescribed holy days man does not ordain for himself were to disappear in favor of the holidays he did so ordain? What would a world be like in which there no longer existed that beauty that was awakened by faith? But let us speak of the present. Every liturgy ought, in reality, to be a kind of holy day, should have about it something of the cheerful, liberating purposelessness of a genuine holy day, liberation from the compulsion of what we plan for ourselves in favor of the answer that already awaits us and that we have only to hear and accept. If that is the case, we must surely say: The Church will have to learn again how to celebrate holy days, how to radiate the brightness of a holy day. Her obeisance to the rational world has been much too deep in latter years; she has thereby let herself be robbed of a piece of herself. The Church should invite us to the holy days she has preserved in faith. In doing so, she will enable even those to rejoice for whom her glad tidings are inaccessible because they are viewed too rationally.

The second comment is this: Faith confers community, vanquishes loneliness. He who believes is not alone. Not only because he knows there is an ear always open to him but because he knows, too, that he has behind him the great community of those who, in every age, have traveled the way he is traveling and have become his brothers and sisters. Augustine, Francis of Assisi, Thomas Aquinas, Vincent de Paul, Maximilian Kolbe are not just important personages of the past. In faith they live, they speak to us, they understand us as we understand them. An individual actively rooted in the faith will not be troubled by the gloomy picture painted by Albert Camus, who, in the end, came to feel that all human relationships resemble the situation of two men talking to each other through the walls of a telephone booth: very near to and yet, in the last analysis, inaccessible and invisible to each other. When an individual has opened his innermost depths in faith, he is no longer inaccessible. Even if he no longer knows himself, there is an essential communication in which all men are open to each other. To this extent, the possibility of community that springs from faith is different from that of every club, every political party, whichever side one may choose. Here, too, we might attempt an examination of conscience with regard to the Church of the present. Today, when natural communities have broken up and the walls of isolation have become higher and higher, human beings seek and need community more than ever before. The Church must reflect again on the possibility that she has the answer; she must learn to offer men the experience of community, to make them open to community. Precisely here lies her potential for making men joyful; if she is actually to do so, she must learn far more than she has until now.

That leads to one final remark. The Church suffers today because of the antagonism of the groups and opinions that are warring within her; as a result, it becomes ever harder for the Christian to know where right lies and to distinguish true prophets from false ones. Our topic has much to do with the discernment of spirits, about which we might formulate this basic rule: where joylessness reigns, where humor dies, the spirit of Jesus Christ is assuredly absent. But the reverse is also true: joy is a sign of grace. One who is cheerful from the bottom of his heart, one who has suffered but not lost joy, cannot be far from the God of the *evangelium,* whose first word on the threshold of the New Testament is "Rejoice!"[102]

---

[102] Cf. on this subject the chapter on the Holy Spirit in my book *Der Gott Jesu Christi. Betrachtungen über den Dreieinigen Gott* [henceforth *Der Gott Jesu Christi*] (Munich: Kösel, 1976), 85–93.

CHAPTER 2

FORMAL PRINCIPLES OF CATHOLICISM

Section I
Scripture and Tradition

A. Anthropological Foundation of the Concept of Tradition

Slogans like traditionalism and progressivism that, some years ago, still seemed adequate to describe the conflicting views of the two basic positions within the Church have since come to be regarded as shallow by all who are seriously engaged in the effort to find a new orientation for the Church, the world and mankind. For it is gradually becoming obvious that we must all work together if we are ever again to establish a proper relationship to the times in which we live. If the past, with its institutions and customs, was once a force to be reckoned with, if it once provided the model by which the present, too, could face the problem of what it means to be human, it is now the future that bears the full burden in the ever faster process of change. Today is no longer what yesterday was, and tomorrow will be different from today. Thus the time span that encompasses "today" grows shorter and shorter. Before we know what is happening, even those things we still consider modern are being labeled "grandpa's movies", "grandpa's refrigerator", "grandpa's day", and so forth. Not just once in our lifetime but a dozen times, we feel ourselves transported into grandpa's time and, if we could, would hurry through two generations in the course of one decade. At the same time, however, there arises the question of the kind of spacesuit we should have in order to sustain the cosmic tempo with which we are fleeing faster and faster from the gravitational pull of tradition, and we wonder what ground controls would be necessary to prevent our burning out in the vast expanse of the universe, our bursting asunder like a homunculus of technology— questions that cannot be brushed aside today as stubborn obscurantism, for they are being raised most urgently by those who know most about the tempo of our alienation from tradition and who are most keenly aware of the problems associated with man's historic space flight.

For a long time now, we have no longer been able to distinguish, in this connection, between those problems that pertain to the Church and those that pertain to mankind. Although there are, of course, questions that are specifically Christian and specifically ecclesial, they must, nevertheless, always be seen in the human perspective. Should the Church ignore this fact, she would fail to recognize the central principle on which she is founded, by which she is ordered to universality, that is, to the service of man, of the humanity of man. In the necessarily fragmentary observations that follow, I should like, therefore, to begin with some general remarks on the relationship of tradition and progress; then to investigate their relationship in the primitive Church; and, on that foundation, by way of conclusion, to offer a few comments about the course the Church should take today.

Tradition and humanity

If we ask first how tradition and the break with tradition can coexist at all in man's life, two antithetical theses suggest themselves. On the one hand, there are grounds for saying that man lives by tradition; indeed, that it is tradition that most truly marks him as man. On the other hand, it is said that the modern age is founded on a break with tradition, that it owes its progress to the fact that it has abandoned tradition in favor of rationality. How are these two theses related? Is it correct to say that the modern age is man's liberation as a person or the beginning of his destruction? Is it a belated but fundamental change in the process by which man becomes man, or is it the beginning of his end? Our answer will depend on the value we set on the phenomenon of tradition. The deep rift that runs through the modern age is attributable to the fact that it is precisely here that man's paths diverge.

1. Tradition as a prerequisite of humanity

Let us examine the two theses separately to ascertain whether they are true or false. On the basis of Köhler's experiments with chimpanzees, in the course of which the chimpanzee Sultan demonstrated his ability to invent a kind of tool but was unable to transmit his ability to the future, Rüstow concluded: "The quality of man that is lacking in animals is, to be precise, not intellect, but tradition—tradition as the possibility of passing on to others the product of the intellect and thus augmenting and enriching it as it is preserved from generation to generation."[1] It is not difficult to detect

---

[1] A. Rüstow, "Kulturtradition und Kulturkritik", in *Studium Generale* 4 (1951): 308; quoted here from Josef Pieper, *Überlieferung*, 37. Anyone familiar with Josef Pieper's work will readily see how much the first part of these remarks is indebted to him.

in this definition a distorted concept of "intellect"; instead of "intellect", it would be more correct to speak of something like "invention". In that case, the sentence might be more accurately stated as follows: Despite the invention of which they are capable, the fact that animals have no intellect is revealed in their inability to transform invention into tradition and so into a historical context. In other words, invention acquires meaning only if it can create tradition, for only thus can history be generated.

This insight sheds significant light on the problem that engages us. The inseparable connection between humanity and history becomes apparent: humanity and historicity, intellect and history, are inextricably related. The human spirit creates history; history conditions human existence. If we attempt to analyze even more precisely the exact nature of history, we might say that the human element—intellect—manifests itself in the transcendence of time, of the moment; intellect is basically memory—a context that fosters unity beyond the limits of the present moment. We have arrived now at a chain of related concepts, the articulation of which we may describe as follows: it is as memory that intellect proves itself *qua* intellect; memory generates tradition; tradition realizes itself in history; as the already existing context of humanity, history makes humanity possible—for without the necessarily transtemporal relationship of person to person, humanity cannot be awakened to itself, cannot express itself. One further fact emerges from our discussion: the ability to keep the past always present is synonymous with the ability to anticipate the future in the present, to shape it even now. For we have seen that the most distinctive characteristic of tradition is, in fact, the ability to recognize my *now* as significant also for the tomorrow of those who come after me and, therefore, to transmit to them for tomorrow what has been discovered today. On the other hand, a capacity for tradition means preserving today what was discovered yesterday, in that way forming the context of a way through time, shaping history. This means that tradition properly understood is, in effect, the transcendence of today in both directions. The past can be discovered as something to be preserved only if the future is regarded as a duty; discovery of the future and discovery of the past are inseparably connected, and it is this discovery of the indivisibility of time that actually makes tradition. The emphasis may vary, but tradition can evolve only if the whole of time has been discovered. In this sense, we can offer, as the first result of our inquiry, the statement that tradition, as the *constitutivum* of history, is constitutive of a humanity that is truly human, of the *humanitas hominis*.

Before turning our attention to the present, it will be helpful to review some further aspects of this thesis in order to make its claim and its limits as comprehensible as possible. We have thus far considered the series:

memory-tradition-history-humanity. We must now examine another component that we have thus far taken for granted: How can memory actually become tradition? How is the transfer accomplished? How else but by communication, by a sharing-with [*Mit-teilung*]? By the transmission of memory to others. Communicability becomes, then, a second mark, along with transtemporality, of the concept "intellect" and, at the same time, a second contextual element of tradition. Human communication is accomplished in many ways, but the element of speech is always central to it. Hence we can say that speech is at once the means and the context of tradition; tradition is dependent on man's ability to speak, which, in turn, makes possible the transtemporal communication of man to man in their common humanity.

When we have said this, our notion of tradition becomes at once more concrete. Together, memory and speech offer a model of the relationship of tradition and time. For memory works to give meaning by establishing unity, by communicating the past to the present and by providing a mode of access to the future. It reveals itself as true memory, on the one hand, by faithfully preserving the past and, on the other hand, by understanding this past in a new way in the light of present experiences and thus facilitating man's advance into the future. As for speech, it is essentially as something bestowed, something received, that it fulfills its function of conferring unity. The condition of its effectiveness is its permanence. Yet, at the same time, it fulfills its function of preserving history only if it is open to the ever new experiences of new generations and so maintains its ability to give expression to the tradition that is continually in the process of formation, to the purification of tradition and hence to the history that is still to be made.

A perception becomes evident here that will prove significant as we conclude our observations on this topic: tradition requires a subject in whom to adhere, a bearer, whom it finds (not only, but basically) in a linguistic community. The matter of tradition relates to both history and community. It is possible only because many subjects become, as it were, *one* subject in the context of a common heritage. The ancient world lived this concept very realistically in the form of clans: there, all stood for one, one for all; what happened to one happened to all; what was done by one was done by all. They were bound together as one subject; they were one: Canaan, Edom, Israel.[2] Even though such concepts have long since become alien to us, we can still discover something of their reality in the linguistic community we share as fellow speakers of the same language, in

[2] Cf. the comprehensive study of the clan theory in Josef Scharbert, *Prolegomena eines Alttestamentlers zur Erbsündenlehre* (Freiburg: Herder, 1968), 31–44; see also bibliographical materials.

the historical community into which we are so incorporated by our heritage that we are inescapably bound to the blessing and the curse of this particular history. It is only when these relationships have been thoroughly examined that we shall be able to understand again the primitive facts that were displaced by an all too individualistic anthropology. What exactly is meant by primordial revelation? by original sin? Obviously, the former cannot be just the transmission of the first man's fragmentary memory of a conversation with God. If this were so, man's history would be quite different. Nor can the latter be regarded as a matter of heredity or of bad example solely from without. From what has been said, we may conclude that the origin of "humanity" coincides in time with the origin of man's capacity for tradition. Primordial revelation would mean, then, that there occurred in the formation of subjects who would be bearers of tradition primordial realities that were beyond the native understanding of any individual but were open to the new revelations experienced in obedience by the great patriarchs, by those great ones who kept themselves open to transcendence and assured its acceptance. On the other hand, it would mean also the possibility of a fall, of infidelity, of pride. And original sin, then, would mean this: the *humanum* is rooted in tradition, to the beginnings of which there belongs, above all, the ability to hear the Other (whom we call God). We must add, however, that, from the start, not only this ability to hear and this actual hearing but also sin were constitutive in the formation of subjects in whom tradition would inhere—a kind of formation that is itself constitutive of mankind per se.

2. Tradition as the endangering of humanity

This apparent digression brings us, therefore, once again to the notion of tradition and, at the same time, to the problems of the modern age. The possibility of a certain reconciliation between the idea of tradition as the basis of what it means to be human and the break with tradition has already suggested itself; we were able to affirm that true tradition is by no means concerned only with the past but is intimately connected also with the future. We come now to a further point. Tradition, which is by nature the foundation of man's humanness, is everywhere mingled with those things that deprive him of his humanity. The basis of man's humanness—tradition—is contaminated. It bears simultaneously within itself both itself and, for this very reason, the seeds of antihumanism. Its source and its destruction are inextricably intermingled—that is the real tragedy of mankind. Man must hold fast to tradition if he is to hold fast to his humanness, but in doing so, he inevitably holds fast also to the forces of alienation. The simple statement with which we began acquires thereby a strange ambiguity, for we must expand it now into the statement: Tradition is the precondition for man's humanness, but it is also its peril. Whoever destroys tradition destroys man—he is like a traveler in space who himself destroys the possibility of ground control, of contact with earth. But even he who would preserve tradition falls likewise into the danger of destroying it.

We must, consequently, analyze tradition from two different perspectives. From the theological point of view, it is necessary first of all to guard tradition against traditions; that is, we must not let ourselves be suffocated by the luxuriant growth of individual traditions but must be assiduous in cutting away what is accidental or temporary, in keeping it within bounds in order to make room for what is really fundamental. This rule of thumb is applicable to any community. A religious order, for instance, must see to it that the individual customs that have multiplied quite logically over the years are cut back from time to time in favor of the true spirit of the order; a nation must be assiduous in purifying its own traditions; the Church must do likewise. But there is, above and beyond all this, a deeper question that is not so readily applicable to the Church but that is all the more surely to be found in the content of human history: Is the basic tradition itself really intact, or is it perhaps itself marked by the forces of alienation? Let us take ancient Rome as an example: when, under the emperors, it opposed the *prisca virtus Romana* to the luxury of the present and its destructive effects, this was, to be sure, an admirable reformatory effort of impressing moral force. But was Ovid really wrong when he attributed to precisely this *prisca virtus* the original sin of fratricide with which Rome had begun under its legendary founders, Romulus and Remus? Was there not in this *prisca virtus* something destructive, something harsh, a national egoism that was contrary to the truth about man and to his true *virtus*? And who would deny that this example, which is far removed from us in time, is, nevertheless, closely akin to the historical conditions of our present day?

3. The basic problem of the modern age: tradition or the break with tradition as the way to humanity?

We have arrived now, by way of antithesis, at the starting point of the modern age. As a new historical state of mankind, the modern age clearly has its origin in a changed attitude toward tradition. Tradition comes to be regarded as a binding of man to the past; it is to be opposed by his orientation to the future. Because man is endowed with critical rationality, tradition is seen as an unwarranted assumption of *auctoritas*; there is only *one auctoritas* to which man must submit himself unconditionally—namely, *ratio*.[3] To the concept of tradition as the basis of man's humanity there is opposed the concept of an emancipated rationality that is hostile to tradition; the present crisis in the Church is due not least of all to the fact that, within her, advocates of both concepts are now engaged in a lively conflict with regard to her own tradition.

What more shall we say? First, it must be plainly stated that, even in the modern age, there are various degrees in the criticism of tradition, not all of which can be subsumed under one heading. The rise of the natural sciences, as exemplified by Kepler, Copernicus and, above all, Galileo, was far from being an uprising against tradition on the part of a reason divorced from tradition. In the case of Galileo, it was clearly an adoption of the tradition of Pythagoras and Plato as against that of Aristotle. As such, it was wholly in conformity with the basic tendency of the Renaissance. A tradition that was purely Greek asserted itself at the expense of the Graeco-Christian synthesis of the Middle Ages; against a rigid, one-sided tradition there was offered an open tradition that seemed, by contrast with a tradition rooted in authority, to be the tradition of reason.[4] From this perspective, it would be possible to establish a parallel between Galileo's way of thinking about the mathematical explanation of nature and what Luther did in the realm of Church and Christianity: Luther's statement was a forceful No to man-made traditions, to which he opposed "Scripture alone" as the pure word of God. Actually, of course, Scripture is also tradition; hence Luther's negation of tradition is, in reality, a protest against a particular form of tradition to which he opposes the primary tradition, which, however, he regarded, not as ecclesial and historical tradition, but as the direct word of God. In somewhat the same way, Platonism was important for Galileo, not as tradition, but as the coming of age of reason. As a first step, we may conclude, then, that the founders of the modern age directed their criticism of tradition, not against tradition as such, but against traditions. Its value lay in the fact that, behind the traditions, it found tradition and so could share in a proc-

---

[3] For several informative quotations on this subject, see Josef Pieper, *Überlieferung*, 112: a break with tradition was the prerequisite for the development of modern science (J. Ritter); 43: "Tradition is in conflict with rationalism" (Adorno); vice versa, 106: "Freedom that slips in by way of forgetfulness is empty" (Iwanow); similarly Leszek Kolakowski, 116; for both views, Jaspers, 44: authority as the real enemy of philosophizing, 106: the outcome of a philosophy without the content of a great tradition is "seriousness that grows empty".

[4] Cf. the translations from Galileo in Werner Heisenberg, *Das Naturbild der heutigen Physik* (Hamburg, 1955), 59–78; Norbert Schiffers, *Fragen der Physik an die Theologie* (Düsseldorf: Patmos, 1968), esp. 25–39; Wilhelm Kamlah, *Utopie, Eschatologie, Geschichtstheologie. Kritische Untersuchungen zum Ursprung und zum futuristischen Denken der Neuzeit* (Mannheim, 1969).

ess of learning that, once assimilated and expanded, could lead to progress. For just as religion could not develop fruitfully without the community of those who had previously experienced the reality of God, so science could not develop without the bond of a learning that had been going on for centuries, that accepted the breakthroughs of the intellect as they occurred and developed them according to their nature. We might also say of the process just described that it replaced a static tradition, fixed by authority, with a dynamic, self-critical tradition under the constant control of reason. But something even more basic has also been revealed here. What was really sought was the pure power of reason, the immediate access to the word of God. That both of these are to be found in tradition, that tradition is not the adversary of reason but its handiwork, its mark and the contingency on which it is founded—these facts were less clearly understood: not so much, perhaps, in Galileo's case as in Luther's very basic polemic against tradition.

Throughout the modern age, the realization that where tradition is wanting, reason is also wanting has served again and again as a critical corrective to this break with tradition. As an example, I cite only the history of the new exegesis. We can date its beginning from Reimarus' radical attack against the traditional concept of Christ. For Reimarus, the Church's faith was no longer the way to find Jesus but a mythical smokescreen that concealed his historical reality.[5] Jesus was to be sought, not *through* dogma, but *against* it, if one wanted to arrive at a historical knowledge of him. Historical reason became the corrective of dogma; critical reason became the antipode of traditional faith. But Reimarus' way proved to be a dead end from which one could emerge only by once again embracing tradition and criticizing his thesis in terms of it. Albert Schweitzer, as we know, traced the tortuous course of research into the life of Jesus from Reimarus' time to the beginning of the twentieth century; during that whole time and even up to the present, its course has remained always the same: historical *ratio* has been fruitful only when it has reverted again and again to tradition, whereas tradition has remained vital and effective only by repeated confrontation in every age with the potentialities of historical speculation.

Nevertheless, there is something in Reimarus' initiative that is symptomatic of the second phase of the modern age. Chronologically, his work

---

[5] On this subject, cf. especially the work edited by Helmut Ristow and Karl Matthiae, *Der historische Jesus und der kerygmatische Christus* (Berlin: Evangelischer Verlagsanstalt, 1960); James M. Robinson, *Kerygma und historischer Jesus* (Zurich: Zwingli, 1960). Werner Georg Kümmel's work, *Das neue Testament. Geschichte der Erforschung seiner Probleme* (Munich: Alber, 1958), is especially valuable as a history of historico-critical exegesis. See, on 299ff., the excerpts from Albert Schweitzer's classic work: *Geschichte der Leben-Jesu-Forschung,* 2d ed. (Tübingen: Mohr, 1913).

more or less parallels that of the French Encyclopedists, whose teachings prepared the way for the French Revolution. The attack on tradition became, with them, ever more fundamental, more conscious, more intense. This movement increased its scope during the age of technical reason. The idea of emancipation is understood today as the radical antithesis of the idea of tradition. All previous value systems are to be unmasked; in his rationality, man becomes the creator not only of himself but also of a world constructed according to his own designs; he forms himself and reality anew in the unconditioned transparency of his own rationality. Philosophically, this concept is expressed in the theory that man was not created according to a preconceived design and is, consequently, free (and, at the same time, obligated by this freedom) to design himself—to determine what man is to be like in the future.[6] This liberation of man from the soil of the earth, from the foreordination to which he owes his existence, is most evident in the notion of perfect dominion over life and death and in elimination of the distinction between man and woman: the goal of total emancipation seems to be reached when man can be propagated by technical means, when he is no longer dependent on the fortuitousness of *bios* but, bringing all hidden things to light, designs himself in a way of thinking that does not look backward but takes as its sole measure the needs and hopes of the future.

Given this full-fledged space flight of the spirit, the Church must be, as it were, something of a "ground control", the seat of tradition, even though she is, properly and under other circumstances, the heavenly terminal that draws man from the closed world of his traditions and teaches him to be self-critical. The Church begins, in fact, with the premise that "original sin" does exist; that is, that tradition is not the unsullied foundation of the human, but rather that every tradition is infected with the forces of the antihuman, which hamper man in his efforts to become himself. It is only to this extent that the Church is involved with the spirit of the modern age or the modern age with the Church. For the Church knows only *one* saving tradition: the tradition of Jesus, who lives his life from the Father, who receives himself from the Father and continually gives himself back to the Father. From this perspective, the Church is, on the one hand, critical of all other traditions, for it is from this perspective that the phenomenon known as "original sin"—that is, the antihuman element in all traditions—makes itself known not just as a statistical but also as a fundamental fact. On the other hand, it is from this perspective also that she must offer resistance to that philosophy of emancipation that regards man as endowed with no nature or truth of his own and so attributes to

---

[6] Josef Pieper has repeatedly discussed this topic. Cf. especially, Josef Pieper, *Wahrheit der Dinge,* 4th ed. (Munich: Hochland, 1966).

him the unlimited freedom to mold himself according to his own design. For one who believes, the person of Jesus means precisely this: that man is not the inconsequential product of evolution but something entirely different. The whole life of Jesus consisted in being an encounter, an exchange, with him whom he called Father. To believe in Jesus means, therefore, to believe that there is a truth from which man proceeds and which is most signally his own, which is his true nature. To emancipate oneself from this truth in favor of an expedient one has designed for oneself is to emancipate oneself from what is human, from the humanity of man. The criticism of tradition is limited by the fact that man remains bound to the truth of his nature, to his creaturehood, and can find himself only when he finds this truth. And that means that technical *ratio* remains bound to the *ratio* of authority, to the tradition of humanity.

I. *The problem of Jesus as the prerequisite for a theological answer to the dilemma of the modern age*

But where does this tradition make itself heard? Our analysis of the dilemma of the modern age has led us directly to the next step in our considerations, for it has caused us to turn our attention to the structure of belief and hence to the person of Jesus Christ. What do we learn, in the process, about the importance of tradition for the shaping of human existence? Against the background of the most recent literature about Jesus, we might be tempted to approach the subject antithetically, as we did above when we contrasted the way in which tradition is usually experienced with the way in which the modern age understands existence, for in doing so, it will be remembered, we were able in the course of our considerations to correct an antithesis that was too strict. It would be possible, then, to present the issue in some such antithetical formula as the following: in Jesus and Paul, the Christianity of the New Testament rests on a radical criticism of tradition; ecclesial Christianity, on the other hand, rests on an equally radical traditionalism. But we must resist the temptation to resort to facile formulas that are as appealing to the public as they are inaccurate; the real issue is more effectively presented in a differentiated approach. I would like, therefore, to explore the question on a progressive scale of three chains of thought.

1. Jesus' affirmation and criticism of tradition

Jesus' message evoked a multiplicity of responses which, in turn, reflected a multiplicity of responses which, in turn, reflected a multiplicity of attitudes toward tradition: Paul's radical criticism of tradition stands side by side with the pious respect for tradition that marked another type of Christianity; somewhere between the two was to be found the Lucan theology, which, though it was based on the freedom from law that characterized Pauline Christianity; also expressly emphasized the historical line that led from the Old Testament to the Church, thus stressing the continuity of the history of faith.

The situation in the early Church, as presented here in rough outline, corresponds to the diversity that is apparent also in the Jesus-tradition. The scale extends from such explicitly traditional texts as the teaching preserved in Matthew that ". . . The man who infringes even one of the least of these commandments . . . will be considered the least in the kingdom of heaven" (Mt 5:19) to the critical intensity of the saying reported in Mark and Matthew: ". . . You have made God's word null and void by means of your tradition" (Mt 15:6; cf. Mk 7:13) or in the admittedly difficult to interpret sentence: "The sabbath was made for man, not man for the sabbath" (Mk 2:27: Mark's special property?).[7] Despite the diversity of tradition, one fact is uniformly recognizable: although Jesus fought determinedly against the dogmatization of a casuistical tradition, he stood firmly rooted in the foundation of Old Testament faith, that is, in the foundation of the law and the prophets. Even apart from content, this seems to me to offer a most significant insight with regard to structure: Jesus did not present his message as something totally new, as the end of all that had preceded it. He was and remained a Jew; that is, he linked his message to the tradition of believing Israel. He did not abandon the Old Testament as something antiquated and now superseded. He lived it and, in doing so, revealed his meaning: his message was the creative referral of tradition to its original foundation. Traditions were criticized in order that genuine tradition might be revealed.

Not without reservations can we characterize Jesus' attitude toward tradition as the opposition of Scripture and tradition. Although he rests his teaching on the Old Testament canon rather than on early Jewish tradition, it would, nevertheless, be anachronistic to attribute to him an Old Testament *sola Scriptura*. To do so would be to affirm at the same time both too much and too little. Too much, because Jesus lived in the living community of Israel and did not share the views of the archaizing groups—nor should it be overlooked in this connection that archaism can be a vehicle as much of liberalism as of sectarianism. The Sadducees represent the one group: they professed allegiance to the most ancient elements of tradition in order to leave themselves free to arrange the

---

[7] Ernst Käsemann's article "War Jesus liberal?", in *Der Ruf der Freiheit*, 3d ed. (Tübingen: Mohr, 1968), 19–53, contains a perceptive discussion of the state of the question.

present as they pleased. Qumran exemplifies the other group: by petrifying tradition at a particular moment in time, they enclosed themselves in the circle of the past. Both groups are well represented in the modern world. Most progressive movements thrive on a quiet archaism, affirming only the ancient Church or only the New Testament or, even, only the twelfth chapter of the first epistle to the Corinthians; sects thrive on archaism by seceding at a certain point in the ongoing history of faith. Nothing of this kind can be discovered in Jesus. He lived in the living community of Israel; he observed the rites of the temple and performed his religious duties; he did not bind the history of Israel to a single moment in time—this is especially clear in the most recent Jewish writings about him.[8] From another point of view, however, it is too little to describe Jesus in terms of *sola Scriptura,* for he also transgressed the letter of the law of Moses; he criticized even the most holy part of the canon—or, more correctly, he claimed to interpret more purely than was done in the written word the will of God that was hidden therein. We can say, then, that he regarded as normative the collection of traditions attributed to Moses and the prophetic tradition even while he recognized that they were transmitted through a living community and had to be reinterpreted in terms of the new claims upon him. Because he did so knowing the fullness of power that resided in him, he took his place consciously in the prophetic tradition and willed not only to create tradition but also to provide an interpretation that would become the heart of tradition.

2. The unifying center: Jesus' awareness of his mission

The question now arises: What led to this claim of Jesus? How are we to explain this remarkable combination of faithfulness to and criticism of tradition? We might begin with the thesis that Jesus' criticism of tradition was the expression of his specific awareness of mission and of the unique fullness of power that had its source therein. Like Jesus himself, in other words, we must not see in that criticism a general or readily generalizable model of behavior. To conclude that one who wishes to belong to Jesus must be, like him, radically critical of tradition is to overlook the fundamental fact of his relationship to God and, because of it, to the traditional form of God's word. The more extreme conclusion that Jesus was a revolutionary, that one is, therefore, following in the footsteps of

---

[8] Cf. the review by Rudolf Pesch, "Christliche und jüdische Jesus-Forschung", in Wilhelm Pesch, ed., *Jesus in den Evangelien* (Stuttgart: Katholisches Bibelwerk, 1972), 10–37; see also Pinchas E. Lapide's review of the literature on the subject, "Jesus in der israelischen Literatur", in IKZ 2 (1973): 375–82; see also the *Freiburger Rundbrief* 23 (1971), nos. 85 / 88, esp. the article by Franz Mussner, "Der Jude Jesus", 3–7.

Jesus if one becomes a revolutionary—or, in another form: as Jesus acted with regard to the synagogue so must the true disciple of Jesus act with regard to the Church—such a conclusion is, in the first place, full of inexactitudes: for, whether we like it or not, Jesus was pious. "Both pious and liberal", is the way Ernst Käsemann expresses it—and in this "both" he sees an inner relationship with the "both" of the teaching of Chalcedon: "both God and man".[9] If we interpret the word "liberal" correctly, and in this context that would mean according to nineteenth-century notions, we must accept this formula. And if Jesus' piety is, even then, unquestionably still very different from many other types of piety, it remains nonetheless true that he was pious: that he prayed, that he attended the synagogue, that he read the Bible. Everything else—a Jesus who consorted with evil companions, a Jesus who was not religious, and so forth—is a more or less tasteless and romantic invention. For against any such conclusion there is not only the factual evidence but, above all, the structural fact that such direct transferences are at variance with the uniqueness of Jesus' mission as Son, for he proves his Sonship precisely by his creative acceptance of tradition and his creative extension of it into the future. This is what we mean when we speak of Jesus' obedience, which is the criterion by which we interpret the content of his Sonship.

We must proceed carefully here, for what we are discussing lies at the very center of the New Testament. What, precisely, is this obedience of Jesus that encompasses, on the one hand, his relationship to tradition and, on the other, his relationship to God as expressed in the formula "Son"? At first glance, we might say: Scripture speaks of the death of the servant of God. Jesus is that servant. Consequently, he must obey Scripture and, ipso facto, the Father. He must die "in order that the Scripture may be fulfilled". But there is, of course no question here of a mechanical fulfillment of a preordained letter of the law, though one might infer this from a superficial reading of the Gospels from Matthew to John. The obedience of the Son, the Son's relationship to tradition—to Scripture—is not something mechanical. The situation is rather this: to affirm at this hour and in all its fullness the truth proclaimed in Scripture, that is, the truth about man that is presented in the words of this central tradition, demands the passion of truth in deadly conflict with those powers that conceal and distort it. Jesus dies because there are forces hostile to truth; his obedience is fidelity to truth in conflict with the tangled web of untruth. But it is precisely by obeying truth that he obeys both the Father and the

---

[9] Ernst Käsemann: "The Chalcedonian doctrine should by no means be reduced to the formula 'both pious and liberal'. It is merely stated that this formula is indispensable for the correct understanding of the teachings of Chalcedon because it names a crucial characteristic of Jesus" (25).

Scripture that he interprets by virtue of his immediate relationship to God, that he thereby opens anew to its inmost foundation, filling it with a new reality by his living of its word. His relationship to the fundamental ground of being is a relationship of real union with the fundamental truth—that is, "Sonship": in this relationship to God, the very letter becomes flesh.

3. The sustaining ground: Jesus' relationship to God

What we Christians must learn from Christ is, therefore, neither revolution nor traditionalism but something quite different: that we are to read Scripture from the Father's perspective, that is, from the perspective of a concrete relationship to God. There both the difference and the similarity between Christ and the Christian are to be found. The difference, because our relationship to God is not the same as that of Jesus; the similarity, because Jesus wants to lead us, by this means, to know the Father from the perspective of tradition and to understand tradition from the perspective of the Father. There, too, lies the key to that combination in Jesus of faithfulness to and criticism of tradition, to that juxtaposition of "liberal" and pious that is so puzzling to us when we view it from without. At first glance, much of what Jesus says and does strikes us as the attitude of a liberal—and, in passage after passage, one thing or another seems to confirm this impression, as, for example, his attitude toward the ritual of purification or his stand on the Sabbath-question. It is admittedly perplexing, then, to discover that his No to the traditions of the Pharisees is by no means the prelude to a generally liberal position with regard to the law but, upon occasion, even heralds an unprecedented intensification of its demands, as, for, example, in his position with regard to the indissolubility of marriage, the demands of love of neighbor or the requirements of discipleship.[10] It is obvious, then, that there is no question, in Jesus' case, of an arbitrary liberalism: rather, both his freedom and his strictness proceed from a common source: from his prayerful intercourse with the Father, from his personal knowledge of God, on the basis of which he draws the dividing line between center and periphery, between the will of God and the work of man. Jesus has spiritualized the letter—which explains his freedom toward tradition; but he has spiritualized it, not in terms of an arbitrary and general enlightenment, but rather in terms of his relationship with God. Adapting Käsemann's argument, we might say, then, that the combination "both liberal and pious" that we observe in Jesus is, in fact, to

---

[10] Cf. ibid., 29; cf. also Günther Bornkamm, *Jesus von Nazareth*, 7th ed. (Stuttgart: Kohlhammer, 1965), 92–100.

be understood *only* in terms of the Chalcedonian mystery "both God and man".

To repeat: we cannot imitate the unique quality of Jesus' relationship to God. On the basis of his intimate communion with God, however, Jesus has given us a new interpretation of tradition, has opened its inmost depths for us and has thereby given us access to tradition. These circumstances, in turn, provide the Christian with a directive for his own relationship to tradition: the Christian sees in Jesus a point of access to the center of tradition, to that place where tradition is, in very fact, a breakthrough to what was in the beginning; where it does not range itself against reason but reveals the ground on which it rests. In other words, he sees himself protected not only against false tradition but also against a false freedom from tradition, for he reads tradition as Jesus does. And that means, in truth, that he shares in Jesus' relationship to the Father, that he interprets tradition in conversation with God, the Father of Jesus Christ. Only that inner acquaintance with God that is made possible by Jesus can open a path through the mountain of tradition that, without this living context, would remain lifeless and perplexing. Where this relationship to God is lacking, both traditionalism and the criticism of tradition become an arbitrary sport. That is why the increasingly popular notion of a "posttheistic Christianity" that seeks to reduce the romanticism of the God–is–dead theology to a conceptual denominator must be vehemently opposed. What Jesus reveals as a basic and central tradition is ultimately, not a multiplicity of tenets, but the simple and ancient credo of Israel: God is. In this sense, Jesus is a radical Jew—it is a question of God's existence as God, which is just as indisputable as Jesus' existence as man, because the latter is wholly dependent on Jesus' personal relationship with the Father. God is precisely what he appears to be in Jesus because, as a Divine Person, Jesus himself belongs to God. The Resurrection is but the most extreme concretization of this statement: God is. It shows that God is in-deed [*wirklich*], for being is doing and God's being is the life that overcomes death. That God is in-deed means that there is a truth of man in which the goals of his intellectual inquiry find their limits and their measure. With this, our analysis has led us back to the point at which we started: in addition to the specifically Christian context, we have laid bare also the basic human and humanitarian option that resides in the message of Jesus. Ultimately, there is but one alternative: the alternative between the absolute dominion of technical reason, which would presuppose the absurdity of being, and belief in creative reason, which, as the tradition on which reason rests, also gives reason its meaning.[11]

---

[11] Cf. the analysis in Robert Spaemann, "Die Frage nach der Bedeutung des Wortes 'Gott' ", in IKZ 1 (1972): 54–72, esp. 65, 69.

II. Survey of the problem: Church, Christianity, tradition

Our topic seems to demand that we take a third step here and speak of the
problem of tradition as it exists in the Church. The reader may perhaps be
disappointed—and may perhaps even regard it as a way of avoiding the
difficulty of what is, in fact, a universal question—that this subject is
dismissed so summarily. I do not deny the difficulty of the question, but it
seems to me that the unsolvability of so many of the controversies that face
us today lies precisely in the fact that we never look beyond the frictions of
the moment and hence remain unaware of the greater issues that are at
stake. Yet it is only this larger context that can make our day-to-day
sufferings bearable, that can provide a thread to guide us through the
labyrinth from which there is otherwise no escape. For that reason, I have
made a conscious effort to show, above all, the broader framework and so
to make plainly visible, above and beyond the irritations of daily living,
the magnitude of the problem that engages us. I am convinced that we can
make no progress until we are ready to look at the *whole* and, from this
perspective, to shape our attitude toward the events of daily life, which
will in any case be wearisome. The question is, not how we can establish a
trouble-free existence, but what is worth the trouble and what is not.

But let us come now to the point. If we are correctly to assess the
meaning of the Church, we must recall an insight at which we had arrived
earlier in our general analysis of the concept of tradition. Tradition, we
said, always presumes a bearer of tradition, that is, a community that
preserves and communicates it, that is the vessel of a comprehensive
common tradition and that becomes, by the oneness of the historical
context in which it exists, the bearer of concrete memory. This bearer of
tradition in the case of Jesus is the Church. That is not a theological
judgment in the true sense of the word but rather a simple statement of
fact. The Church's role as bearer of tradition rests on the oneness of the
historical context and the communal character of the basic experiences that
constitute the tradition.[12] This bearer is, consequently, the *sine qua non* of
the possibility of a genuine participation in the *traditio* of Jesus, which,
without it, would be, not a historical and history-making reality, but only
a private memory.

The Church is tradition, the concrete situs of the *traditio* of Jesus, into
which—let us admit it—much human pseudotradition has found its way;
so much so, in fact, that even, and even precisely, the Church has
contributed to the general crisis of tradition that afflicts mankind. What,
then, are we to do? Where shall we turn?

---

[12] Cf. ITK, *Pluralismus* (Einsiedeln, 1973), commentary on theses 4, 5 and 6.

It has become clear, I think, that two roads have led us to this crisis: it is absurd to seek to destroy the bearer of tradition as such, to undertake an ecclesiastical space flight with no ground station, to attempt to produce a new and purer Christianity in the test tube of the mere intellect: a Church that is nothing but a manager is nothing at all; she is no longer tradition, and, in an intellect that knows no tradition, she becomes pure nothingness, a monster of meaninglessness.

False, too, is the closely related attempt to cut tradition off at a given point, to try to save the Church by a liberal or conservative archaeologism. It is important, in my opinion, to realize that the most rabid forms of progressivism are forms of archaeologism: they are no longer satisfied with limiting tradition to *sola Scriptura*; they regard with suspicion everything that comes after Paul—especially, then, the writings of St. Luke and, *a fortiori*, the pastoral epistles. The difference between such progressivisms and a false traditionalism is not a fundamental one; it is merely a question of when tradition ends. True tradition is thus completely and totally falsified. Nor should we overlook the fact that precisely the most progressive archaeologisms are dishonest, for they define tradition according to the need of the moment and depend extensively on reconstructions that are but the reflections of their own *a priori* conceptions: Faust's mockery of historians—that it is only their own spirit that lurks behind the so-called spirit of the times—is a case in point. But this does not help the person who finds himself mired today in a crisis that is in very fact a question of being or nonbeing: I find it almost uncanny that theology is so often engaged in banal and egotistic frictions today when the waters have risen to humanity's very neck and the death knell of theology may actually have sounded. To repeat: salvation comes, not from the destruction of tradition or the archaeological neutralization of tradition, but only when the Church, the bearer of tradition, penetrates to its true center, to the life at the heart of tradition, to that community with God, the Father of Jesus Christ, that is revealed only through faith and prayer. Only when this occurs can there be that true progress that leads to the goal of history: to the God-man who is humanity's humanization.

B. Baptism and the Formulation of the Content of Faith— Liturgy and the Development of Tradition

It makes a considerable difference whether we view the topic "Baptism and the Formulation of the Content of Faith" from the perspective of early Christianity or from that of modern theology. In the latter case, it is almost impossible to discover a relationship between baptism and the

verbal formula of faith; to all intents and purposes, the "and" of our title is
without substance. In the early Church, on the other hand, we find a close
relationship between the two. In the tension that thus becomes obvious
between the beginnings of Christianity and its present state are to be found
also the tension and significance of our topic.

Let us look first at contemporary Catholic theology as it is systemati-
cally presented in, for example, the lengthy article on "Baptism" in the
Dictionnaire de théologie catholique.[13] The treatment of baptism is determined there by the basic framework developed at the height of Scholasticism for teaching about the sacraments in general: the study of the meaning and essence of baptism is subdivided into questions about the minister
and recipient, the matter, form and effect of the sacrament.[14] The topic
baptism and the formulation of the content of faith could, perhaps, be subsumed here under the question of sacramental form, that is, of the word
that determines the sacrament. But its scope would then be limited—not
only by being restricted to this category but also, and for that very reason,
by being forced into the schema of matter and form. For the word of faith
is still regarded there solely as the "form"—or, more accurately, as the
formula—that is the one decisive and determinative factor for the validity
of the sacrament as a whole. When, on the other hand, the concept of a
sacramental formula is allowed its full scope, it is linked with the concept
of the establishment of this formula by Jesus Christ himself, so that the
question of its determinative power is completely eliminated: the formula
exists as something preordained and inviolable, not as an expression of
faith, but as "institution". A discussion of baptism and the formulation of
the content of faith might also be appropriately introduced into the discussion of the recipient of faith, for, in receiving the sacrament of faith, one
must also be questioned about one's own faith. When we analyze more
closely what has been said on this subject, we discover that this preliminary conjecture is, in fact, largely confirmed. For it becomes clear that the
topic of faith is divisible into two categories, in which it exists in a singu-
larly truncated form that is either abstractly doctrinal or cultically rituralis-
tic.

---

[13] J. Bellamy et al., "Baptême", in DTC 2:167–378. This monumental article has yet to be
surpassed for comprehensiveness. In its systematization, it reflects the classic form of thought
that preceded Vatican Council II. Valuable material is also contained in DACL 2:1:251–346
(de Puniet). The article "Baptême" by G. Jacquemet and André Bride in *Catholicisme: hier,
aujourd'hui, demain* 1 [henceforth *Catholicisme hier*] (Paris: Letouzey et Ané, 1948): 1207–27),
is also an excellent comprehensive study but contains little that is not to be found in DTC.

[14] Cf., for example, the subdivisions in the section about baptism and the Fathers of the
Church: Noms, Matière, Forme, Mode de collation, Ministre, Sujet, Symbolisme et figures,
effets, Nécessité, Rites de l'administration solennelle (179); similar subdivisions in other
sections.

1. *Interrelationship of baptism and the formulation of the content of faith in the theology of the second Christian millenium*

a. Faith as a necessary precondition for baptism

Faith first makes its appearance when the adult neophyte is questioned about the prerequisites for baptism. It must be admitted, however, that the connection is much looser there than might have been expected in an event that has been designated the *sacramentum fidei,* the *obsignatio fidei,* that is, the cultic and ecclesial expression of the profession of faith.[15] There is, to begin with, the fundamental distinction that faith is a prerequisite, not of the validity, but only of the licitness of baptism.[16] For the whole of Scholastic teaching on the sacraments, this means that faith is relegated to a position of secondary importance: from the realm of *opus operatum* (= validity) to that of *opus operantis* (= licitness)—from the realm of the sacraments per se to that of the subjective predisposition necessary for their reception. With regard to the effect of the sacraments, to the properly intended *res sacramenti,* it means, in turn, that one who is baptized without having the corresponding Christian faith is indeed marked with the *character sacramentalis* but does not receive the grace of the sacrament, although he would do so at a later date if he then had the proper dispositions.[17] Thus the sacrament is, to a large extent, removed from the sphere of faith and into the sphere of an automatic rite, on the one hand, and, on the other, of an ontology of the soul.

The situation becomes worse when we discover that, even among the necessary preconditions for the licitness of baptism, faith enjoys no special prerogative but is simply one of a series of conditions including, above all, sorrow for sin—in which connection we must note that the moral decision indicated by the expression "sorrow for sin" is plainly understood as a second distinct requirement alongside faith, while the latter, for its part, seems to consist mainly in the acceptance of a series of propositions.[18] A

---

[15] "Fidei sacramentum", see *Adversus Marcionem,* sec. 28, 2, in *Tertulliani opera,* pars I, *Corpus Christianorum* [henceforth CChr], series latina (Turnhout: Brepols, 1954), 1:472; "obsignatio fidei", see *De poenitentia,* sec. 6, 16, in ibid., 331. Cf. *Catholicisme hier* 1:1216, and further texts. For patristic designations of baptism, see DTC 2:179–80.

[16] DTC 2:279–81; *Catholicisme hier* 1:1217: "S'il arrivait que quelqu'un vienne au baptême sans croire, le sacrement n'aurait pas d'utilité pour son salut. S'il avait cependant l'intention véritable de recevoir le sacrement tel que le Christ l'a institué et tel que l'Église le donne, il pourrait être marqué du caractère baptismal (c'est ce qu'on exprime en disant que le sacrement serait alors valide)".

[17] See n. 16.

[18] DTC 2:280. The following prerequisites are named: "la foi, l'*espérance* et le *repentir* des péchés. . . . L'absence de l'une ou de l'autre de ces conditions empêcherait le baptise de

relationship that the Council of Trent sought to maintain is thus obviously destroyed. Admittedly, Trent referred to faith as a "preparation for justification" and placed it first among the acts required for that purpose: with hope, with the beginning of charity and with *paenitentia* (penance and sorrow for sin), as well as with the intention of receiving baptism.[19] But the Council then united this diversified complex, which was governed and bound together by the fundamental motivation of the three theological virtues, by reference to the inner unity of the theological acts of faith, hope and charity. When it is stated in the rite of baptism that the catechumen desires faith, which bestows eternal life, the reference is to a faith that is, at the same time, hope and charity, for a faith divorced from hope and charity cannot bestow eternal life.[20] Thus there emerges at this point a comprehensive concept of faith that includes the whole process of preparation for justification. In this sense, faith is to be understood as the correspondence between the subject and the objective event of baptism, as the spiritual sphere in which this occurs. In order to refute the Reformation concept of *fides-fiducia,* on the other hand, the separateness of the acts is so strongly emphasized, and faith as an individual act distinct from hope, charity and penance is consequently so strongly accented, that the fragmentation of the whole into a series of individual requirements, of which faith is but one, becomes inevitable.[21]

Our theme, which is concerned, not with the relationship between faith and baptism as such, but with the relationship between baptism and the

---

recevoir la grâce sanctifiante et le pardon de ses péchés". Faith as "connaissance des vérités de foi", ibid., 354.

[19] Henricus Denzinger and Adolfus Schönmetzer, *Enchiridion symbolorum, definitionum et declarationum de rebus fidei et morum* (Freiburg: Herder, 1973), 1526. [This work will henceforth be cited as DS. (Trans.)]

[20] Ibid., 1531. It is regrettable, in my opinion, that, for this profound answer—the catechumen desires of the Church faith and the bestowal of eternal life—the new baptismal rite has substituted the bland response: the candidate desires baptism. The *Rituale Romanum* also permits, among other alternatives, the former answer: "fidem". In the official German text, it is, for some reason or other, not even offered as an alternative. With this change from *fidem* to *baptismum,* the transcendence of the event has been removed from the baptismal dialogue; only the empirical act of the conferral of baptism is still mentioned as the purpose of the action. In the former answer, on the other hand, the whole breadth of the event, its mysterious paradox, is present. What is bestowed in baptism is far more than "baptism", more than sacrament—in contrast to a faith that one must, in some sense, have oneself; what is given is precisely that faith that one receives from the Church. With the addition of "eternal life", it was clear at the same time that what was meant was what man really wants: life, not just some particular liturgical action. Consequently, the formula expressed a union of Pauline and Johannine theology. Liturgically, it kept alive the Reformation's concern that justification be conceived as proceding entirely from faith.

[21] Emphasis on the unity of faith-hope-love: especially in DS 1531; emphasis on the separateness of the individual acts, 1533–34.

formulation of the content of faith, requires that we ask ourselves now how the meaning of faith and the formulation of the content of faith can be more exactly defined within this narrower perspective. A decree of the Congregation for the Propagation of the Faith from the year 1703 casts light on this subject. It forbids, in missionary countries, the baptism of an individual, even though he be in danger of death, who is ignorant of the truths necessary for salvation.[22] Following Hebrews 11:6, these truths are defined as the existence of God—the concept of God being frequently extended to include Trinity and Incarnation—and the reward or punishment (μισθαποδότης) he bestows in the life to come. For the ordinary administration of baptism in missionary countries (except where there is danger of death), Benedict XIV established as prerequisites: knowledge of the principal mysteries of faith, of the Creed, the Our Father, the decalogue, the precepts of the Church, the effect of baptism, the acts of faith, hope and charity and their motivation.[23] It is interesting that the second part of these prerequisites—which is largely a matter of memorization—corresponds rather exactly to the medieval "catechism" which derives from the early Church and to which Luther also subscribed in his Catechisms, in which, while rejecting systematization, he presented the principal elements that had been handed down: decalogue, (Apostles') Creed, Our Father, baptism + confession + Sacrament of the Altar, daily prayers, catechism table of domestic duties [Haustafel]. We can establish the following as the principal elements of the catechism of the early Church: creed, Our Father, doctrine of the "two ways" (instead of the decalogue, which can be traced only to the thirteenth century as part of the catechism), sacraments.[24] With the enumeration of these elements, we are again reminded of the ancient catechumenate and thus of the connection between baptism and the formulation of the content of faith; at the same time, the bridge between the rite of administration of the sacrament and the formulation of the content of faith becomes evident. Although the link with ancient Christianity and, with it, the unity of the dogmatic history, the unity of the sacrament, becomes clear at this point (and not by chance in the context of the missionary task of the Church), the whole continues to be truncated. Not only does the question about faith and baptism re-

---

[22] DTC 2:354.

[23] Ibid. C. Ruch refers here, above all, to an instruction of October 18, 1883, that summarized what had been said earlier.

[24] On this subject, see the instructive article "Katechismus" by H. W. Surkau, in Die Religion in Geschichte und Gegenwart [henceforth RGG], 3d ed., vol. 3 (Tübingen: Mohr, 1959): 1179–86. Surkau calls attention (1180) to the fact that Augustine, for instance, in "De fidei et operibus", 9:14 and 13:19 (PL 40: 206 and 210), mentions the baptismal instructions of John the Baptist and the Philippus catechismus (the latter expression undoubtedly a coinage of North African Church Latin). On the structure of the catechismus of the ancient Church, see Surkau, 1181–82.

solve itself, on the one hand, into a question of the above-mentioned material for memorization and, on the other hand, into a question of the ideal (or doctrinal) minimum of prerequisites; it also, by reason of its culmination in a question about the nature of baptism of desire, falls into an ever more independent and abstract existence through which not only baptism but even concrete, ecclesial Christianity as such appears to be a more and more elegant (or, depending on one's point of view, a particularly unscrupulous) form of religious existence, as opposed to the far simpler perspectives to be found in Hebrews 11:6.

b. The role of faith in the liturgy of baptism

If, in what has been said above, we have described the dogmatic and theological aspect of the whole, it must now be noted that faith also makes an appearance in the framework of the liturgical rite of baptism. Just as it seemed, in the first instance, to be consigned to the abstract and doctrinal realm of the ideal, so we now find it embedded in ritualism. More precisely, it appears there three times in the rite so long prescribed in the *Rituale Romanum*:

1. In the recitation of the *symbolum,* which, with the Our Father, incorporates the basic teachings of the ancient catechumenate. In the rite of baptism, the *symbolum* represents the surviving remnant of the former double rite of *traditio et redditio symboli*.

2. In the interrogatory formula of baptism, which counterbalances the renunciation of Satan and his kingdom and, as the positive *pactio,* expresses the covenant of faith. In conjunction with the renunciation of Satan, it is the ritual form of the doctrine of the two ways. It leads to the act of covenant, which is consummated in the triple Yes of faith. It is worth noting that the text preserved here is considerably more archaic than the *textus receptus* of the *Apostolicum*. It retains throughout the form to be found in the *Gelasianum,* a form that assuredly antedated, in liturgical practice, the compilation of this sixth-century Sacramentary.[25] Not only, then, is this interrogatory formula of baptism with its creed in question form to be counted among the oldest parts of the only recently superseded Roman rite; it is also its most essential part, corresponding, as it does, to the central action of all the ancient Christian baptismal forms that have come down to us (Hippolytus, Ambrose, Augustine, the Oriental Church before Gregory of Nyssa) and in which the baptismal event itself is linked

---

[25] DS 36, with bibliography and information about sources. In the new *Rituale,* the article on Christology has been improved, but the first and second articles have been retained in their original form. The German *Rituale* requires also the recitation of the *Apostolicum,* which is no longer required in the Roman *Rituale*.

with this process of *pactio*.[26] Here we see plainly the difference between the first stage in the development of the baptismal rite and the last stage as it was described above. *Pactio* and *mersio* have been separated since the Middle Ages; the baptismal interrogation with its triple *credo* is no longer at the center of the baptismal event but has been relegated to the catechumenate and hence to the "preparation for justification", thereby reducing its importance. As a result, the ritualization of the former catechumenate once again brings with it a regrettable loss.

3. In the sacramental formula, based on Matthew 28:19, which was itself originally a "short formula of faith", a concentrated reference to the fundamental structure and essential form of the faith expressed in the *symbolum*. In its present form and against the background of Scholastic theology, it has, admittedly, to a large degree lost this meaning, appearing now simply as a sacramental formula, a purely administrative formula, basically identical with that prescribed for all the sacraments in the fundamental schema of matter and form. Not only is its character as a *symbolum* thereby overlooked but, at the same time, the reciprocity that existed in the baptismal interrogation and in the interrogatory form of the *symbolum* is destroyed. Through the transformation of the interrogatory *symbolum* into a "formula", the whole becomes a unilateral act of administration that, on the juridical model of valid documentation, requires no answer but is valid as posited. When we realize, in addition, that the minimal requirements for valid baptism have been reduced to the pouring of water and the concomitant recitation of the baptismal formula, that everything else is, consequently, to be regarded as "preparation", it becomes evident that there is no place in current theological and liturgical thought for a discussion of baptism and the formulation of the content of faith.[27]

But this means that both the concept of faith and that of baptism have fallen into a kind of isolation in consequence of which their relationship has become problematic—to the detriment not only of baptism but also of the right understanding of faith. For in Catholicism this has the effect of doctrinalizing faith, of bestowing on the formulations of faith an

---

[26] Cf. Alois Stenzel, *Die Taufe* (Innsbruck: Rauch, 1958), esp. 73ff. and 79–98.

[27] I regard these facts as highly significant both for a proper view of the relationship of institution and person, of priest and "laity", in the Church and for the beginning of the process of the development of dogma. As for the former, there is automatically corrected there a one-sidedly "magisterial" view of Church life. There exists no antithesis between purely active conferral and purely passive reception; the conferral in the baptismal dialogue refers, rather, to an active reception—perhaps there can be developed on this basis a properly Christian concept of dialogue. At the same time, it is obvious that the indispensable prerequisite of faith is not to be sought in a firmly fixed form but in a living spiritual nexus that creates its form historically.

increasingly theoretical character, with the result that today, when the question of the *symbola* is assuming a new importance, there are appearing short formulas of faith that are in reality nothing but abstract recapitulations of theology, of doctrinal structure, and that have lost all sense of the original meaning of the formulas of faith.[28] Luther, it is true, strongly opposed this doctrinalization and sought to restore to faith its entirely personal character as the confident certainty that my sins have been forgiven, but this did not restore the ecclesial context of faith that was apparent in its original partnership with baptism. Moreover, the possibility of understanding the meaning of the sacraments became even more remote. The question of the relationship of faith and baptism has consequently become increasingly unanswerable for contemporary theology. Even Luther's solution is not particularly convincing. Baptism is widely regarded as no more than a positive dispensation of God, who intended in this way to give faith a necessary and meaningful support—but, from the perspective of our century, we must ask if he did not, in fact, burden rather than support it. It is understandable, then, that for many exegetes the level of baptism and that of faith seem, in Pauline theology, to be two wholly distinct paths that are fundamentally incapable of meeting. What is genuinely Christian is strangely intermingled with what has been borrowed from the mystery religions. The fact that baptism took place long before Paul makes it even more difficult to separate what refers to Christianity as a whole from what refers solely to the sacraments.[29]

2. Baptism and the formulation of the content of faith in the ancient Church

But what was the original relationship? The question about "faith and baptism" that has become so difficult to answer seems to me, in fact, to be

---

[28] This is especially clear in the various "short formulas" proposed by Karl Rahner, *Schriften zur Theologie* [henceforth *Schriften*], 14 vols. (Einsiedeln: Benziger, 1961–1980), 8 (1967): 153–64. Naturally, there are also, in the history of the *symbolum*, texts with a strongly doctrinaire tendency, as, for instance, the *symbolum Quicumque*. This is due to the varying functions of the texts—from *symbola* for catechumenate and baptism to those for ordination. The fact that the question of the concrete value of the texts, of their relationship to the framework of Christian and ecclesial life, is so seldom asked is one of the chief weaknesses of the discussion about short formulas—apart from the fact that they are almost always summaries of theology, not of faith. Cf. the more thorough discussion of this topic in Part One, Chapter 2, Section 1D of the present work.

[29] On the exegetical discussion, cf. Rudolf Bultmann, *Theologie des Neuen Testaments*, 3d ed. (Tübingen: Mohr, 1958), 311ff.; Otto Kuss, *Paulus* (Regensburg: Pustet, 1971), 243–44; 411–14.

susceptible of an answer only in terms of the question about baptism and the formulation of the content of faith. Since the main directions in the history of the dogmatic and liturgical process have been so convincingly elucidated in recent studies, it will suffice here briefly to recall the principal facts.[30] What is so striking about the oldest baptismal rituals available to us—Tertullian, Hippolytus, Ambrose—is this: they contain no baptismal formula as we understand the term today but, instead, a baptismal interrogation in which the *symbolum* is divided into three questions, and the three responses thereto and concomitant triple immersion of the neophyte comprise the form in which the sacrament is administered. This baptismal dialogue is, at the same time, the oldest extant form of the confession of faith.

We can state with certainty, then, that the formulation of the content of faith in fixed formulas—*symbola*—originally occurred primarily in the context of baptism: it is referred to the baptismal event in which it originates, which occasions the need for such formulas and to which they continue to be referred. They are to be understood in the context of the administration of baptism.[31] Some differentiation is, of course, necessary here. In actual fact, the complex process of baptism led, in its various stages, to the development of two different types of confessions of faith. The catechumenate gave rise to instructional manuals, to a *regula*; the administration of baptism gave rise to *symbola* ("declarative" and "interrogatory" confessions of faith). The two types reflect the different tasks and functions from which they emanate.[32] They likewise express different levels in the process of faith, different stages in its realization. Faith encompasses the level of the *didascalia*, the comprehensive instructional manual, which is standardized and fixed in its overall structure but flexible and not susceptible of standardization in its

[30] I agree here to a large extent with the careful study by Alois Stenzel.

[31] This is by no means to say that baptism was the only occasion on which a creed could be formulated; it points merely to the primary importance of baptism in the development of the confession of faith. On other significant stages, see especially: Oscar Cullmann, *Die ersten christlichen Glaubensbekenntnisse* (Zurich: Evangelischer Verlag, 1942); for a comprehensive review of the state of research, see Karl Lehmann, *Auferweckt*, 27–67. On the basic ways in which *symbola* were formed and on their relationship to the *evangelium* as such, see Heinrich Schlier, "Die Anfänge der christologischen Credo", in Bernhard Welte, ed., *Zur Frühgeschichte der Christologie* (Freiburg: Herder, 1970), 13–58.

[32] Stenzel, 79–98; 157–64, esp. 160–64; 160: "on the particular character of the *symbolum* . . . .: it is a short formula of baptismal instruction (specifically, of instruction for the φωτιζόμενοι = the 'enlightened'). Its role (when recited from memory) was not formally, then, a confession of faith as is suggested by the nature of *pactio, sponsio,* etc., but a bearing witness to the correctness of faith (= *fides quae*)"; 163: "Since there were two different confessions in the baptismal ritual, the declaratory creed was the place both for accommodation of the continuing explication of dogma and for rejection of actual heresies."

individual ramifications. Faith also encompasses the level of the act of *pactio,* of the neophyte's Yes to the summons of the *credo,* and is here, in its trinitarian and salvation-historical structure, an organically constructed form, a *symbolum,* in which question and answer are united in the indissolubility of a definitive event. The formulation of the content of faith takes place, on the one hand, in the *didascalia,* which is oriented to baptism and for which the baptismal interrogation, which it then develops concretely in its separate propositions, is normative; it occurs, on the other hand, in the act of decision itself: it is ordered to the confession of faith that likewise represents acceptance of new life.[33]

Two questions are still to be answered. First, the historical problem: What led to the separation of the *symbolum* and the baptismal formula, that is, to the relegation of the *symbolum* to the preparatory stage of baptism, thereby at the same time obliterating the distinction between *didascalia* (*regula*) and *symbolum* and, in doing so, paradoxically establishing a new separation: the congealing of sacrament into rite, of theology into doctrine, with the consequent devaluation of the *symbolum,* on the one hand, and, on the other, the transformation of the concept of *symbolum* into the basis of the later concept of dogma? Secondly, we must ask: What relationship exists between faith-formula and sacrament where this obliteration has not yet taken place?

Despite the research of Stenzel, who has made a special study of the matter, it seems to me that the historical process by which the *symbolum* was relegated to the liturgy of preparation has yet to be fully explained. What is clear is that the evolution of the rites of *traditio* and *redditio symboli* in the last stage of the catechumenate (the stage of those who were called θωτιζόμενοι in the East, *competentes* in the West, and *electi* in Rome) had already somewhat obscured the distinction between *regula* and *symbolum,* in so doing, reducing to some extent the importance of the interrogatory *symbolum,* which had once been the essential element of baptism. Stenzel has attempted to show that the rite of *apotaxis* (renunciation) prescribed by the doctrine of the two ways resulted, by a kind of inner necessity, in the formation of a corresponding *syntaxis* (affirmation), and that this *syntaxis* inevitably absorbed the baptismal interrogation and affirmation, which then came to be redundant in the structure of the baptismal event and were replaced by the simple formula of baptism. The process was hastened, moreover, by the tendency to make the central formula of the sacrament as dependent as possible on the language of Holy Scripture;[34] it was revealed

---

[33] For a comprehensive and historical elucidation of these connections, see Henri de Lubac, *La Foi chrétienne.*

[34] Stenzel, 114: "Baptism is not alone in its tendency to adapt the inherited formulae increasingly to the language of Scripture: a significant example is the linguistic development

clearly, however, only with the disappearance of the catechumenate, on the one hand, and, on the other, with the absorption of sacramental theology into the schema of matter and form in which the *pactio* disappeared in favor of a mere administration of the sacrament that makes all but unrecognizable the specific relationship of baptism, confession of faith and faith.

But how are we to interpret this relationship? To explain it, we must, I think, review the whole structure of baptism from the perspective of the various steps of the catechumenate. The latter began with instruction by, for the most part, private teachers (private schools), inaugurated by Christians who vouched for the newcomer and made themselves responsible for him. In this way, there followed, at first hesitantly, cautiously, but without official participation, an introduction to the thought and life of Christians. Then, step by step, the Church entered more directly into the process. There was, on the one hand, the catechumen's contact with the word through participation in the liturgy of the word and thus in the official teaching of the Church and, on the other hand, the action of the Church in the required exorcisms. This concretization achieved its ultimate goal in the night of the baptism itself with its No, its Yes, its sealing by immersion and its anointing with oil. In all this, the conviction was operative that faith is, on the one hand, the decision of the individual (in the framework of the concept of the two ways [exorcism] and the *regula*), but that it is far from being just that; that it is also a meeting, a being received, a letting oneself be received, by the community of the faithful; that one cannot achieve fullness of being by one's own private decision; that one becomes oneself by becoming a confession of faith, an open Yes, when one is received by the community of the faithful, when one is incorporated into that community, when one is immersed and allows oneself to be immersed in it. Thus the act of faith can take place and be what it is supposed to be in no other way than by referring itself publicly to the Church and letting itself be received in the mutuality of question and answer, letting itself be buried, immersed, made one with the one subject of the *credo: Mater Ecclesia.*[35] To this twofold process of receiving and letting oneself be received must be added also the fact that the Church knows and confesses, in the act of receiving, that she does not act in her own right as a separate and independent subject but in the name of Father, Son and Holy Spirit; that her act of receiving is, in its

---

of the canon or the *anaphora.*" On 112, Stenzel shows that the beginnings of baptism with indicative formulas, at least in the Syrian church, can be dated with certainty to the last years of the fourth century.

[35] In *Catholicisme,* 50–51, de Lubac shows that the "I" of the *symbolum* refers to the Church as subject.

turn, contained in the act by which she, too, is received and lets herself be received. To this triple interaction, the sacrament is witness; it is not, therefore, something secondary to the act of faith but its ecclesial dimension and, at the same time, the theo-logical dimension of the ecclesial. With respect to our questions, this means that faith is ordered to the confession of faith, the confession of faith is ordered to the community, and the community is ordered to the liturgy. In this circle, in the circle of the true and complete structure of the sacrament of baptism, the formulation of the content of faith has its original and central place.

C. The Creeds of Nicaea and Constantinople: History, Structure, Content

Sixteen hundred years ago, at the Second Ecumenical Council of Constantinople, that confession of faith was formulated that, even today, is the common possession of nearly all Christian churches and ecclesial communities. Memorial celebrations in Rome and Constantinople reminded us of the date; in Germany, it was underscored by a joint statement of the Catholic, Orthodox and Protestant churches. The ancient Creed became, for separated Christians, a signpost on the road to unity. It will be rewarding, therefore, to examine it more closely. How did it originate? What does it mean?

The question seems even more relevant when we consider that the situation of the Church prior to that Council was anything but ideal. Basil, the great Bishop of Caesaria (in present-day Turkey), who is justly regarded as one of the architects of this Council, which, in fact, he did not live to attend, compared the state of the Church at that time with a night battle at sea: everything is in turmoil; friend and foe are no longer distinguishable in the encompassing gloom and the incessant and desolate shouting; both sides strike out randomly. The Church, according to Basil,[36] was in a state of indescribable confusion. I shall attempt to explain, as briefly as possible, how this situation came about and then to ask how the Council of Constantinople succeeded in rescuing and reuniting the Church that had fallen prey to divisive factions. However, it is not my intention in these remarks simply to scrutinize more or less curiously a past now distant but, rather, to speak of our own fate, of the Church of today with her hopes and needs.

[36] Basil, *De Spiritu Sancto*, German translation by M. Blum (Freiburg, 1967), 112–17. An introduction to Basil's thought and the literature will be found in Benoît Pruche, *Sur le Saint Esprit*, in *Sources chrétiennes*, no. 17, 2d ed. (Paris: Éditions du Cerf, 1968), 9–248.

It is in this spirit that we turn now to the history of the fourth century,[37] at the beginning of which the Emperor Constantine brought about such a great change in the religious policy of the Roman Empire, putting an end to the three-hundred-year-old struggle against Christianity, which he declared an officially legal and, soon thereafter, specially favored religion. In doing so, he was responding not only to the actual strength that Christianity had meanwhile acquired in the Roman Empire but also to the mood of his own century. The gods of Greece and Rome had ceased to be credible; they no longer existed outside of poetry or served any legitimate political purpose; they could no longer offer either individuals or society a moral foundation for their way of life. The turn to monotheism was in the air; it was, in fact, long overdue. On the other hand, it was also clear that one could not pray to a god who was just the product of the philosophers and that, from such a god, no fullness of power was to be expected either in politics or in ethics. The belief in one God had to have a genuinely religious origin, that is, it had to rest on revelation, if it was to bind and be accepted as binding. For that reason, the eyes of the intelligentsia had long been turned toward Judaism, which could point to a monotheism with a strongly religious foundation. But Jewish monotheism was so linked to national traditions and ritual prescriptions that Judaism was unthinkable as the common religion of the Mediterranean world. The young Christian religion, on the other hand, had demonstrated more and more clearly, in its hard struggle against the great variety of spiritual movements that proceeded from Judaism, its potential as a new world religion. Constantine recognized this and began, circumspectly but nevertheless determinedly, to smooth its way toward becoming the new universal religion.

In the meantime, it soon became apparent that, while Christianity was indeed a belief in only one God, it was, at the same time, far more than a purely philosophical monotheism. This was clear, above all, in its confession of Jesus Christ as the Son of God. At a time when Christendom was, as it were, officially acknowledged as heir to the ancient philosophy and as a rational religion, the conflict about the meaning of the concept "Son of God" could not fail to reach dramatic proportions. The struggle

[37] The following presentation owes much to an unpublished lecture delivered by W. D. Hauschild at the 1981 spring meeting of the ecumenical discussion group founded by Cardinal Jaeger and the Protestant Bishop Stählin on the topic "Das trinitarische Dogma von 381 als Ergebnis verbindlicher Konsensusbildung". Cf. also Hauschild's work *Die Pneumatomachen. Eine Untersuchung zur Dogmengeschichte des 4. Jahrhunderts* (Hamburg, 1967). Also important for this topic are, above all, Louis Bouyer, *Le Consolateur. Esprit-Saint et vie de grâce* (Paris: Éditions du Cerf, 1980)—for the theology of the fourth century, see especially 167–214; Yves Congar, *Je crois en l'Esprit Saint* 3 (Paris: Éditions du Cerf, 1980): esp. 55–67; P. Luislampe, *Spiritus vivificans. Grundzüge einer Theologie des Heiligen Geistes nach Basilius von Caesarea* (Münster, 1980).

between political accommodation, philosophical enlightenment and the resistance of religion to both of them began to affect the Church more deeply than she had ever been affected by external persecution. Constantine observed with consternation this movement that was diametrically counter to his plans for a new unity of the Empire on the basis of the unity of Christian belief. The incipient schism in the Church was for him a political problem; he was, however, farseeing enough to recognize that the unity of the Church could not be achieved by political measures but only by religious ones, that is, by awakening the unitive forces within the Christian faith itself. Consequently, he convoked the first ecumenical council in history, an assemblage of the bishops of the world, in Nicaea, a city in Asia Minor not far from the metropolis he had founded in Constantinople. This Council definitively rejected the notion of a Christianity of accommodation. In the years preceding the Council, the theologian Arius of Alexandria in Egypt had offered a very attractive model of such a Christendom. He explained Christian belief as monotheism in the strictest sense of philosophical thought. That meant, above all, that the designation of Christ as "Son of God" was not to be taken literally. According to philosophical monothism, Christ could not be God in the true sense of the word but only an intermediate being whom God used for the creation of the world and for his relationships with human beings. The word "God" as a designation for Christ was to be used only, as it were, in quotation marks; with the necessary restrictions, however, its use could be permitted the faithful for reasons of piety.[38]

This solution was extraordinarily appealing. The philosophical offensiveness of the expression "Son of God" was thereby avoided, and Christology was fully embedded in a framework acceptable to the ruling modes of thought. The biblical texts could also be explained in this way while holding fast to the language of tradition. The Nicene Fathers rejected this possibility: they insisted that the Bible could and must be taken literally in what concerned its most crucial point—its witness to Jesus Christ. If it says "Son", it means "Son". The Fathers translated the expression "Son of God" by the formula: Christ is one in Being with the Father; he is God in the literal sense, not just in quotation marks. They incorporated the formula "one in Being with the Father" into their confession of faith, their creed. If a philosophical concept was thus joined to the biblical words, it was only for the purpose of saying, without fear of misunderstanding, that the Bible is to be taken seriously in its literal meaning and is not to be modified by philosophical accommodations to a mode of thought that is more

[38] See Aloys Grillmeier, *Jesus der Christus im Glauben der Kirche* I (Freiburg: Herder, 1979): 356–85, for a thorough treatment of the subject. [For an English translation of vol. I, see Aloys Grillmeier, *Christ in Christian Tradition,* vol. I, trans. John Bowden, 2d ed. (London: Mowbrays, 1975). (Trans.)]

widely acceptable. Thus the appropriation of philosophy by faith occurs here in a way exactly opposite to the way in which Arius had appropriated it: whereas he measured Christianity by the norms of enlightened understanding and altered it accordingly, the Council Fathers used philosophy in order to clarify, beyond the possibility of misunderstanding, the belief that is the essence of Christianity.[39]

By this decision, Christianity's right to be taken seriously as a religion and its role as a spiritual entity in its own right were both vindicated. But this was more than the enlightened world of that time was prepared to accept. Although the Nicene Creed was protected by the authority of both Emperor and bishops, that is, by the ranking authorities of both Church and state, it found acceptance at first only in the West, where the supremacy of the bishop of Rome was fully recognized; moreover, the West lay outside the great philosophical movements of the age and was, in consequence, not so affected by their intellectual upheavals as was the Greek-speaking East. There, the eminent Alexandrian Bishop Athanasius stood almost alone in his acceptance of Nicaea. Throughout the Eastern Church, there arose that indescribable confusion of which Basil speaks. More and more new formulas were invented by way of compromise, but, instead of uniting, they served only to increase the number of factions.

In view of this situation, Constantine had begun to distance himself from the unenforceable decision of the Council of Nicaea. His son Constantius II pursued a policy of deliberate rejection of the Nicene Creed. As a politician, he attempted to establish unity on the basis of the least common denominator. The Council had, it was true, declared that Christ was one in Being with the Father, but did there not now exist a number of formulas that spoke instead of the Son's *similarity* to the Father? Constantius adopted the version that said Christ was "like the Father in accordance with the Scripture" and had this formula approved in 360 by the Synod of Constantinople, thus formally annulling the Nicene Creed.[40] From a political point of view, this must have been regarded as an exceptionally clever compromise, since faith was in this way firmly referred to the Bible. For did not the formula explicitly say: Christ is as the Bible says he is? An apparently pious solution was thereby reached that based faith simply and solely on the word of Scripture. But it also deprived the Church of the right to make her own decisions and placed the concrete ordering of ecclesial matters in the hands of the state.

It soon became apparent that this escape into biblicism was far from

---

[39] For a further explanation, cf. Joseph Ratzinger, *Der Gott Jesu Christi*, 70–76. On the historical aspects, see Grillmeier, 386–413.

[40] On the religious policies of Constantius, cf. *Handbuch der Kirchengeschichte*, ed. Hubert Jedin, 2:1: Karl Baus and Eugen Ewig, *Die Reichskirche nach Konstantin dem Grossen* (Freiburg: Herder, 1973), 42–51.

establishing the dominance of the word of Scripture. For Nicaea had not ranged itself against the Bible; on the contrary, it had officially expounded the Bible in terms of the universal faith of the Church, thus making it effective in its full strength. Now, however, the Church was disavowing her own decision, and, consequently, her right to make her own decisions, by referring the individual to the word of the Bible but, at the same time, leaving in doubt what was actually being said about this central question. In consequence, the Church no longer had a voice of her own, and the Bible ceased to be a universal word: it was delivered over to contending theological factions, thus surrendering the Church to the power of politics, which must now make the decisions that the Church no longer claimed the authority to make. By a kind of inner necessity, biblicism was followed by the domination of theological factions and the Church's surrender to politics.

But a Church that has, to this extent, lost her inner strength is no longer of any political interest because no spiritual force emanates from her. Theodosius, the new Emperor from the West, was well aware of this fact. He therefore altered the politico-religious course of the Empire, directing it once again toward Nicaea, which, shortly after his assumption of office in 379, he again confirmed as the valid foundation of Church unity. He clearly rejected both the purely political and the biblicist norms by declaring as normative the faith of the pope in Rome and of the bishop of Alexandria.[41] By this action, the Church was again recognized as the maker of her own decisions and the source of the universal and binding interpretation of the Bible. She was freed from her bondage to the political structure and placed anew under her own control. For the Council of Nicaea had declared that the bishops of Rome, Alexandria and Antioch were the authoritative guardians of the universal faith of the Church.[42] Because Antioch was floundering in a vortex of politically determined theologies, the Emperor was compelled, however, to turn to Rome and Alexandria; hence this imperial decree likewise marks for us a stage in the development of the authority of the bishop of Rome with regard to the faith of the whole Church. The Emperor's decision was a step in the right direction to the extent that it returned the Church to herself. On the other hand, the function of politics in matters of faith was once again overvalued; for if Nicaea was to be accepted as valid in the East, that

---

[41] *Theodosiani libri XVI cum constitutionibus sirmondianis et leges novellae ad Theodosianum pertinentes,* ed. Th. Mommsen et Paulus M. Meyer, vol. 1, pars posterior (Berlin: Weidmann, 1905), liber decimus sextus, "De Fide Catholica", 16:1, 2 (February 27, 380), "Cunctos Populos", 833.

[42] Canon 1. Text in *Conciliorum oecumenicorum decreta,* ed. Josepho Alberigo et al., 3d ed. (Bologna: Istituto per le Scienze Religiose, 1973), 6.

acceptance had to come from the inner conviction of the Church in the East. In February 380, therefore, the Emperor was obliged to temper his too precipitate action and to make an even greater effort to strengthen and reconcile the inner regenerative powers of the Church in the East.

These powers had, in fact, been developed during the years in which the Nicene faith was under harassment. We have, from the year 382, a shocking letter addressed to Pope Damasus in Rome by the bishops once again assembled in Constantinople in which they report how many bishops in the East had suffered for the faith during the years of suppression. Many had gone into exile and had died there. Others had suffered at home rather than in exile. They had been stoned and tortured; those who survived could indeed say of themselves that they bore the wounds of Christ in their bodies (cf. Gal 6:17).[43] Faith like this, which proved itself in suffering, was possessed of an inner radiance that the political opportunists among the bishops could not appreciate. Since the middle of the fourth century, however, a new theological power had been increasingly in evidence. At first, it had been philosophical and political accommodation in the face of biblicism that rules almost exclusively; Nicaea found little resonance and, therefore, few followers among the intelligentsia. Then there arose three individuals whose words retain even today their power to enlighten: the above-mentioned Bishop Basil of Caesarea; his brother, Gregory of Nyssa; and the friend of his well-remembered student days in Athens, Gregory of Nazianzus.[44] These three theologians of Asia Minor became a stabilizing force for the second generation of theologians after Nicaea, which succeeded in so broadening and deepening the intellectual bases of the Nicene faith as to make it more readily comprehensible to a wider circle of seeking individuals. Through the efforts of these men, Nicaean orthodoxy also regained its appeal even in the politico-religious realm. For the achieving of a new consensus, it was certainly of decisive importance that Meletius, Bishop of Antioch and a bitter opponent of the older Nicaean bishops of Rome and Alexandria, joined the younger generation, providing a basis for the formation of a majority that would ultimately unify the East once again under the aegis of the Nicene faith.[45] This unification occurred at the Council of Constantinople in 381. To make this understandable, we must prefix a short explanation.

The increased scrutiny of the intellectual bases of the Nicene faith that

[43] See text in ibid, 25–30.

[44] Cf. Bouyer, 178–92; Baus, 66–70.

[45] The figure of Meletius is undoubtedly viewed too positively by Baus, 68–70. For a more critical treatment, see W. Schneemelcher, "Meletius", in RGG 4 (1960): 845; E. Amann in DTC 10:520–31; cf. also Henri I. Marrou, in Jean Daniélou and Henri I. Marrou, *Geschichte der Kirche* 1 (Einsiedeln, 1953): 273.

took place in the circle of the younger generation of Nicaeans led not only to a new understanding but also to new difficulties. At the beginning of the fourth century, the question about Christ had been the principal problem of Christian monotheism. Christ was either excluded from the concept of God as required by philosophical monotheism or included as required by biblical tradition. But in the attempt to think through the Christian concept of God in these terms, one inevitably encountered the question of the Holy Spirit. In its confession of faith, Nicaea had dealt thoroughly with the question of Christ. About the Holy Spirit, however, it had merely repeated the ancient baptismal confession: ". . . and in the Holy Spirit". That was no longer enough. There was reason to fear that the debate about the Holy Spirit would lead anew to the same drama as had arisen in connection with the question about the Son. With its confession of belief in the Holy Spirit, which it added to the already existing Nicene Creed, the Council of Constantinople avoided this eventuality and restored unity to the Church. How did it accomplish this? The answer is not an easy one.

In the year 379, a Synod at Antioch had already worked toward a new consensus; it was possible to rely on 150 bishops of the Near East. By a clever move on the part of the Emperor, the extremists of both sides were not invited to the Council. He excluded representatives of the West, whose hard line in favor of Nicaea had made it difficult to win over those who had thus far resisted it; but he also omitted from the Council the irreconcilable opponents of Nicaea, thus eliminating *a priori* the possibility of violent tensions among the participants. But such a tactic could have had the opposite effect of evoking opposition; hence, while it can go far toward explaining the reaching of a consensus, it cannot explain the wide acceptance of this consensus. For this we must look for deeper causes.[46] I see four principal ones:

1. The philosophical achievement of the younger generation of Nicaeans lay principally in the fact that they attacked the problem of Christian monotheism from a new angle. In the initial debate at the beginning of the fourth century, the concept of monotheism, on the one hand, had been opposed to the confession of the divinity of Jesus Christ, on the other. It was not easy to combine the two. The theologians of the second generation after Nicaea realized that the question of monotheism had to be completely rethought. They understood that belief in Christ and the Holy Spirit was not in opposition to monotheism but rather revealed, for the first time, its true greatness. They adopted the Platonic model of the three hypostases and recognized, on that basis, that the oneness of God consisted precisely in the oneness of Father, Son and Holy Spirit. The

---

[46] On the ecumenicity of the Council, Baus, 79–80.

oneness of being, wisdom and love is a higher oneness than the oneness of undifferentiatedness. They recognized that the true oneness of God was to be understood in terms of the spiritual, not of the atom, the material; they recognized that it was precisely this confession of the divinity of Christ and of the Holy Spirit, which seemed to run counter to monotheism, that actually revealed the nature of the divine oneness and allowed the great and illuminating notion of a God who is divine to emerge in contrast to the notion of a God conceived by man. In this way, the Holy Spirit did not become an additional problem to be reconciled with monotheism but rather—since the Holy Spirit opened the way to the doctrine of the Trinity and, with it, to a new appropriation of the deepest thought of antiquity—the solution of the christological problem and the door to Christian monotheism.

Gregory of Nazianzus combined this new, personalistic and spiritual understanding of being, of reality as such, with a new philosophy of history, which he interpreted as progressive history, as the history of a continuing revelation and, therefore, of a progressive education of mankind by faith. He identified the first stage in this progress as the leading of the human race out of the darkness of the worship of false gods and into the knowledge of the one true God—as the transition from human beliefs to revelation. The second stage, which coincided with the transition from the Old to the New Testament, from law to grace, from the particularity of Israel to the universality of the salvation of all peoples, led to knowledge of the Son of God; it was, as it were, the passage from Father to Son. Now, in the third stage, the Holy Spirit and, along with him, the whole mystery of God was revealed. The trinitarian nature of God is reflected in the historicity of human existence, which, for its part, parallels the history of revelation. The present era of the Church thus became comprehensible to man as fulfillment, as a time in which a long journey reached its goal.[47]

2. The decrees of Constantinople corresponded, then, to a certain confidence of thought as well as to the self-assurance of an age in which, as it were, a new threshold of history was crossed. But it is impossible for philosophy alone to keep the Church in existence. Generally speaking, an intensification of thought is possible only if it has been preceded by an intensification of experience. The new theology of the Cappadocians, which made possible the triumph of Constantinople, rested in fact on the new intellectual experience that owed its existence to the Nicene faith. It is

---

[47] S. P. N. Gregorii Theologi, *Opera quae exstant omnia,* "Orationes XXVII–XLV", Oratio 31 (Theologia Quinta), PG 36:159–65. ("Grégoire de Nazianze, Discours 27–31", in *Sources chrétiennes,* no. 250 [Paris: Éditions du Cerf, 1978]: 322–30). For a French translation, see Henri de Lubac, *Catholicisme,* 384–86. See also Joseph Barbel, *Gregor von Nazanz, Die fünf theologischen Reden* (Düsseldorf, 1963), 260–67.

unthinkable without the suffering of the martyrs who defended their faith against the state church and, in a time of crisis, had recourse to a deep-rooted reliance on prayer and on the liturgy of the Church. Basil developed his doctrine of the Holy Spirit, his concept of Christian monotheism, entirely from the liturgy of the Church; his book about the Holy Spirit is, at bottom, nothing other than a theology of liturgy. He begins with a discussion of baptism: Christ commissioned the apostles to make all people his disciples by baptizing them "in the name of the Father and of the Son and of the Holy Spirit" (Mt 28:19). In the biblical context of baptism, Basil found the fundamental law of Christian life and prayer. Thus the reality of Christian prayer was the guideline for philosophy. One does not first form a mental image of God and then try to pray to it; on the contrary, there exists first the experience of prayer, which, in turn, rests on the sacrament, that is, on the experience of God that was communicated to the apostles and continues to exist in the Church—the experience of Jesus Christ himself, who could make God known to us only because God was known to him.

Another definitive element originated also with Basil, the real pioneer of the new unity. Confession of the Holy Spirit goes hand in hand, in this theology, with the theme of Church reform. Devotion to the Holy Spirit is for him, not a theological theory, but a search for the spirit of faith, a search for divine life and for the renewal of the Church through the Spirit. It is a criticism of the state church and a search for the Church of faith, for a truly spiritual community of faith and life. Thus Basil became the Father of Monasticism, which he wanted to establish in the Church, not as a unique group separated from the rest of Christianity, but as the model of a brotherhood of faith, in which the ideals that gave it birth continue to thrive: "The whole group of believers was united, heart and soul; . . . everything they owned was held in common" (Acts 4:32; cf. 2:42–47). The foundation of this ecclesial life and this concept of the Church was belief in the Holy Spirit. On the other hand, from this lived confession of the Holy Spirit proceeded a persuasive power that was stronger than any rationalistic accommodation or decree of the state.[48]

3. From this depth of faith and thought, Basil patiently sought the dialogue and accomplished the work of persuasion without which the crevasses of separation could not have been filled. Many found that he went too far. His friend Gregory of Nazianzus saw in his arguments a tendency toward indecisiveness and ambiguity that he could not condone. Athanasius, who, with noble inflexibility, had supported the Nicene faith

---

[48] For the relationship between spiritual life (monasticism) and pneumatology in Basil's writings, cf. Bouyer, 197–98. Cf. also Werner Löser, *Im Geiste des Origenes. Hans Urs von Balthasar als Interpret der Theologie der Kirchenväter* (Frankfurt: Josef Knecht, 1976), 128–33.

singlehandedly for half a century amidst a flood of contumely and contradiction, was better able to understand Basil on this point. He realized that, in this way, the Bishop of Caesarea had, in truly apostolic manner, become weak with the weak. At the Council of Constantinople, it was the arguments of Basil, who had meantime died, that led to the choice of relatively open formulations of faith in the Holy Spirit, a language of religious experience that was intended to and did in fact make it possible for as many as possible to accept these words. Such compromises can be dangerous and Gregory of Nazianzus rejected them with sharp words.[49] In this case, the compromise was protected by the liturgical witness and the spiritual life that made it possible and, at the same time, gave it its unequivocal meaning.[50]

4. The Church of the West was at first indignant at the autocratic and unilateral action of the Emperor, who, as we saw above, had invited only the East to the Council. The bishops of the Council were well aware of the problem thus created: a new dependence on the state. They tried to free themselves from this bondage at another assembly in 382 by sending a moving letter to Pope Damasus and asking his approval of the results of the Council.[51] Representatives of the West did not, in fact, attend the Council until seventy years later at the Council of Chalcedon, but the action of the Eastern bishops is important in its own right. It recognizes the predominance of the ecclesiastical over the political structure and gives expression to their intention of binding themselves to the whole Church in a union that can exist only in union with the bishop of Rome. Here, too, Constantinople offered a meaningful sign that contributed to the healing of the rift that already existed between East and West and to the restoration to the whole Church of a unity that persisted for centuries.

It is not difficult, I think, to see how much we can learn today from this long history. Today, too, the Church cannot be saved by compromise and accommodation or by mere theorizing but only by self-reflection and a depth of faith that opens the door to the Holy Spirit and his unifying power. However numerous the human factors that were necessary for the achievement of unity at the Council of Constantinople, it is also ultimately through these factors that it becomes clear that the unity of the Church is not to be brought about by human effort but can be effected only by the Holy Spirit. Anyone who looks back on this Council knows that this is not a denial of individual effort, not an expression of resignation, but the strongest word of hope that can be conceived.

---

[49] Gregory of Nazianzus, *De vita sua*, 1703–64, ed. H. G. Jungk (Heidelberg, 1974).
[50] Cf. Baus, 75–76.
[51] Cf. n. 42 above.

D. Short Formulas of Faith? On the Relationship between Formula and Interpretation

It is not easy for faith to express itself today. Its traditional formulas sound foreign to our contemporaries; their meaning remains obscure. It is against this background that we are to understand the extraordinary resonance found by Karl Rahner's suggestion that new "short formulas of faith" be composed. Since then, innumerable such texts have proliferated, but there has been little reflection on the fundamental problem. That is what we shall consider in the following remarks, in which we shall also turn our attention to the question of pluralism in the Church and in theology—a question that is closely related to the demand for short formulas.

Starting from his initial premise, which is the need for greater comprehensibility, Rahner establishes the following as essential characteristics of the "short formulas" he recommends:

a. They must be intelligible to their hearers.

b. They must be capable of being immediately assimilated by those for whom they are intended.

c. Given the pluralism of intellectual trends in contemporary society, there must be a large number of such formulas because of the many different mentalities to be addressed.

d. The need for brevity arises from the fact that the contemporary individual is a "very busy" person.

e. Given the rapid fluctuation of intellectual outlooks that characterizes the modern age, it must be expected that the short formulas will themselves be short-lived; in other words, pluralism is to be understood not only as synchronous but also as diachronous.

For purposes of classification:

a. the short formulas are compared to advertising slogans, or also to party programs and manifestoes;

b. their relationship to the classic *symbola* remains unclear, although there are many indications that they are intended to substitute for them. At times, however, they seem to be merely explanations of the ancient *symbola,* which continue to exist alongside them.[52]

---

[52] All the above statements are based on Karl Rahner's article "Die Forderung nach einer 'Kurzformel' des christlichen Glaubens", in *Schriften,* 8 (1967): 153–64, which inaugurated the debate about "short formulas". Despite many valuable observations by others, the fast-growing literature on the subject remains basically within the framework set by Rahner. Consequently, it will not be necessary to review it here. See my comments in the first section of the present work: "What Constitutes Christian Faith Today?" [For an English translation of two articles by Karl Rahner on the need for short formulas of the faith, see "The Need for a

If the notion of short formulas is to be examined in the context of pluralism, the emphasis must undoubtedly be on the question of classification,
for the justification of these formulas and, consequently, the theological
status of the whole concept depends entirely on this classification. To begin with, we must point out that there is a clear contradiction in the classifications formulated under a. and b.: the *symbola* never had the function of
advertising slogans or of party programs or manifestoes. For that matter,
neither is a party program an advertising slogan, nor is it usually intended
solely for advertising purposes. It is regarded as a guideline for the party
rather than as material for advertising. What the classifications in a. and b.
have in common is their attempt to explain the *symbolum* sociologically in
terms of modern society by interpreting it on the basis of the two social
factors "advertising" and "party" and, in that way, determining its linguistic classification. Against this attempt to determine the linguistic classification of the *symbolum* in terms of its sociological function there can be
no basic objection, though we must ask ourselves whether it has been successful. I think it has not. The classification "advertising" belongs to the
consumer world of industrial society and is by its very nature something
quite different from the "propagation of truth" that is the goal of the
Christian mission. Truth is not a product. It is not subject to the legalism
of consumerism, and the approach to it is not, therefore, to be determined
according to the ground rules of consumer advertising. In like manner, the
classification "party" (and "party language"), which has developed from
the rivalry of political powers and the interests that are ordered to them, is
fundamentally different from the formation of groups as the Church tries,
at least, to form them.

It should be clear, then, that the concept "short formula" and the
classification *symbolum* were formulated with totally different goals in
mind and must consequently be ordered to totally different sociological
communities. The common element of relative brevity must not be
allowed to obfuscate the fact that the notion "short formula" and the
traditional form of the *symbolum* are anchored in two fundamentally
different intellectual environments and cannot, therefore, be meaningfully
coordinated unless in doing so each system is elucidated in its entirety.
Our next question, then, must be about the purpose and background of
the traditional *symbolum*. When we attempt to answer this question, we
discover that we must distinguish among the different types of *symbola*.
Without too much simplification, we can name four basic ones:

'Short Formula' of Christian Faith", in *Theological Investigations,* 9, trans. Graham Harrison
(London: Darton, Longman and Todd, 1972): 117–26, and "Reflections on the Problems
Involved in Devising a Short Formula of the Faith", in ibid., 11 (1974): 230–44. (Trans.)]

1. The baptismal *symbolum*. Traditionally, this *symbolum* differed in individual detail from congregation to congregation even while its basic formulation remained unchanged. It provided a summary of the doctrinal teachings of the catechumenate formulated with a view to its goal, which is baptism. Structurally, therefore, the baptismal *symbolum* is an extension of the trinitarian formula (Mt 28:19): that is, an amplification of the content of the trinitarian invocation with, in particular, a salvation-historical Christology and a reference to both the fundamental predications of ecclesiology and the eschatological goal of Christian hope. In saying this, we have said all that is necessary for an understanding of the *symbolum* and have identified the sociological and linguistic community in which it is rooted.

a. The *symbolum* presupposes the way of the catechumenate, which is itself not merely a process of intellectual instruction but, above all, a process of conversion that requires the active cooperation of the candidate and also prays for and, in the exorcisms, manifests the healing action of God. The baptismal *symbolum* presumes for the whole human race, then, a process of maturation and decision in which its teaching is generally assimilated; it understands itself as the expression of a process of decision that is comprehended both as the end of the present way of the catechumenate and, at the same time, as the never-ending beginning of a new way.

b. In terms of its linguistic form, the *symbolum* is a confession of faith. Its language is not an objectification of doctrine as that of the so-called short formulas so often is ("Man is always . . .";[53] the "incomprehensible 'whither' of human transcendence";[54] "Man realizes himself truly . . . only . . .";[55] "Christianity is . . .").[56] Rather, it is—more modestly yet, at the same time, more demandingly—the expression of a personal decision (made by a whole community) for a way that is attainable only by means of such a decision. To use the terminology of linguistic theory, it combines informatory and performatory language, the emphasis being on the performatory element.

c. The way of the catechumenate, which it presupposes and summarizes, means, at the same time, an entering into the life of the ecclesial community. In saying this, we have named the linguistic bearer (and, linguistically speaking, the linguistic "context") of the *symbolum*, which, like any language, exists, not in a vacuum, but against a sociological background: in this case, the community of believers, which must not, of course, be

[53] *Schriften*, 8:159 (beginning of the first draft of a short formula.
[54] *Schriften*, 9 (1970): 250 (beginning of the "theological" short formula).
[55] Ibid., 252 (beginning of the "sociological" short formula).
[56] Ibid., 254 (beginning of the "futurological" short formula).

allowed to become a linguistic island but is rather to be understood as the area in which are realized the particular experience and the way of life proper to it that make certain linguistic concepts accessible at all. No one disputes the fact that the link with a linguistic context is characteristic of all types of short formulas; it is obvious that a formulation such as the "incomprehensible 'whither' of human transcendence" will be comprehensible only within a quite definite (and very limited) linguistic context. The difference between the linguistic context of the *symbola* and that of the "short formulas" is that the theory of short formulas disputes the right of the Church as such to have a language of her own and measures her formulations by the standard of secular comprehensibility (advertising slogans!); that it seeks to reduce this language radically to secular language yet, at the same time, places under the label of pluralism arbitrary linguistic groups from which there is no way that leads outside themselves or to other groups because pluralism is, in the last analysis, not to be done away with. By way of contrast, the *symbolum* sees in the Church as a whole an independent linguistic subject that is united by the common basic experience of faith and is thus possessed of a common understanding. In this respect, the Ephphrata-rite is rich in meaning: it sees the human individual as deaf and dumb before God the Father, before Christ and before the Holy Spirit who speak to him; at the same time, it expresses the belief that this deafness and dumbness can be overcome by the Holy Spirit who acts concretely in the community of the Church to make the process by which the individual becomes capable of speech a part of the process by which he is incorporated into the Church.

2. The conciliar *symbolum,* of which the classic form is the so-called Creed of Nicaea-Constantinople.

a. We must observe that what we are discussing here is a *symbolum* formulated on the episcopal level[57] to serve as a clarification for the whole Church and revealing in its entirety the mark of this linguistic bearer. It is neither suitable for nor intended as a baptismal *symbolum* but serves, rather, on the episcopal level, to provide—for the "control" and regula-

---

[57] This does not mean, of course, that the *symbolum* concerns only the bishops. By its incorporation into the eucharistic celebration as *credo,* it also became the immediate *credo* of all the faithful. Thus it continues to be distinct from the baptismal *credo* in terms of type. Against the background of the catechumenate, the baptismal *credo* formulates the decision in favor of faith; the eucharistic *credo* is spoken from within the decision that has been taken, from within the linguistic and existential community of the faith. The fact that this originally episcopal *credo* was able to establish itself as the confession of the congregation assembled in faith shows that it had succeeded in remaining in the language of prayer and in formulating the norm of proclamation in a way suitable to prayer—a way that could also be adopted by the congregation without having to refer directly to such problems as *homoousios.* Cf. Part One, Chapter Two, Section 1C of the present work, which deals thoroughly with this topic.

tion of the proper understanding of the baptismal decision—explanations that are indispensable for proclaiming it but not of themselves a necessary content of such a proclamation.

b. As an episcopal *symbolum*, the text is an instrument of unity for the whole Church in what concerns the fundamental understanding of the faith proclaimed at baptism. The ecumenical ("catholic") character is essential to it. Only the episcopacy of the whole Church can be the official channel for the formulation of such a text. It must be said that even after the schism of 1054 this includes also the episcopacy of the Eastern churches, for, as a legitimate episcopacy of churches that have preserved intact the heritage of faith, they continue to be an integral part of the Church as a whole. A council consisting only of the churches of the West could, therefore, never formulate a text with such a claim. If we consider the structural character of the Church of the Fathers, we will realize that the Council of Nicaea cannot be dismissed in this way and that ecumenical formulations of faith are still possible in principle.

As for the linguistic form of such a *symbolum* of the whole episcopacy, we should observe that it is an integral part of the faith inaugurated by baptism and seeks to lead it further on the level of reflection—admittedly of a reflection that does not enter into details of scientific analysis but establishes basic reference points for an understanding of the faith.

3. The ordination *symbolum*, as it appears, for instance, in the writings of Athanasius. The Tridentine (or Vatican) *symbolum* may also be classified here. From the perspective of the history of the *symbolum*, the *symbolum* of Paul VI also belongs in this category. In view of its purpose, the ordination *symbolum* might be designated as a program of study.

a. This would explain its more theoretical character. Nevertheless, the texts are consistently referred to the confession and decision [of faith]. They do not give the impression of being objective secular formulas that can be used arbitrarily.

b. Their use as a program of study explains also the regional and temporal character of such texts. The basic doctrinal structure is, of course, determined by the baptismal and conciliar *symbola*. But, under certain circumstances of time and place, special doctrinal contents can make their appearance and be deemed especially worthy of retention while others lose in importance. For this type of *symbolum*, variability in individual detail—"pluralism"—is a necessity. That it can also be a danger is evidenced by the entrenchment of anti-Protestant emphases in the post-Tridentine era. For that reason, reflection on the basic *symbola* and the regular reexamination of such texts is indispensable—a reexamination not just at certain intervals of time but also between and among ecclesiastical localities. It is imperative that pluralism be combined with a common standard; in this regard, the mutual monitoring through bishops' conferences and the service of the papacy can play a significant role.

4. The *Confessio Augustana* (Augsburg Confession) represents a kind of confession that, despite its preponderantly Catholic content, severs itself structurally from the historically "Catholic" *symbolum* and creates a new type of Christian community—the denomination [*Konfession*]: this fact alone should indicate how precarious it is to use the term "confession" [*Bekenntnis*]. What happened is well known. A reform group attempted to eliminate the link that had existed since the time of Justinian between imperial proscription and the ecclesial classification "heretic" by laying before the emperor a legal declaration ("confession") of their Catholicity. The recipient of this confession was, then, the emperor; the confession itself was the statement of a doctrinal structure that was theoretically Catholic. The door was thus opened for both the theorizing and the secularizing of the confession of faith—and this is true even though we must evaluate the contents of the text quite positively and not deny the historical necessity that led to its composition. Although, in its content, the *Confessio Tridentina* was a refutation of the *Confessio Augustana* and a certain "confessionalizing" of the Catholic Church of the West was, therefore, unavoidable under the circumstances, the Tridentine text remains structurally within the tradition of the Catholic *symbolum*; it is strictly an ordination *symbolum* for use within the Church and has never aspired to or been able to achieve the same significance for Catholicism as the Augsburg Confession enjoys in its own sphere. For our purposes, this fourth type of *symbolum* need not be further discussed since it forms no part of the history of the *symbolum* of the undivided Church. Where it served in the formation of a church, it had, for all practical purposes, the function of an ordination *symbolum*.

If we wish to form a judgment as to the possible positive significance of short formulas, we must weigh them against the whole spectrum of the *symbolum*. When we attempt this, we discover anew how vague the classification "short formula" really is, whether it is considered theologically, linguistically or socio-linguistically. Neither its relationship to the traditional *symbolum* nor its own sociological and linguistic context has been taken into account. On the one hand, its criticism of ecclesial language continues to be naive because it is based on the fiction of a commonly understood universal language; on the other hand, this fiction leads to an equally unconsidered pluralism because, in the search for a modern (= "more comprehensible") formulation, only separate and largely unstable groups have been used as linguistics frameworks. The split into an unlimited synchronous and diachronous pluralism characterized by great rapidity of disintegration and an extremely limited radius of comprehensibility is due, in the long run, to the fact that the whole question of a linguistic community has simply been ignored. We must say, then, that, in the attempt to give Christianity a new interpretation through the use of short formulas, the wrong end of the problem has been seized: the slogan, a borrowing from the *instrumentarium* of consumer economics, explains nothing where there is question of transmitting knowledge of the faith. We must ask, rather, how one enters into a particular linguistic context or community and, on the other hand, how this community is able to reconcile itself with the whole. That, however, is a very comprehensive problem that involves the whole question of the inner and outer relationship of faith and of the openness and oneness of the Church as well as of the fundamental problem of human communication as such. The search for the "formula" can be but one aspect of this more far-reaching task.

Nevertheless, the question arises here as to how the ancient Church actually carried out her "advertising"; the notion of advertising seems to be the only thing that is clear about the classification "short formula", so it is on this point that our effort to compare *symbolum* and short formula must be concentrated and defined. Let us say at once that none of the various types of *symbola* has the meaning of a "promotional text" or a "party program". No one has ever used the formulas of faith in the Old or New Testament for purposes of "advertising". To do so would have been impossible, in any case, since they are concentrated summaries of the faith and can, therefore, be understood only from within the faith. It is not just today that the question about the meaning of the word "God" is unanswerable; it was no less so for the early Church. In a world full of gods, the word "God" could not be unambiguous.

a. The Christian propagation of the faith occurred through the believing community as such. Its existence was a reality that attracted men or, at least, posed questions for them. In general, we can assume that the beginning of a conversion to Christianity was not likely to consist in a request for a program but rather in a favorable attitude—that was frequently directly fostered by personal relationships with Christians (cf. the custom of having witnesses or "guarantors" for the catechumen, from which springs our custom of having sponsors for baptism)—toward the Church that formed the believing community. Here, the sociological interrelationships of antiquity (*domus*) could extend the radius correspondingly. Even today, we must admit that education in the faith is unthinkable without a believing community that—however fragmentarily—confirms this faith.

b. Conversion to the faith is not, obviously, simply a turning to the shelter of a community but a purposeful turning to the truth that the community has received and that is its distinctive characteristic. That, in fact, is why the community, as a formal entity, seeks converts through the catechumenate, which discloses the content and manner of Christian life. The catechesis may vary in individual detail, but its classification is always the same, including, of necessity, an introduction that attempts to interpret the fundamental concepts of Christianity; this introduction uses the schema of the Jewish proselytizing sermon, that is, the interpretation of the faith of Israel as modified by Hellenistic Judaism to satisfy the nostalgia for monotheism that marked the ancient culture.

We seem now to have reached a point at which it is possible to give an understandable and realizable meaning to the concept "short formula". First we must state that, with the catechumenate, the early Church solved the problem of propagation of the faith in the only way appropriate to the comprehensive requirements of what the Church represents. "Propagation of truth" can occur only through initiation into a way of life: truth does not "sell" itself for less. Next we must say that the demand for short formulas can have two positive functions today.

a. The attempt to develop a catechetical model and, in particular, a basic precatechetical model (on the analogy of the Jewish proselytizing sermon). "Pluralism" reveals itself readily here in a twofold form; there can, in any event, be a question only of a discussion model that must be adapted to circumstances. On the one hand, we cannot (as we do now) expect every preacher and catechist to deal with everything from reflection on the principles of faith to their proclamation. He needs preparation in the basic truths to be considered before he can communicate these to others. On the other hand, one cannot project a given situation onto the drawing board beforehand; the enfleshment of the model can occur only in concrete instances. To this pluralism of situations must be added, then, a pluralism of catechetical models: in a society that bears the imprint of neo-Marxism, the way of reflection will be different from that in a society determined by existential philosophy or in one marked by Hindu religiosity, and so forth. Clearly, one cannot speak of "formulas" in all these instances but rather of models—on the analogy of the widely spread common style of catechesis in the early Church, which aimed, not at formulas, but at conceptual context.

b. It is conceivable, too, I think, that a meaningful effort to shorten theological statements is also taking place in connection with the ordination *symbolum*. It is obvious that a great number of the modern "short formulas" are not, as they mistakenly claim to be, short formulas of faith but short formulas of theology. In other words, whereas the baptismal *symbolum* names, without commentary, the articles of faith as such, these texts offer, not the articles of faith themselves, but a reflection on them. For this reason, they are closer to the understanding of those to whom the relevant form of reflection is familiar than are the *symbola,* but they are, by the same token, limited to one form of reflection. That is, they are, and are intended to be, interpretations, whereas the *symbolum* is the "real thing". The ordination *symbolum* is not intended as a special kind of theology, although it will probably contain a basic form of interpretation. In any event, it would undoubtedly be helpful if contemporary theology would try to condense in a clear way not only its precatechetical preambles, but also its efforts to present a summary of Christian beliefs and, in doing so, would let it be more plainly understood wherein it sees the unifying logic of faith. We have already pointed out that not only pluralism but also the constant mutual monitoring that proceeds from and leads to unity are essential ingredients of such an effort.

The actual existence of such a unity is an indispensable prerequisite if these efforts are to be meaningful. Access to the "linguistic context" of the Church and her faith would be impossible if the identity of the Church as a linguistic subject were not recognizable. The classification of conceptual contexts in the area of faith, which is suggested here as a substitute for the vague concept of "short formulas of faith", has, in this connection, a firmly defined meaning: it claims to be, not a substitute for the *symbolum,* but a guide to the fundamental decision of faith that is inconvertibly expressed in the *symbolum.*

Appendix. Changeability and unchangeability in the Church

We know from experience that there is changeability in the Church. On the other hand, if there were not also unchangeability and permanence, it would be meaningless for us to continue to designate her through the ages by the one word "Church", for, in that case, there would be lacking to her the identity that keeps changeability in check. But how are we to describe the interrelationship of the two? Above all, at a time when the debate about what changes are permissible in the Church and what are not—the debate about the identity of the Church and her boundaries—no longer poses a merely academic problem but is a crucial question even for the ordinary Christian, it becomes imperative that we search for standards by which to determine where these boundaries lie. Consequently, those attempts will not suffice that aim simply at compiling a quantitative list of what is or is not susceptible of change; we want to know the reasons. Granted such attempts have their value not only because they provide manageable and practical data but also because there are, in fact, a number of realities that clearly belong—or even more clearly do not belong—to the essence of Christianity. In this connection, it is assuredly worthy of note that Luther, for instance, based his Catechisms, not on a carefully considered system of proofs, but quite simply on what are called the *loci,* the principal deposits, of faith, which he gathered together and explained: the Ten Commandments, the Our Father, the sacraments, the confession of faith. In doing so, it might be added, he followed the most ancient catechetical traditions and thus differed in no formal way from the Catholic Church. To be honest, I do not understand why we are no longer capable of such moderation today but must insist on basing our textbooks on the most sophisticated structural systems, which are as transitory as their authors and the intricacies of which are, for the most part, not comprehensible to our students.[58] By pointing to the principal situs of classic catechesis, we give a fundamental guideline that is as useful and solid a criterion today as it was in the past: inseparable from the Christian identity is the Church's confession of faith: that is, what the Church has designated, over and above the vicissitudes of theological interpretation, as the genuine word of faith ("dogma"); inseparable from the Christian identity is, for the Catholic, the essential content of the Christian liturgy, which is independent of the Church's own volition, that is, the sacraments and the relationship of the Christian to God as exemplarily formulated in the Our Father, the prayer of the Christian; inseparable from the Christian identity, finally, is that fundamental deposit of moral tenets taught by the Church on the basis of the decalogue and its impact on the Sermon on the Mount and the admonitions of the apostles.

To conclude, these cornerstones of the Christian identity, established by the catechetical tradition in the course of centuries, precede reflection, for Christianity is not something we devise for ourselves but something we receive as a reality that is antecedent to anything of our own devising. But if we cannot devise faith, we can certainly—and indeed we must—ponder it, for only the faith that has been inwardly assimilated can be passed on to others. But how, in our pondering, are we to understand the matter of Christian identity as we have just described it? That is the question that inspires these remarks. There are various possibilities for such an understanding. The following suggests itself to me: we always find the Church in the tension between what is changeable and what is unchangeable. On the one hand, she is that which is changeable, for she bears within herself the mark of all the changing generations of mankind throughout the centuries. Yet she must, for all that, remain ever "the Church" and, for that reason, be also the subject in which change occurs

[58] In the meantime, two catechisms—*Botschaft des Glaubens* and *Grundriss des Glaubens*—have been published that, fortunately, do not fall under this criticism but, once again, present the fullness of faith in terms of the classic *loci.* That is a step forward which, after the fiasco of the late sixties, may succeed in launching a new and positive phase of catechetical development.

but which, nevertheless, remains alway identical with herself. Hence she is, in a certain respect, comparable to a human being, who, by physiological and psychological norms, is but a succession of states yet who knows, for all that, that he is always himself. We must ask, then: What constitutes the Church as a subject? What makes her what she is? If we recall that Paul formulated the concept of the Church as a subject that remains constant in the midst of change when he called her a "body" (a "self"), we can look to him also for the answer. From being an amorphous mass of individuals, the Church is constituted a subject by him whom Paul names the Head, namely, Christ. That means: she continues to be a unified entity only by his grace. She exists as the Church by reason of her union with him. She is the Church because she lets herself be formed by him as her Lord and, in return, gives herself to him. She is not a subject by virtue of her own power but by the relationship that makes her a subject.

This apparently very speculative answer becomes at once entirely practical when we ask: How does this take place? In practice, union with Christ can mean only that the Church as a whole and in her individual members prays to Christ and with him. She becomes the Church in the celebration of the liturgy through which she enters into the prayer of Jesus Christ and thus stands with him in the presence of the Holy Spirit and speaks with him to the Father. She becomes the Church by adoration, but adoration, if it is to be christological, must be trinitarian. This is her real life force, without which her lifeblood will dry up. But there is also a reciprocal relationship. It is only the active participation of the individual that can make the liturgy, the divine service of the community, meaningful. But only the liturgy has the power to sustain the prayer of the individual and to give him strength. We should be very certain of this latter point if we want to establish a hierarchy of truths, as the Council understood it, a nodal point, as it were, from which the other point follows. For it really does follow. On the one hand, a liturgy oriented to Christ includes also the Trinity and, thus, a fundamental confession of faith. On the other hand, as we saw, it expresses also the orientation of every individual to God; the sacraments, too, have their place in it, for they bear witness not only to the fact that mankind takes here its tentative step toward transcendence but also to the fact that the "other side" has broken in upon us and has commerce with us. It is this that makes possible, ultimately, the following of Christ, the entering into his action—for in Christ the Word is act in the highest degree: when he says, "This is my body", it is an anticipation of his death and, consequently, the most radical of human acts—such as can be consummated only by him who is, at the same time, also the Son.

In what has been said, we have already answered the question of whether all this is not too narrowly Christian and pietistic, too far from the hard realities of the present. After our reference to the eucharistic words of Jesus, we need hardly elaborate on the intensity and depth of the actions and sufferings that follow from such an attitude. But I would like, nevertheless, to add to the question about the degree of human realism that is reflected in such an understanding of Christianity a closing remark that will compel us to ask ourselves again what actually constitutes reality for mankind. Recently, I entertained two South American bishops, with whom I discussed both their social projects and their pastoral experiences and efforts. They told me of the intensive proselytizing with which the hundred or so Christian denominations of the reformed churches have encroached upon the traditional Catholicism of the land and are changing its religious face. In the course of the conversation, they spoke of a remarkable event that they considered symptomatic and that had forced them to examine their conscience as to the course taken by the Catholic Church of South America since the end of Vatican Council II. They related that representatives of several villages had come to the Catholic bishop to tell him that they had now joined a Protestant community. They took the opportunity to thank the bishop for all the social undertakings by which he had accomplished many fine things for them through the years and which they greatly appreciated. "But we need a religion, too," they said, "and that is why we have become Protestants." Through such encounters, my two guests averred, they had become aware again of the deep religious sentiment which exists in the Indians, in all the people of their countries, and which they had more or less ignored when they decided that these countries should first be developed and then evangelized. But men really do not live by bread alone and cannot wait to have their other need fulfilled until bread is no longer a problem. There are more realities than we, with our Western mentalities, usually understand by that word. And what is essential and unchanging in Christianity leads us far beyond what we generally call reality. Therein lies its power to save.

E. Importance of the Fathers for the Structure of Faith

Anyone who attempts to assess the importance of the Fathers of the Church for modern theology will be faced immediately with strange inconsistencies. The movement toward renewal, which has been observable in the field of Catholic theology since the end of World War I, understood itself basically as *ressourcement*, as a return to sources that were no longer to be seen through the eyes of Scholastic philosophy but were to be read in themselves, in their own original form and breadth. Granted, the sources that were to be discovered anew flowed first and above all in Holy Scripture; but the search for a new way in which theology could assimilate what was said in the Scriptures and realize it in the Church led of its own accord to the Fathers, to the era of the early Church, in which the waters of faith still flowed unpolluted and in all their freshness. We need only recall the names of Odo Casel, Hugo Rahner, Henri de Lubac, Jean Daniélou to have before our eyes a theology that knew—and knows—that it was close to the Scriptures because it was close to the Fathers. This situation seems, in the meantime, to have ceased to exist. In the course of a few years a new awareness has arisen that is so filled with the burning importance of the present moment that it regards any recourse to the past as a kind of romanticism that might have been appropriate in less stirring times but has no meaning today. Instead of *ressourcement,* we have *aggiornamento,* a confrontation with today and tomorrow in which the content of theology is to be made current and effective. The Fathers have been pushed far into the background; a vague impression of allegorical exegesis remains behind and leaves a bad taste and, indeed, a feeling of superiority that regards it as progress to keep yesterday as far as possible from today and so seems to promise an even better tomorrow.

I. *The* aporia *of the topic*

1. Interpretation of Scripture and patristic theology

Have the Fathers of the Church a significance for contemporary theology or not? Should they have such a significance, or should they, for the sake of the content of theology, be relegated to the purely historical, to the investigation of what has been, with only a very indirect relevance—if, indeed, any at all—for today? If we examine the question more closely, we shall soon see that it is by no means simply a rhetorical one but rather a highly complex problem in which is reflected the whole dilemma of theology, its predicament between *ressourcement* and *aggiornamento,* between turning back to the sources and responsibility to today for the fate of tomorrow. At first glance, there seems indeed to be a very satisfactory answer: Of course! Back to the sources. But why the Fathers of the Church? Is not Scripture enough? From the opposite perspective, one might just as easily argue that there can be no problem here since the matter has long ago been decided for us. In fact, Vatican Council I expressly followed the Council of Trent in decreeing that in ecclesiological matters and in matters of faith that meaning is to be accepted as the true meaning of Scripture "which Holy Mother Church has held and still holds. She has the right to judge concerning the true sense and interpretation of the Sacred Scriptures. No one, therefore, is permitted to interpret Sacred Scripture contrary to this sense or contrary to the unanimous consent of the Fathers."[59] Vatican Council II did not, it is true, repeat these statements, but neither did it retract them; a muted echo can, in fact, be detected when the *Dogmatic Constitution on Revelation,* after its approval of research regarding literary forms and so, in principle, of the application of historical-critical methods to the explanation of the Bible, continues: "But since Sacred Scripture must be read and interpreted with its divine authorship in mind, no less attention must be devoted to the content and unity of the whole of Scripture, taking into account the tradition of the entire Church and the analogy of faith, if we are to derive their true meaning from the sacred texts."[60] The same attitude is again in evidence in the sixth chapter of this text, in which the meaning of Holy Scripture in the life of the Church is continually unfolded in close relationship to ecclesial tradition, especially when it is stated: "The spouse of the incarnate Word, which is the Church, is taught by the Holy Spirit. She strives to reach day by day a more profound understanding of the Sacred Scriptures in order to provide her children with food from the divine words. For this reason also she duly fosters the study of the Fathers, both Eastern and Western, and of the sacred liturgies."[61]

In view of such texts, we might seem justified in asserting that the importance of the Fathers for Catholic theology has been, as it were, dogmatized. But does this help to solve the problem? On the contrary, it does precisely the opposite by letting it be seen for the first time in all its complexity. In the *Dogmatic Constitution on Divine Revelation,* as we have seen, affirmation of the historical-critical method stands in peaceful juxtaposition to affirmation of interpretation on the basis of the tradition and faith of the Church; but this twofold affirmation conceals the antagonism of two basic attitudes that are diametrically opposed to one another in both origin and purpose. The Council text regards, as the essence of the second method, the understanding of Holy Scripture as an inner unity in which one part sustains the other, has its existence in it, so

---

[59] DS 3007; 1507 (Trent). These statements are anticipated in the formulations of the *Constantinopolitanum* 2, DS 438. [The English translation of this text is quoted here from "Dogmatic Constitution *Dei Filius,* on the Catholic Faith", chap. 2, "Revelation", in *Documents of Vatican Council I, 1869–1870,* selected and translated by John F. Broderick, S. J. (Collegeville: The Liturgical Press, 1971), 9, 43. (Trans.)]

[60] "Dogmatic Constitution on Divine Revelation", chap. 3, 12, in *Vatican Council II. The Conciliar and Post Conciliar Documents,* Austin Flannery, O. P., gen. ed. (Northport, N. Y.: Costello Publishing Co., 1975).

[61] Ibid., chap. 6, 23.

that each part can be read and understood only in terms of the whole. With this, we have in fact touched upon the fundamental concept of patristic exegesis, of which the central exegetical idea was unity—the unity that is Christ himself, who permeates and sustains all Scripture. "To read Holy Scripture in the light of grace is to unite it. If one reads it according to the flesh as the Jews read it, the law stands as a second entity beside the New Testament; but if it is read according to the spirit, it becomes itself a gospel"—so wrote M. Pontet in his commentary on texts from Augustine and Origen.[62] The task of the historian, however, is not first of all to unite but to distinguish; not to seek for a pneuma that faith knows is actively present in the whole Bible, but to ask about the many individuals who, each in his own way, have worked on this many-faceted composition. His task is, then, precisely that which the Fathers called "reading according to the flesh as the Jews read" and of which Jerome once warned with the words: "Si litteram sequimur, possumus et nos quoque nobis novum dogma componere".[63] Thus every "both-and" seems to be denied us and only a strict either–or to be possible here. And this applies to historians as well as exegetes, for the converse is true of the historian—that exegesis can be either historical *or* dogmatic but never both at once. Dogmatic interpretation—the interpretation of a text from the perspective of dogma—is, for him, the exact opposite of historical interpretation, which accepts no other norm than the text that lies before it. This does not mean, of course, that all of patristic and contemporary exegesis is comprised in these antitheses. But if—which cannot be further investigated here—something like a deeper unity or, at least, a complementarity of the two ways should lie concealed here, it is certain that it can be brought to light only by means of this antithesis. Assuredly, the Fathers are not, then, devoid of all significance for the modern scriptural exegete. At the very least, he will have to acknowledge them as witnesses to the text and as

---

[62] Maurice Pontet, *L'Exégèse de St. Augustin prédicateur* (Paris: Aubier, 1944), 377. Pontet refers to Augustine's Sermo 25, 2, PL 38: 168: "Lex . . . ad servitutem generat (Gal 4:24). Quare? Quia carnaliter intelligitur a Judaeis. Nam spiritualiter intellecta, Evangelium est." He refers also to the beautiful passage in Origen's commentary on Jn 1:15: πῶς γὰρ ἀρχόμενος ἀπὸ τοῦ προφήτου εὐαγγελίζεται Ἰησοῦν (the reference is to Philip in Acts 8:35), εἰ μὴ τῆς ἀρχῆς τοῦ εὐαγγελίου μέρος τι ὁ Ἡσαίας ἦν; . . . εἰ ὁ εὐαγγελιζόμενος "ἀγαθὰ εὐαγγελίζεται", πάντες δὲ οἱ πρὸ τῆς σωματικῆς Χριστοῦ ἐπιδημίας Χριστὸν εὐαγγελίζονται . . . πάντων πῶς εἰσιν οἱ λόγοι τοῦ εὐαγγελίου μέρος, . . . "Johanneskommentar", bk. 1, 15, in *Die griechischen christlichen Schriftsteller* [henceforth GCS], *Origenes Werke*, 4:19, ed. Erwin Preuschen (Leipzig: Hinrich, 1903).

[63] *Dialogus adversus Luciferianos*, sec. 202, PL 23: 182. Cf. Pontet, 183; Joseph Ratzinger, *Die Geschichtstheologie des heiligen Bonaventura* (Munich, 1959), 64–65, which shows that the same idea is characteristic for Bonaventure. Extensive material on this subject is to be found especially in Henri de Lubac, *Der geistige Sinn der Schrift* (Einsiedeln, 1956); Henri de Lubac, *Exégèse médiévale* (Paris: Aubier, 1959–1963).

members of an age that was relatively close to the origin of the Scriptures; but the role that thus falls to them is a modest one that is, in any event, quite different from the concept of the normative power of the *unanimis consensus Patrum* with which we began.

Our reflections thus far have yielded a first result that we can express in the following statement: the Tridentine pronouncement about scriptural interpretation according to the Fathers—which, by the way, is based essentially on the decrees of the Second Council of Nicaea[64]—represents today a problem of systematic, and only indirectly of exegetical, theology. In the irreconcilable discrepancy between the Tridentine pronouncement and the actual course of exegesis, both the *theological* problem of *historical-critical* exegesis and the problem associated, in today's intellectual climate, with the concept of tradition and of dogmatic thought per se become surprisingly clear. The question of the relevance of the Fathers has thus brought us face to face with the touchstone of contemporary theology as a whole—a touchstone that is the inevitable concomitant of its stressful position between two worlds: faith and knowledge. Granted, it is not something new with which theology has here to contend but only an intensified recurrence of the old dilemma of *auctoritas* and *ratio,* which has always pursued its own course and raised its own difficulties.

2. The concept of tradition and the question of the relevance of the Fathers

But let us return to our topic. Thus far, we have been able to establish the relevance of the Fathers in the sphere of scriptural exegesis at best in a very modest degree, partly because, paradoxically, modern historical science shares in a certain sense in the ahistorical orientation of technology. For natural science and technology, the history of their discoveries is not an essential part of themselves but only a prehistory. Only the datum is significant, not how it came to be. In much the same way, the history of exegesis has degenerated for the exegetes into a prehistory with which their own efforts are not directly concerned. Despite all that has thus far been said, we have by no means exhausted the problem of the Tridentine and Roman texts with which we started. For we might now say: All right, then; the scriptural interpretations of the Fathers are no longer as important as they once were. But these same texts show that, for the teachings of Catholic theology, both Scripture *and* tradition are normative; hence, we might say, even if the Fathers are perhaps of secondary importance as interpreters of Scripture, they are unquestionably of primary importance as witnesses to tradition. Nevertheless, even in this way we do not find a so-

[64] DS 600–609.

lution as easily as we might have expected. For we must now ask whether a person can be a witness to tradition in any other way than by being a witness to the interpretation of Scripture, to the discovery of its true meaning. Perhaps, indeed, the wisdom of the pronouncements of Trent and of 1870 consists precisely in the fact that they allow tradition to bear upon scriptural interpretation; that they recognize the Fathers as the expression of tradition because they are revealers of the Bible. Be that as it may, with respect to tradition, modern Catholic theology has arrived, by both the irreconcilable paths it has followed, at what amounts to an almost total dissolution of the bond between the concept of tradition and patristic theology. On the one hand, there is the direction best designated by the name of Geiselmann; essentially, it regards tradition as but the living presence of Scripture, which adds nothing to Scripture but is merely the translation of Scripture into the living present of the Church. Hence it is, in all ages, whole and entire, and, because every age can relate to Scripture directly in its own way, any appeal to the past is fundamentally meaningless. Certainly the richness of scriptural exegesis through the ages can help every age to a deeper understanding of the breadth of the biblical testimony, but, for that very reason, there is even less justification for limiting tradition to a particular early period. Such a limitation—as, for instance, to the first five centuries—seems now to be "romantic" or "classicist".[65] Against this objection, it might, of course, be argued that the dispute about the Fathers did not originate with romanticism or classicism. It reaches back to the fourth century and seems to have experienced its first climax,[66] at the beginning of the fifth century, simultaneously in the East, with the controversy between Cyril of Alexandria and Nestorius, and in the West, with the controversy over the doctrine of original sin between Augustine and Julian of Eclanum. It persisted throughout the whole period of Scholasticism and, after being submerged by the rationalism of the Enlightenment, emerged again to usher in a new era of theology with men like Möhler and Drey.

The other direction taken by the more recent theology of tradition

---

[65] Cf. Josef Geiselmann, "Das Konzil von Trient über das Verhältnis der Heiligen Schrift und der nicht geschriebenen Traditionen", in Michael Schmaus, *Die mündliche Überlieferung* (Munich, 1957), 123–206, esp. 184–93. On the importance of classicism for the reawakening of the debate about the Fathers, see also the careful study by P. Stockmeier, "Die alte Kirche—Leitbild der Erneuerung", in *Theologische Quartalschrift* 146 (1966): 385–408.

[66] Cf. the survey by Alfred Stuiber, "Kirchenväter", in LTK 6:272–74 (with bibliography); André Benoît, *L'Actualité des Pères de l'église* (Neuchâtel: Delachaux & Niestlé, 1961), 5–9, and the important dissertation by E. Nacke, *Das Zeugnis der Väter in der theologischen Beweisführung Cyrills von A.* (Münster, 1964).

developed, principally in connection with the dogmas of 1854 and 1950, as an attempt to fill the lacunae in their historical foundation by means of systematic reflection. The result of this effort may be seen in, for instance, the proposition that to prove that a predication belongs to tradition it is not necessary to adduce proof that reaches all the way back to the beginning; it is sufficient to take a cross section of the Church's awareness of faith at any given time in her history, for whatever the whole Church holds to have been revealed *has* been revealed and belongs to the authentic tradition of the Church.[67] Implicit, though not expressly stated, in this "dehistoricizing" of the concept of tradition was a minimizing of the importance of the Fathers; it is even more difficult to justify a special role for them on the basis of this assessment than on the basis of Geiselmann's theorizing. What happened here is of decisive importance, for the connection between the concept of tradition and patristic theology, which had so long been impregnable,[68] is thus severed, and the importance of the Fathers, which, as we have already seen, had been reduced to a minimum by the historical-critical method of scriptural interpretation, is now being questioned from the perspective of dogma and in the sphere of tradition. Or, at least, the Fathers seem to be relegated to one and the same level as the rest of history and theology, so that they would have, in any event, no special meaning within this history, and the question of their role in theology would be reduced to the general question of what proportion of the present age theology can claim as its own history, to what extent it can raise to its way of thinking the deliberate ignoring of history that characterizes the natural sciences and is, in them, a postulate of their own methodology or to what extent it is referred by its nature to a different orientation toward history.

[67] Cf. Albert Lang, *Der Auftrag der Kirche*, in *Fundamentaltheologie* 2 (Munich: Hueber, 1962): 290f.; O. Müller, "Zum Begriff der Tradition in der Theologie der letzten hundert Jahre", in *Münchener Theologische Zeitschrift* 4 (1953): 164–86; Damiano van den Eynde, "Tradizione e Magistero", in *Problemi e orientamenti di teologia dommatica* (Milan: Marzorati, 1957), 1:231–52.

[68] Many texts in support of this statement are to be found in Heribert Schauf, *Die Lehre der Kirche über Schrift und Tradition in den Katechismen* (Essen: Driewer, 1963). Cf. also the Denzinger texts cited in n. 59 and 64 of this chapter: in *Constantinopolitanum* 2 as well as in *Nicanum* 2, tradition seems to be equated with διδασκαλία πατέρων and πίστις ἁγίων τεσσάρων συνόδων. Cf. also the *Decretum Gelasianum*: "Romana Ecclesia post illas Veteris vel Novi Testamenti, quas regulariter suscipimus, etiam has suscipi non prohibet Scripturas, id est: Sanctam Synodum Nicaenam . . . Constantinopolitanum . . . Ephesinam . . . Chalcedonensem" DS 352. See also the sixth-century addition: "Sed et si qua sunt concilia a s. Patribus hactenus instituta, post istorum quattuor auctoritatem et custodienda et recipienda decrevimus" (DS 352).

3. The separated churches and the "Fathers of the Church"

Let us disregard for the moment the thoughts that press upon us at this point in order to examine a third *aporia,* which once again expands the range of our questioning and brings the whole problem closer to a solution. Even if the Fathers seem to be losing stature as interpreters of Holy Scripture and witnesses to tradition, do they not, at least, have a distinguished ecumenical significance? Thomas Aquinas and the other great Scholastics of the thirteenth century are "Fathers" of a specifically Roman Catholic theology from which the Christian churches of the Reformation consider themselves completely separated and which, for the churches of the East, also expresses an alien mentality. But the teachers of the ancient Church represent a common past that, precisely as such, may well be a promise for the future.[69] This thought must not be esteemed too lightly, for it is, in fact, to be regarded as the catalyst that can help to solve the problem of the relationship between patristic and modern theology. Here, too, however, we must not seek an easy answer by overlooking the obstacles that lie in the way. Whereas the theology of the Eastern Churches has never aspired to be anything but a patristic theology, the attitude of the Reformation toward the Fathers was, from the beginning— and still is—ambiguous. Melanchthon strove emphatically to prove that the heritage of the ancient Church, which had been abandoned by medieval Catholicism, was restored in the *Confessio Augustana;*[70] Flaccius Illyricus, the first great historian of the Reformation, followed in his footsteps,[71] and the work of Calvin, with its radical reliance on Augustine, takes the same direction.[72] By contrast, Luther's attitude to the Fathers, including Augustine, was always more critical. The conviction seemed to grow ever stronger in him that the defection from the Gospels occurred at a very early date. It will suffice to quote one typical text: "I say this because I myself wasted and lost much time on Gregory, Cyprian, Augustine, Origen. For the Fathers, in their time, had a remarkable attraction to and liking for allegories; they used them constantly, and their books are full of them. . . . The reason is this, that they all followed their own conceit, mind and opinion, as they thought right, and not St. Paul, who wanted to

---

[69] A. Benoît, 81–84.

[70] A. Benoît, 17–18. Cf. especially the passage Benoît quotes in n. 4 from Pontien Polman, *L'Elément historique dans la controverse religieuse du XVIᵉ siècle* (Gembloux: Duculot, 1932), 37: "On peut presque dire que l'idée fondamentale de Mélanchton dans toute son oeuvre polémique est de démontrer l' ancienneté du luthéranisme, sa concordance avec l'Église des premiers siècles."

[71] Ibid., 22. Cf. Peter Meinhold, "Flacius", in LTK 4:161–62.

[72] A. Benoît, 19–22.

let the Holy Spirit act there from within."[73] Even here, the Fathers seem to be discredited for their use of allegory, and the study of them seems to be regarded as a waste of time by comparison with a direct attention to the word of Scripture.

The dichotomy just discovered within reformational thinking exists, indeed, even to the present time. Nor is it removed when Benoît, following the direction indicated by Melanchthon, seeks to define the Fathers no longer—in the manner of Catholic theology—as ecclesial, because of their significance for the Church, but rather as scriptural, because of their position with regard to Scripture, and describes them as those Christian authors "who, consciously or not, sought to express and interpret the revelation of God in Jesus Christ as it is retold in the Scriptures."[74] But this does not solve the basic problem of whether the Fathers are a way, a byway or a false way to the Scriptures, except that, for the Fathers themselves, their scriptural way was not distinguishable from their ecclesial way, and to separate them is to open an unhistorical perspective. And in precisely this bond lies ultimately the question that concerns us.

In many respects, a decision about the role of the Fathers seems, in fact, to have been reached today. But, since it is more unfavorable than favorable to a greater reliance upon them, it does nothing to lead us out of our present *aporia*. For, in the debate about what constitutes greater fidelity to the Church of the Fathers, Luther's historical instinct is clearly proving itself right. We are fairly certain today that, while the Fathers were not Roman Catholic as the thirteenth or nineteenth century would have understood the term, they were, nonetheless, "Catholic", and their Catholicism extended to the very canon of the New Testament itself.[75] With this assessment, paradoxically, the Fathers have lost ground on *both* sides of the argument because, in the controversy about the fundamental

---

[73] Sermons on the Second Book of Moses, Alleg. 1, Wittenberger Ausgabe, 16, 67. Cited in A. Benoît, 16, n. 1.

[74] A. Benoît, 50. Cf. all of chap. 2: "Les Pères de l'église: Essai de définition", 31–52.

[75] Cf. Ph. Vielhauer, "Zum 'Paulinismus' der Apostelgeschichte", in *Evangelische Theologie* 10 (1950–1951): 1–15; Hans Conzelmann, *Die Mitte der Zeit* (Tübingen: Mohr, 1960); Ernst Käsemann, "Paulus und der Frühkatholizismus", in *Exegetische Versuche und Besinnungen* [henceforth *Exegetische Versuche*], 2 vols. (Göttingen: Vandenhoeck und Ruprecht, 1960–1964), 2 (1964): 239–52; Hans Küng, "Der Frühkatholizismus im Neuen Testament als Kontroverstheologisches Problem", in *Theologische Quartalschrift* (1962), 385–424. See also, the informative text by Karlmann Beyschlag, *Clemens Romanus und der Frühkatholizismus* (Tübingen: Mohr, 1966). A still valuable work is Adolf Harnack, *Dogmengeschichte* 1 (Tübingen: Mohr, 1931): 239–43; 337–425. On the other side, R. Sohn, *Wesen und Ursprung des Katholizismus* (Leipzig, 1912). On the classic position as a whole, Erik Peterson, "Die Kirche", in *Theologische Traktate* (Munich: Kösel, 1951), 411–29.

basis for understanding Scripture, there is nothing more to be proved or disproved by reference to them. But neither have they become totally unimportant in this domain, for, even after the relativization they have suffered in the process we have described, the difference between the Catholicism of an Augustine and a Thomas Aquinas, or even between that of a Cardinal Manning and a Cyprian, still opens a broad field of theological investigation. Granted, only one side can consider them its own Fathers, and the proof of continuity, which once led directly back to them, seems no longer worth the effort for a concept of history and faith that sees continuity as made possible and communicated only in terms of discontinuity.[76]

II. *Attempt at an answer*

1. Fathers and "Fathers of the Church"

Nevertheless, a fact is emerging from these reflections that can guide us in our search for an answer. For we must admit, on the one hand, that, even for Catholic theology, the so-called Fathers of the Church have, for a long time, been "Fathers" only in an indirect sense, whereas the real "Father" of the form that ultimately dominated nineteenth-century theology was Thomas Aquinas, with his classic systematization of the thirteenth-century *doctrina media,* which, it must be added, was in its turn based on the "authority" of the Fathers.[77] On the other hand, it is evident that Protestant theology is also not without its "Fathers", insofar as the leaders of the Reformation have, for it, a position comparable to the role of the Fathers of the Church. The perspective from which Scripture is studied and the point of departure for ecclesial life bear their mark and are inconceivable without them.[78] Indeed, we must go a step farther and say

[76] Ernst Käsemann, *Exegetische Versuche,* 2:45: "I must answer that constancy simply does not exist in the realm of history and that all one can say about continuity in this context is that discontinuity is dialectically linked with it." [For a translation of parts of Käsemann's text, see *Essays on New Testament Themes,* trans. W. J. Montagne (Naperville, Ill.: Allenson, 1964). (Trans.)] Cf. Rudolf Bultmann, *Glauben und Verstehen* 2 (Tübingen: Mohr, 1952): 162–86, esp. 183–86.

[77] On the relationship between medieval and patristic theology, see especially Joseph de Ghellinck, *Patristique et Moyen Age,* 3 vols. (Gembloux: Duculot, 1959, 1961). On the medieval understanding of *auctoritas,* see Marie Dominique Chenu, *La Théologie au douzième siècle* (Paris: Vrin, 1957), 353–57.

[78] In the meantime, of course, a second "level" of Fathers has made its appearance: the liberally oriented founders of the historico-critical method in theology. The awareness that they are "Fathers", that we cannot ignore our Fathers without finding ourselves "in empty

that the division in the Church is revealed above all in the fact that the Fathers of the one side are not the Fathers of the other. And the ever more observable inability of the one side to understand the other even in language and mode of thought stems from the fact that each has learned to think and speak at the knees of totally different Fathers. The differences among the sects do not have their source in the New Testament. They arise from the fact that the New Testament is read under the tutelage of different Fathers.

Here, from a quite unexpected angle, we have stumbled upon the immense significance the Fathers have for the Church, even though we are not speaking, in the narrower sense, of the so-called "Fathers of the Church". But does this not force us to a further thought? Who would deny that Thomas Aquinas and Luther are each Father of only one part of Christianity? Granted, under very different circumstances and in such a way that neither of the two sides can comfortably mention both of them in one breath. But even if we give full weight to this difference in evaluation and legitimacy, what we have just said is still valid. Certainly, if Christians of both traditions are not indifferent to each other, neither will they be indifferent toward those whom the other regards as Fathers. They will attempt to understand them in order to understand each other.[79] But even this understanding will not make the Fathers of one group the Fathers of the other. And so the question remains: If these Fathers can be Fathers for only a part of Christianity, must we not turn our attention to those who were once the Fathers of all?

2. Who is a "Father of the Church"?

We have reached a point now at which we can form a positive concept of the Fathers and obtain a proper view of their actual importance. Who, exactly, is a "Father of the Church"? We have touched earlier upon the new attempt at a definition by André Benoît, the patrologist of the Department of Evangelical Theology at the University of Strasbourg.

---

air and a space without history", is emphatically stated by Käsemann in *Exegetische Versuche*, 2:36.

[79] In this respect, the increasing number of important Catholic writings about Luther and of Protestant studies of Thomas Aquinas is a hopeful sign. Cf., on the one side, Harry J. McSorley, *Luthers Lehre vom unfreien Willen* (Munich: Hueber, 1967); Otto Hermann Pesch, *Theologie der Rechtfertigung bei Martin Luther und Thomas von Aquin* (Mainz: Grünewald, 1967); on the other side, Ulrich Kühn, *Via caritatis. Theologie des Gesetzes bei Thomas von Aquin* (Göttingen: Vandenhoeck & Ruprecht, 1963); Thomas Bonhoeffer, *Die Gotteslehre bei Thomas von Aquin als Sprachproblem* (Tübingen: Mohr, 1961); Hans Vorster, *Das Freiheits-*

Though it contains much that is important and worthy of note, it cannot, as we saw, serve as a fundamental principle. Benoît himself rejects the purely historical definition advanced by F. Overbeck and A. Mandouze,[80] whose efforts are not relevant for our own inquiry because they regard the Fathers *per definitionem* as belonging only to the past and so exclude the question of their significance for the present and the future, which is our primary concern. Benoît also directs his criticism, with some well-founded arguments, to the Catholic view of the Fathers, in which the Fathers are characterized by the following marks: adherence to doctrinal orthodoxy, holiness in the sense of the early Christian concept of holiness, implicit or explicit ecclesial recognition and, finally, *antiquitas,* that is, belonging to Christian antiquity.[81] Though it would be rewarding, we cannot undertake in this short study a comprehensive discussion of Benoît's views; we must be content to ponder briefly the key points in his far from unproblematical definition and, in that way, to assimilate as much as possible the positive ideas of the Strasbourg patrologist.

What is most questionable in Benoît's definition are the concepts of "orthodoxy" and "antiquity". For our purpose, it will suffice to analyze the latter point more closely. Apart from the fact that it is difficult to say up to what point it is permissible to speak of antiquity in the Church, the question also arises of whether the fact of antiquity per se can be a criterion for the Christian, or whether, with the emphasis on antiquity, we are not dealing again with a basic mythological category that Plato expressed in the concepts πάλαι and ἀρχαῖοι and was thus able to say of the ancients that "they were superior to us and lived closer to the gods".[82] At work here is a natural concept of age for which what is earlier is per se always better and closer to the gods, while the constantly forward-moving era of those born later grows ever more distant from the source and, for that reason, compels them more urgently to guard that which was in the beginning and which communicates to their late hour the tidings of a distant truth. For the self-understanding of Christian theology, an almost

verständnis bei Thomas von Aquin und Martin Luther (Göttingen: Vandenhoeck & Ruprecht, 1964).

[80] A. Benoît, 36–43, with references to F. Overbeck, "Über die Anfänge der patristischen Literatur", in *Historische Zeitschrift* 48 (1882): 417–72, and to André Mandouze, *Mesure et demesure de la patristique*: speech at the third Congress of Patrologists at Oxford in 1959 (= *Studia Patristica* 3, pt. I, ed. Cross [Berlin, 1961]; *Texte und Untersuchungen zur Geschichte der altchristlichen Literatur* 78:3–19).

[81] A. Benoît, 31–36. Cf. the introductions in the various patrologies (Quasten, Cayré, Altaner-Stuiber); see also, summary by Stuiber in LTK 6:274.

[82] *Platonis opera,* ex recensione R. B. Hirschhigii, vol. I (Paris: Ambrosio Firmin Didot, 1856), "Philebus", 16c, line 7, 402. See also, Josef Pieper, *Über den Begriff der Tradition* (Cologne-Opladen: Westdeutscher Verlag, 1958); Josef Pieper, *Über die platonischen Mythen* (Munich: Kösel, 1965).

passing remark of St. Benedict has been for centuries a kind of programmatic answer to this attitude. All monks, young and old, are called to the monks' chapter, he said, "because the Lord often reveals to a younger monk what is better".[83] This sentence made it possible for medieval theology to delimit the principle of *auctoritas* and to give expression to the actuality of Christian revelation, which has not only its πάλαι but, from its belief in the Spirit, also its today. Granted, the Christian, too, is bound to a primeval event and, to this extent, to the normativeness of what once was, of the "ancient". But this "ancient" is not to be defined, as it is in myth, as the primordial, for which whatever is more ancient is ipso facto more authentic. It is determined by history, by the new action of God that succeeds and cancels the myth of "antiquity". To this must be added those already mentioned factors of the present day, whose tension-filled unity with the primeval must be constantly reemphasized.[84]

We have drawn a fundamental distinction here between the mythical concept of tradition and the Christian concept of patrology. It cannot be denied, however, that, despite all the differences between the two, there exists also an analogy in the Christian link with a normative primeval event. The Fathers, we must now say, are not marked out simply because they belong to "antiquity"; the fact that they stand near *in time* to the origin of the New Testament does not necessarily prove that they are *inwardly* close to it. But that inner closeness is what matters. If their temporal proximity is to have a positive meaning, it can come only from the fact that they are in a special way a part of the primeval event or are somehow linked to it by a common bond, the significance of which is distinctive in a theological sense.

In fact, both may well be the case. Let us recall a thought on which we have already dwelt. The Fathers are the teachers of the as yet undivided

---

[83] *Regula S. P. Benedicti et Constitutiones congregationis Sancti Mauri* (Paris: Typis Guillelmi Desprez, Regis et Cleri Gallicani Typographia, 1770), C 3, 14. For an account of the effect of this sentence on the medieval theory of the development of dogma, see Joseph Ratzinger, "Offenbarung—Schrift—Überlieferung", in *Trierer Theologische Zeitschrift* 67 (1958): 13–27.

[84] On this whole topic, cf. the debate between Josef Pieper and Jürgen Moltmann on the question of promise and tradition, which space does not permit us to discuss here. See J. Moltmann, *Theologie der Hoffnung,* 5th ed. (Munich: Kaiser, 1966), 268–79, and Pieper's answer: "Hoffnungslose Zukunft und Hoffnung ohne Grund?", in *Hochland* (1967), 575–89. Cf. also my discussion with Pieper, in Joseph Ratzinger, *Das Problem der Dogmengeschichte in der Sicht der katholischen Theologie* (Cologne-Opladen, 1966), 35–59 and 42ff. Important material on the problem as a whole is to be found in N. Brox, "Antignostische Polemik bei Christen und Heiden", in *Münchener Theologische Zeitschrift* 18 (1967): 265–91, esp. "5: Wahrheit und Überlieferung", 277–91.

Church. Benoît rightly places great emphasis on this fact,[85] which should either replace the criterion of *antiquitas* or form its inner theological content and so help to determine the temporal limits of the patristic age. His attempt to establish the year 1054 as the end of the patristic age on the basis of this criterion seems to me, however, to be too mechanical. On the other hand, Basil Studer surely cuts the time too short with his suggestion that the patristic age ended in 451.[86] Admittedly, the controversy over Canon 28 of the Council of Chalcedon is the first warning sign of the separation between East and West;[87] admittedly, too, we must not be tempted to undervalue the significance of the quarrels that followed Chalcedon: they brought about the separation of the whole Semitic or non-Graeco-Roman element from the Church as a whole. To that degree, the end of the Fourth Ecumenical Council does indeed represent a certain watershed. Nevertheless, the era of Church councils approved by both East and West persisted; the unity of faith and *communio* continued to express itself in the unity of common theological thought.[88] The year 1054, on the other hand, is too peripheral and incidental a date to be meaningful as a reference point; the event of that year only made clear outwardly what had long existed in fact: that East and West spoke different languages, thought in different theologies—that, in other words, there still existed particular theologies but no "ecumenical theology" such as had existed in the time of the Fathers. We would have to say, then, that the patristic age ended with the changed intellectual climate marked by the Migrations and by the hostile spread of Islam; as an outward sign of the latter, we can point to the pope's turning to the Carolingian Empire, by which the old ecumenism was finally destroyed and—together with the creation of the church-state—the new self-understanding of the West, the fundamental constellation of the Middle Ages, was created.[89]

[85] A. Benoît, 81–82.

[86] Basil Studer, "Die Kirchenväter", in *Mysterium salutis* 1, Johannes Feiner and Magnus Löhrer, eds. (Einsiedeln: Benziger, 1965), 588–99, esp. 594.

[87] Cf. Thomas Owen Martin, "The Twenty-Eighth Canon of Chalcedon: A Background Note", in Aloys Grillmeier and Heinrich Bacht, *Das Konzil von Chalkedon*, vol. 2: *Entscheidung um Chalkedon* (Würzburg: Echter, 1953): 433–58; Joseph Olsr and Joseph Gill, "The Twenty-Eighth Canon of Chalcedon in Dispute between Constantinople and Moscow", in ibid., vol. 3: *Chalkedon Heute* (Würzburg: Echter, 1954): 765–83. For the text of the canon, see *Conciliorum Oecumenicorum Decreta,* canon 28, 99–100.

[88] Above all, we must be aware that the following councils were deeply concerned— though not always for pure reasons of faith—with healing the wounds caused by the Council of Chalcedon and hence form a historical unit with that council. Cf. Georg Kretschmar, "Die Konzile der alten Kirche", in Hans Jochen Margull, ed., *Die ökumenischen Konzile der Christenheit* (Stuttgart: Evangelisches Verlagswerk, 1961), 13–74.

[89] Cf. the survey in Franz Xavier Seppelt and Georg Schwaiger, *Geschichte der Päpste von den Anfängen bis zur Gegenwart* (Munich: Kösel, 1964), 75–109. I am indebted to P. Hacker of Münster for calling my attention to this change.

We have now gained not only a chronological but also the germ of a theological determination of what is to be understood by the terms Fathers, patristic age and patristic theology. The Fathers, we can now say, were the theological teachers of the undivided Church; their theology was, in the original sense of the word, an "ecumenical theology" that belonged to all; they were "Fathers" not only of a part but also of the whole and are, therefore, to be called "Fathers" in a distinctive sense that is peculiarly their own.

3. Basic reflection on the function of the Fathers in the synthesis of faith

This insight can be deepened and its content enriched. The fact already mentioned, namely, that Scripture is always read in some way under the tutelage of certain "Fathers", can now be expressed in the more general formula that Scripture and the Fathers belong together as do word and answer. The two are not identical, are not of equal importance, do not possess the same normative power. The word is always first; the response, second—the order is not to be reversed. Yet, despite the difference between them and the fact that they permit no intermingling, the two concepts are also not to be separated. Only because the word has found its answering word [Ant-wort] does it continue to be a word and to become effective. From the ontological perspective, the word is a referential reality: it assumes the presence of one who speaks as well as of one who receives the word by hearing it; it ceases to exist not only if no one speaks but also if no one hears: there is a silence that is also a response—the silence of hearing; but there is also a silence in which the word is stifled—that silence, namely, in which no one hears. Hence the word exists only in conjunction with—by means of—the response. This is true also of the word of God, Scripture. Granted, this word infinitely transcends all our responses, its word is never completely exhausted [aus-gewortet], as Augustine expressed it once in a wonderful image in his interpretation of Psalm 103:11: "[You set springs gushing in ravines] . . . supplying water for wild animals, attracting the thirsty wild donkeys." The waters from which the wild animals drink become for Augustine an image of Holy Scripture, which is open to all, large and small, learned and unlearned, and gives drink to all who thirst. "The hare comes there to drink, and the wild donkeys; the hare is small, the wild donkey is large; the hare is timid, the donkey is fierce; yet both drink—each as much as it needs to slake its thirst".[90] The word is greater than any response. That is why the effort of theology and of the Church to understand what was in the beginning must

---

[90] St. Augustine, "Enarratio in Ps. CIII", 3, 4, in CChr 40 (1956): 1501. Cf. M. Pontet, 136, n. 117.

be constantly renewed, must not be allowed to dry up at any point. At the same time, we must not forget the inseparability of word and response, must not forget that we cannot read or hear the word except in conjunction with the response, which has first received the word and is indispensable for its existence. Even if the response is criticized or rejected, it is still the horizon from which the word is to be understood. That is perhaps most clear when we consider the limitations on the response that actually was given. This response, that is, the historical synthesis of Christianity, would doubtless have been altogether different if the faith had undergone its definitive development, not in the Graeco-Roman world, but in the East, in the Semitic world or in India. Instead of the ontological theology and Christology of the Greeks, instead of the anthropological orientation of Augustine, in which the questions of the Reformation are anticipated, totally other considerations would almost certainly have made their appearance.[91] In one respect, such a speculation may serve to make visible the breadth of possibilities that are inherent in Christianity and are the hope of its mission; but it also illuminates the irrevocability of that first response that gave the word its historical form.

4. Historical concretizations

Word and response: the content of this formula by which we have attempted to express the relationship between Scripture and the Fathers can be made more concrete from the perspective of history. At the same time, it will become even clearer wherein lies the permanent value, the indispensability, of these ecumenical teachers of the faith whom we call Fathers of the Church. The uniqueness of their proto-response can be summarized in four fundamental facts.

a. The canon of Holy Scripture can be traced back to them, or, at least, to the undivided Church of the first centuries of which they were the representatives. It is through their efforts that precisely those books that today we call the "New Testament" were chosen as such from among a multitude of other available literary texts, that the Greek canon of the Jewish Bible was joined to them as the "Old Testament", that it was interpreted in terms of them and that, together, the two Testaments came to be known as "Holy Scripture". The establishment of the canon and the establishment of the early Church are one and the same process but viewed from different perspectives. A book was recognized as "canonical" if it was sanctioned by the Church for use in public worship. By the Church: that meant that the numerous Eastern Churches which, in the beginning,

---

[91] Cf. the opinions expressed by Jean Daniélou in *Das Judentum und die Anfänge der Kirche* (Cologne-Opladen, 1964) and *Théologie du Judéo-Christianisme* (Tournai, 1958).

each had her own custom with regard to liturgical reading, all came, in the end, to accept this one book.[92] The fact that a given book was selected while another was rejected presumes, however, a process of intellectual winnowing and deciding and a dramatic tension such as we can hardly conceive today when we read, on the one hand, the Gnostic gospels that aspired to become Scripture and, on the other hand, the anti-Gnostic writings of the Fathers in which what seems to us such a clearly drawn dividing line then divided the Church in two and for the recognition of which she had to struggle and suffer.

By the end of the second century, this process of winnowing and deciding—Augustine compares it to the dividing of the waters above from the waters below by the vault that turned chaos into cosmos[93]—had already more or less come to an end, although its offshoots extended far into the following centuries, which expanded, deepened and gave final form to the earlier decisions. This means that the canon, as canon, would be inconceivable without the intellectual movement to which patristic theology bears witness. The canon is the product of this movement: to accept it is, therefore, of necessity to accept also those basic intellectual decisions that formed it. Word and response are here inseparably united— and this despite the fact that the Fathers were always careful to keep their response distinct from the proclaimed word in contrast to the intermingling of the two that was so characteristic of *gnosis* and appears, in a particularly classic manner, in the mixture of tradition and interpretation in the so-called Gospel of St. Thomas.[94] Where the writings of the New Testament are read as canon and the Old Testament is read as the Christian Bible, there we find ourselves in the intellectual ambience of the struggle of the first centuries; there we have as Fathers those who were then teachers of the Church.

b. In selecting the writings that were to be recognized as constituting the Bible, the early Church made use of a norm that she designated, in her own words, as the κανὼν τῆς πίστεως, *regula fidei*. Certainly not the least of the functions of this canon was to lead to a discrimination between false and genuine sacred writings and, in this way, to help establish the canon of "the" Scripture. The *regula,* for its part, continued to function in the many different *symbola,* whether conciliar or extraconciliar, in which the effort of the ancient Church to determine what actually constituted Christianity found its binding expression. In addition to her role in laying down the canon of the Bible, then, the Church of the Fathers may also be

---

[92] Cf. Alfred Adam, *Lehrbuch der Dogmengeschichte* (Gütersloh, Mohn, 1965), 87–91.

[93] St. Augustine, "Confessionum Libri XIII," bk. 13, chap. 15, sec. 18 (251–52) and sec. 22 (253–54) in CChr 27 (1981); "Enarratio in Ps. CIII", 8, in CChr 40 (1956): 1479.

[94] Cf. J. B. Bauer, "Echte Jesusworte?", in W. van Ulnik, *Evangelien aus dem Nilsand* (Frankfurt, 1960), 108–50.

characterized as the time that gave birth to the fundamental *symbola* of all Christendom. As long as these *symbola* continue to be prayed, as long as Christianity continues to confess Jesus Christ as both God and man and to worship God as one God in three Persons, just as long are these Fathers its Fathers. When the "basis" of the ecumenical council of the Church of Jesus Christ speaks of Jesus as "God and Savior" and determines the mission of the Church as being, in the language of the doxology, "to the glory of God the Father, the Son and the Holy Spirit",[95] the heritage of the great early Christian *symbola* is present in and basic to this new attempt at a kind of minimum-*symbolum*. Whenever the Church confesses her Lord in the words of the *symbolum,* she is always reminded of those who first made this confession of faith and, in the affirmation of faith that it signifies, likewise formulated the renunciation of a faith that was false.

c. In the ancient Church, the reading of Scripture and the confession of faith were primarily liturgical acts of the whole assembly gathered around the Risen Lord. That brings us to our third point: the ancient Church created the fundamental forms of the Christian liturgical service, which are to be regarded as the permanent basis and indispensable reference point of every liturgical renewal. The liturgical movement between the two world wars, which, in Catholic as well as in Protestant Christianity, led to a new concentration on the nature and form of the Christian liturgy, resulted, on both sides, in a decisive orientation toward the great liturgies of the ancient Church. Today, however, when so much of what was then hoped for has become a reality, a new tendency is making itself felt: the desire to compose for this technical age a liturgy that will not only transcend the exuberance of the Middle Ages but will also consider it necessary to begin again from the beginning and to free itself from the heritage of the ancient Church. If war is thereby declared on a certain archaism, a romantic glorification of antiquity that certainly existed in the liturgical movement, and, in its place, a spiritual freedom is proposed that would not be bound to antiquity and would not feel compelled to adopt what is old just because it is old—if all this is true, we can only applaud it. But if the bond with the basic forms of ancient Christian prayer and ecclesial prayer through the centuries is thereby to be severed, we must be firm in our resistance. The findings of Protestant liturgists of our own time, who have long since made similar experiments and can speak from their own experience, can stand us in good stead here. Of the many judgments available to us, two will suffice. First, that of so unromantic a theologian as Wellhausen, who came to the conclusion that the Protestant

---

[95] Wolfdieter Theurer, *Die trinitarische Basis des ökumenischen Rates der Kirchen* (Bergen-Enkheim: Kaffke, 1967).

liturgical service is, at bottom, Catholic, but with the heart cut out.[96] Secondly, the opinion of A. Benoît: "The sixteenth century was too brutal in destroying the bridges that linked it to the past, and the liturgical tradition of Protestantism found itself, in consequence, not merely impoverished but reduced almost to nothing."[97] Liturgical renewal that does not seek to disintegrate and destroy or to replace the unifying power of the liturgical service by a general antagonism cannot ignore the liturgical heritage of the patristic age. Benoît is right in summarizing his reflections on patrology and liturgy in the words: "The return to the ancient tradition, to the tradition of the as yet undivided Church, is one of the ways that lead to unity."[98]

d. To these three facts—that we owe to the Church of the Fathers the canon of Scripture, the *symbola* and the basic forms of liturgical worship—a final comment may be added as a kind of appendix. By comprehending faith as a *philosophia* and placing it under the rubric *Credo ut intelligam,* the Fathers acknowledged their rational responsibility for the faith and thus created theology as we understand it today, despite all the differences in individual methodologies. This turning to a rational responsibility, moreover, is not to be regarded lightly. It was, in fact, the precondition for the survival of Christendom in the ancient West, and it is the precondition for the survival of the Christian way of life today and tomorrow. This "rationalism" of the Fathers has been often enough criticized, but its critics have, nevertheless, been unable to abandon the course it set, as we see most clearly in the work of Karl Barth, with its radical protest against every effort to find rational explanations and its simultaneous and fascinating struggle to find a deep-rooted understanding of what God has revealed. Thus, by its very existence, theology will always be indebted to the Fathers and will have cause to return again and again to these masters.

We have now considered the most important formal perspectives on which is based the lasting significance of the Fathers for contemporary theology and for every theology of the future. In many respects, it would be desirable now to begin again from the beginning in order to make the whole content as concrete as possible. We should discuss the problem of patristic exegesis;[99] we should comment on the structure of patristic

[96] Quoted in Wilhelm Averbeck, *Der Opfercharakter des Abendmahls in der neueren evangelischen Theologie* (Paderborn: Bonifacius Druckerei, 1967), 151.

[97] Ibid., 75.

[98] Ibid., 77.

[99] Cf. especially, in this context, the various writings of Henri de Lubac (see n. 63 to this chapter) and Jean Daniélou (especially *Sacramentum futuri* [Paris: Beauchesne, 1950]); Rolf Gögler, *Zur Theologie des biblischen Wortes bei Origenes* (Düsseldorf: Patmos, 1963). See also the bibliographical material in all of the above.

thought, its unique union of biblical, liturgical and theological attitudes; we should deal with the question of the relationship between critical thinking and thinking based on faith. Some secondary, but not therefore unimportant, aspects of the questions should be included, for instance, the fact that, even in a purely historical way of thinking, no satisfactory conclusion can be reached if we place a vacuum between ourselves and the Bible and try to forget that the Bible comes to us by way of history. Only by acknowledging history can we transcend it. If we try to ignore it, we remain entangled in it;[100] we cannot possibly read the Bible in a way that is truly historical however much we may seem to be applying historical methods. In reality, we remain bound to the horizon of our own thinking and reflect only ourselves. But to do all this would be to exceed by far the limits of this small work. Instead, I should like to conclude these reflections with the thought with which André Benoît concludes his important study of the relevance of the Fathers and with which I am in total agreement. He says there: "The patrologist is, without doubt, the individual who studies the first centuries of the Church, but he should likewise be the individual who prepares the future of the Church. That, at least, is his mission."[101] Indeed, working with the Fathers is not just a matter of cataloguing in a museum dedicated to what has been. The Fathers are the common past of all Christians. And in the rediscovery of this common possession lies the hope for the future of the Church, the task for her—and our—present.

[100] Cf. A. Benoît, 29–30; 56–57: "Elle (= the Church) peut, par suite de l'ignorance de son histoire, se croire libre, libre d'entamer un dialogue immédiat et direct avec l'Écriture. Mais en fait parce que, sans qu'elle s'en rende compte, son passé pèse sur elle, elle en dépendra presque totalement. Et plus cette dépendance sera inconsciente, plus elle sera lourde et pesante" (57).

[101] A. Benoît, 84. In this connection, reference must be made again to the interesting reflections on the contemporary function of patrology in U. Wickert, "Glauben und Denken bei Tertullian und Origenes", in Zeitschrift für Theologie und Kirche 62 (1965): 153–77.

Section 2
Faith and History

A. Salvation and History

I. *Premise of the question*

1. Basic experience of the connection between salvation and history

History always becomes problematical for us when a crisis occurs in a particular historical configuration. When that happens, we become conscious of the distance—or, indeed, the contradiction—between history and being, between our historical and our ontological nature; we must search again for the union between our being and history, either by invalidating history as it has been up to the present or by conceiving it anew from its roots. In saying this, we have discovered, in essence, where the problem of salvation history begins as well as the basis of its present relevance. Wherever men escape from their daily confrontation with the saving and threatening powers of the cosmos and apprehend themselves as a community that meets the pressing needs of existence together and builds a sheltering and protective form of existence that perdures through generations, there history as a form of salvation has its origin: the individual is no longer exposed alone to the abysses of his own existence but sees himself as the member of a race, a nation, a culture that bestows directly upon him the form and direction of that existence, that guarantees him safety, freedom, life—that are "salvation". It is race that makes possible for him the peaceful management of his daily existence; that provides him with the external means of mastering that existence and, in the structuring of marriage and family as well as in the ordering of social relationships in general, supplies him with answers to the question about his own existence; that enables him to form and interpret in terms that are essentially human the open riddle of existence. History becomes his salvation, the makers of history become for him those special divine powers in whom he has more confidence than in the distant cosmic divinities: "God-Son" is nearer than "God-Father", the distant and mysterious Being who becomes near and gracious through the mediation of the Son.[102]

---

[102] Cf. G. van der Leeuw, *Phänomenologie der Religion* (Tübingen, 1956), 103. A typical example is the myth of Athena, who sprang from the head of Zeus. As Aeschylus's *Eumenides*

This is, in essence, the principle of "salvation history": salvation comes through history, which, therefore, represents the immediate form of religious experience. History is thus a shelter; it gives existence its true character (not its alienation), because this history is divinely established and it is precisely in the reception of the historical that that which transcends history—the eternal—becomes present. Basically, it is possible to find this structure even in peaceful periods of Christian history: the human individual entrusts himself directly to the faith of the Church, not because he has come, through historical proofs, to the conviction that the events recorded in the New Testament are the indisputable center of all history, but because he finds in a world formed by and filled with faith a firm basis that gives his life meaning, salvation and shelter. The community of belief and prayer in which he grew up, the unfolding of the world and its values, the direction his own life has taken, the answer to the question about the form of human existence—all this assures him of the peaceful security he needs to fulfill his existence and for which he is ready to pay the price of much effort; the concrete presence of Christian history gives form and freedom to his life and is, therefore, accepted as salvation. Only when this history begins to contradict the fundamental experiences of his life, when, instead of sheltering him, it begins to divide and rend him, when, instead of offering a way, it increases almost beyond endurance the dilemma of existence, when its own structure begins to topple, when it becomes unquestionable in itself—only then does such history become a problem. The suspicion arises that history does not lead to being but confuses it; that it is not healing but opium; not the way to what is essential but a form of alienation. When historical consciousness is affected to this extent, then the human individual, who exists in history, also undergoes a crisis; he must seek and struggle to construct for himself a new way.

But we must not stop here. We have just tried to understand how one can come to experience history as salvation; now we must see that experience of salvation can, at the same time, be a revolt against history.

---

shows with particular clarity, Athena was honored as the foundress of law. She is, therefore, a complete recapitulation of that "culture" and that form of history that give salvation to the individual. She is the expression of the divine origin of salvation in history. By the above-mentioned myth of her birth, Athena's particular role as a founding divinity was referred back to the universal God of the heavens, who thus lost his mysterious remoteness and, as the father of Athena, became near and trusted, whereas Athena, by the same token, gained universal meaning and power and her history was raised to the level of the universal. On Aeschylus's *Eumenides,* cf. Hans von Balthasar, *Herrlichkeit: Eine theologische Ästhetik,* vol. 3:1, "Im Raum der Metaphysik" (Einsiedeln: Johannes Verlag, 1965): 111–12. On the changes in the Athena-image, see Ulrich von Wilamovitz-Moellendorff, *Der Glaube der Hellenen,* new printing (Darmstadt, 1955), vols. 1 and 2, passim; consult index.

This revolt may take many forms. In Buddhism, it manifests itself as a general turning-away from history and from being as it exists in history, so that nonbeing actually becomes God. The revolution at which it aims is so radical that it is no longer to be regarded as just an attack against what constitutes history per se but rather as the complete antithesis to history, as turning toward "nothingness".[103] In the case of Plato—in the crisis of Greek historical consciousness that was revealed in the execution of Socrates, when the wretched condition to which the piety of the state had been reduced became apparent to the disciple of him who was filled by God and put to death as one hostile to God—the negation is of a quieter kind: a turning to that eternal and essential element in man that transcends history. Being and history are thus separated by a gap that history will never again be able to close. As a result, obedience to prevailing laws persists despite the realization of their inadequacy, thus relativizing history to the utmost and divesting it, as a whole, of its salvational character, even though there is no lack of activity or even any neutrality with regard to it: the effort to purify it on the basis of ancient tradition and to leave only what is essential goes hand in hand with the glimpsing of that essential. For Karl Marx, on the other hand (I venture to leap ahead here), the understanding of history as alienation is a challenge to destroy the old history and create a new one. Here, again, salvation is expected and understood in terms of history, but as a history to be made, not as an already existing history.

2. The beginnings of the problem in its Christian form

Where exactly does the Christian faith belong in this context? There is no single answer to this question; the division of Christianity is inseparably linked to a division in the relationship to history and finds its principal expression in the opposing forms of historical consciousness. Let us proceed slowly here, considering the faith first in relationship to the great structures of man's historical experience that I have indicated above and, in that way, perhaps, gradually discovering what is proper and peculiar to it. Proceeding in this way, we can affirm that the Christian faith itself arose in a time of historical turmoil, in the invalidation of historical consciousness as it had existed up to that time. The message of Jesus presumes a loss of credibility on the part of the late Judaic concept of history. Its interpretation by Paul gives radical expression to this historico-critical fact; it completes the break with the former concept of history and, at the

---

[103] Cf., for example, the discussion in Helmer Ringgren and Ake v. Ström, *Die Religionen der Völker. Gundriss der allgemeinen Religionsgeschichte* (Stuttgart: Kröner, 1959), 262–314, and the references given here.

same time, understands Jesus' message as the foundation of a new history, which, paradoxically, is experienced as the end of all history and, for that reason, affects all mankind. It would not be difficult to identify, on this basis, two criteria of the rising Christian historical consciousness, which, in their paradoxical tension, bring into focus the paradox of this consciousness itself: it is characterized simultaneously by both personalization (individualization) and universalization. The beginning and end of this new history is the Person of Jesus of Nazareth, who is recognized as the last man (the second Adam), that is, as the long-awaited manifestation of what is truly human and the definitive revelation to man of his hidden nature; for this very reason, it is oriented toward the whole human race and presumes the abrogation of all partial histories, whose partial salvation is looked upon as essentially an absence of salvation. By offering temporary salvation, all these histories cut man off from his last end, from his very humanness, which they concealed and kept from him by lulling him with what was provisional.

It is not our purpose to pursue further these inner perspectives of biblical thought but rather to complete the ordering of them to history as a whole with which we began. We may say here that the message of Jesus is offered to the various peoples of the world as the history that alone gives salvation, and that it is concretely organized into ἐκκλησίαι or παροικίαι. Neither term is free from problems. Ἐκκλησία designates the chosen community that exists, as it were, alongside the ordinary and, as such, ongoing everyday community; παροικία refers even more explicitly to a society of sojourners, of those who have not here a lasting city, yet who, in practice, still live with—and from—the past. In many respects, this notion of themselves as sojourners may have been what gave Christians their strength. In a history that was vanishing, they knew that they were the embodiment of a history that was just beginning—a history that was already theirs. In this context, we can understand the "already and not yet" as a concrete historical experience. Nevertheless, their character as faith reduced to nonhistory and nonsalvation both its own prehistory and the concrete contemporary history of the present. But it did not abrogate this contemporary history; it merely lowered its status. On the other hand, the new history that came into being was just a secondary history (of sojourners!); it could preserve its salvational character only by hope, that is, in the relationship of what was experienced to what was not yet experienced.

We see in this a certain parallel to Platonic thought. While remaining in history, one nevertheless always transcends history but in such a way that this "transcending" actually enters into history as source and hope. Hence the contact with Platonic thought very early determined the future course of the Christian faith, which was able to sustain the shattering of its expectation of a proximate *eschaton* by accepting the Platonic concept of the transcendence of history and, on that basis, giving Christian hope a new form.

Was this an ill-conceived development? That is the question that has plagued Western consciousness with burning trenchancy ever since Luther. Luther's appearance signaled the collapse of the prevailing Christian historical consciousness. In the Christian West, the "sojourner" character of this consciousness had largely disappeared in favor of the identification of present history with Christian history, which continued to exist as such only in its character as the one undivided, salvation-bringing orbit of mankind. Granted, the history in which one lived in this way was distinguished by the fact that its stage embraced heaven and hell, but both had become, in fact, a real part of the existing historical order. Christianity thus no longer appeared as an alternative to history but as the form of its definitiveness and insurmountability. Inevitably, seeds of discontent gathered wherever this history was experienced as oppressive and harmful, wherever escape from it was regarded as one's only hope. As we know, that was the case in many heretical movements of the Middle Ages, but such an experience produced genuinely historical change only with Luther, who considered this heavenly-earthly, Christian-secular history no longer as salvation-bringing and Christian but as anti-Christian, and who sought Christianity, not in it, but against it, even though he remained imprisoned in it in all his thinking.

We have just described a form of Christian self-understanding in which history and salvation are closely linked. What we have now to consider is the totally different way of regarding the relationship between faith and history that has its origin with Luther. Whereas the very continuity of history had previously been the constitutive factor for the understanding of Christendom as salvation history, Christendom now appears under the sign of discontinuity. Whereas Christianity had previously depicted itself as community and Church, it was now the *pro me,* the ultimate discontinuity of a personalist orientation, that was determinative for Luther, and responsibility for the Christian order was deliberately referred to the world, to the princes, in order, precisely in this way, to expose the lack of historical actuality in the Church that was herself unable to form her own history or communicate salvation by her continuity.

This transition from continuity to discontinuity can be demonstrated in all the essential and basic elements of ecclesial form: in place of *successio,* the expression and safeguard of continuity, there appears now the charismatic power of the Spirit that acts here and now; in place of typology, which pointed to the continuity of history in promise and fulfillment, there appears now the spoken appeal to what was in the beginning; history, once understood as the union of promise and fulfillment, is interpreted now as the contradiction between law and gospel. Because ontology is the basic philosophical expression of the concept of continuity, *it* is opposed first as a Scholastic and later as a Hellenistic perversion of Christianity and is contrasted with the idea of history. In modern histories of theology, the concept of salvation history is treated as a Protestant antithesis to the ontological assessment in Catholic theology. Even today, discussion of the question of salvation history is not free of this assessment. Finally, since the concept of the Incarnation is the real anchor-point of ontology in theology, it is opposed antithetically by emphasis on the Cross as the real axis of the Christ-event—the Cross as the expression of radical discontinuity, as the permanent escape from organized historical forms (even if they are Christian) into the *extra portam* of a faith that is ultimately not to be institutionalized.[104]

II. *Present form of the question*

1. Stages of the discussion

We have now outlined the basic presuppositions on which the present study of the topic of salvation history must rest and that are to be regarded as its roots if we are to make clear its scope and the universal human context in which it takes place. Let us turn our attention, in this second part, to the present form of the question. The shocks to historical consciousness produced in our century first by two world wars and then by the transition—more or less in fits and starts—to the new form of civilization we know as the "secular city" pushed the problem of "salvation history" with a new urgency into the center of theological speculation. Today, we can already distinguish two stages of the dispute: first, a more "conventional" treatment of the theme that remains within the bounds of the traditional nexus and is characterized by such problems as Platonism and Christendom, Hellenization and de-Hellenization, ontology and history, institution and event, incarnational theology and theology of the Cross, but collectively by the problem of the relationship of history and ontology, of the mediation of history in the realm of ontology; secondly, a more revolutionary kind of questioning, which, through the intermediate stage of a theology of hope, refers in history essentially to the future and is, therefore, at the same time depreciated or

---

[104] The problem of continuity-discontinuity has been discussed in great detail especially by Käsemann, *Exegetische Versuche*, 2:45–46.

rejected as a history of events that have come to pass; its questioning has much in common with that of Marxism. In the form of a theology of revolution (or, to put it more mildly, in the form of political theology), the theme of discontinuity is molded into a new form: where history is salvation only on the basis of hope, past history is rejected as a form of existence; talk of the historically conditioned becomes the antipode of a turning to the historical. Thinking "historically" becomes thinking anti-historically—nowhere is this more clearly observable than in the works of J. B. Metz, in which the enthusiastic option for history represents, at the same time, an equally decisive rejection of the past, a suspension of all reference to tradition in favor of a program of what is to be done.[105]

Structurally, it is true, political theology undoubtedly offers a variation on the theme of salvation history; materially, however, it more or less abandons the ground of theological tradition—to the extent, namely, that it abandons theological traditions and rests on immanently political considerations. The real difference between political theology and the theology of salvation history as we know it becomes apparent only when we look closely at the central thesis of each of them and search there for an answer. As we are well aware, the central theme of salvation-historical theology has always been the question of the relationship between ontology and history: How can history play a role in the molding of being, and when is it alien to being? For Christian history, which in its external parameters is a particular phenomenon concentrated in a single individual who comes to meet us bound by time and place to a past that, at the same time, claims universality—claims that this particular is the universal—for such a history, the problem of mediating between particular and general was especially explosive. It reached its peak in the struggle about "*salus extra ecclesiam. . . .*" What is being attacked here is the universality of the particular history, opposition to which flows from the actual nonuniversality of Christianity. The attempt to reconcile the two—to support the attack and, at the same time, to affirm the universality of Christianity—can serve as a concentrated example of a historical problem that is specifically Christian: its ranking of history and ontology.[106] If the problem is broached to the radical forms of political theology, their answer is simply to ignore it. To maintain the existence of human nature as such is, for them, the essence of alienation; no human nature exists for

[105] Cf. the following works by Johannes Baptist Metz: *Zur Theologie der Welt* (Mainz: Grünewald, 1968), esp. 77–78 and 90–91; *Glaube in Geschichte und Gesellschaft* (Mainz: Grünewald, 1977); *Jenseits bürgerlicher Religionen. Reden über die Zukunft des Christentums* (Munich: Kaiser, 1980). On Metz's philosophical and theological orientation, see Richard Schäffler, *Was dürfen wir hoffen?* (Darmstadt: Wissenschaftliche Buchgesellschaft, 1979).

[106] For a more comprehensive treatment, see Joseph Ratzinger, *Das neue Volk Gottes. Entwürfe zur Ekklesiologie* (Düsseldorf: Patmos, 1972).

which history is the mediator but only the rough-draft *man*, the ultimate
form and scope of which is determined by *this* particular individual who,
out of the rough draft, creates a man.[107] Thus, the antithesis to ontology
and the affirmation of discontinuity here reach their greatest intensity:
man as the measure of all human realities simply does not exist; man is
what he makes himself to be; there are ultimately no limits to this
manipulation except those set by his own ability, even though, in the
humanized world, purified of all alienation, there still shines a glimmer of
the concept of permanence.

2. History as the antithesis of ontology

This means that the current discussion, by its radicalness, has given a new
form to the basic problem behind the term salvation history. The problem
of history's role in the realm of being has become a question about being as
such: Is there a continuity of "humanness"? And, if there is, at what
point does the mediation of history begin? If we consider this question,
which, I believe, expresses the fundamental crisis of our age, from a
strictly theological viewpoint as befits our subject, everything seems at
first to end in the realization, which almost no one would contest today,
that, except in a few passages, the Bible contains no ontological reflection,
that it is, in fact, actually antithetical to the Greek mode of ontological
thought. If we look more closely, however, we shall soon see that this
notion is a superficial one and can do justice neither to the multiplicity of
biblical forms nor to the many possible forms in which the ontological
question may be stated. One more observation: with its interpretation of
Jesus as the eschatological Adam, who is himself the image of God—that
is, God's translation into human form and man's translation into God, the
Bible establishes a definitive standard for the being *man,* which, it is true,
looks to man's future, but to a future that is also fulfillment because it
restores him to his essential nature. If we were to believe that, with the
concept of Christ as Adam, which expresses the essential unity that is man,
the matter has been positively decided in favor of the continuity of "humanness", we would only be deceiving ourselves, for it is precisely here
that the contradiction begins again.

The Bible does, it is true, recognize the distinction between the first and
the second Adam, that is, it sees historically existing man as man alienated

[107] For a good introduction to the various movements in political theology, see Siegfried
Wiedenhofer, *Politische Theologie* (Stuttgart, 1976). For a fundamental treatment of liberation
theology, see Karl Lehmann et al., *Theologie der Befreiung,* ITK (Einsiedeln, Johannes Verlag:
1977), which also contains an extensive bibliography.

from himself precisely by his history; in fact, the doctrine of original sin says basically only this: that man's history is the history of an alienation that is contrary to his nature, so that he can become himself only by faith, which marks him as a "sojourner" in relation to current history, and can come into contact with even this essential part of his self only by way of the tension between his political existence and his existence as a "sojourner". At least in some of his works, Luther, as we know, so greatly intensified the problem of alienation that is expressed in the model of the two Adams that the historical Adam is but wood and stone compared with the new existence opened by faith. In his early work, he believed that man would remain thus even after his earthly existence so that all his efforts to attain salvation could be nothing but sin; on the other hand, even sin would not be able to abolish this new existence. Both are regarded here in strict discontinuity; in principle, therefore, ontology—that is, a continuity and identity of being that embraces the differences of history—no longer exists. To this assessments are due all those often very contradictory efforts to reconstruct salvation history in radical contrast to metaphysics— whether the early Barth, who describes faith as an act of God in and with respect to man that presumes no true encounter between God and man; or Rudolf Bultmann, who, rejecting linear continuity, describes faith as the momentary "now" of decision, a "now" that exists only at the moment of acting;[108] or Moltmann's theology of hope,[109] which concentrates on the collective dimensions and forms the starting point for political theology and the theology of revolution. All these, however, are but variations of the one effort to reject the categories of being and describe faith as salvation in purely historical terms, to solve the problem of history's mediation in the realm of ontology by canceling it and declaring history alone to be that which is and is essential.

3. The search for the unity of history and being

Here, we are brought face to face once more with the alternative with which we started. Is there or is there not a continuity of "humanness"? Is history mediation or end? To pursue this aspect of the question further, we would have to deal exhaustively with the *aporiae* of both possibilities—but that would be to exceed the bounds of the present study. I shall limit myself, therefore, to clarifying in as exact and differentiated a manner as

[108] For a further discussion of Barth and Bultmann, and for some commentary on Oscar Cullmann's criticism of Bultmann, see, in the present work, Part One, Chapter One, Section 2b: "Salvation History, Metaphysics and Eschatology".

[109] Moltmann, *Theologie der Hoffnung*.

possible the present state of the question. Having addressed the theme of discontinuity and its roots, I propose, in a final train of thought, to say something more about the counter-effort, about the attempt to comprehend history as mediation in such a way that even the future can be hope only because it promises the freedom to be. This thesis is supported by the fact that, in the naming of Christ as the second Adam, with the differentiation that distinguishes him from the first Adam, the whole Christian tradition of antiquity understood also the unity of Adam's being—the unity that lies in creatureliness, in the creative thought of God, which is not to be nullified. In contrast to the Greek concept of being, then, creatureliness means having one's origin, not in a passive idea, but in a creative freedom; it includes, therefore, in a positive way, the temporality of being as the mode of its self-fulfillment, history as substantiality, not mere accidentality, but in such a way that time has its unity in the *Creator Spiritus* and, because it is sequential, is still a continuity of being by way of succession.[110]

It must be admitted that, in many respects, the problem is made more complex by this line of reasoning than by the rejection of ontology. For there arises here with special clarity the dilemma between the general and the particular, between particular history and the claim to universality. Is it even possible, philosophically, to maintain this tension in the face of the radical views about historical relevance to which we are exposed today? This, it seems to me, is the form in which the question of salvation history is being asked in Catholic theology today, and it is here that we should discover the contribution that Catholic theology can and ought to make to the study of this question.

The attempts to find an answer are not so numerous as one might hope. I propose to outline here the most effective and surely the most penetrating of these attempts: that of Karl Rahner, who wrestled with the problem in his early work *Hörer des Wortes*[111] and later undertook to build on that beginning, particularly with his concept of the anonymous Christian.[112] The critique of Rahner's contribution with which this chapter closes will

---

[110] The special theme of an ontology that originates in the belief in a Creator God is discussed by Claude Trésmontant, particularly in *Biblisches Denken und hellenische Überlieferung* (Düsseldorf, 1959) and *Die Vernunft des Glaubens* (Düsseldorf, 1964).

[111] Karl Rahner, *Hörer des Wortes,* 1st ed. (Munich: Kösel, 1941); 2d ed., newly revised by Johannes Baptist Metz (Munich: Kösel, 1963). [For an English translation, see *Hearers of the Word,* trans. Michael Richards (New York: Herder and Herder, 1969). (Trans.)] For the debate about this work, see especially Eberhard Simons, *Philosophie der Offenbarung* (Stuttgart: Kohlhammer, 1966), and Alexander Gerken, *Offenbarung und Transcendenzerfahrung* (Düsseldorf: Patmos, 1969). Important insights are also to be found in Hansjürgen Verweyen, *Ontologische Voraussetzungen des Glaubensaktes* (Düsseldorf, 1969).

[112] Cf., for example, *Schriften,* 6:545–54.

also serve to clarify the work that still remains to be done in this area. The problem with which Rahner begins has been discussed above: the dichotomy between the particularity of Christian history and its claim to the whole being *man*. Can a particular history justly claim to be salvation not just for a particular historical period but for man precisely *qua* man? We can distinguish two stages in Rahner's answer. The first consists in his description of man as hearer of the word, that is, as a being who waits for something that comes to him from without, for the word spoken in history, for revelation. He is the being who lives not just from the depths of his own being, who finds his fulfillment, not in what issues from himself, from his very nature, but, by reason of this nature, keeps watch for what can come to him only in freedom and from without. What is accidental is, for him, the necessary; what is free and must be given in freedom is, for him, the indispensable. In other words, what is necessary to his being is ordered to that which is accidental in history; this accidental in the history that comes to him from without as "particular" is for him an indispensable accident that can neither add to nor subtract from his being but is precisely the form in which his being becomes most fully itself. The paradox of the being *man* is that he can find the "universal" in himself only in tension with the "particular", with a history that comes from without, so that man can be described and postulated, as it were, *a priori,* as the receiver of a revelation history, as a "hearer of the word": Christian history thus loses its extrinsic character; it is, rather, a necessarily free answer to the free necessity and the necessary freedom of the being *man*.

Up to this point, we have been able to follow Rahner's thought without difficulty and even to acknowledge it as an exposition both of our present experience of existence and of the basic direction of christological dogma. It becomes problematic, however, when we reach the second stage, which became more and more the principal motif of his later work. If revelation history is not to be understood as categorically extrinsic but refers, rather, to the human race as a whole, Rahner argues, then it must also be present in the human race as a whole. Let us look more closely at this conclusion. Rahner says of the human being "that he is historical *as* the subject of transcendence; his subjective being . . . is mediated *by history* to its autonomous fulfillment".[113] In simpler language, this means that man's being itself is historical in character. The limitation of this basically

---

[113] In the following remarks, I refer essentially to Rahner's comprehensive Summa, *Grundkurs des Glaubens. Einführung in den Begriff des Christentums* [henceforth *Grundkurs*] (Freiburg: Herder, 1976). For quotation, see 145. I return here to the reflections first presented in my review of this work: "Vom Verstehen des Glaubens", in *Theologische Revue* 74 (1978): 165–86. For an evaluation of the work as a whole, I refer the reader especially to this review. It is not the work as such that is being discussed in the present pages but only

important insight is that it refers, of course, only to this historical character in general. It follows that the role of history in the shaping of man's being is shown to be necessary in a universal sense. However, that is not the real problem, which is, rather, that the Christian faith claims universality for a *particular* history. But the conclusion about universality cannot lead to the particularity of Christianity. The limits of the universal only seem to have been overcome. In reality, however, "the historical character" as such is subsumed in the universal. History is "salvation history" because it is everywhere and because it has always the role of forming man to his true nature. Rahner has quite obviously drawn this conclusion when he says that "salvation history is coexistent with the totality of human history".[114] "By world history, then, we mean salvation history."[115] Or again: "Revelation history" is "coextensive with the totality of world and salvation history".[116]

Rahner knows, of course, that he would turn theology into a philosophy of history if he did not develop his thought further. In his comments on universality, he attempts, therefore, to arrive at the particularity of Christianity without, at the same time, sacrificing the identification of particular and universal. To achieve this squaring of the circle, he offers two thoughts. The first consists in designating Christianity as a particularly successful apprehension of what is always more or less consciously acknowledged. He calls Christendom "a very definite and successful historical reflection and the historically reflexive self-awareness of a revelation history . . . that is itself completely coextensive with world history."[117] In other words, "This kind of revelation history"—that is, Christendom—is "only a species, a segment, of universal, categorical revelation history, the most successful instance of the necessary self-explication of transcendental revelation. . . ."[118] Here he affirms a certain superiority of Christian history within the whole of world history—a superiority that lies, admittedly, not on the level of the event, but of consciousness: the particularity of Christianity with respect to the rest of history is now located in the realm of reflection; in Christianity is reflected that which, in itself, is always and everywhere.

Again, Rahner himself obviously felt that he had not done justice to what is peculiarly Christian. He makes, therefore, a second attempt to

---

certain aspects of it. [For an English translation of Rahner's text, see *Foundations of Christian Faith. An Introduction to the Idea of Christianity*, trans. William V. Dych (London: Darton, Longman and Todd, 1978). (Trans.)]

[114] *Grundkurs*, 147.
[115] Ibid., 148.
[116] Ibid., 149.
[117] Ibid., 151.
[118] Ibid., 159.

express the particularity of Christianity and of Christian history. In the process, he excludes much that had hitherto been subsumed under these headings. About the Old Testament he says, for instance: "We see, then, that such a history could and, indeed, did occur also in the history of other nations. . . "[119] The person of Jesus is, for him, the only distinctive aspect of Christian history. In this way, the specific historical claim of the Christian faith can be reduced to the uniqueness of the "Absolute Bringer of salvation". In him, Rahner sees the only caesura in history as such, which, as a whole, is the transition "from a being hidden in nature and immediately threatened by it" to "the now just beginning era of hominized existence that follows upon the first period of natural existence. . . ."[120]

From this standpoint, the Savior is the only unique element in Christian history—and Rahner can present him as such only because he has already demonstrated on general principles that this figure is necessary and universal. For Rahner, man is, in fact, self-transcendent being; hence the God-man can be deduced as the true Savior of mankind in terms of man's own being: the Incarnation of God is the highest instance of the ontological fulfillment of human reality, the successful, perfect transcendence.[121] As the successful form of human self-transcendence, or, in other words, as the utterance of God in a finite subject, Christ, the Redeemer, is the expression and realization of the human universal.

We come thus to a final point. From what has been said, it follows "that in the meeting with him [Christ] . . . the mystery of reality itself . . . 'is present'."[122] Even more clearly: "The relationship to Jesus Christ, in which an individual . . . makes Jesus, present within him, the mediator of his direct relationship to God" is such "that man in his existence . . . is always already within this . . . relationship whether he is explicitly aware of it or not."[123] From this, Rahner develops his basic formula of Christian existence, in which he seeks to express its simplicity and greatness, its full universality as present in its apparent particularity: "He who . . . accepts his existence . . . says . . . Yes to Christ."[124] This is the unifying point in Rahner's concept of Christianity, in which his whole reflection is contained in summary: "The Christian and the Church do not say something that can be opposed. Rather, they say that the Unutterable . . . that reveals itself . . . is Nearness."[125] To be a Christian is to accept one's

[119] Ibid., 171.
[120] Ibid., 172.
[121] Ibid., 216.
[122] Ibid., 204.
[123] Ibid., 205–6.
[124] Ibid., 225–26.
[125] Ibid., 387.

existence in its unconditionality. Ultimately, therefore, it is but the explicit reflection of what it means to be human.[126] In the last analysis, this means "that the Christian is not so much an exception among men as simply man as he is".[127]

This broadly outlined thesis of Rahner's has something dazzling, something stupendous, about it. The particular and the universal, history and being, seem to be reconciled. The uniqueness of Christianity and the universality of man's being coincide. If one accepts the uniqueness, one has the universality as well; if one has the universality, one possesses also the uniqueness. But is that really the answer? Is it true that Christianity adds nothing to the universal but merely makes it known? Is the Christian really just man as he is? Is that what he is supposed to be? Is not man as he is that which is insufficient, that which must be mastered and transcended? Does not the whole dynamism of history stem from the pressure to rise above man as he is? Is it not the main point of the faith of both Testaments that man is what he ought to be only by conversion, that is, when he ceases to be what he is? Does not Christianity become meaningless when it is reinstated in the universal, whereas what we really want is the new, the other, the saving trans-formation [Ver-änderung]? Does not such a concept, which turns being into history but also history into being, result in a vast stagnation despite the talk of self-transcendence as the content of man's being? A Christianity that is no more than a reflected universality may be innocuous, but is it not also superfluous? And, it might be noted in passing, it is simply not empirically true that Christians do not say anything particular that can be opposed; that they say only what is universal. They say much that is particular. Otherwise, how could they be a "sign that is rejected" (Lk 2:34)?

Rahner could, of course, refute all this by saying that he, too, takes as his point of departure that which is inconceivably new, the *Event* that *is* the Savior. He could say that what is universal has now become that which saves only because, in this Savior, a universality of being has come to pass that could not emanate from being itself. I prefer to leave open the question of whether this does justice, on a conceptual level, to what is particular and unique in the salvation history that has its center in Christ. The real problem seems to me to be with the spiritual formulation, for it is only in the spiritual formulation, which has its source in the abstract concept, that we find the real test of theological speculation. Spiritually, however, this intermingling of universal and particular, of history and being, of being a Christian and being man "as he is", amounts to man's self-affirmation. To be a Christian is to accept oneself. Let us recall again

---

[126] Ibid.
[127] Ibid., 388.

the formula: "He who . . . accepts his existence . . . says . . . Yes to Christ."[128] In this spiritual transposition of transcendental deduction—which was its hidden starting point—I see a resolution of the particular into the universal that is at variance with the newness of Christianity and reduces Christian liberation to pseudoliberation. For the theologian who struggles with the particularity of Christianity, there is, to be sure, a tremendous liberation in being able to say at the end: No, the particular is the universal. He is freed from the burden of Christian particularity, led into the freedom of universal philosophy and its rationalism (although he will soon discover that no one will accept his identification of the Christian with the universal and that he is being called upon to do away with this ballast if it has nothing special to offer). The weary Christian who groans under the burden of Christian history and ecclesial bonds is also freed by these theories. Self-acceptance—just being human—is all that is required. But he, too, will soon ask: Can I do away with ecclesial positivity when it is always there anyway, whether it is reflected upon or not? Can I ignore what is different from what others say when, after all, we only are and do the universal? Or is it enough to declare that all Christian positivity is a realization of the human per se? But will not this explanation, if it is to have no consequences, soon become just a palliative that does not dispense me from fulfilling my Christian duties but makes it more difficult for me to do so by telling me that there are other ways of doing it?

In other words, this liberation is not very far-reaching. One who escapes into the pure rationality of the human will have either to reestablish the particularity of the Christian claim or to acknowledge the emptiness of the universal rationalism that leaves man without a way yet challenges him again and again to seek for a concrete—for a particular—option. The Christian who groans under the burden of being a Christian will have either to accept anew—as everyone else must—the burden that, in any event, he will find quite different from the mere awareness of it or to free himself of his burden and then likewise stand in the emptiness of a humanity the acceptance of which, as it is in itself, now seems to him to be none other than his eternal enslavement. The enslavement of nihilism is not less than that of mere facticity. Just to accept one's humanity as it is (or, even, "in its ultimate unconditionality")—that is not redemption; it is damnation. For what does it mean to be human? Not that merely accepting humanity is the last word. Against such a conclusion, the question arises: Why are we as we are? And from that there flows the longing to become other than we are.

The inadequacy of the spiritual formulation in which Rahner's theology of history finds its concrete expression clarifies for me the at first

[128] Ibid., 225–26.

unexpected conversion of this transcendental deduction into Marx-inspired theologies in the generation after Rahner. From the populariza-tion of his findings, it is possible to conclude that the contents of Christian-ity must be interchangeable with the universal knowledge of mankind as a whole; that they are, accordingly, susceptible of an interpretation that equates them with the commonly held views of universal reason. Admit-tedly, this is a reversal of the direction of Rahner's thought, but it cannot be denied that there is a certain logic in it. Rahner appropriated universal reason for Christianity and tried to prove that universal reason leads ultimately to the teachings of Christianity and that the teachings of Chris-tianity are the universally human, the rational par excellence. Now the di-rection of his thought has been reversed. If the teachings of Christianity are the universally human, the generally held views of man's reason, then it follows that these generally held views are what is Christian. In that case, one can—in fact, one must—interpret what is Christian in terms of the universal findings of man's reason. It follows that the "materialistic read-ing of the Bible" will be something quite normal, however recondite it may be in terms of the original meaning of the texts. It becomes apparent, at the same time, that man cannot rest in the universally human. The norm that what is Christian is what is human leads to the option of understand-ing, as the core of Christianity, that which can claim to be grounded in reason. In the works of Gutierrez, for instance, we can see the conviction that Marxism is a science, the scientific analysis of the human individual and his economic situation. What Gutierrez understands by "science" thus automatically becomes also the criterion for interpreting what is Chris-tian, since this "science" presents itself, at the same time, as the fulfillment of the real moral postulate of mankind. Granted, all this cannot be imputed to Rahner, and it would be unfair to hold an author responsible for the conclusions that others draw from his works unilaterally and against the whole tenor of his thought. On the other hand, such a factual misinterpre-tation can, nevertheless, help him to isolate the weak spots and critical points of his synthesis and, from that perspective, to give a new orienta-tion to his theological reflection.

Let us return to our topic. We said above that Rahner's intermingling of history and being in the concept of the "Absolute Bringer of salvation" leads to a spirituality of self-affirmation and the identification of "humanness" as such with the notion of what it means to be Christian. We saw also that the liberation from Christian particularity that was accomplished in that way is not a satisfactory outcome since reality as such—man as he is—cannot be the object of unconditional acceptance but rather bears within itself the seeds of a profound nonacceptance. We must, therefore, look for a different expression, a better formula. I would say, to begin with, that we should look in the direction of a spirituality of conversion, of ec-stasy [Ek-stase], of self-transcendence, which is also one of Rahner's basic concepts, although, for the most part, he loses sight of its concrete meaning in his synthesis. But we cannot begin at the end. We must ask: What is the really critical point in Rahner's deduction? Where does it go wrong and, as a result, lead to a false formula of existence? Given the seriousness of the matter, the debate on the subject must give evidence of the same thoroughness and penetrating radicality as Rahner's own work. For that reason, it cannot be brought here to an appropriate conclusion but can only be shown to be necessary. If, despite this fact, I do not simply refrain from an answer here, what I say can, nevertheless, be no more than a suggestion, a first indication, of the direction such an answer must take. It seems to me that the real problem with Rahner's synthesis is that he has attempted too much. He has, so to speak, sought for a philosophical and theological world formula on the basis of which the whole of reality can be deduced cohesively from necessary causes. Granted, he does this not just on the basis of his own thought but as an interpretation of what we know through Christian faith and the revelation on which it rests. This revelation seems to him to reveal the horizon from which man—taught by God's own word—can begin to reflect on the divine mysteries and come to understand with God's own understanding, can gain an understanding of the cohesion of reality as a whole. This basic intention is unimpeachable. Theology is just such an attempt to find an understanding of reality itself. But revelation has given us no world formula. Such a concept is plainly counter to the mystery of freedom. Even science is aware today that it will find no world formula because, even in the realm of nature, there exists the nonnecessary.[129] A fortiori, there can be no spiritual world formula—that was also Hegel's basic error. Under the title Das Ganze im Fragment, Hans Urs von Balthasar has consciously opposed this concept in his theology of history in order to emphasize in advance that it is not given to man to see and express the whole in itself; at best, he can have but an intimation of it in the fragmentary, the positive, the particular.

To put it briefly, I believe the nucleus of the problem with Rahner's synthesis lies in his understanding of freedom. There are, to be sure, impressive passages in his work in which the Christian concept of human freedom—that freedom that combines disposing-of-oneself and disponibility—is clearly unfolded. Basically, however, Rahner has, to a great extent, adopted the concept of freedom that is proper to idealistic

---

[129] This is forcefully stated in J. Monod, Zufall und Notwendigkeit. Philosophische Fragen der modernen Biologie (Munich, 1970), 56–57; cf. 178–79.

philosophy, a concept that, in reality, is appropriate to the absolute
Spirit—to God—but not to man. He says, for instance, that freedom is
"the ultimate self-responsibility of the person . . . as self-action."[130]
Freedom is defined as the ability "to be oneself".[131] Parallel to the concept
of an almost godlike ability for self-action, we observe a withdrawal from
empirical reality that raises the question of where this freedom takes place
if it is categorically so undiscoverable, especially since it is said elsewhere
that man's self-realization occurs in and through the categorical. In
relation to the concept of God, finally, human freedom seems actually to
have been absorbed into divine freedom so that, formally, the impression
arises of an efficacy that belongs to God alone: "That we do not know, as
subjects of a freedom that is still becoming, whether or not God has placed
all freedom in [the making of] a good decision is a . . fact to be accepted
with obedience, just as we must accept our existence with obedience."[132]
In the same vein, Rahner calls man's freedom an "always already accomplished freedom"[133]—freedom seems to pass into and be assimilated by
predestination. In fact, the attempt to depict cohesively with a logical necessity the unity and totality of the real leads unquestionably to an identification of freedom and necessity: if the whole of history is to be portrayed
in a single necessary logic, then it is a history of necessity, of what is necessary, and scarcely leaves room for a freedom that resists systematization.

Ultimately, then, a synthesis that combines being and history in a single, compelling logic of the understanding becomes, by the universality of
its claim, a philosophy of necessity, even though this necessity is then explained as a process of freedom. By its very nature, insistence on freedom
involves the rejection of a closed system. The logic of the whole is not
something we can deduce. A synthesis adequate to the spiritual tension of
Christianity must, therefore, be an open synthesis that rejects a definitive
and all-embracing logic. From a purely philosophical standpoint, that will
be its weakness; it puts Christendom in an unsatisfactory position with regard to Marxism. But precisely in Marxism we see that a system that can
know and order all things, that claims perfect rationality, soon turns the
force of logic into the force of a police state that it explains as a necessary
vehicle of freedom. The weakness of the Christian synthesis is its strength.
The key thought of a Christian philosophy and theology would, therefore, have to be freedom—that true freedom that includes also the nonde-
ducible and hence excludes perfect conceptual cohesion. The person of
Jesus Christ, as the Event of the new and unexpected, is, then, the central

---

[130] *Grundkurs,* 47.
[131] Ibid., 49.
[132] Ibid., 112.
[133] Ibid., 138.

expression of this freedom, which, for that reason, becomes the central figure in history. Such freedom can be, at the same time, the model for understanding that God can freely lead every freedom to salvation without our knowing in what context he acts—at least, in what context other than that which tells us that freedom always has to do with love, and love with redemption. This means, in turn, that man does not find salvation in a reflective finding of himself but in the being-taken-out-of-himself that goes beyond reflection—not in continuing to be himself, but in going out from himself.[134] It means that the liberation of man consists in his being freed from himself and, in relinquishing himself, truly finding himself. It means that by accepting the other, the particular, the apparently not-necessary and free, he finds what is whole and real.

Such a philosophy of freedom and love is, at the same time, a philosophy of conversion, of going out from oneself, of transformation; it is, therefore, also a philosophy of community and history, of a history that is truly free. Man finds his center of gravity, not inside, but outside himself. The place to which he is anchored is not, as it were, within himself but without. This explains that remnant that remains always to be explained, the fragmentary character of all his efforts to comprehend the unity of history and being. Ultimately, the tension between ontology and history has its foundation in the tension within human nature itself, which must go out of itself in order to find itself; it has its foundation in the mystery of God, which is freedom and which, therefore, calls each individual by a name that is known to no other. Thus, the whole is communicated to him in the particular.

B. Salvation History, Metaphysics and Eschatology

The turbulent process of change that, for some decades now, has been holding Catholic theology in its grip and compelling it to reflect upon itself with a comprehensiveness and depth that have not been known since the great crisis of the thirteenth century—this change is nowhere more obvious than in the area of salvation history, which includes the question of the orientation of theology. For Catholic theology, the question is a rather recent one, although—simply in terms of the structure of Christianity,

---

[134] I have discussed the concept of ecstasy as the basic spiritual form of Christian existence more fully in relation to the thought of pseudo-Dionysius the Areopagite in the first version of these remarks, which appeared in *Wort und Wahrheit* 25 (1970): 11–14. Cf. also the material presented by René Roques, "Dionysius Areopagita", in RAC 3:1075–121; Endre von Ivánka, *Plato christianus* (Einsiedeln: Johannes Verlag, 1964), 223–89. In particular, I recommend the entire work of Hans Urs von Balthasar as the expression of a broad synthesis.

which appeared as the good tidings of God's action in history—the question that lies behind it has always been present in one form or another and, as the relationship of οἰκονομία and θεολογία, of *dispositio* and *natura*, even stands at the center of the Church Fathers' reflections on Christian reality.[135] Nevertheless, we can judge the extent to which the question, as it is posed today, was and is regarded as something new from the fact that Vatican Council II did not link its debate on salvation to the already existing patristic term *dispositio* but rather coined for itself, as a borrowing from the German, the expression *historia salutis*. Therewith we have also an indication of the source of the problem that, in our century, has entered Catholic theology by way of Protestant thought. In what follows, we shall attempt, first, to outline the development of this thought during the last three decades and then to sketch elements of an answer, which can be, of course, just a suggestion of the direction such an answer might take, not a comprehensive analysis.

I. *The first phase of the discussion: salvation history as the antithesis of metaphysics*

To the best of my knowledge, the question of when and where the acceptance of the concept of salvation history took place in Catholic circles has not yet been investigated. So far as I can see, it was Gottlieb Söhngen who first raised the issue in German-speaking countries in a debate with Karl Barth and Emil Brunner;[136] in France, it was especially Jean Daniélou who addressed the question in response to the work of Oscar Cullmann.[137] In this first stage of the debate, the term *salvation history* had an antithetical meaning: salvation-historical theology was introduced as the opposite of metaphysics or of theology from a metaphysical standpoint; salvation

---

[135] Cf. Stephan Otto, *"Natura" und "Dispositio". Untersuchungen zum Naturbegriff und zur Denkform Tertullians* (Munich: Hueber, 1960); Auguste Luneau, *L'Histoire du salut chez les Pères de l'Église* (Paris: Beauchesne, 1964); M. J. Marmann, *Praeambula ad gratiam. Entstehungsgeschichte des Axioms "Gratia praesupponit naturam"*, dissertation (Regensburg, 1974).

[136] Cf. especially Gottlieb Söhngen, "Natürliche Theologie und Heilsgeschichte. Antwort an Emil Brunner", in *Catholica* 4 (1935): 97–114; "Analogia fidei", in ibid., 3 (1934): 113–36 and 176–208. The response to Emil Brunner is also contained in *Die Einheit in der Theologie* (Munich: Karl Zink, 1952), 248–64.

[137] Especially Jean Daniélou, "Réponse à O. Cullmann", in *Dieu vivant*, n. 24 (1953), 107–16; *Essai sur le mystère de l'histoire* (Paris: du Seuil, 1953); "Christologie et eschatologie", in Aloys Grillmeier and Heinrich Bacht, *Das Konzil von Chalkedon*, 3 (Würzburg: Echter Verlag, 1954): 269–86. See also, Jean Frisque and Oscar Cullmann, *Une Théologie de l'histoire du salut* (Paris: Casterman, 1960); Hans-Georg Hermesmann, *Zeit und Heil. Oscar Cullmanns Theologie der Heilsgeschichte* (Paderborn: Bonifacius Druckerei, 1979).

history and metaphysics were regarded as contradictory and their relationship as something to be studied. A statement by Cullmann probably shows most plainly the depth of the question that thus entered Catholic theology: "If, today, the radical distinction between Hellenistic metaphysics and Christian revelation has been to a large extent completely eradicated for most people, this is due to the fact that the Greek concept of time very early suppressed the biblical one. . . . The resolution into metaphysics of the primitive Christian concept of a salvation history linked to a rising time-line is the root of the heresy, if apostasy from primitive Christianity can be called heresy".[138] The old problem of Protestant dogmatic historiography, which understands Catholicism as the product of an illegitimate combination of the Greek and biblical spirit, makes its appearance here with renewed vigor as a question about the legitimacy of metaphysics in theology.[139] The same theme is discernible when Karl Barth thunders his inflexible No against *theologia naturalis* and when Emil Brunner, in a less radical way, accepts a *theologia naturalis* but firmly distinguishes the salvation-historical *theologia naturalis* of Protestant thought from what, in his opinion, is the ahistorical, purely metaphysical Catholic form of natural theology.[140]

As can readily be seen, the antithesis that exists between salvation-historical and metaphysical theology is not a question of the concepts and constructions of the theology of history but of a basic principle of methodology: of the link between history and faith, of the link between faith and the *factum historicum* of the saving act of God in Jesus Christ and in the whole history of God's covenant with man, whose great Yes he is. But there is, at the same time, also a question of the *prae* of the divine word in relation to human thought, or, in the language of scientific theory, of the historical in relation to the speculative. As Gottlieb Söhngen has said: "Speculative theology is not true theology nor is historical theology a more or less propaedeutic theology. How did the Enlightenment express it? Factual truths serve as a propaedeutic for rational truths. Hence Christian theology cannot, with a clear conscience, speak of the propaedeutic

---

[138] Oscar Cullmann, *Christus und die Zeit*, 2d ed. (Zurich: Evangelischer Verlag, 1948), 46–47. [For an English translation, see Oscar Cullmann, *Christ and Time*, trans. Floyd V. Filson (London: SCM Press, 1962). (Trans.)]

[139] Cf. Aloys Grillmeier, "Hellenisierung und Judaisierung des Christentums als Deuteprinzipien der Geschichte des kirchlichen Dogmas" in *Scholastik* 33 (1958): 321–55 and 528–58; contains extensive bibliographical material. For a well-conceived and profound discussion of the question from the standpoint of Bultmann and his eschatological thought, see W. Kamlah, *Christentum und Geschichtlichkeit*, 2d ed. (Stuttgart, 1951).

[140] See works of Gottlieb Söhngen mentioned in n. 136 above; cf. also Hans Urs von Balthasar, *Karl Barth. Darstellung und Deutung seiner Theologie* (Cologne: Jakob Hegney, 1951).

character of historical theology. . . ."[141] Following salvation-historical thought, Söhngen states emphatically that the truth of Christianity is not the truth of a universally accepted idea but the truth of a unique fact. The sharp distinction from myth that is expressed in the following statement is thus made possible: "The *logos* of myth is beyond history, and the mythical event is meta-history in a more than human domain. The mystery of Christianity, however, raises a claim that must be historically substantiated."[142] Here we discover an inner demand of salvation-historical theology in which its antithesis to the understanding of history by Bultmann and his disciples is already apparent inasmuch as the link between faith and history requires that faith be susceptible of historical substantiation—not as though historical reason would of itself be able to found or establish faith, but faith must be able to coexist with it. Thus salvation-historical theology in this first phase of the debate is to be defined as a theology that knows itself bound to Scripture as to the witness of the historical acts of God that are man's salvation. In other words, two concepts are combined here that will later be separated: the link to Scripture is essentially also a link to the events it records and to the historical character of these actions, which are the bearers of salvation and, consequently, truly "salvation history".

The critical question that arises here for Catholic theology has already been indicated: the problem of how this whole—as opposed to the limited antithesis of Barth, Brunner and Cullmann—is compatible with the metaphysical heritage of Catholic theology. This question was soon expanded into the broader one of the extent to which *scriptural* mediation could exist together with *ecclesial* mediation.[143] Söhngen attempted to approach the first question by constructing two philosophical models— the abstract-metaphysical and the concrete-historical—whose mutual complementarity became for him the key to the Catholic-Protestant debate as well as a kind of hermeneutic for disclosing the relationship between Scripture and dogma. Statements that had previously seemed irreconcilable could now be understood to be related. The justification and boundary of such a reconciliation of two modes of thought will, of course, have to be studied further; but, above all, there is opposed to such an emphasis on the link between salvation and a historical event the question of its reactualization [*Vergegenwärtigung*] (its "simultaneity", as Kierkegaard would say), which, as it happened, was being discussed at the same time from a different perspective in Catholic theology in Odo Casel's

---

[141] In *Die Einheit in der Theologie*, 347.

[142] Ibid., 348. For a classic discussion of the antithesis between salvation history and myth, see Gustav Stählin, "μῦθος", in ThWNT 4:769–803.

[143] This question is emphasized again in Oscar Cullmann, *Die Tradition als exegetisches, historisches und theologisches Problem* (Zurich: Zwingli, 1954).

study of mysteries. Here, paradoxically, the nonhistorical concept of mystery in the Greek mystery religions, that is, the cultic reactualization of the mythos, was in the foreground of attention, not the historical form of reactualization that the Old Testament offered with the concept of remembrance, of memory.[144]

II. The new front: eschatology as the antithesis of salvation history

1. Position of Bultmann and his followers

Acceptance of the concept of salvation history as a corrective for a view that was all too strongly oriented toward metaphysics is still operative in Catholic theology; its most significant fruit was the appearance, in the years after Vatican Council II, of a "salvation-historical dogmatics" that sought to apply the guidelines of salvation-historical thought to the whole range of Catholic dogmatics and that had its source, especially in German-speaking countries, in the collaboration of widely known scholars.[145] In the meantime, however, there had arisen in Protestant theology a new attitude toward salvation history that led to a direct reversal of its former position. This attitude, too, which derives from the theology of Rudolf Bultmann and has been elaborated in its details by Bultmann's followers, Vielhauer and Conzelmann,[146] can be traced to a certain extent to the impetus given by Karl Barth, who, by his radical counterpoising of God's

[144] Odo Casel even takes a decidedly negative attitude toward the Old Testament; cf. Theodor Filthaut, *Die Kontroverse über die Mysterienlehre* (Warendorf: Schnell, 1947). That may well be the crucial and not sufficiently recognized weakness in his theory. Söhngen's works on the theology of the mysteries (*Symbol und Wirklichkeit im Kultmysterium* [Bonn: Hanstein, 1937]; *Der Wesensaufbau des Mysteriums* [Bonn: Hanstein, 1938]) are linked to the theme of salvation history by way of the problem of analogy but do not carry the thought to its conclusion. Max Thurian, on the other hand, attempted to offer a theory of reactualization in terms of the Old Testament "memorial" in *Eucharistie* (Paris: Delachaux et Niestlé, 1959) without referring to Casel. The subject has been thoroughly treated by Louis Bouyer in *Eucharistie. Théologie et spiritualité de la prière eucharistique,* 2d ed. (Tournai: Desclée et Cie, 1968).

[145] *Mysterium Salutis. Grundriss heilsgeschichtlicher Dogmatik,* Johannes Feiner and Magnus Löhrer, eds., 5 vols. (Einsiedeln: Benziger, 1965–1976). On the basis of Rahner's thought, a theory of salvation history was presented by Adolf Darlap in 1:3–156, as the foundation of the whole series. Unfortunately, the editors did not succeed in maintaining a unified concept throughout. Almost the only evidence of it in the work as a whole is their preceding organizational schema, which often seems somewhat contrived.

[146] Ph. Vielhauer, "Zum 'Paulinismus' der Apostelgeschichte", in *Evangelische Theologie* 10 (1950–1951): 1–15; Hans Conzelmann, *Die Mitte der Zeit,* 3d ed. (Tübingen: Mohr, 1960). The strongest expression of the trend away from the idea of salvation history is undoubtedly the text by Franz Hesse, *Abschied von der Heilsgeschichte* (Zurich, 1971), which raises a blunt

word and all human efforts in the sphere of religion, was the first to point out the possibility of accepting in a theologically positive way the strongly eschatological interpretation of the message of Jesus that was initiated by J. Weiss and developed further by A. Schweitzer and of making it the nucleus of a contemporary expression of Christianity. "A Christianity that is not wholly, entirely and absolutely eschatology has wholly, entirely and absolutely nothing to do with Christ", Barth stated in the forceful language of his early career.[147] The consistent carrying out of this program, which led of necessity to the concentration of theology on a single theme, was reserved for Bultmann, for whom—in contrast to Barth—the question of reactualization, the problem of the "presentness" of the Christian message, became the crucial springboard of his whole theological effort, and who led his followers to a definite rejection of the idea of salvation history. It must be assumed here that the contents of Bultmann's theology are already known; our purpose is to review briefly those methodological points that indicate a connection with our theme.

We can say, then, that the first significant point to be discussed here is Bultmann's emphasis on the preeminence of word over event. It might even be maintained that the word, the kerygma, is the real salvation-event, the "eschatological event", that leads man from the alienation of his existence to its essence. This word is present wherever it makes itself heard; it is the always-present possibility of salvation for mankind. It is clear that, in the last analysis, this primacy of the word that, as such, can always be spoken and thus can be posited as always present, cancels the notion of a continuous series of salvation-historical events; salvation is to a large extent detemporalized just as the notion of the eschatological is expressly divested of all temporal determinatives. With this, another point makes its appearance: the distinction between historical conditioning and history: from a theological perspective, the event-context is neutralized as "historical conditioning"; as a word-event, on the other hand, theologically meaningful "history" is withdrawn from the objectively determinable realism of historical events and moved into the nonobjectifiable.[148]

---

war cry against the concept of salvation history. In the same vein, see G. Klein, "Bibel und Heilsgeschichte. Die Fragwürdigket einer Idee", in *Zeitschrift für die neutestamentliche Wissenschaft und die Kunde der älteren Kirche* 62 (1971): 1–47.

[147] Karl Barth, *Der Römerbrief* (Bern, 1919); quoted here from the 2d ed. (Munich: Kaiser, 1922), 298. On the whole subject of the reversal with regard to eschatology, see Folke Holmström, *Das eschatologische Denken der Gegenwart* (Gütersloh: Bertelsmann, 1936); François-Marie Braun, *Neues Licht auf die Kirche* (Cologne: Benziger, 1946), 103–32.

[148] Cf. the conclusion of the classic article "Neues Testament und Mythos", in *Kerygma und Mythos,* vol. 1, 3d ed. (Hamburg: Reich, 1954), 46ff. See also Oscar Cullmann's sharp

This view of Christian reality led logically to a division in the canon itself that has since had a highly paradoxical effect on the controversial positions in theology. Paul and John emerge as the authentic interpreters of Jesus' message because, from the time-conditioned form of his temporal proclamation of the approaching eschaton, they have released the true meaning that appears in the Pauline doctrine of the justification of the sinner and, in another way, in John's concept of the eschaton as always present. By way of contrast, the presentation of Jesus' message in the framework of salvation-history, as in Luke, could appear only as a misinterpretation of what is essential in that message—a misinterpretation in which the outer rim of the temporal becomes the center but the true center is deeply hidden and forgotten. The salvation-historical view of the third Gospel is now appraised as the beginning of the lapse from the eschatological attitude of primitive Christianity into Catholicism, into the continuation—also institutionally perpetuated—of the history of God's covenant with men.[149] This means, however, that the positions are exactly the opposite of what they were in the first phase of the debate: if the lapse from salvation history into metaphysics was then branded as the Catholic error, it is now the preoccupation with a continuous historical line that progresses by way of a determinable sequence of events that is regarded as the Catholic misinterpretation of the original intention of the New Testament. Instead of the antithesis between salvation history and metaphysics, there arises the antithesis between salvation history and eschatology, which is based on an exactly opposite evaluation of the phenomenon "salvation history". But the attitude to Scripture and, above all, to the historical valence of that to which it bears witness has also changed. The ecclesial-critical meaning of Scripture, which salvation-historical thought had already exposed more or less incisively, did, in fact, continue to exist and was even considerably heightened insofar as the actuality of the individual word-event was opposed to the continuity of

---

criticism of this viewpoint in *Heil als Geschichte* (Tübingen: Mohr, 1965). [For an English translation of this work, see Oscar Cullmann, *Salvation in History,* trans. Sidney G. Sowers and editorial staff of SCM Press (London: SCM Press, 1967). (Trans.)] In the meantime, this rejection of hsitorical reality has had what can only be called a disastrous effect, especially in the realm of catechetical literature, as, for instance, when, in a work such as *Jesuskurs* by B. Blasius and K. H. Ohlig (Munich-Düsseldorf, 1973), the Resurrection tradition is traced back to a conversation among the apostles. The transfer of these attitudes to the catechetical realm was fundamentally revealed in Hubertus Halbfas, *Fundamentalkatechetik* (Düsseldorf: Patmos, 1968).

[149] Cf. the studies by Vielhauer and Conzelmann that are mentioned in n. 146 above; see also the contributions by Käsemann on the subject of early Catholicism, in *Exegetische Versuche,* 1:214–23; 2:239–52.

the salvation-historical concept. But while the defenders of salvation history had assumed a position practically in line with old Protestant Scripturism, one was, nevertheless, more reminded of Luther's *"urgemus Christum contra scripturam"*.[150] Concentration on the word forced the events into almost total meaninglessness. The dominance of the problem of reactualization, which we have already seen as operative in the background, of necessity brought with it a new attitude toward the historical: the basic problem of interpretation for theology is precisely the reactualization, not the historical form, of what took place in the past; the latter can now be freely investigated as a theologically neutral entity and has, in fact, lost its preoccupation with what is immediately oriented to existence.[151]

2. Catholic approaches to the problem

It was inevitable that the twofold liberation thus gained with regard to the pressing questions of the modern spirit should be regarded by Catholic theologians, too, as offering the possibility of a new approach: for one thing, the problem of the "present-ness" of the Christian message seemed to have been solved by such a view; Christian faith seemed to have been recalled from a distant past into the midst of today; for another thing, they felt free to leave historical criticism to its own devices without having to worry about its theological implications. The promise of such a solution must have been all the more attractive to Catholic theologians because the accommodation of the metaphysical approach to the basic position of the salvation-historical concept had never been really successful and because they had never been able to free themselves of a certain uneasiness with regard to the claim of the historical in theology, of which they seemed, in an unexpected way, to be able to free themselves by retreating from mere history into existential history, leaving the former to the historians as an exercise ground that had now ceased to be dangerous. The philosophi-cal Thomistic interpretation had very early sought to build a bridge from Thomas to Heidegger: nothing was more desirable than to transform his metaphysical position by interpretation into an eschatological-existential one, thereby establishing an unexpected consensus of Bultmann and Thomas against salvation history and, at the same time, reducing *ad absur-*

---

[150] Cf. on this question Paul Hacker, *Das Ich im Glauben bei Martin Luther* (Graz: Styria, 1966), 65–96, esp. 68–72.

[151] Bultmann's late work, *Das Verhältnis der urchristlichen Christusbotschaft zum historischen Jesus* (Heidelberg: Winter, 1960), is typical of this development, as is the development of his thought by his disciples H. Braun and H. Conzelmann. The criticism of this position from within Bultmann's circle by Ernst Käsemann in *Exegetische Versuche*, 1:187–214; 2:31–68, is especially important.

dum all those attempts that had struggled to interpret Thomas himself as the philosopher of salvation history.[152]

Did not Thomas himself also make the distinction between history and historicity that is being made today? As evidence, one might point to the question in traditional Scholastic form: "Utrum obiectum fidei sit aliquid complexum per modum enuntiabilis", which can be traced by way of Peter Lombard to Hugo of St. Victor, who, in turn, borrowed it from a text of St. Augustine.[153] The content of the question stems from Augustine's proposition that faith is at all times—from Abel to the last of the elect—always one and the same faith and that its temporal determination is, consequently, completely extrinsic; it is concerned with the realities of salvation as such, independent of the temporal factor.[154] Among medieval theologians, this concept led to the objection that, if that were the case, the Jews could not be blamed for supposing that the Incarnation was yet to take place, nor could the Gnostics be blamed for supposing that the Resurrection had already occurred. But if neither supposition is correct, then precisely that which occurred in time must be, as such, the substance of faith.[155] This is not the place to review the complicated distinctions with which this line of reasoning was countered; it will suffice to point to the formula with which Bonaventure—in complete accord, here, with the mind of Thomas Aquinas—resolved the question: ". . . explicatio accidit fidei nec mutat essentiam fidei, sic et variatio temporis determinat, non variat fidem. . . ."[156] We might well

---

[152] For an attempt to present Thomas Aquinas from the standpoint of salvation history, see Ghislain Lafont, *Structures et méthode dans la Somme théologique de St. Thomas d'Aquin* (Paris: Desclée de Brouwer, 1961); the interpretations by Congar and Schillebeeckx are in the same vein. For a very enlightening critical discussion of the problem of salvation history in Thomas, see Gustave Martelet, "Theologie und Heilsökonomie in der Christologie der 'Tertia' ", in *Gott in Welt,* Festgabe für Karl Rahner, 2 vols. (Freiburg: Herder, 1964), 2:3–42. See also, M. Seckler, *Das Heil in der Geschichte* (Munich, 1964). For a more "existential" interpretation of Thomas, see Gisbert Greshake *Historie wird Geschichte* (Essen: Ludgerus, 1964). Because of the increasing radicalization and dehistoricizing of theology, attempts to interpret Thomas in this way have become less and less numerous.

[153] St. Thomas Aquinas, *Summa theologiae* [henceforth ST] 31 (New York: McGraw-Hill, 1974), II-II q 1 a 2, 10. On the prehistory of the question, cf. Martin Grabmann, *Die Geschichte der scholastischen Methode* 2 (Freiburg: Herder, 1911): 276–79, as well as the information in the *Scholion* in the Quaracchi edition of the works of St. Bonaventure: St. Bonaventure, *Sententiarum Liber III,* d 24 a 1 q 3 c, n. 6: "Utrum fides sit circa complexum, an circa incomplexum", *Opera omnia* 3 (Ad claras Aquas: ex typographia Collegii S. Bonaventurae, 1887): 514–15.

[154] Cf., for example, St. Augustine, "Retractionum Libri II", lib. 1, caput 13, 3, PL 32:603: "Nam res ipsa, quae nunc christiana religio nuncupatur, erat apud antiquos, nec defuit ab initio generis humani, quousque ipse Christus veniret in carne, unde vera religio, quae jam erat, coepit appellari christiana."

[155] The arguments are given in great detail in Bonaventure, 515, col. c.

[156] Ibid., 516, cols. a and b.

say that this is one of the crucial texts for illuminating the way in which medieval theologians—whose Augustinian-Platonic bent is plainly seen here despite their Scholasticism—determined the relationship between faith and history. History was consigned to the realm of *explicatio,* which, in turn, was subsumed under the concept *accidere* and thus removed from the realm of "substance", only to be then assigned, under the pressure of biblical evidence, to *perfectio,* the promised fullness of faith. Granted, there are certain points of contact between the way in which the interrelationship of faith and history is treated here and in Bultmann; nor is the deep-rooted difference in the total concept in terms of which the individual statements are to be read any less clear. But that seemed relatively unimportant at a time when the theology of controversy was being transformed into a theology of concord. The proffered liberation from the burden of history seemed more important than exactness of historical detail. Thus it almost seems, at the moment, as though the idea of salvation history, which has only recently made its appearance in Catholic theology, will soon be extinguished. In fact, it was not really pursued in the form in which Cullmann understood it but was converted almost at once into the new guise of a theology of hope, which, in turn, quickly assumed concrete form as political theology, theology of liberation, theology of revolution. Bultmann's existential formalism was, in fact, abandoned, but, though it-self unable to survive because of its total contentual hollowness, it had prepared the way for the new concept by its relativization of past history and, ipso facto, of its Christian content. With political "theologies", theology as theology has been abandoned, the self-destruction of theology has been accomplished. At the same time, however, its fundamental question has been raised anew, for it is obvious that it can exist neither on an exclusively salvation-historical nor on a strongly existential base.

3. Preamble to further questioning

We have reached the point now at which there arises with critical urgency the question of the future course of Catholic theology. Two facts emerge clearly from what has already been said. First, it should be clear from the synopsis above that, for pursuing the dialogue with Protestant theology, Catholic theology requires that there be, despite all divisions and antitheses, a common theological motive; that, whether they accept or reject each other's views, the two sides be sensitive and responsive to each other. Second, it should likewise be clear that Catholic theology must not regard its role in this dialogue to be that of trying to agree with whatever is currently the strongest position of the other side but must rather look, in its own way, for whatever common ground there may be and, in doing so, not be afraid to learn from its partner.

But how are we to increase our understanding of the double antithesis *metaphysics-salvation history* and *salvation history-eschatology* that we have just uncovered and which contains in itself the basic decision as to the course theology should take? A further comment seems in order: we must neither over- nor underestimate the value of theological programs. The formula "explicatio accidit fidei", in which we located the medieval formulation of the relationship between faith and history, offers a very extensive program; for medieval theology, nevertheless, history was able to play not just an accidental but a far more strongly essential role with regard to faith than could have been deduced on the basis of this program. None other than Thomas, the metaphysicist, who, in one respect, brought about the rejection of the salvation-historical concept, especially as it was elaborated by the Victorines, took the first critical step toward the age of history by replacing the hitherto basic classic rule of hermeneutics: "Quid credas docet allegoria" by its direct opposite: "Ex solo sensu litterali potest trahi argumentum".[157] The change in hermeneutic method, the revolution in the approach to theology, that is positively and negatively (yes, negatively!) indicated in the antithesis of the two formulas, has never been sufficiently studied. Similar inconsequences, as we have shown, exist also today. Fortunately, theology has always been richer in its achievements than in its programs.

III. *Basic prerequisite for an answer: the question as to the core of Christianity*

But let us be done with preambles. It is time to take the first step toward the problem itself. How can we decide between the antitheses we have encountered? In that context, we must first recall that the antithetical positions we have discovered always rest on a basic concept of what is essentially Christian—what is the "core of the gospel". According to Cullmann, the decisive factor is a series of events that have been brought about by God and into which I incorporate myself by faith. Faith, then, is essentially the fitting-of-oneself into a history that precedes the individual, into which the believer enters and which brings him thereby to his mission and to salvation. According to Bultmann, the decisive factor in faith is the sense of eschatological existence, that is, it is a concept that Bultmann

---

[157] Cf. the Scholastic maxim of Nicholas of Lyra: "Littera gesta docet, quid credas allegoria, Moralis quid agas, quo tendas anagogia (quoted in the Quaracchi edition of Bonaventure's works, 5:205, n. 5). I have written at some length about Bonaventure in my book *Die Geschichtstheologie des hl. Bonaventura* (Munich, 1959); see, for example, 63ff. and

himself understood as a new formulation of the Pauline doctrine of the *iustificatio impii* that Luther had made the core of his teaching. In modern times, *Catholic* theology has consistently rejected the Protestant quest for the core of the gospel—a quest that has become visible to us here as the background of the present problem—as an attempt to pick and choose and has opposed to the concern about the focus of the *one* gospel the breadth of the *whole* faith. Nevertheless, the question now being asked was by no means strange to Catholic theology even in its primitive stage when the Catholic mode of interpretation had to prove itself the authentic way of the Christian message as opposed to that of Gnosis; the *regula fidei*—the κανὼν τῆς πίστεως—was formulated as the Christian answer to this question.[158]

But just what does this canon say? If, today, we were to ask Catholic Christians what they consider the absolutely crucial constituent of the Catholic faith, the most frequently heard answer would be a reference to the divinity of Christ, that is, to the christological confession in the form given it by the Council of Chalcedon some 1500 years ago. The core for which we are seeking would lie, then, in the statement: Jesus, the man, is God. If we were to stop here, we would have an "is", an ontological statement, as the core of Christianity, and it may indeed be said that the theology of St. Thomas—in fact, the Catholic theology of West and East—circles around this axis. Does that mean a No to the historical understanding of Christianity? To draw such a conclusion would be to ignore the fact that the "is" of Chalcedon includes an event: the Incarnation of God, the σάρξ ἐγένετο that presumes as the ground of its possibility the twofold ὁμοούσιος of Chalcedon—ὁμοούσιος τῷ πατρί and ὁμοούσιος ἡμῖν—and the theological metaphysics expressed therein. It would be to overlook the fact that the Chalcedonian ὁμοούσιος is intended to be but an interpretation of the σάρξ ἐγένετο and to ensure its significance in world history against the Docetic theology of interpretation, in which reality is reduced to the interpreting word so that we can speak of it as though it were reality, although it is in fact only appearance. It would be, finally, to overlook the existential meaning of the statement that is the actual driving force behind the formation of christological dogma, which is itself motivated by the question: What depth of reality does the word that is proclaimed to us by Christ actually have?

---

the further bibliographical references suggested there. The quotation from Thomas Aquinas is from ST I q 1 a 10 ad 1. Cf., in this connection, the study by Maximino Arias-Reyero, *Thomas von Aquin als Exeget* (Einsiedeln: Johannes, 1971).

[158] Joseph Ratzinger, *Das Problem der Dogmengeschichte in der Sicht der katholischen Theologie*, esp. 20 and further bibliographical references. In the present work, cf. especially Part One, Chapter 1, Section 1B and Chapter 2, Sections 1B and 1C.

All this makes it clear that we cannot stop at the confession of Chalcedon, for it is to be understood only in the context of the earlier confessions that it attempts to interpret, just as these confessions, in turn, cannot be read apart from the formulation of Chalcedon and the question that is irrevocably raised there. As the antecedent core of every Christian *confessio*, as the root of the formation of the *regula fidei*, there offers itself that original *confessio* in the New Testament that we find, as it were, in brief form in the name of Jesus Christ: Jesus is the Christ, or, translated into its Hellenistic form: Jesus is the *Kyrios*, the Lord, in which form the Old Testament background of the *Kyrios*-title, which is a paraphrase of the name of God, already affords a distant anticipation of Chalcedon. Jesus is the Christ—again we stand before an "is"-statement that, we must grant, bears in itself more clearly than the Chalcedonian formula the reference to an event: to the event of investiture in the office of king, of the "anointing" that makes this Jesus the "Anointed One", the Christ of God.

Realization of this fact advances us another step and enables us to reach, as it were, the last level of excavation by asking: When and where, according to New Testament belief, did Jesus' "anointing", his installation as king, take place? When it spoke of "anointing", the theology of the Fathers of the Church was usually referring to the Incarnation—which corresponds to the model of Chalcedonian thought as we have just seen it;[159] Gnosis, on the one hand, insisted on the baptism of Jesus as the crucial event and based its Docetic—or, as we would say today, its phenomenological—Christology upon it.[160] Although there are biblical foundations for both concepts, they do not reveal the answer of the first witnesses of the faith. It is, however, clearly visible in the early Christian type of sermon that Luke has preserved for us in the Pentecost sermon of St. Peter. In its most crucial section, this sermon is the good tidings of the Resurrection of the Crucified One and draws from the fact of the Resurrection the following conclusion: "For this reason the whole House of Israel can be certain that God has made this Jesus whom you crucified both Lord and Christ" (Acts 2:36). The same fact is even more trenchantly expressed in the ancient confessional formula that is preserved for us in Romans 1:3–4,[161] which says of Jesus that ". . . according to the human nat-

---

[159] Cf. H. Mühlen, *Der Heilige Geist als Person* (Münster: Aschendorff, 1963), 175–76.

[160] Cf. Jean Daniélou and H. J. Marrou, *Geschichte der Kirche* I (Einsiedeln, 1963): 85; Johannes Betz, *Die Eucharistie in der Zeit der griechischen Väter* 2:1 (Freiburg: Herder, 1961): 193ff. Where it does not continue to be method but becomes a point of view, the exclusion of the ontological question, as happens in the phenomenological method, leads of necessity to a restriction to the φαίνεσθαι and hence to a construction that is close to Docetism.

[161] Cf., in this context, the thorough study by Heinrich Schlier, "Eine christologische Credo-Formel der römischen Gemeinde", in *Der Geist und die Kirche. Exegetische Aufsätze und Vorträge* (Freiburg: Herder, 1980), 56–69; see also, Heinrich Schlier, "Die Anfänge des

ure he took, [he] was a descendant of David: . . . in the order of the spirit, the spirit of holiness that was in him, [he] was proclaimed Son of God in all his power through his Resurrection from the dead". The raising of Jesus from the dead is portrayed as his elevation over all the powers of this world, including the hitherto invincible power of death, and as his investiture in the eschatological kingdom of God, toward which all the hope of the Old Testament is directed. The sentence "Jesus has risen" thus expresses that primitive experience on which all Christian faith is grounded; all further confessions are interpretations of this original one, including the confession of Jesus as the Messiah, of the "Christ-ness" of Jesus, however strongly an understanding of the previously uncomprehended message of the historical Jesus as it is later remembered may be operative here. "Jesus has risen"—this sentence is thus, above all, the true *articulus stantis et cadentis ecclesiae* by which the structure of faith and theology are chiefly to be determined.[162]

With this statement we seem to be again at the heart of the conflict with which we started, since the Resurrection is understood by one group as a historical event and as part of the long line of salvation history but by the other as the eschatological event that transcends all history, that leaves history shattered in its wake and is present in the *kerygma* as the totally other. Although the futility of expecting an unqualified interpretation where there is question of what is ultimate and essential has thus again been confirmed, I believe, nonetheless, that, in the last part of these reflections, I can draw from the doctrinal core we have defined a few guidelines for the course theology should take between salvation history and metaphysics, between salvation history and eschatology.

IV. *Attempt at an answer*

1. From what has been said, it is clear that all Christian theology, if it is to be true to its origin, must be first and foremost a theology of Resurrection. It must be a theology of Resurrection before it is a theology of the justification of the sinner; it must be a theology of Resurrection before it is a theology of the metaphysical Sonship of God. It can be a theology of the

---

christologischen Credo", in Bernhard Welte, ed., *Zur Frühgeschichte der Christologie* (Freiburg: Herder, 1970), 13–58. Cf. also Part One, Chapter One, Section 1A in the present work: "What Constitutes Christian Faith Today?"

[162] Willi Marxsen's attempt to prove that belief in the Resurrection is a dispensable fabrication founders on the unequivocal contrary evidence of the exegetical findings. Cf. Jacob Kremer, *Das älteste Zeugnis von der Auferstehung* (Stuttgart: Katholisches Bibelwerk,

Cross but only as and within the framework of a theology of Resurrection. Its first and primordial statement is the good tidings that the power of death, the one constant of history, has, in a single instance, been broken by the power of God and that history has thus been imbued with an entirely new hope. In other words, the core of the gospel consists in the good tidings of the Resurrection and, consequently, in the good tidings of God's action, which precedes all human doing.

This seems to me an important insight that will repay further investigation. For if it is true that the *prae* of God's action is significant for theology, that faith in an *actio Dei* is antecedent to all other declarations of faith, then the primacy of history over metaphysics, over all theologies of being and existence, becomes immediately obvious. It thus becomes obvious also that the concept of God is removed from the realm of a mere οὐσία. I believe it was here that the definitive boundary between the biblical and the Greek concept of God became obfuscated, that this obfuscation was the crux of the repeated patristic attempts to combine Greek thought with biblical faith and that from this arose for Christian theology a task that is still far from being accomplished. Decisive for the Greek concept of God was the belief in God as a pure and changeless being of whom, consequently, no action could be predicated; his utter changelessness meant that he was completely self-contained and referred wholly to himself without any relationship to what was changeable.[163] For the biblical God, on the other hand, it is precisely relationship and action that are the essential marks; creation and revelation are the two basic statements about him, and when revelation is fulfilled in the Resurrection, it is thus confirmed once again that he is not just one who is timeless but also one who is above time, whose existence is known to us only through his action.

The *prae* of God's action: this means not just the preeminence of history over metaphysics but also the rejection of a purely existential version of the gospel message—quite simply because the gospel message means the primacy of the "in itself" over the "for me", because it excludes the intermingling of the "in itself" with the "for me" that was introduced by Luther and reached its utmost radicality in existential theology; that was

---

1966), esp. 115–31; Willi Marxsen, G. Delling, H. G. Geyer, *Die Bedeutung der Auferstehungsbotschaft für den Glauben an Jesus Christus* (Tübingen, 1966).

[163] Cf., for example, Aristotle, Πολ. ἡ 3, in *Aristotelis opera,* ex recensione Immanuelis Bekkeris 2 (Berlin: Gruyter, 1960): 1325 b, 29: οὐκ εἰσὶν αὐτῷ πράξεις ἐξωτερικαί; and Μετ. 7, in ibid., 1074 b, 25–35: . . . δῆλον τοίνυν ὅτι τὸ θειότατον καὶ τιμιώτατον νοεῖ, καὶ οὐ μεταβάλλει. εἰς χεῖρον γὰρ ἡ μεταβολή . . . αὐτὸν ἄρα νοεῖ, εἴπερ ἐστὶ τὸ κράτιστον, καὶ ἔστιν ἡ νόησις νοήσεως νόησις.

eventually forced to conclude that there is no "in itself" outside the "for me", so that, ultimately, the existential interpretation becomes identified with what is interpreted. To seek another independent reality behind it would be foolish objectivism.[164] God acted: this was said before anything was said about man, about his sin, about his search for a gracious God.

Thus the *prae* of God's action means, ultimately, that *actio* is antecedent to *verbum,* reality to the tidings of it. In other words, the level of reality of the revelation-event is deeper than that of the proclamation-event, which seeks to interpret God's action in human language. Precisely this is the origin of the sacramental principle, the reason why the word of God, which is also action, must be received by man in words *and* signs.

2. If we were able to establish, as our first point, that the Resurrection is an action of God, so now we must extend this statement by saying as our second point: the Resurrection is an eschatological action of God. No other word in the language of theology today has assumed such a wide range of meanings as the word "eschatological"; hence we must immediately ask ourselves: What does it mean in this context when we designate the action of God as eschatological? The answer must be given in several stages. The starting point is the fact that Israel awaited the awakening of the dead as the end of history, that is, quite literally as the *eschaton,* as the final action of God. Using the stylistic devices of the apocalyptic writers, therefore, the Evangelists, and especially Matthew, described Christ's Cross and Resurrection as the final hour; they wanted to make it plain that this was not just any resurrection, such as an Elias or some other miracle-worker might have brought about, but a resurrection of a kind never before known, after which death would be no more.[165] That means also, then, that in this awakening the realm of history has been transcended, that he who arose from the dead did not return, as anyone else might have done, to a this-worldly history but stands above it, though by no means without relationship to it.

Thus the Resurrection cannot be a historical event in the same sense as the Crucifixion is. For that matter, there is no account that depicts it as such, nor is it circumscribed in time otherwise than by the eschatological-symbolical expression "the third day".[166] On the one hand, it belongs

---

[164] On the subject of Luther's "pro me" and the surprising anticipation of "existential interpretation" that is included in it, see Paul Hacker, *Das Ich im Glauben bei Martin Luther* (Graz: Styria, 1966). Oscar Cullmann (*Das Heil als Geschichte,* 97), has attempted to express the ultimate form of existential theology in these words: "We should not say: Christ is Christ 'for me' because he is Christ. We should say, rather, that he is Christ because he is Christ 'for me'."

[165] Günther Bornkamm, "σείω σεισμός", in ThWNT 7:195–99, esp. 198–99.

[166] Cf. here the critical analyses by Jacob Kremer (see n. 162), 38, 47–48, 52, 53; and by Karl Lehmann, *Auferweckt.*

intrinsically to the totality and ultimate greatness of this event that it is "eschatological", that is, that it transcends history; on the other hand, it belongs just as intrinsically to its inherent importance that it also touches upon history, that is, that this person who was dead is now no longer dead; he—really he himself and as such—is eternally alive in his individuality and uniqueness. Thus, it belongs, at the same time, to this event that it both reaches above history and is founded and anchored in history. Indeed, we could almost say that the definitive transformation that eschatology underwent by virtue of the Christian belief in the Resurrection is its transposition into history. For late Judaic expectation, eschatology lay at the end of history. To believe in the Resurrection of Jesus means, on the contrary, to believe in the *eschaton in* history, in the historicity of God's eschatological action.

3. If what we have said thus far is correct, it means that, as God's eschatological action, the Resurrection has both a cosmic and a future-oriented character and that the corresponding Christian faith is a faith of hope in the fullness of a promise that encompasses the whole cosmos. That means, in turn, a rejection of the individualization of man, the ordering of the "I" to the "we", the orientation of Christianity to the future as much as to the past. In less academic language, we might say: Christology is concerned not with just freeing the individual *qua* individual from his sins in a way that can then only be described in a highly qualified manner; it is most deeply concerned with the future of man, which can be accomplished only as the future of the whole human race. It is concerned with the future of the whole human race, which can become itself only by rising above itself. In Scholastic as well as in patristic theology, Christology has two basic points: one in the past, which finds its expression in the doctrine of original sin; the other in the future, which has its critical constant in the biblical concept of Christ as the "last man", that is, as the revelation and the beginning of the definitive mode of human existence.[167] If we can say, with reference to the first, that Christ is necessary in order that the burden of the past—original guilt—may be

---

[167] The second basic point is to be found in all those theologians who reject the Scotist idea of the *praedestinatio absoluta Christi*. It appears regularly, for instance, in the interpretation of Gen 2:24 and Eph 5:32, in which even these theologians who otherwise see a strong relationship between the Incarnation of Christ and man's fall into sin reveal a different view of Christology. Cf., for instance, Thomas Aquinas, ST, II-II q 2 a 7 c: . . . Nam ante statum peccati homo habuit explicitam fidem de Christi incarnatione secundum quod ordinabatur ad consummationem gloriae: non autem secundum quod ordinabatur ad liberationem a peccato per passionem et resurrectionem, quia homo non fuit praescius peccati futuri. Videtur autem incarnationis Christi praescius fuisse per hoc quod dixit: Propter hoc relinquet homo patrem et matrem et adhaerebit uxori suae, ut habetur Gen 2:24; et hoc Apostolus, ad Ephesios 5:32 dicit sacramentum magnum esse in Christo et Ecclesia; quod quidem sacramentum non est

overcome, we must say with reference to the second that Christ is necessary in order that the human race may come into its future, which it is not able to do unaided. This second point does not cancel the first; it gives it its context, the place from which it is to be understood. It does not mean that sin is regarded as trivial or is minimized in its terrible power to destroy—against such an interpretation there stands the Cross of Christ, the humanly effected death of God as the shocking revelation of the sinister destructive power of human wickedness, of that perversion of human justice and piety in the name of which Jesus was condemned to death. But it means, also, that God conquers man's past—conquers sin—by calling him into the future—into Christ. And it means, certainly, that any theology is ultimately to be rejected as inadequate that confines salvation to a pure, nonobjectifiable subjectivity, when, in reality, it is precisely a liberation from isolation into subjectivity in the service of the whole.

All this can also be regarded from another standpoint. The fact that the Christian *eschaton* already takes place *in* history rather than just at its end considerably alters the nature of the eschatological as such. Cullmann speaks of a separation that thus occurs between mid-time and end-time and emphasizes the continuing line of salvation history that results therefrom and stands henceforth under the double sign of "already" and "not yet".[168] More important, however, than this linearity or the wavelike movement that represented Cullmann's later concept is the changed understanding of salvation that is inherent in the separation between middle and end, τέλος and πέρας, as Daniélou expresses it.[169] This separation signifies at one and the same time the Christian *aporia* and the Christian answer. The Christian *aporia*, because this separation says, in fact, that, from a worldly point of view, nothing has been changed, that Christian salvation does not occur as a change of relationships; but even this appearance that Christianity makes no difference, this embarrassment of faith before the world's reckoning, is a Christian answer that directs man, beyond all his relationships, to what is essentially himself. Perhaps a

---

credibile primum hominem ingorasse.—The emphasis shifted in the course of the debate about *praedestinatio absoluta* so that now the metaphysical (*praedestinatio absoluta*) and the salvation-historical ("*propter nostram salutem*") constructions are mutually exclusive, and the latter is confined to the purely retrospective understanding of the fall into sin. The whole question needs further and more exhaustive investigation. Some comments are to be found in Hans Urs von Balthasar, *Karl Barth* (Cologne: Kegner, 1951), 337. The subject is treated more thoroughly in W. Haubst, *Vom Sinn der Menschwerdung. Cur Deus homo* (Munich, 1969). Important aspects of the question are also found in V. Marcolino, *Das Alte Testament in der Heilsgeschichte* (Munich, 1970).

[168] See his two salvation-historical texts: *Christus und die Zeit*, 2d ed. (1948), and *Heil als Geschichte* (1965). Cf. Joseph Ratzinger, *Eschatologie* (Regensburg, 1977), 49–64.

[169] Jean Daniélou, "Christologie et eschatologie" (see above, n. 137), 275.

theology of salvation history should regard it as its primary task to inquire into the inner form of this separation into middle and end and, thereby, to address the question that is so worrisome to existential theology.

4. With this, it is already apparent that the Resurrection of Jesus Christ from the dead, which, as God's action, is antecedent to every theology, does not insist on an empty "in–itself–ness" but is oriented to the center of human existence. Let us attempt to reflect again, briefly, on this existential aspect of God's action, which is not accidental but *essential* to its cosmic and eschatological character. The Resurrection is the reawakening of him who had first died on the Cross; its "hour" is the Passover of the Jews, the remembrance of the leading of the House of Israel out of slavery. Jesus' Cross and Resurrection are seen by faith in the context of the inner meaning of the Passover, as the ultimate Passover in which what has always been meant by that is seen for the first time in its true light. All salvation history is gathered here, as it were, in the one point of this ultimate Passover that thus includes and interprets salvation history, just as it is itself interpreted and illumined by salvation history. For it is evident now that this whole history is likewise an exodus history:[170] a history that begins with the call to Abraham to go out from his country—and this going-out-from has been, ever since, its characteristic movement. It attains its deepest significance in the Passover of Jesus Christ: in the ἀγάπη εἰς τέλος, in the radical love that became a total exodus from himself, a going-out-from-himself toward the other even to the radical delivery of himself to death so that it can be explained in the words: "I am going away and shall return" (Jn 14:28)—by going, I come. The "living opening through the curtain", as the epistle to the Hebrews explains the Lord's going-away on the Cross (Heb 10:20), reveals itself in this way as the true exodus that is meant by all the exoduses of history. Thus we see how the theology of Resurrection gathers all salvation history within itself and concentrates it on its existence-oriented meaning so that, in a very literal sense, it becomes a theology of existence, a theology of *ex-sistere,* of that exodus by which the human individual goes out from himself and through which alone he can find himself. In this movement of *ex-sistere,* faith and love are ultimately united—the deepest significance of each is that *Exi,* that call to transcend and sacrifice the *I* that is the basic law of the history of God's covenant with man and, ipso facto, the truly basic law of all human existence.[171]

A point seems to become visible here at which salvation history and

---

[170] Jürgen Moltmann has pursued this idea with great energy in *Theologie der Hoffnung.*

[171] Cf. Joseph Ratzinger, "Gratia praesupponit naturam", in Joseph Ratzinger and Heinrich Fries, *Einsicht und Glaube,* Festschrift für Gottlieb Söhngen, 2d ed. (Freiburg: Herder, 1963), 151–65, esp. 164–65.

eschatology, the theology of the great acts of God in history and the theology of existence, can coincide if they are willing to reflect deeply on themselves and to open themselves to this reflection. God's action is, precisely in the objectivity of its "in-itself-ness", not a hopeless objectivity, but the true formula of human existence, which has its "in-itself-ness" outside itself and can find its true center only in *ex-sistere,* in going-out-from itself. It is also no empty past but that "perfect tense" that is therefore man's true "present tense" because it is always antecedent to it, always at the same time its promise and its future. Thus it implies, of necessity, that "is" that faith soon formulated explicitly: Jesus *is* Christ, God *is* man. Hence man's future means being one with God and so being one with mankind, which will be a single, final man in the manifold unity that is created by the exodus of love. God "is" man—it is in this formula that the whole greatness of the Easter reality has first been fully apprehended and has become, from a passing point in history, its axis, which bears us all.[172]

[172] In view of the fundamental meaning of this "is", I would stress more strongly today than I have in these pages the irreplaceability and preeminence of the ontological aspect and, therefore, of metaphysics as the basis of any history. Precisely as a confession of Jesus Christ, Christian faith—and in this it is completely loyal to the faith of Abraham—is faith in a living God. The fact that the first article of faith forms the basis of all Christian belief includes, theologically, the basic character of the ontological statements and the indispensability of the metaphysical, that is, of the Creator God who *is* before all becoming. Cf. on this subject my *Einführung in das Christentum,* 84–124; *Der Gott Jesu Christi* (Munich, 1976), 22–23 and 30–40; in the present work, see especially Part One, Chapter One, Section 2b and Part Three, Chapter One, Section A.

PART TWO

FORMAL PRINCIPLES OF CHRISTIANITY IN THE ECUMENICAL DISPUTE

GENERAL ORIENTATION WITH REGARD TO THE ECUMENICAL DISPUTE ABOUT THE FORMAL PRINCIPLES OF FAITH

A. The Ecumenical Situation—Orthodoxy, Catholicism and Protestantism

Anyone who wants to make a prognosis for the future of ecumenism must first clarify what he understands by ecumenism, that is, how he sees the division of Christianity and what model of unity he has in mind. It seems to me that, among the incalculable number of divisions by which Christianity is torn, there are two basic types to which two different models of unity correspond. We encounter the first type in the divisions in the ancient Church between Chalcedonian and non-Chalcedonian churches; it is also typical of the split between East and West, although ecclesial differences of a hitherto unknown radicality played a role there. We encounter the second type in the divisions that have been formed in the wake of the reform movements of the sixteenth century.

The basic historical types of division in the Church

Let us attempt to analyze the two types in somewhat greater detail so that we may know what models of unity are appropriate to them and, thus, the hopes as well as the obstacles for ecumenism today. The split between the Chalcedonian and pre-Chalcedonian churches concerned the confession of Jesus Christ and was thus obviously central in nature: where there is no unity in confessing Christ, there can also be no unity with regard to the sacrament of Christ's presence, and thus the Body of the Lord is rent. We should note, however, that this confessional split refers only to a very recondite point in the conceptual elucidation of the mystery of Christ, for both sides are united in their acceptance of the Council of Nicaea as well as in confessing the consubstantiality of the Son with the Father and the Incarnation of God in Jesus. But this unity in accepting Nicaea assumes the unity of ecclesial and doctrinal structure that underlay Nicaea. It means

---

This lecture, which was delivered in Graz in 1976, is purposely reprinted here in its original form because, precisely in that form, it has meaning for the current dialogue about the "recognition" of the *Confessio Augustana*.

unity not only with regard to a particular point but unity in the way in which the Church was formed from the word of Jesus and of the apostles, in the way in which Christianity was historically fashioned. This means that, along with Scripture, the Church that came into existence from and in Scripture is also truly and irrevocably accepted, in the basic form in which she had developed before Nicaea, as a vessel of the word. It belongs to this basic form that the bishops, by virtue of their sacramental consecration and the ecclesial tradition they received with it, personify the Church's unity with her source. In other words, that basic factor that has been expressed since the second century in the concept of the *successio apostolica,* the apostolic succession, belongs intrinsically to this structure. This means, in turn, that the structural unity has not been destroyed. Although the point at issue is a central one and thus brings about a separation, the basic form of the acceptance of the word in history, that is, the supporting nexus as such, is not disputed.[1]

All this, as we have said, is basically true also of the separation between Rome and Constantinople that became the starting point of the division between East and West. Not everyone, it is true, especially on the Orthodox side, would agree with this opinion—which shows how time has served to intensify the gravity of the dispute. For, from the Orthodox point of view, at least according to one interpretation, the *monarchia papae* means a destruction of the ecclesial structure as such, in consequence of which something different and new replaces the primitive Christian form. Because this aspect of the problem is, generally speaking, more or less foreign to us in the West, I should like to indicate in a few words how this impression has arisen in the East. For such a view, the Church in the West is no longer, under the leadership of her bishops, a nexus of local churches that, in their collegial unity, go back to the community of the twelve apostles; she is seen, rather, as a centrally organized monolith in which the new legal concept of a "perfect society" has superseded the old idea of succession in the community. In her, the faith that was handed down no longer (so it seems) serves as the sole normative rule—a rule that can be newly interpreted only with the consensus of all the local churches; in her, the will of the absolute sovereign creates a new authority. Precisely this difference in the concept of authority grew steadily more intense and reached its climax in 1870 with the proclamation of the primacy of jurisdiction: in one case, only the tradition that has been handed down serves as a valid source of law, and only the consensus of all is the normative criterion for determining and interpreting it. In the other case, the source of law appears to be the will of the sovereign, which creates on

---

[1] On the question of the non-Chalcedonian churches, cf. especially *Wort und Wahrheit. Revue for Religion and Culture,* supplementary issue, no. 2 (Vienna, 1974), and, in particular, the contributions by V. C. Samuel and A. Grillmeier, 19–40.

its own authority (*ex sese*) new laws that then have the power to bind. The old sacramental structure seems overgrown, even choked, by this new concept of law: the papacy is not a sacrament; it is "only" a juridical institution; but this juridical institution has set itself above the sacramental order.

At this point, we should also call attention to the fact that the division regarding the concept of the relationship of sacrament and law was not something new in the second millenium; it reached deep into the history of the ancient Church. Rome had always acknowledged the validity of baptism even outside the orthodox community and, correspondingly, also the validity of ordination outside it, thus recognizing a certain distinction between the sacrament and the legal entity of the Church. For the East, the link between sacrament and Church had always been so total that it could never feel comfortable with this interpretation, which, in fact, also left it theologically somewhat helpless vis-à-vis the Christian reality of heresy; nor was the gradually evolving distinction between οἰκονομία and ἀκριβεία particularly helpful. Be that as it may, it is clear from our reflections that, in the second millenium, the suspicion was increasing in the East that the split with Rome was more extensive than earlier ones had been, that it destroyed the basic structure of the Church herself.

On the other side, the judgments of Rome regarding the East were becoming noticeably more stringent. The more primacy was seen to be a prerequisite for Church membership and, consequently, a prerequisite for salvation, the more inevitable was the question about the degree to which one could speak of real Church membership where this central prerequisite was wanting. As for the Western distinction between the validity and the liceity of the sacraments, the validity, it is true, was generally not questioned, but the more liceity came to be regarded as crucial, the less significant validity became. In summary, we must say that the division between East and West contained a fearful danger—that of growing into a break that would raise the question of the existence of Christian attitudes on either side. Behind the threatening cloud, however, the elements of healing remained. Unlike the East, Rome, it is true, placed great weight on those passages of the New Testament that speak of Peter, thus actually remaining true to the original tradition, of which a more apt and concrete expression exists nowhere else. The applications of these passages have, it must be admitted, in many respects outgrown their initial heritage so that, at first glance, they may seem to overlook the basic sacramental structure. But, in the real life of the Church and at the solid core of her constitution, the relationship with the sacraments remained always vital and, precisely by reason of its union with the office of Peter, sustained the whole structure. A closer approach to and awareness of one another can hardly ignore this fundamental unity, which, in the whole course of the dispute, has never been impugned. The West may point to the absence of the office of Peter in the East—it must, nevertheless, admit that, in the Eastern Church, the form and content of the Church of the Fathers is present in unbroken continuity. The East may criticize the existence and function of the office of Peter in the West, but it must also be aware that, because of it, no other Church exists in Rome than that of the first millenium—of the time when a common Eucharist was celebrated and when but one Church existed.[2]

With Luther another kind of division that had its roots in Augustine appeared in the Church. The split between Donatists and Catholics that rent the Church of his African homeland caused the great doctor of the Church to distinguish with a sharpness until then unknown between the theological greatness of the Church as a salvific reality and her empirical existence: many who seem to be in the Church are outside her; many who seem to be outside her are in her. The true Church is the number of the predestined who, on the one hand, transcend the visible Church while, on the other hand, the reprobate are present at her very center. For Augustine, it must be admitted, this concept had no adverse repercussions with regard to the value of the sacramental and apostolic structure of the Church and her tradition. But the great Western schism of the fourteenth and fifteenth centuries had imbued it with a degree of realism that would have been inconceivable up to that time. For nearly half a century, the Church was split into two or three obediences that excommunicated one another, so that every Catholic lived under excommunication by one pope or another, and, in the last analysis, no one could say with certainty which of the contenders had right on his side. The Church no longer offered certainty of salvation; she had become questionable in her whole objective form—the true Church, the true pledge of salvation, had to be sought outside the institution. It is against this background of a profoundly shaken ecclesial consciousness that we are to understand that Luther, in the conflict between his search for salvation and the tradition of the Church, ultimately came to experience the Church, not as the guarantor, but as the adversary of salvation. The concept of the Church was limited, on the one hand, to the local community; on the other hand, it embraced the community of the faithful throughout the ages who are known only to God. But the community of the whole Church as such is no longer the

---

[2] On the historical and factual problems discussed in this section, cf. especially Louis Bouyer, *L'Église de Dieu. Corps du Christ et Temple de l'Esprit* (Paris: Cerf, 1970), in particular 45–65, 163–89, 373–93; Yves Congar, *L'Ecclésiologie du haut Moyen Âge* (Paris: Cerf, 1968), esp. 324–93; *Koinonia. Premier Colloque ecclésiologique entre théologiens orthodoxes et catholiques* [henceforth *Koinonia*] (Istina, Paris, 1975); St. Harkianakis, *Orthodoxe Kirche und Katholizismus* (Munich, 1975).

bearer of a positively meaningful theological content. Ecclesial organization is now borrowed from the political realm because it does not otherwise exist as a spiritually significant entity. Thus there does, it is true, exist an important community of belief with the ancient Church wherever the credal texts are taken seriously, but its ecclesial anchor and, therefore, the binding authority that sustains its agreements or disagreements remain unclear although, in the ecclesiological development of the Protestant community, much has been restored as a matter of actual necessity that has in principle lost its *raison d'être*.[3]

Against this background we can now weigh the possibilities that are open to Christian ecumenism. The maximum demands on which the search for unity must certainly founder are immediately clear. On the part of the West, the maximum demand would be that the East recognize the primacy of the bishop of Rome in the full scope of the definition of 1870 and in so doing submit in practice, to a primacy such as been accepted by the Uniate churches. On the part of the East, the maximum demand would be that the West declare the 1870 doctrine of primacy erroneous and in so doing submit, in practice, to a primacy such as been accepted with the removal of the *Filioque* from the Creed and including the Marian dogmas of the nineteenth and twentieth centuries. As regards Protestantism, the maximum demand of the Catholic Church would be that the Protestant ecclesiological ministries be regarded as totally invalid and that Protestants be converted to Catholicism; the maximum demand of Protestants, on the other hand, would be that the Catholic Church accept, along with the unconditional acknowledgement of all Protestant ministries, the Protestant concept of ministry and their understanding of the Church and thus, in practice, renounce the apostolic and sacramental structure of the Church, which would mean, in practice, the conversion of Catholics to Protestantism and their acceptance of a multiplicity of distinct community structures as the historical form of the Church. While the first three maximum demands are today rather unanimously rejected by Christian consciousness, the fourth exercises a kind of fascination for it—as it were, a certain conclusiveness that makes it appear to be the real solution to the problem. This is all the more true since there is joined to it the expectation that a Parliament of Churches, a "truly ecumenical council", could then harmonize this pluralism and promote a Christian unity of action. That no real union would result from this, but that its very impossibility

[3] On this subject, cf. Part Two, Chapter 2B of the present work: "Sacrifice, Sacrament and Priesthood in the Development of the Church"; Yves Congar, "Die Lehre von der Kirche", in *Handbuch der Dogmengeschichte,* ed. Michael Schmaus, Aloys Grillmeier, Leo Scheffczyk, vol. 3, 3c and 3d (Freiburg: Herder, 1971), esp. 3, 3d ("Vom Abendländischen Schisma bis zur Gegenwart"), 1–51.

would become a single common dogma, should convince anyone who examines the suggestion closely that such a way would not bring Church unity but only a final renunciation of it.

As a result, none of the maximum solutions offers any real hope of unity. In any event, church unity is not a political problem that can be solved by means of compromise or the weighing of what is regarded as possible or acceptable. What is at stake here is unity of belief, that is, the question of truth, which cannot be the object of political maneuvering. As long as and to the extent that the maximum solution must be regarded as a requirement of truth itself, just so long and to just that extent will there be no other recourse than simply to strive to convert one's partner in the debate. In other words, the claim of truth ought not to be raised where there is not a compelling and indisputable reason for doing so. We may not interpret as truth that which is, in reality, a historical development with a more or less close relationship to truth. Whenever, then, the weight of truth and its incontrovertibility are involved, they must be met by a corresponding sincerity that avoids laying claim to truth prematurely and is ready to search for the inner fullness of truth with the eyes of love.

On the question of reunion between East and West

How, then, are the maximum demands to be decided in advance? Certainly, no one who claims allegiance to Catholic theology can simply declare the doctrine of primacy null and void, especially not if he seeks to understand the objections and evaluates with an open mind the relative weight of what can be determined historically. Nor is it possible, on the other hand, for him to regard as the only possible form and, consequently, as binding on all Christians the form this primacy has taken in the nineteenth and twentieth centuries. The symbolic gestures of Pope Paul VI and, in particular, his kneeling before the representative of the Ecumenical Patriarch were an attempt to express precisely this and, by such signs, to point the way out of the historical impasse. Although it is not given us to halt the flight of history, to change the course of centuries, we may say, nevertheless, that what was possible for a thousand years is not impossible for Christians today. After all, Cardinal Humbert of Silva Candida, in the same bull in which he excommunicated the Patriarch Michael Cerularius and thus inaugurated the schism between East and West, designated the Emperor and people of Constantinople as "very Christian and orthodox", although their concept of the Roman primacy was certainly far less different from that of Cerularius than from that, let us say, of the First Vatican Council.[4] In other words, Rome must not require more from the East with respect to the doctrine of primacy than had been formulated and was lived in the first millenium. When the Patriarch Athenagoras, on July 25, 1967, on the occasion of the Pope's visit to Phanar, designated him as the successor of St. Peter, as the most esteemed among us, as one who presides in charity, this great Church leader was expressing the essential content of the doctrine of primacy as it was known in the first millenium. Rome need not ask for more. Reunion could take place in this context if, on the one hand, the East would cease to oppose as heretical the developments that took place in the West in the second millenium and would accept the Catholic Church as legitimate and orthodox in the form she had acquired in the course of that development, while, on the other hand, the West would recognize the Church of the East as orthodox and legitimate in the form she has always had.

Such a mutual act of acceptance and recognition, in the Catholicity that is common to and still possessed by each side, is assuredly no light matter. It is an act of self-conquest, of self-renunciation and, certainly, also of self-discovery. It is an act that cannot be brought about by diplomacy but must be a spiritual undertaking of the whole Church in both East and West. If what is theologically possible is also to be actually possible in the Church, the theological aspect must be spiritually prepared and spiritually accepted. My diagnosis of the relationship between East and West in the Church is as follows: from a theological perspective, the union of the Churches of East and West is fundamentally possible, but the spiritual preparation is not yet sufficiently far advanced and, therefore, not yet ready in practice. When I say it is fundamentally possible from a theological perspective, I do not overlook the fact that, on closer inspection, a number of obstacles still exist with respect to the theological possibility: from the *Filioque* to the question of the indissolubility of marriage. Despite these difficulties, some of which are present more strongly in the West, some in the East, we must learn that unity, for its part, is a Christian truth, an essentially Christian concept, of so high a rank that it can be sacrificed only to safeguard what is most fundamental, not where the way to it is obstructed by formulations and practices that, however important they may be, do not destroy community in the faith of the Fathers and in the basic form of the Church as they saw her.[5]

[4] Cf. J. Meyendorff, "Églises soeurs. Implications ecclésiologiques du Tomos Agapes", in *Koinonia*, 35–46 (German translation in IKZ 3 [1974]: 308–22, esp. 309–10.

[5] Louis Bouyer offers a plan for the gradual restoration of unity between East and West in "Réflexions sur le rétablissement possible de la communion entre les Églises orthodoxe et catholique. Perspectives actuelles", in *Koinonia*, 112–15.

Because it has two elements, the above-mentioned diagnosis admits of quite opposing prognostications. What is theologically possible can miscarry spiritually and, in consequence, become once again theologically impossible. What is theologically possible can also be spiritually possible and, in consequence, become theologically deeper and purer. Which prognostication will prove to be the correct one cannot be foretold at the present time: the factors pointing to one or other of them are almost equally strong.

But the opposing prognostications that are expressed in this diagnosis should be construed not just as a theorizing about theoretical possibilities but as a practical imperative: it is the task of every responsible Christian and, in a particular way, of theologians and leaders of the Church to create a spiritual climate for the theologically possible; under the compelling mandate of a unity without sameness, to see and experience the antithetical at all times without specious superficiality; to inquire always not just about the defensibility of union, of mutual recognition, but even more urgently about the defensibility of remaining separate, for it is not unity that requires justification but the absence of it.[6] The fact that opposing prognostications are possible means that the prognostication is also dependent on ourselves, that it exists in the form of a mandate and that to make us aware of this fact should be the sole meaning of any encounter that does not simply impart information but makes known a task and demands an examination of conscience that compels us to action.

On the question of Catholic-Protestant ecumenism

Prognostications as to the future of ecumenism—the question is only half answered as long as we have said nothing about the prospects of unity between the Catholic Church and the Protestant denominations. In view of the overwhelming plurality of world Protestantism, the question is admittedly much more difficult to answer than that regarding Catholicism and Orthodoxy, which can be approached uniformly, as it were, from a common and consistent model. In any event, one thing should be clear: unity between Catholicism and Orthodoxy would not hinder but rather facilitate unity with the Protestant churches. Granted, the solution that is being proposed, in this context, in the suggestion of the Ecumenical Institute of the Faculties of German Universities,[7] seeks a healing of the

---

[6] Papandreou shows emphatically that this is the right perspective, in Raymund Erni and Damaskinos Papandreou, *Eucharistiegemeinschaft. Der Standpunkt der Orthodoxie* (Freiburg/ Schweiz, 1974), 68–96, esp. 91–92.

[7] *Reform und Anerkennung kirchlicher Ämter. Ein Memorandum der Arbeitsgemeinschaft*

division in the rejection of the dogma and structure of the ancient Church. But we have already seen that such a solution would not lead to unity but would constitute its ultimate rejection. In view of the variety of positions and situations that exist in the individual Protestant denominations, I shall limit my remarks here to those churches that bear the stamp of Luther, but a model that will serve for all Protestant churches should become recognizable in the process. Logically, the search for church unity must begin with the denominational and ecclesial structure, however much it will also respect and appreciate precisely those sources of a quite personal piety and the spiritual strength and depth that are provided for the individual. But if what we are discussing is not a union between individuals but a community of churches, then what is at stake is the confession and faith of the church of which the individual is a member and in which he is opened to a personal encounter with God. That means: the reference point of such an effort must be the confessional writings of the Evangelical Lutheran Church; writings of private theologians will be taken into account only insofar as they contribute to denominational theology.[8] Research in recent years has led to the conclusion that it was not just for diplomatic reasons that the *Confessio Augustana* [henceforth CA] was composed as the fundamental Lutheran confessional text; it was intended to be interpreted under the law of the empire as a Catholic confession; it was understood with inner conviction as a search for evangelical Catholicity—as an effort to filter the seething discontent of the early reform movement in a way that would make it a Catholic reform.[9] Efforts are being made, accordingly, to bring about a Catholic recognition of the CA—or, more accurately, a recognition of the CA as Catholic—that would establish the Catholicity of the churches of the Augsburg Confession and thus make possible a corporate union despite existing differences.[10] Certainly such a recognition of the CA by the Catholic

---

ökumenischer Universitätsinstitute (Munich-Mainz, 1973); the text of the memorandum is on 11–25. For several responses to this, see *Catholica* 27 (1973), esp. the contribution by Karl Lehmann, 248–62; cf. also, Heinz Schütte, *Amt, Ordination und Sukzession in Verständnis evangelischer und katholischer Exegeten und Dogmatiker der Gegenwart sowie in Dokumenten ökumenischer Gespräche* (Düsseldorf: Patmos, 1974).

[8] In this context, we must ask ourselves above all what significance Luther's theology has in relation to the confessional writings. Until there is a more or less universally accepted answer to that question, everything else will continue to be uncertain.

[9] Cf. Vinzenz Pfnür, *Einig in der Rechtfertigungslehre? Die Rechtfertigungslehre der Confessio Augustana (1530) und die Stellungnahme der katholischen Kontroverstheologie zwischen 1530 und 1535* (Wiesbaden: Steiner, 1970).

[10] A concrete program in this direction was proposed in the journal *Bausteine* (1975), vol. 58, 9–20, and vol. 59, 3–22. See also the fundamental article by Vinzenz Pfnür,

Church would be far more than a theoretical theological action that could be worked out by historians and church politicians. It would be, rather, a concrete historical step on both sides. It would mean that the Catholic Church recognized, in the beginnings thus made, an appropriate form for realizing the common faith with the independence that was its due. On the other hand, it would mean that the Protestant churches would accept and understand this text, which is susceptible of many interpretations, in the way that was originally intended: in unity with the dogma and basic structure of the ancient Church. It would mean for both sides that the open question as to the center of the Reformation would be solved in a spiritual decision that would recognize the Catholic orientation of the CA and that the heritage of that time would be experienced and accepted in accordance with this interpretation.

The question of the practical possibility of such a development—the prognosis on the basis of the diagnosis—is much more difficult than it was with regard to a *rapprochement* between the Catholic Church and Orthodoxy. This, too, is a question that can be answered better by action than by speculation. What action? Generally speaking, certainly, a manner of thinking and acting that respects the other in his search for the true essence of Christianity; an attitude that regards unity as an urgent good that demands sacrifice, whereas separation demands justification in every single instance. But we can define the required action even more clearly in terms of the above diagnosis. It means that the Catholic does not insist on the dissolution of the Protestant confessions and the demolishing of their churches but hopes, rather, that they will be strengthened in their confessions and in their ecclesial reality. There is, of course, a confessionalism that divides and that must be overcome: on whatever side it occurs, we must speak of confessionalism in a pejorative sense wherever the noncommunal, the anti-, is experienced as an essential constituent and thus intensifies the division. We must oppose to this confessionalism of separation a hermeneutics of union that sees the confession of faith as that which unites. Our interest, that is, the interest of ecumenism, cannot be linked to the precondition that the confession will simply disappear but rather that it will be translated from its banishment to the realm of the nonbinding into the full meaning of a binding community of faith in the Church. For only

---

"Anerkennung der Confessio Augustana durch die katholische Kirche? Zu einer aktuellen Frage des katholisch-lutherischen Dialogs", in IKZ (1975), 298–307. Objections to this article by Paul Hacker and T. Beer (in ibid., 1976) rest on the problematic historical and fundamental ("juridical") relationship of the *Confessio Augustana* to Luther's work and to the remaining work of Melanchthon (especially the defense [*Apologia*] of the Augsburg Confession). In any event, the question cannot be solved by a historically favorable interpretation of the CA but only by a spiritual and ecclesial decision that is beyond the competence of historians. Cf. below, Part Two, Chapter 1C in the present work.

where this happens is a mutually binding community possible; only thus does an ecumenism of faith possess the necessary stability.

The question about the prognosis for ecumenism is, ultimately, a question about the forces that are operative in Christianity today and that may be expected to leave their mark on the future. Two obstacles are opposed to the realization of Church unity: on the one hand, a confessional chauvinism that orients itself primarily, not according to truth, but according to custom and, in its obsession with what is its own, puts emphasis primarily on what is directed against others. On the other hand, an indifferentism with regard to faith that sees the question of truth as an obstacle, measures unity by expediency and thus turns it into an external pact that bears always within itself the seeds of new divisions. The guarantee of unity is a Christianity of faith and fidelity that lives the faith as a decision with a definite content but precisely for that reason is always searching for unity, lets itself be constantly purified and deepened as a preparation for it and, in so doing, helps the other to recognize the common center and to find himself there by the same process of purification and deepening. It is clear that the first two attitudes are closer and more immediate to man than the third, which challenges him to excel himself and, at the same time, reduces him to utter helplessness, demands from him inexhaustible patience and a readiness to be constantly purified and deepened anew. But Christianity, as a whole, rests on the victory of the improbable, on the impulse of the Holy Spirit, who leads man beyond himself and precisely in this way brings him to himself. Because we have confidence in the power of the Holy Spirit, we hope also for the unity of the Church and dedicate ourselves to an ecumenism of faith.

B. Rome and the Churches of the East after the Removal of the Ban of Excommunication of 1054

Anyone who reads the documents in *Tomos Agapes*[11] that reflect twelve years of contact between the two Churches can hardly escape a certain sadness. He will see a hesitant and reserved beginning, a dramatic rise to a *fortissimo* of hopes, of closeness, so that the moment of full union seems almost within reach; but the final threshold is not crossed, and the last days witness to a decline that, while it does not extinguish all confidence, nevertheless lets a certain doubt appear that is far from the mood of those

[11] In 1971, under the title *Tomos Agapes* (Book of Love), the Ecumenical Patriarch in Constantinople and the Vatican Secretariate for the Unity of Christians published jointly a volume in which were collected the written documents and the addresses exchanged by the Vatican and Phanar between 1958 and 1970.

moments in which the movement was at its height. The reader wonders what consequences can actually result from a lifting of the anathema of 1054 and whether there actually are consequences of any significance. I propose to address these questions solely on the basis of the documents that are collected in the *Tomos Agapes*. I shall not discuss the resonance the proceedings found in the various realms of Christian ecumenism but shall deal exclusively with the question: How is the lifting of the anathema explained and evaluated in the official texts themselves; what consequences are foreseen? Such a methodological limitation has, of course, the disadvantage that it pursues the actual course of events only within the narrow confines of what has been officially retained; on the other hand, however, it can present with all the more clarity the formal version of what occurred.

I. *The course of events*

Hesitant Beginnings

If this study of the central issue is not to prove futile, it will be helpful to preface it with a short description of the events themselves that will likewise be limited to the sources assembled in the *Tomos Agapes*. In the beginning, there was courtesy but also reserve. The Patriarchal Synod, in agreement with the other autocephalous Orthodox churches, decided that it "was not possible" to send observers to the Second Vatican Council; at the same time, however, they expressed the wish that the work of the Council, which the Orthodox churches would follow with intense interest and befitting attention, might be successful in the true spirit of Christ. The autocephalous Orthodox churches nourished the hope that wider horizons of the Christian spirit and of mutual understanding would be opened and that, in consequence, conditions would arise in the near future that would promote useful contacts and fruitful dialogues "in the spirit of the Lord and in fraternal charity for the benefit of that unity of all Christians for which Our Lord Jesus Christ prayed".[12]

Nor did the second invitation, in 1963, meet with a different reception.[13] The first personal letter of Pope Paul VI to Patriarch Athenagoras, dated September 20, 1963, brought about a notable caesura. It sounded a note that the Patriarch later repeated in a critical text: in it is to be found the thought that underlies everything that follows, the theological leitmotif of

[12] Τόμος Ἀγάπης: *Vatican-Phanar (1958–1970)* (Rome/Istanbul: Typis Polyglottis Vaticanis, 1971), no. 22, 62.

[13] No. 30, 74–77; no. 31, 78–79.

the whole proceedings, as it were, already formulated: "Let us entrust what is past to the mercy of God and heed the advice of the Apostle: '. . . I forget the past and I strain ahead for what is still to come . . . trying to capture the prize for which Christ Jesus captured me' (Phil 3:13, 12)."[14] The Patriarch's answer of November 22, 1963, takes up this thought and continues it with a quotation from the thirteenth chapter of the first epistle to the Corinthians; the mutual endeavor is incorporated into the framework of the concept of the one Body of Christ and thus leads quite naturally to the introduction of the motif of *communio*: "We believe we can give one another no better gift than that of the communion of love (κοινωνίας τῆς ἀγάπης), which, in the words of the Apostle, 'is always ready to excuse, to trust, to hope and to endure whatever comes' (1 Cor 13:7). Once, this communion was firmly entrenched in the bond of peace of our holy churches; now it is renewed through the grace of the Lord 'to the praise of his glory' (Eph 1:14)."[15] The two motifs of forgetting—of striking from the memory—and of "excusing", which would form the core of the events of December 1965, have thus already been formulated. The Patriarch's communiqué of December 6, 1963, after the announcement of the plan for a papal visit to the Holy Land, strengthened the hopes that had been awakened: it reported that the Patriarch, in his address, had expressed the thought that, by meeting in the places where Christ had lived and died, a work of Divine Providence could be accomplished—a way could be opened to the full restoration of Christian unity.[16]

From the meeting in Jerusalem to the removal of the anathema

The next stage was the meeting of Pope and Patriarch on the Mount of Olives. The Patriarch saw in the event the dawn of a new day in which future generations would together praise the one Lord and Redeemer of the world in the participation of the same chalice of the Body and Blood of the Lord.[17] The Pope, too, spoke of a turning of the ways in the meeting between the "Catholic Church and the Patriarch of Constantinople" but offered, as well, precise distinctions as to what was and was not signified by the present proceedings—for instance, the reciprocal kiss of peace.[18] At such an exalted moment, such distinctions might seem to have a sobering effect, but they were also an expression of the fact that the point had now

[14] No. 33, 83; cf. no. 94 (Address of Patriarch Athenagoras at the reception of Cardinal Bea, April 3, 1965), 206.
[15] No. 35, 86–88.
[16] No. 36, 90.
[17] No. 48, 110.
[18] No. 49, 112–19.

been reached at which wishes were not sufficient and something concrete had to be done. In fact, the ideas expressed here were repeated with even more precision when the anathema was lifted; they are, therefore, central to our discussion, for there began, at this point, the delimiting of what could and could not result from the whole process.

The first concrete result of the meeting in the Holy Land occurred on September 8, 1964: the Holy Synod decided that it could now send observers to the Council in Rome.[19] The immediate prehistory of the lifting of the ban of excommunication took place, according to the documents, on February 16, 1965, with an address on the occasion of a visit to the Pope by Metropolitan Meliton of Hilioupolis and Theira. A letter of Cardinal Bea on October 18 of the same year assuredly refers to this visit. In discussing the concrete arrangements for the approaching ceremony, the Cardinal refers to a thought expressed verbally by this Metropolitan during his visit to Rome.[20] Meliton brought to the κυρίαρχος Ἐπίσκοπος of ancient Rome the kiss of peace in the Lord from his brothers in the East. While the Pope had spoken in Jerusalem of a turning of the ways and of meeting at the sources of the gospel— metaphorically, in view of the place of that meeting, but also more than metaphorically, the Metropolitan spoke of rekindling the fire of nostalgia for the early happiness of the Church.[21] Above all, however, he expressed the wish that a systematic endeavor might begin for the development "of fraternal relations between our two Churches", in the course of which the obstacles that stood in the way would be removed. In this manner, they would come quickly to a genuinely theological dialogue and, by abandoning themselves to the action of the Holy Spirit, would prepare for the dawning of the bright day of the Lord on which East and West "would eat the same Bread, drink from the same chalice and confess the same faith in 'the Spirit that we have in common' (Phil 2:1) for the glory of Christ and his one, holy, Catholic and apostolic Church".[22] On April 3, Cardinal Bea developed this thought on his visit to Phanar,[23] but it was especially the reply of the Patriarch that furthered the discussion during this audience. The thoughts and concepts he used belong to the very heart of the matter; they must, therefore, be analyzed when, after tracing the prehistory, we turn to the events themselves.

With the above, the more remote prehistory of the whole proceedings

---

[19] No. 72, 153.

[20] No. 87, 172–77 (Address of Metropolitan Meliton); no. 119, 250–51 (Letter of Cardinal Bea).

[21] No. 49, 116 (Paul VI: "ad Evangelii fontes"); no. 87, 174 (Meliton: τὸ ἱερὸν πῦρ τῆς νοσταλγίας).

[22] No. 87, 176.

[23] No. 93, 192–99.

has been described. A letter from Cardinal Bea to the Ecumenical
Patriarch, dated October 18, 1965, marks the immediate beginning of the
events themselves. Referring to the ideas that Metropolitan Meliton and
Metropolitan Chrysostom of Myra had expressed during their visit to
Rome, he suggested that a commission of four members from each side be
named to study the question.[24] The agreement of the Patriarch came in a
telegram, the contents and date of which are unfortunately not preserved
in the documents.[25] On November 16, Cardinal Bea named the Roman
members of the commission;[26] on November 22, a meeting was held in
Phanar. The programmatic address of Metropolitan Meliton at the
beginning of the commission's sessions offered also the official
interpretation of the proceedings, on the basis of which all conclusions will
have to be drawn; it will, therefore, be examined in detail.[27] The answer of
Archbishop Willebrands was in the same vein and added some further
points. The minutes of the meeting contain the official statements and
confirm at the same time the interpretation given in these addresses.[29] On
December 7, the historic event took place in St. Peter's in Rome and in the
Cathedral of Phanar in Constantinople. The joint declarations of Pope and
Patriarch, the brief *Ambulate in dilectione* of Pope Paul VI and the patriarchal *Tomos* of Patriarch Athenagoras with his Synod as well as the address
of Metropolitan Meliton in Rome complete and define the event.[30]

Posthistory

The Christmas messages of Pope and Patriarch on the holy night of 1965
are the first documents in the posthistory of that day. The thrill of the great
event still vibrates, especially in the words of the Ecumenical Patriarch. He
surpassed the passage in Philippians about forgetting the past by referring
to 2 Corinthians 5:18: ". . . the old creation has gone, and now the new
one is here. It is all God's work. It was God who reconciled us to himself
through Christ and gave us the work of handing on this reconciliation".

---

[24] No. 119, 250–51.

[25] The fact of the telegram is known from no. 121, 254.

[26] No. 121, 254. The members of the Roman Commission were: Msgr. Michael
Maccarrone, Alphonse Raes, S. J., Alphonse Stickler, Christophe Dumont, O. P. The
meeting was presided over by Msgr. Jean Willebrands, who was accompanied by Pierre
Duprey. According to the minutes, the Orthodox participants were Metropolitan Meliton,
Metropolitan Chrysostom of Myra, P. Gabriel (Chief Secretary of the Holy Synod),
Georges Anastasiades, Archdeacon Evangelos. In addition to Pierre Duprey, the Secretaries
were André Scrima and P. Paul (Undersecretary of the Holy Synod).

[27] No. 122, 256–65.

[28] No. 123, 266–69.

[29] No. 124, 270–75.

[30] Nos. 127–30, 278–97.

For him, there had begun "a new period" that was the fruit of that light that let the birth of the Lord shine in the world "for the unity and peace of his holy Church and of all men".[31] The fact that, for the Patriarch, matters were not at an end but had begun in a way that carried with it an obligation is clear from his programmatic explanation on December 7, 1966, the first anniversary of the lifting of the ban: this text cannot be considered just "posthistory"; its challenging dynamism belongs to the interpretation of the event itself and will have to be considered later. Let us quote here a sentence that is central to its whole theme: "December 7, 1965, means a light that scatters the darkness that dimmed a whole era of Church history that is now past; this light illumines the present and future course of the Church."[32] Paul VI was, for the Patriarch, "the apostle of unity and peace".[33]

Another text of great importance is the address of the Patriarch Athenagoras on the visit of the Pope to Phanar on July 25, 1967. With its almost hymnic and, at the same time, exhortative language, it has the effect of a dramatic attempt by this great Church leader to complete without further ado the beginning that had been made in 1965 and to achieve full unity of the Churches of East and West by virtue of what had then taken place. That Athenagoras remained true to the end to this passion for reconciliation we know from his Christmas messages of 1967,[34] 1968[35] and 1969,[36] to which the responses from Rome were, for the most part, somewhat more reserved but, nevertheless, endorsed the same goal of sacramental community. But the great highlights are now things of the past, and there is no evidence of new progress. That is why it is so imperative today that we inquire into what has actually taken place and not relegate it to oblivion, causing that bad conscience to rage again that should properly be filled with new purpose.

2. Meaning and consequences of the lifting of the ban of excommunication

Restoration of charity as the central intention

After this outline of events, let us turn now to the question that is our main concern: What was the theological purpose of the act by which the

---

[31] No. 132, 303.
[32] No. 142, 319.
[33] Ibid., p. 321.
[34] Nos. 200 and 201, 454–55.
[35] Nos. 236 and 237, 518–19.
[36] Nos. 277, 602–3, and no. 279, 606–7.

anathema of 1054 was removed? What results were foreseen in the act as it was intended? The first fundamental perspectives appear in the address delivered by Patriarch Athenagoras when he received Cardinal Bea on April 3, 1965. What is happening here, he said, reflects a holy and historic responsibility—that means we have gone beyond mere politeness and have entered the realm of historic action, of responsible performance, that will leave its mark on the history of the Church. There are two stages to be considered: the dialogue of love and the theological dialogue. Our present task is to engage directly in the former, to prepare carefully for the latter.[37] With these words, a distinction was drawn that persisted throughout the whole proceedings and is doubtless to be counted among the basic categories by which it was attempted to determine precisely the merit of the whole—its theological and ecclesiological role. Pope Paul VI had already interpreted in the same way the kiss of peace that was exchanged by the two Church leaders at their meeting in Jerusalem: the dogmatic, liturgical and disciplinary distinctions would have to be stated in their proper place and discussed in a spirit that paid due attention to the demands of truth without prejudice to charity. "But what can and must happen now is this: fraternal love must grow."[38] In the Metropolitan Meliton's official interpretation of the act of reconciliation, the same distinction was stated authoritatively: The act of lifting the ban brings "no modification whatever in the status of dogma, in the existing canonical order, in the liturgy or in the life of the Church. . . . It does not mean a restoration of the sacramental community".[39] What it intends is this: "We meet for the purpose of restoring love between the Orthodox Church and the Roman Catholic Church."[40]

But what does this mean? How is this separation of theology and love—of dogma, cult and law, on the one hand, and of love, on the other—to be understood? Is this love to be ranked as ecclesial and therefore theological or only as humanitarian? Does it stand totally outside of theology or is it, as *agape,* a New Testament love in the true sense of the word and, therefore, to be understood as ecclesial? The central question is: Should we assume that faith is here excluded from love and love from theology? But, from a Christian standpoint, what would that *agape* be from which faith was absent, that theology that had nothing to do with *agape*? It is clear—from the same address of Metropolitan Meliton—that a meaning so fatal to both *agape* and theology is not what was intended. The events of 1053–1054 had caused the love between the bishoprics of Rome and Constantinople to

[37] No. 94, 202.
[38] No. 49, 116.
[39] No. 122, 262–64.
[40] Ibid., 260.

grow cold—but, according to Matthew 24:12, the cooling of love is an eschatological phenomenon; its restoration, consequently, has to do with salvation history; it is not something external. If it can be objected that this interpretation does violence to the text, it is all the more significant that the speaker defined the planned event as the "confiding of ourselves to the mystery of love and the economy of God". Here there is an express attribution to the "economy" of salvation history: at the same time, there is an allusion to a possible theological and legal aspect of the whole that should be neither over- nor undervalued: the event is to be interpreted according to the principle of economy. Even though there is question here, not of ecclesial "economy", but of the economy of God to which the Church confides herself, it is permissible to find in these words a certain line of communication and, therefore, a certain categorical clarification of the proceedings.[41] Pope Paul was even more explicit in his brief of December 7, 1965, on the occasion of the lifting of the anathema. He quoted the phrase about the cooling of charity from a letter of Pope Gregory VII to the Patriarch Michael Cerularius: "Just as harmony once served us well, so it later served us ill that on both sides . . . charity grew cold."[42] Now, however, it was important that "we be bound together by love, 'the sweet and healing bond of spirit to spirit' (Augustine). Therefore, we want to follow the path of fraternal love on which we may be led to full union. . . ."[43]

Let us be convinced of this fact: the fundamental category of the event was the "restoration of love". The reference was to ecclesial love—not to private or theological or purely humanitarian love, but to a community of love between bishopric and bishopric, between Church and Church. This ecclesial *agape* is not yet a sacramental community but possesses in itself the necessary dynamism to become such. It is to be regarded as an actual ecclesial union that binds churches as churches.

Purification of memory

Let us return to the address of Patriarch Athenagoras in April 1965 with which we started. The theme of the restoration of love after a "yesterday on which lay the burden of antithesis, mistrust and antagonism" led naturally to a second theme: "By overcoming the alienation and filling in

---

[41] Ibid., 258. Cf., for the theological character of the "Dialogue of Love", an address by Metropolitan Meliton in June 1968, quoted in Pierre Duprey, *La Théologie et le rapprochement entre les Églises catholiques et orthodoxes*, in Yves Congar, *Mélange* (1974), 37–50, quotation on 39.

[42] No. 128, 286.

[43] Ibid.

the trenches that separate us, we shall be able to consider our difficulties in quite a new light. If we stay close to one another, we shall also seek the best way to a tomorrow that will make possible the remedying of the past and the restoration (ἀποκατάστασις in Greek!) of the former beauty of the one undivided Church."[44] It is a question of changing the past, of creating a new present and a new future. But how is the past to be changed? As we noted earlier in these pages, the Pauline text: "I forget the past . . ." plays here a crucial role: past is present through memory. Memory gives it its dangerous power in the present and causes the poison of yesterday to become the poisoning of today. Reparation of the past can take place through a purification of memory. Thus, in a letter dated December 20, 1965, Paul VI spoke of the desire "to leave the past in God's hands so that we may direct all our energies to preparing a better future".[45] In all texts that directly interpret the action of December 7, the key reference is to the concept of forgetting, of the "purification of memory" that will also serve "to heal".[46] It is represented as the negative prerequisite for the positive process, which is the restoration of love: love is made possible by a changed memory. In the joint official declaration of December 7, the essential point is this: both sides erase from memory and from the midst of the Church the excommunication that once took place and consign it to oblivion.[47] I find the most penetrating interpretation of the event to be that of Metropolitan Meliton, who said: The symbol of separation has been destroyed and has been replaced by love as the symbol of our self-discovery. The sacramental community has, it is true, not been restored, but "the fundamental prerequisite for a continuing resolution of differences has been fulfilled: that is, fraternal love has been officially and ecclesially established between the two primary sees of East and West".[48] This, in the last analysis, is the deepest meaning of such forgetting. It is called forgiving.[49]

Again we must ask: What does all this mean? And again we must answer: Certainly more than a mere exchange of courtesies. The character of the events of 1054 in the history of the Church has been changed. But again the objection is raised: Is it possible to confer retroactively on historical acts a different legal character? Can history be changed by legal

---

[44] No. 94, 204. The concept of ἀποκατάστασις (restoration) also appears among other places in the programmatic address of Metropolitan Meliton on November 22, 1965: no. 122, 262.

[45] No. 131, 298.

[46] No. 123, 268.

[47] No. 127, 4b, 280 and 281.

[48] No. 130, 296.

[49] No. 127, 282 and 283.

action, or must strict historical cognizance be taken of it precisely because it happened? It can be changed to the extent that in the continuing identity of the subject *Church* certain events have a continuing legal effect. In international law, the retroactive nullification of a contract would represent a comparable situation (as we have recently experienced in the historic settlement between Germany and Czechoslovakia); in the realm of Church history, the history of the councils offers a point of comparison: the situation of the Church changes when a council that at first had been considered valid is, after some time, definitively and universally labeled a "Robber Synod" and excluded from the official history of the faith; or, vice versa, when an originally local council is recognized as ecumenical. A similar process of the new evaluation of history that leads to a new evaluation of the present has taken place here with full binding power: the reciprocal anathema of 1054 no longer belongs to the official roster of the Church. It has been nullified by the act of forgiveness. The old memory must be replaced by a new one—a memory of love. In one of his letters to his order, St. Francis of Paola once warned strenuously against the power of remembering evil: "Memory of evil is an injustice, . . . a sentinel who protects sins, . . . alienation of love, a nail that pierces the soul, wickedness that never sleeps, . . . a daily death."[50] He knew this from the often tragic experiences of religious orders; the Church knows it from her own history. By the act of December 7, 1965, this poison was drawn out of the ecclesial organism, which must never again give it place—that is the very concrete and urgent challenge of the event. The Church has a new memory; she must support this new memory and strengthen it: that is true of every teacher of theology, of every preacher, of the catechumen, of the bishops—the renewal of memory became, from that day on, the solemnly sealed, mutual duty of the Church in East and West.

Removal of ban—an ecclesial-legal and theo-logical process

We turn now to a third viewpoint that promises to bear fruit for our inquiry. We must ask: Who is the subject of the act of December 7, 1965? What is its precise object? What is its purpose? Again it is, above all, the address of Metropolitan Meliton at the beginning of the work of the joint commission that offers precise guidelines. The events of the years 1053–1054, he points out, involved the sees of Rome and of Constantinople; the protagonists in that drama belonged to the two Churches (Rome and Constantinople); consequently, they were the

---

[50] In Alessandro Galuzzi, *Origini dell' Ordine dei Minimi* (Rome: Libr. della Pont. Univ. Lateranense, 1967), 121–22. Quoted here from *Liturgia horarum iuxta ritum Romanum* (Typis Polyglottis Vaticanis, 1972), 1326.

immediate partners in those events. At this point, there is a slight difference between the original text, which is in Greek, and the French translation. In the Greek, there is mention twice of the episcopal sees of Rome and Constantinople and, at other times, of "these two Churches"; the word "Church" must here be given a narrow interpretation. It refers to the two local churches, though certainly not excluding their patriarchal responsibility and extension. The French translation, on the contrary, designates the partners as "the Catholic Church" and "the Church of Constantinople", thus seeing the word "Rome" more clearly than does the Greek text as including the whole realm of papal jurisdiction. The unsolved problem of the relationship between the local church and the universal Church, which distinguishes the understanding of the Church in East and West, here has its effect on the linguistic form of the whole. There is no real difference. On the one side, the Patriarch of Constantinople with his Synod[51] acts for his jurisdiction, that is, for the jurisdiction that is under him; on the other side, the Pope acts for the jurisdiction that is under him, that is, for the whole Roman Catholic Church. But Constantinople, too, hoped for an effect on the whole Church of the East. Just as the negative consequences of the past were assimilated by the whole Christian East, so they were confident "that, in the same way, the present happy results would accrue to the whole Eastern Church".[52] There was question, then, of a legal act in which each Church would act "according to her tradition and customs".[53] Rome would act for her jurisdiction, Constantinople for hers: "Thus it depends on the jurisdiction of each side and falls under her responsibility; the accomplishment of these acts is for each jurisdiction a work of justice that is the duty of her office and ministry."[54] On the very day of the lifting of the ban, the address of Patriarch Athenagoras, which, in conformity with this outline, names the old and the new Rome as the subject of the act, adds to this canonical aspect one that is essentially theological: "We declare in writing, so that all may know, that the anathema . . . is from now on removed from memory and from the midst of the Church by the mercy of the all-merciful God. By the intercession of our most blessed Lord, of the ever-virgin Mary, Mother of God, of the holy Apostle Peter, the first *coryphaeus,* and Andrew, the first-called, and of all the saints, may he bestow peace on his Church and protect her for all eternity."[55] Ultimately, then, the ecclesial act was interpreted as the

[51] The Τόμος Πατριαρχικός of December 7, 1965, is signed accordingly by the Patriarch and the members of his Synod: *Tomos Agapes,* no. 129, 294.
[52] No. 122, 3, 262.
[53] No. 122, 4, 262.
[54] No. 122, 3, 262.
[55] No. 129, 292.

outpouring of divine mercy—the fruit of God's own action. It seems thus to be an eschatological act: to the extent that the present time is a time of peace, it merges with the time of salvation, which as such is an eschatological time: "In these last days, the goodness of God has been revealed to us in that it has shown us the way of reconciliation and peace."[56]

This theo-logical accentuation of the whole made it possible, at the same time, to link the indicative of the present canonical act very closely with the optative of the hoped-for goal. The act itself came from God's hands, in which lay also its future development toward a happy ending; by its origin, it was united with the future. If we pause here for a moment, we can say that in the event of December 7, 1965, there was question—again in the words of Metropolitan Meliton—"not merely of wishes and fine words but of deeds",[57] of an event in which the jurisdictions of both episcopal sees would participate. On the other hand, however, there was question of a process not solely of ecclesiological law but of an essentially theological character, and this likewise conditioned the dynamism of the whole, which pointed to something beyond.

Sacramental community as proximate goal—kingdom of God as ultimate telos

To what did it point? What was expected from it? Two groups of mutually interpretive answers suggest themselves. One was the urgent desire—expressed ever more strongly and ever more emphatically as time went by—for the restoration of full eucharistic communion. It was heard for the first time in an address delivered on February 16, 1965, by Patriarch Meliton, which we have established as the beginning of the immediate prehistory of the lifting of the ban.[58] The reciprocal telegrams of Pope and

[56] Ibid. The Greek expression "ἐν τοῖς ἐσχάτοις τούτοις καιροῖς" is freely translated into French as "de nos jours". As a direct translation, this is undoubtedly correct; but there is a nuance in the Greek phrasing, which echoes the biblical and patristic tradition, that is difficult to render in a Western language: it would have to be either appropriated or omitted entirely. Cf. also no. 173 (address of Patriarch Athenagoras at the Pope's visit to Phanar on July 25, 1967), 380. "He (= Christ) has given us the task of removing from our midst and from the midst of the Church—yes, even from memory—the curtain that separates us." Linguistically, this sentence is close to the epistle to the Ephesians and so can be considered a reference to the universal obligation of Christian unity that has its source in the mystery of Christ. But the expression "ἀπὸ τῆς μνήμης" (out of the memory), which refers explicitly to December 7, 1965, gives the sentence a much more definite meaning. The removal of the anathema is either described as the fulfillment of this task or viewed as a mission of Christ and so acquires a christological and eschatological character.

[57] No. 130, 296.

[58] No. 87, 176.

Patriarch on December 7, 1967, expressed the wish for a common chalice, for a common communion;[59] one year later, the Patriarch repeated the same wish; a year later again, he urged anew: "The hour for Christian courage has come. We love one another; we confess the same common ancient faith; let us make our way together before the glory of a common holy altar."[60] The Pope's answer preserved the same tone: "We are determined to move forward with prudent audacity and to do everything possible that the day may come when we can go together to the altar of the Lord."[61]

While this is the central canonical and ecclesial perspective, there is present also a comprehensive theological and anthropological context, which was apparent at the very beginning of the contacts in the communiqué of the Ecumenical Patriarch on the occasion of the announcement of the Pope's visit to the Holy Land. The move toward unity takes place, he said, "for the glorification of the Holy Name of Christ and for the benefit of the whole human race".[62] Ecumenism is expressed here in terms that are hardly ecclesiological but almost purely doxological. Later, the ecclesiological aspect would become stronger, but the doxological and anthropological elements would not therefore disappear; they would be noticeably strengthened. The address of Patriarch Athenagoras on the first anniversary of the lifting of the ban contained the sentence: "Modern man and the world can no longer afford the luxury of a divided Christendom, of sophistries and provisos that are not inspired by the gospel, of comfortable and endless academic discussions." Already with this appeal, ecumenism was to be understood as a duty of bearing witness to the faith in the world of today; the thought was linked to the kingdom of God: "The kingdom of God suffers violence."[63] With the visit of the Pope to Phanar, the theme was intensified to the very limits of the possible. There was question not just "of the unity of our two holy Churches but also of a higher service: to offer ourselves . . . to all our beloved fellow Christians . . . as an example of the fulfillment of the entire will of our Lord, who came to bring unity to all so that the world might believe that Christ was sent by God. Yes, even more. We include all who believe in a Creator God. . . . And, in cooperation with them, we will serve all men without distinction of race, creed or

---

[59] Nos. 200 and 201, 454–55.

[60] No. 277, 602.

[61] No. 279, 606. Cf. no. 173, 380, where, in conjunction with the words about the "concelebration of the common chalice of Christ", the Patriarch speaks of "impatient expectation".

[62] No. 36, 90.

[63] No. 142, 320.

ideology in order to advance well-being and peace on earth and to establish the kingdom of God on earth."[64] The text comes close here to the mistake of envisioning an eschatology in this world. But its meaning, nevertheless, is clear from the context. There is question, ultimately, of God's all-embracing plan of salvation, of his kingdom. The simple patience that awaits salvation from God's hands and that very concrete impatience that wants to remove all obstacles to the kingdom and put itself wholly at the disposal of God's salvific plan belong together here in a necessary paradox. The result that Patriarch and Pope envisioned in the lifting of the ban is entirely clear in this context. The event requires "prudent audacity", courage, even impatience—for mankind is waiting, God is waiting. To fall back into endless academic disputes would be an outright contradiction of what has been done and determined by Church to Church.

Andrew and Peter—the new and the old Rome

A final word: the dynamism of the event affects even the language. The reference to the brother apostles Peter and Andrew gains increased importance in the dialogue not only as a means of juxtaposing the Churches of the old and new Rome as sister Churches but also of emphasizing the special closeness of the roles of the two bishops who are the successors of "the first *coryphaeus*" and "the first-called".[65] So far as I am able to determine, it was Metropolitan Athenagoras of Thyatira who, on December 28, 1963, just before the Pope's significant visit to the Holy Land, first spoke of the two apostles in terms of the present and, in doing so, addressed the Pope as the "first bishop of the Church among equals".[66] Meliton of Hilioupolis went a step further after the ban had been lifted. He turned to the Pope with these words: "You, the first bishop of Christianity, and your brother, the second in rank, the bishop of Constantinople, can for the first time in long centuries, by reason of the holy event of this day, turn to mankind with one voice and one heart to proclaim to them the good tidings of Christmas: Glory to God in the highest and peace on earth to the people he loves."[67] Patriarch Athenagoras himself spoke even more strongly when he greeted the Pope in Phanar: "Against all expectation, the

---

[64] No. 173, 382. The reference to mankind occurs again in no. 44, 102–5; no. 50, 120–21 (end); no. 94, 206–7 (Christians and the whole world await from Pope and Patriarch "the liberating word to set aside the wall of schism"); no. 122, 6, 264.

[65] No. 44, 102 (Athenagoras of Thyatria); no. 93, 194 (Cardinal Bea); no. 108, 232 (Pope Paul VI); no. 173, 378 (Patriarch Athenagoras).

[66] No. 44, 102. The French translation renders the text ὡς πρῶτος ἐν ἴσοις Ἐπίσκοπος τῆς Ἐκκλησίας simply as "en sa qualité de premier évêque de l'Eglise."

[67] No. 130, 296.

bishop of Rome is among us, the first among us in honor, 'he who presides in love' (Ignatius of Antioch, epistola "Ad Romanos", PG 5, col. 801, prologue)."[68] It is clear that, in saying this, the Patriarch did not abandon the claims of the Eastern Churches or acknowledge the primacy of the West. Rather, he stated plainly what the East understood as the order, the rank and title, of the equal bishops in the Church—and it would be worth our while to consider whether this archaic confession, which has nothing to do with the "primacy of jurisdiction" but confesses a primacy of "honor" (τιμή) and *agape,* might not be recognized as a formula that adequately reflects the position Rome occupies in the Church—"holy courage" requires that prudence be combined with "audacity": "The kingdom of God suffers violence."[69]

3. Outcome

By way of conclusion, let us ask again: What remains and what will be the consequences of the whole proceedings? The key event is this: the relationship "of a love grown cold",[70] of "antitheses, mistrust and antagonism",[71] has been replaced by a relationship of love, of fraternity, the symbol of which is the fraternal embrace.[72] The symbol of separation has been replaced by the symbol of love. Granted, the sacramental

[68] No. 173, 380.

[69] No. 142, 320 (kingdom of God suffers violence); no. 277, 602 (The hour of Christian courage has come: Εἶναι ἡ ὥρα τοῦ Χριστιανικοῦ θάρρους); no. 279, 606 (kluge Kühneit: prudente audace). Cf. on this question the very provocative contribution of Pierre Duprey, "Brèves réflexions sur l'adage 'Primus inter pares' ", in *Unité des chrétiens* (October 1972), 39–40.

[70] Cf., for example, no. 129, 290.

[71] No. 94, 204. "Absence of love" is, in this text, the all-embracing characterization of the relationship between the Churches of East and West between 1054 and 1965.

[72] In his address, Paul VI explicitly interpreted the fraternal embrace exchanged in Jerusalem by Pope and Patriarch as a sign of the *fraterna caritas* that can increase with resumption of the theological dialogue: "Huius caritatis signum et specimen esto pacis osculum, quod ex Dei beneficio nobis licet in hac sanctissima terra invicem dare" (no. 49, 118; on the relationship of *caritas* and *doctrina,* see 116). The theme of the kiss of peace occurs again in a letter from Patriarch Athenagoras to Pope Paul VI on June 13, 1965: Ἐπὶ δὲ τούτοις φιλήματι ἁγίῳ κατασπαζόμενοι Αὐτὴν ἐν Χριστῷ . . . Phanar (July 25, 1967), it appears in the French text (Nous vous rendons, au sein même de l'Église, le baiser d'amour du Christ; no. 173, 79) but is not found in the printed Greek text (378) although, on the attached plate, the reproduction of the original document, the following sentence appears: Ἀποδίδομεν σοι ἐν μέσῳ ἐκκλησίας τὸν ἀσπασμὸν τῆς ἀγάπης τοῦ Χριστοῦ. The words appear again in the telegram sent to the Pope by the Patriarch on December 7, 1969, 602 and 603; the French text reads: "À l'occasion de ce saint anniversaire Nous embrassons aujourd'hui Votre Sainteté vénérée d'un saint baiser."

community has not yet been restored. But, after the "dialogue of love" has reached its first goal, the "theological dialogue" is expected to follow— not as a quiet academic skirmish that need arrive at no particular goal and is, basically, sufficient unto itself, but under the sign of "impatient expectation", which knows that "the hour has come". *Agape* and fraternal embrace are, in themselves, the *terminus* and *ritus* of eucharistic unity. Where *agape* is a reality in the Church, it must become a eucharistic *agape*. That must be the goal of every effort. That the goal may be reached, the most immediate result of the whole proceedings must be the unremitting effort to bring about the "healing of memory". The legal fact of forgetting must be followed by the actual historical fact of a new memory. That is the inescapable challenge—at once legal and theological—that is inseparable from the event of December 7, 1965.[73]

C. Elucidations of the Question of a "Recognition" of the *Confessio Augustana* by the Catholic Church

Since Vinzenz Pfnür published his definitive article on this subject in 1975,[74] the question of a Catholic recognition of the *Confessio Augustana* [henceforth CA] has been the subject of impassioned debate, even giving rise to the hope that, through such recognition, there could come about, possibly as early as 1980 (the anniversary of the CA), a reciprocal recognition of ministries and, in consequence, the formation of a eucharistic community, thus, after 450 years of separation, healing the rift that began with the misunderstanding of this text, the real purpose of which was in fact unification. At the same time, however, the question of such recognition and of the immediate ecumenical goal toward which it seemed to be directed caused both sides to be uneasy about the threatened dissolution of what was peculiarly their own and led, consequently, to a cooling of the ecumenical climate. From this we see how, under certain circumstances, even well-meaning efforts may be harmful. The experience confirms what was learned in the aftermath of the Council of Florence (1442)—that unification requires of the whole faith community a

[73] In accordance with this inner necessity, a commission composed of both Orthodox and Catholic bishops and theologians took up the work in the summer of 1980. Their task—after the phase of the dialogue of love—is a strictly theological dialogue and, along with that, the preparation for the full union of East and West in a eucharistic community.

[74] Vinzenz Pfnür, "Anerkennung der Confessio Augustana durch die katholische Kirche? Zu einer aktuellen Frage des katholisch-lutherischen Dialogs", in IKZ 4 (1975): 298–307; 5 (1976): 374–81, 477–78.

thorough state of inner readiness for which neither theological nor ecclesiological authority is an adequate substitute.

In a lecture in Graz in January 1976, I commended Pfnür's thesis in principle—and still do commend it—as a goal for ecumenism and hence as an indication of the right course for it to follow.[75] As a result, I was deluged with questions about my concrete attitude toward the issue. My responses form the genesis of the present chapter, the limits of which are thus clearly defined: it is not a scientific treatise and need not, therefore, enter into difficult and complex questions of detail; it consists, rather, of a few comments which, I hope, will elucidate the main aspects of the problem precisely by not going into detail. Its purpose is to clarify the tasks, possibilities and limits of the dispute—nothing more. In order not to exceed this goal, I have consciously renounced all attempts at stylistic elegance and every temptation to confront the vast literature that has since come into existence on the subject.[76]

But let us come to the point! I see the question of recognition as subdivided into four main issues.

1. Position of the CA in the totality of Lutheran confessional writings

We must first ask to what extent the CA is to be regarded as a valid and adequate expression of the faith and life of the ecclesiological communities that trace their origin to Luther. The immediate historical import of the text is clear. It was intended to show the Emperor that the new form of Christian ecclesial life, as it had spread far and wide under the impact of

---

[75] Joseph Ratzinger, "Prognosen für die Zukunft des Ökumenismus", in *Ökumenisches Forum, Grazer Hefte für konkrete Ökumene*, no. 1 (1977), 31–41 (= Part Two, Chapter 1A of the present work).

[76] Mention will be made here of only one representative text: Harding Meyer, Heinz Schütte and H. J. Mund, *Katholische Anerkennung des Augsburgischen Bekenntnisses? Ein Vorstoss zur Einheit zwischen katholischer und lutherischer Kirche* (Frankfurt: Lembeck, 1977). Among later works, I consider the following especially helpful: Wolfhart Pannenberg, "Die Augsburger Konfession und die Einheit der Kirche", in *Ökumenische Rundschau* 28 (1979): 99–114; Heinrich Fries, Erwin Iserloh et al., *Confessio Augustana, Hindernis oder Hilfe?* (Regensburg, 1979); Peter Gauly, *Katholisches Ja zum Augsburger Bekenntnis?* (Freiburg: Herder, 1980). The volume *Confessio Augustana. Bekenntnis des einen Glaubens. Gemeinsame Untersuchung lutherischer und katholischer Theologen,* ed. Harding Meyer and Heinz Schütte (Paderborn-Frankfurt: Bonifacius Druckerei, 1980), is semi-official in character. The following work, which comes from the German Democratic Republic, is worthy of note: F. Hoffmann and U. Kühn, *Die Confessio Augustana im ökumenischen Gespräch* (Berlin, 1980). I quote throughout this chapter from the classic text of the CA that was first published in 1930: *Die Bekenntnisschriften der evangelisch-lutherischen Kirche* [henceforth *Bekenntnisschriften*], 2

Luther's teachings, still fell juridically under the concept "Catholic". At the same time, the new movement drew a careful distinction between itself and the radical sects, attempting in this way to state, even for itself, its purpose and foundations. But the movement continued to develop, with the result that the CA became just *one* confessional text among many others in which, in a changed historical context, the polemical accent against the Catholic Church grew increasingly strong. Even the defense (*apologia*) of the CA abandoned the attempt at unification and drew dogmatic boundaries—which is true to an even greater degree of Melanchthon's *Tractatus de potestate papae* (1537), which, however, is more open to the concept of reconciliation than are the Schmalkaldic Articles, in which the Pope is designated as Antichrist and an understanding with Rome is declared impossible in itself and unthinkable.[77] The CA is the oldest personal statement of Protestant faith to be included in the corpus of confessional writings. The question is: Are the later texts to be interpreted as further developments and definitions that elucidate what was previously unclear, or is the direction of the CA the normative one? How strong is the inner unity of the confessional texts?

In discussing this first basic issue about the CA, that is, its place in the totality of the confessional writings, we must turn our attention also to a second issue that is neither less complicated nor less important: To what extent are Luther's writings to be regarded as the real foundation of the Reformation, as the normative basis for interpretation, in terms of which we are to decide the true meaning of the confessional writings? Peter Manns, as we know, objected to "recognition of the CA" on the grounds that it was an attempt to bypass Luther in order to achieve a cheap ecumenism with the more flexible but less profound Melanchthon.[78] It is as dangerous as it is false to argue, as Manns does, that the real strength lies with Luther and that it is to his writings that reference must be made in ecumenical endeavors, not to the derivative texts of Melanchthon, including the CA. This objection seems to me to be beside the point; interest in the CA is aimed, not at choosing between Luther and Melanchthon, but at coming to a genuinely ecclesial encounter above and beyond the disputes of theologians. Focus on the CA is due, not to the fact

---

vols. (Göttingen: Vandenhoeck and Ruprecht, 1952). A translation into modern German has been published by Siebenstern Pocket Books: Heinrich Bornkamm, *Das Augsburger Bekenntnis* (Gütersloh, 1978). [For an English translation, see "The Augsburg Confession (1530)", in *Creeds of the Churches,* ed. John H. Leith, rev. ed. (Richmond: John Knox Press, 1973), 63–107. (Trans.)]

[77] *Bekenntnisschriften,* second part of art. 4, 428–33.

[78] Peter Manns, "Zum Vorhaben einer katholischen Anerkennung der Confessio Augustana: Ökumene auf Kosten Martin Luthers?", in *Ökumenische Rundschau* 26 (1977): 426–50.

that it stems from Melanchthon, but that, as an official ecclesiological text, it ranks higher than do the texts of other theologians, however important. Manns' work does, however, call our attention to two important problems:

a. The distinction between theology and statements of church doctrine cannot be so clearly drawn in the sphere of the Lutheran Reformation as it can in Catholic theology. In fact, the Reformation rests, to a large extent, on the fact that that distinction has been eliminated and that, in consequence, statements of church doctrine can have no higher or different rank in principle than the findings of scientific theology.[79]

b. Luther, however, regarded himself not merely as a theologian but as possessed of an *auctoritas* comparable to that of the Apostle Paul,[80] and he has, in fact, always been looked upon in the Lutheran tradition as a kind of prophetic founder. Luther is the norm even for Melanchthon, so that we are justified in asking: To what extent, in practice, is the CA to be read according to the norm of Luther's writings, and to what extent may it be regarded as a separate "ecclesiological" text and, therefore, as a norm in its own right? The answer is by no means clear, nor can it be formulated in purely historical terms. We meet here with contradictory possibilities of development, with the option of deciding in one direction or the other. We must, therefore, ask: According to what norm is Luther himself to be read and interpreted—solely according to the ecclesiological norm[81] or, in a more revolutionary fashion, as fundamentally critical of the Church and her institutions?[82] This question, too, cannot be answered in purely historical terms although, in my opinion, the interpretations that regard his works as critical of the Church and her institutions are clearly superior to the bland ecclesiological interpretations of, for instance, Meinhold and Kinder, however sympathetic they may be to Catholicism. Nevertheless, there is still room for decisions that must be recognized as such. I regard it as a positive factor that history does not have the last word here. The possibility remains of taking this or that position with regard to the many-faceted legacy of the Reformation and of thus actually taking new steps to

---

[79] Cf. Siegfried Wiedenhofer, *Formalstrukturen humanistischer und reformatorischer Theologie bei Philipp Melanchthon*, Regensburger Studien zu Theologie 2 (Munich: Peter Lang, 1976): esp. 282–347.

[80] On this subject, cf. the instructive contribution of Helmut Feld, "Lutherus Apostolus. Kirchliches Amt und apostolische Verantwortung in der Galaterbrief-Auslegung Martin Luthers", in *Wort Gottes in der Zeit*, Festschrift für Karl Hermann Schelkle zum 65. Geburtstag, Helmut Feld and Josef Nolte, eds. (Düsseldorf: Patmos, 1973), 288–304.

[81] That is, in the direction taken in their interpretations by Schlink, Althaus, Kinder, Meinhold, Joest, to which, on the Catholic side, Lortz, Manns and, to a certain extent, Iserloh also subscribe.

[82] That is, in the line pursued in very different ways by, for example, Gogarten, von Loewenich, K. G. Steck and, most convincingly, E. Bizer.

leave the past behind or, on the other hand, of assimilating from that legacy whatever is of permanent value.

2. The question of the authority of the confession

All this leads to the second basic issue raised by the debate about recognition. Given the structure of Luther's reform and of the communities that derived from it, what would be the actual character of a confessional text? To what subject would it be responsible and by what claim would this be the case? In the *Confessio* itself, the subject is defined as *nos* (I), *nostri* (XX), *ecclesiae nostrae* (XXIV). The identity of this *"nos"* is clarified in the *Praefatio: nos infra scripti* (= a number of princes and mayors) *perinde ut alii Electores, Principes et Status.* From this we are to understand the meaning of Article I: *Ecclesiae magno consensu apud nos docent.* If we prescind from the impressive political faction in this identification of the subject, the theological bearer of the *Confessio* is the consensus of a number of local churches: more accurately, congregations. This consensus is presented as a factual theological situation. Such a self–interpretation raises two questions for the present discussion:

a. To what extent does there exist today a factual consensus of *"ecclesiae nostrae"*, as the expression is used in the CA? Precisely in view of the inner structure of this text, the question about its recognition must first be raised as a question about its actual value and application. The second question is even more important.

b. Given the prerequisite of *sola Scriptura,* to what extent can a confessional text have more than factual validity, that is, to what extent can it have binding power in its own right as an ecclesiological statement of doctrine? The effect of Luther's *sola Scriptura* is that an ecclesiological statement of doctrine has no other theological quality than that of being a correct interpretation of Scripture and, therefore, subject to correction by better interpretations. Consequently, the Church has a factual regulatory function but no theological voice of her own. In the last analysis, she cannot, *qua* Church, speak in matters of faith with any more authority than can the theologian. That comes with the exclusion of tradition, which thus becomes a more or less meaningful "custom", but cannot be a binding and definitive teaching of the Church as Church. In CA XXVIII, this viewpoint is formulated as unobtrusively as possible and, in consequence, the fact is somewhat obscured that *traditiones* (as at the Council of Trent only the plural is used) are consigned automatically to the level of "customs" about which it is then positively stated: "It is fitting (*"convenit"*) for the Christian assembly to observe such ordinances for the sake of love and peace, . . . but in such a way that consciences are not burdened, that no one believes . . . he has committed sin if he breaks them. . . ."[83]

The problem associated with the *reductio ecclesiae ad Scripturam* is obscured in the case of Luther and Melanchthon by the infallibility they ascribe to their interpretations of Scripture. But wherever the ambiguity of history makes its appearance, we must ask about the role of *traditio* as *auctoritas*. The dispute about the CA involves the basic problem: Is the CA more than a theology? And, if so, on what grounds? In what does the binding power of ecclesial doctrine consist? A prerequisite for Catholic "recognition" of the CA is its Protestant "recognition", that is, recognition of the fact that here the church teaches and can teach precisely as church. Such a Protestant recognition means a decision as to the formal principle of faith (Scripture and tradition), and this formal aspect of the whole is, in many respects, more important than the material one. The Catholic reaction toward "recognition" is a question about recognition in the Protestant sphere and, as such, an effort to determine the place the Protestant church occupies with respect to faith. In this sense, there is question here not just of a scholarly problem that could be worked out by specialists in the field but of the dynamism of a spiritual process that can succeed only by decisions of a spiritual nature. Theologically, Protestant "recognition", as it has been described, would turn the actual ecclesial teaching and life that now exist in the Protestant sphere concretely into that ecclesiality that has been concealed up to now—and, in fact, questioned again and again in principle—under the one-sided *sola Scriptura* and the consequent fundamental susceptibility of the church to change on the basis of scholarly theological opinions.

We might say, then, that Protestant "recognition" would be, in any event, the first inner prerequisite for Catholic recognition and, at the same time, a spiritual process that would create ecumenical reality. It would bring the incipient ecclesiality of the *"ecclesiae nostrae"* to a new level and, in doing so, would not draw boundaries but would restore the official realm of *"ecclesia"* in which official unity would be possible.

3. *The question of the reconcilability of the content of the CA with the Catholic faith*

Only on this third level do we come, finally, to the question of whether, in terms of its content, the CA itself actually can be reconciled with the

---

[83] CA XXVIII 55, in Bornkamm, 67; *Bekenntnisschriften*, 129.

Catholic faith. A line-by-line commentary of the text is, it is clear, among the tasks inherent in the question of recognition, but it can, for obvious reasons, not be undertaken here. It is certain that, in making such a commentary, one should keep constantly before oneself the statements in the *Confutatio Pontificia*.[84]

I shall limit myself to a few basic remarks. The CA itself answers the question posed here unambiguously in the affirmative when it diagnoses the nature of the division that has taken place with the sentence: "The dispute and quarrel are chiefly about certain traditions and abuses" that have crept in "without any firm basis in divine command or in Scripture".[85] It is, thus, plainly contradictory to the Schmalkaldic Articles, which regard the dissension as basic and declare unification to be completely impossible per se.[86] There can be no doubt that, even up to the present, Lutheran tradition, in this particular respect, follows, not the diagnosis of the CA, but that of the Schmalkaldic Articles and that, on this point, even the *Defense* of the CA departs notably from the CA itself.

How, then, is the diagnosis of the CA itself to be understood and evaluated? What possibilities does it offer for reunion, for demolishing the Schmalkaldic wall? The psychological question about Melanchthon's sincerity, which is constantly raised in this connection, is an idle one and does nothing to further our inquiry; we should simply assume here that the text means what it says.[87] The explanation of the dichotomy must be sought in what the texts actually say. It lies, in my opinion, in the fact that Melanchthon included in the concept of *usus* and *abusus* a wide range of ecclesial forms of doctrine and life that, in the Catholic view, are not *"usus"* but belong, rather, to the realm of official ecclesial faith. Thus the contradiction lay, for him, only in the realm of *usus* while, for the Catholic Church, what he called *abusus* is, in fact, a part of her faith. But Luther was well aware of what the real issue was. He knew that only one side could regard the downgrading of *traditio* to *(ab-)usus* as a mere dispute about customs; that, from the perspective of the whole, it had to be evaluated as a quarrel in principle and about principles.

When the issue is stated in this way, it is clear that the dogmatic articles of the CA are, in fact, relatively unequivocal and clear only in drawing the boundaries against the "fanatics"—as a statement that can certainly not be

---

[84] Since this article was first published, the long-awaited critical addition of this important text has finally made its appearance: Herbert Immenkötter, *Die Confutatio der Confessio Augustana vom 3. August 1530*, in *Corpus Catholicorum* 33 (Münster: Aschendorff, 1979). In the Introduction (1–72), Immenkötter has carefully analyzed the historical position of the text. Cf. also, Vinzenz Pfnür, *Einig in der Rechtfertigungslehre?*, 222–50.

[85] CA, end of pt. 1, 2, in Bornkamm, 32; *Bekenntnisschriften*, art. XXI, 83.

[86] Cf. especially, pt. 2, art. 2 and 4, in *Bekenntnisschriften*, 416–33.

[87] Cf. here the comprehensive treatment by Pfnür in *Einig in der Rechtfertigungslehre?*

evaluated as "obsequiousness" in any negative sense: to establish this boundary was, beyond a doubt, the one aspect of the spiritual struggle of twenty years that was clearly stated in the CA.[88] The quarrel with the Catholic Church is not reflected in a concrete way until the second part of the CA: it can be seen—especially in the articles "On the Mass" (XXIV), "On Confession" (XXV), and "On the Power of Bishops" (XXVIII)—in what sense the new interpretation of the doctrine of justification ran counter to the teaching of the Church and, with it, to the understanding of the sacraments, especially the Eucharist and the spiritual ministry. I propose to demonstrate this by two examples: the Mass and the binding force of ecclesial doctrine (in which the question of spiritual ministry and the problem of *traditio* are intertwined).

With respect to the Mass, it is possible to distinguish quite clearly in the CA two levels of argumentation. In the beginning, Melanchthon remains true to his initial position and discusses the question of private Masses, which had been criticized by the reformers exclusively in terms of stipends, that is, of the avarice of the clergy, and, consequently, in terms of *abusus*.[89] Then, however, he states that the teaching has crept in that the Passion of Christ brought redemption only for original sin and that Christ instituted the Mass in order that satisfaction could in that way be made for all other sins—*mortalibus et venialibus*. This, he continues, is how the universal opinion arose that the Mass is an *"opus delens peccata vivorum et mortuorum ex opere operato."*[90] Whereas it had been stated earlier that stipends were the reason for private Masses, it says now: *"Haec disputatio peperit istam multitudinem missarum."*[91] That is, a theological reason is given in which the relatively rare private opinion of some theologians about the ordering of the Mass to *peccata actualia* was combined with the question of the Mass as satisfaction for sins and of the *opus operatum*.[92] Here we can see the basic shifting of levels that led to the varying classification as *usus* or *traditio*: the question of justification, which is identical with the theology of the Mass, is transferred from the ontological level to that of experience; we might indeed say that in the CA, the new component in the doctrine of justification, by which theology as a whole was revolutionized to its very core, lies in the fact that justification has thus become a question of experience, that is, of the experienced certainty of salvation—in other words, the *consolatio perterrefactae conscientiae*.[93] The key concepts of the

[88] Pfnür has demonstrated this convincingly.

[89] XXIV, 16 (Latin text), *Bekenntnisschriften*, 92. Unless otherwise stated, page references in nn. 89–95 are to the *Bekenntnisschriften*.

[90] XXIV, 21 and 22, 93.

[91] XXIV, 23, 93.

[92] Cf. especially XXIV, 29, 94.

[93] Cf. XXV, 4, 98; XX, 15, 74; and, especially, XX, 17, 75.

doctrine of justification and of the theology of the sacraments, which is identical with it, are fear and consolation, that is, concepts on the level of experience, on which level the ontological statements of the Catholic Church as well as the effect of her liturgy are measured and in terms of which they are necessarily criticized, even rejected. Of the Eucharist, it is said that it was instituted "to soothe the troubled conscience".[94] As a result of this ordering of the whole of theology to the concept of consolation, the communal liturgy of the Church was subsumed *in toto* under the heading of *caeremoniae*, which, in turn, were measured by their pedagogical effect: "For ceremonies are necessary above all so that, by them, the unlearned may be taught."[95]

From this there results automatically the changed view of ecclesial ministry and the fundamentally different classification of ecclesial doctrine that we see in Article XXVIII. This article, like Article XXIV, begins by presenting a genuine problem of (*ab-*)*usus*: the combination of spiritual and secular power in the case of bishops and in the ecclesial practice of excommunication. Here too, however, a properly theological problem moves into the foreground: just as the liturgical celebration can be no more than a *caeremonia*, so ecclesial doctrine can be no more than "ordinances for the sake of love and peace".[96]

At this point, the problem in the content of the CA touches upon the fundamental question (discussed above in 2b) of the possibility of binding doctrine in and through the Church. It is thus revealed to be the really central question. If we were to prescind from the inner self-understanding of the CA and concentrate instead on the proper nature of an ecclesial confession, the emphasis on experience would appear in a new light: "*consolatio*", as the immediate counterpart of "gospel" and as its ultimate norm, would be incorporated into the normativeness of the common faith of the Church; experience would not be deprived of meaning by this but would be relativized in importance and linked to the objective teaching of the Church. Obviously, the text of the CA would thus be transgressed. But, on the other hand, it would be recognized that, by virtue of the CA, the Church had transcended her own self-evaluation and that ecclesial doctrine had, in fact, evolved. This would be in complete accord with the inner meaning of Melanchthon's theology, in which, under the aegis of the Reformation, essential elements of the previously rejected Catholic structure had grown up and had made possible a church structure with the necessary permanence historically to preserve and develop the spiritual impetus received from Luther.[97]

---

[94] XXIV, 26–33, 93–94.

[95] XXIV, 3, 91; Bornkamm, 39.

[96] XXVIII, 55, 129: *ordinatio propter caritatem et tranquillitatem*.

[97] Wiedenhofer (see n. 77) has thoroughly demonstrated this fact on the basis of the texts

4. *The concept of "recognition"*

We are now in a position to state, by way of summary, what "recognition of the CA" does and does not mean. It certainly does not mean that this document would be shown, by historical textual analysis, to be a correct or, at least, a dogmatically unobjectionable and permissible statement of Catholic doctrine. To attempt to do so would be to fail to give cognizance to the actual content of the CA, which, it is true, does in a certain respect strive for such correctness but fails to achieve it because of the shift of levels with regard to the concept of "(*ab-*)*usus*", thus—with the best of intentions—concealing a factual difference that the Schmalkaldic Articles are correct in stating openly. Such a procedure would have to be called sham scholarship and, for a twofold reason, would be not only historically but also ecumenically futile.

a. By it, the CA would be isolated from the corpus of confessional writings and totally divorced from Luther's work. It would thus be enclosed in a fictitious existence of its own that would have no relationship to reality.

b. A CA so understood would be not only without historical validity but also without any corresponding entity in the present ecclesial reality. Sham battles would be waged over the year 1530, for it is well known that today the CA does not (and cannot) have an isolated or isolatable binding force. Hence, a CA so understood would coincide with no concrete ecclesial reality of today but would be revealed as an academic fiction.

If "recognition of the CA" cannot be construed as a verification of history, then (as we saw above in 2) it must be understood as a (certainly historically founded and accounted for) spiritual process that demands new decisions on both sides and that must be regarded, therefore, not as explanatory, but as judgmental in character. From what has been said above, it is clear, however, that such decisions presume a process of maturation that is not easy and must not be expected to be of short duration. There is room for these processes that lead to decision since the reformation legacy itself admits of developments in many directions, above all in two that are diametrically opposed: the ecclesial direction and the direction of emphasis on religious experience, which, if it is made an absolute, can split any institution. Corresponding to this, on the other hand, is the fact that ecclesiality in the Catholic sense also admits of a variety of spiritual and religious forms.

By way of conclusion, let us say that anyone who expects "recognition of the CA" to come about quickly is operating from a false premise. What

---

themselves (384–404); note especially his discussion of the changing schemata of theological systems (397–98).

is at issue here is a very demanding process based on the fact that this text has opened a way that gives it a new meaning which, in turn, can be the starting point of a new way. Since the notion of "recognition" almost of necessity awakens false expectations, it should, in my opinion, be abandoned; since, in addition, the CA cannot be considered in isolation, it would be better to speak of a dialogue about the theological and ecclesial structure of the Protestant-Lutheran confessional writings and their reconcilability with the doctrine of the Catholic Church.[98]

D. Ecumenism at a Standstill? Explanatory Comments on *Mysterium Ecclesiae*

On June 24, 1973, a text was issued in Rome, the official English translation of which bears the title: "Declaration in Defense of Catholic Doctrine against Certain Errors of the Present Day".[99] There is question here, not of a papal encyclical, but—one step lower—of a statement of the Congregation for the Doctrine of the Faith, signed by its prefect, Cardinal

---

[98] All this should not, of course, be taken to mean that the matter of ecumenism should now be postponed indefinitely. Only a superficial attitude can give rise to the opinion that the urgency of a task is irreconcilable with patience in carrying it out. In reality, patience is the only proper response to what is truly urgent. Often by an attitude of patience can it be accepted as urgent, whereas impatience signifies an absence of preparedness. For patience is strength, impatience is weakness. A further reflection is in order here: it is not fitting for either the Church or the Christian to set deadlines for unity. Deadlines can be set only for what is subject to one's own discretion. To refrain from setting our own deadline means to acknowledge ecumenism as God's concern and, for that reason, to give it priority among our own concerns.

In the present case, the meaning of these distinctions is clear: an attitude oriented toward quick action can have only one result: that, with the end of the anniversary year of 1980 and its consequent promulgations, the subject of the Augsburg Confession and its possibilities for unity will be consigned *ad acta*. Only an attitude whose urgency cannot be met by deadlines can give the matter the emphasis that is its due. That is why it seemed right to me to reprint the present article as it was composed on the eve of the Augustana anniversary—as an expression of the unaltered importance of the theme it addresses. In the meantime, the ecumenical commission formed after the Pope's visit to Germany has been carrying out its task to a large degree along the lines envisioned here. By concerning itself with the meaning of the censures and anathemas of the sixteenth century as they are understood in the churches today, it attempts to accomplish that purification and elucidation of the legacy of the past that will prepare the way for the spiritual decisions that were intended, but not clearly described, by the word "recognition".

[99] Ratzinger uses the official German title: "Erklärung zur katholischen Lehre über die Kirche, die gegen einige heutige Irrtümer zu verteidigen ist". I have quoted throughout from the official English translation: "In Defense of Catholic Doctrine" [*Mysterium Ecclesiae*], in *Origins* 3, no. 7 (July 19, 1973): 97, 99–100, 110–23. [Trans.]

Šeper, and its secretary, the Belgian Archbishop Hamer, and provided as well with an explicit ratification, dated May 11, 1973, by Pope Paul VI, at whose order the text was published. It is clear that the Catholic Church has entered today upon a time of great tension and turmoil. It should be equally clear that the hierarchy of the Church cannot simply remain silent in this situation but must do what they can to overcome the crisis. Members of the Church are calling today, with increasing emphasis, for a clear drawing of lines, but the Pope and bishops have been unable as yet to decide in favor of such an action. The resentment that has grown up in the last half-century because of innumerable faulty decisions and, above all, because of a too-narrow handling of Church discipline is like an inward-growing boil on the ecclesial conscience; it has created an allergy to condemnation from which we can more readily expect an increase of the evil than its cure. That is why, despite dramatic tensions that extend to denial of a personal, hearing and answering God and, thus, to the very marrow of Christian belief, the maxim uttered by John XXIII has continued, after Vatican Council II, to be a basic guide for the Church: It is better to use the means of mercy than of condemnation. After the Council, this point of view led, in Germany, to the publication of two important doctrinal texts by the Conference of German Bishops: one on the priestly ministry and, before that, a more general text addressed to all to whom the Church has confided the task of making the faith known. The statement of the Congregation for the Doctrine of the Faith belongs basically to this latter category. It proposes to meet the crisis by a positive presentation especially of those points of Church doctrine that are under dispute and to establish the identity of Catholicism, not by excluding those who hold opposing views, but by an official enunciation of the constituent elements of Catholicism, obviously in the hope that such a statement will prove its effectiveness and lead to a clarification in one direction or another. We shall have to see whether these expectations are fulfilled; at least it will be clear whether or not this approach to discipline in matters of doctrine can serve as a model for the future.

It should be clear from what has been said above that the text we are discussing is an instrument developed from within the Catholic Church in response to an internal crisis. In this connection, it should be noted that it would be false to depict the whole process as a kind of *Lex Küng* directed solely against the Tübingen theologian. That is certainly not the case, although Küng's much-read books and their polemical bent were the immediate catalyst that led to the publication of the text. The quality of the whole as an intraecclesial communication as well as its real purpose are abundantly clear from the last sentence of the document itself, which specifies both those to whom it is addressed and the purpose for which it was written: the "Explanation" is directed to bishops and to all other guardians of the truth; in addition, it is directed to the faithful and, especially, to priests and theologians, "that all may be of one mind in the faith and may be in sincere harmony with the Church". Its purpose is the restoration of harmony and inner sincerity within the Church as the basis of trust, without which there can be no harmony. It is possible to speak only indirectly of an ecumenical purpose—that is, only insofar as the inner division of any church is an obstacle to ecumenical dialogue, and ecumenism would certainly not be served by continuing discord within the Catholic Church.

Unexpectedly, nevertheless, the text led to an ecumenical controversy; it was regarded by many as an attack on already realized ecumenical goals, as a rejection of the outcomes of bilateral dialogues, which, in many instances, had produced mutual clarifications. Hence we may ask: What does the document really say? It deals, in six points, with three principal themes: the question of the oneness of the Church; questions related to the problem of "infallibility"; and questions about priesthood in the Church. Even the first of these themes caused considerable ecumenical consternation, although, in dealing with a topic that was recognized as being especially explosive from an ecumenical point of view, the text purposely speaks only in quotations from Vatican Council II and exercises particular care not to use formulas of its own devising or those of earlier Church proclamations in order to avoid any suggestion that it might be reverting to positions held before the Council or that it was holding obdurately to any new postconciliar position. Consequently, the fundamental elements of the conciliar concept of the unity of the Church and the plurality of Christian communities are skillfully combined in a montage of quotations. The central passages about the Church's constant need of renewal as well as of the presence of Christian truth and holiness in non-Catholic communities are joined to a fundamental conciliar statement which says that the spiritual and visible entities of the Church are inseparable. The visible Church is herself also the spiritual Church, the Church of Jesus Christ. And even more strongly: this one and only Church, which is at once spiritual and earthly, is so concrete that she can be called by name: she "subsists in the Catholic Church, which is governed by the successor of Peter and the bishops in union with that successor". No translation can fully capture the sublime nuance of the Latin text in which the unconditional equation of the first conciliar drafts—the full identity between the Church of Jesus Christ and the Roman Catholic Church—is clearly set forth: nothing of the concreteness of the conciliar concept of the Church is lost—the Church is there present where the successors of the Apostle Peter and of the other apostles visibly incorporate her continuity with her source; but this full concreteness of the Church does not mean that every other Church can be only a non-Church.[100] The equation is not mathematical because the Holy Spirit cannot be reduced to a mathematical symbol, not even where he concretely binds and bestows himself. Mathematics is an abstraction even in the physical sphere but especially where there is question of God and man. Abstractions are clear, but one cannot build one's life on them. The working of the Holy Spirit is admittedly not clear, but it can be trusted: the equation is valid even though it cannot be stated mathematically.

It is not easy to describe the tension aroused by this new reminder of the conciliar text. General awareness had very quickly soothed itself with the assumption that the equation between the Church of Jesus Christ and the Catholic Church was no longer valid even though it was still maintained in certain special Roman pronouncements, the disappearance of which, it was believed, could be confidently expected in the course of further developments. As a result, the concrete churches came increasingly to be regarded, singly and together, as external institutionalizations in whose unavoidable plurality the unity of the Church was mirrored in a more or less fragmented fashion. The "Declaration" of the Congregation for the Doctrine of the Faith addresses this attitude in the following words: "The followers of Christ are not permitted to imagine that Christ's Church is nothing more than a collection (divided but still possessing a certain unity) of churches and ecclesial communities. Nor are they free to hold that Christ's Church nowhere exists today and that she is to be considered only as an end which all churches and ecclesial communities must strive to reach." These sentences evoked the wrath of Bishop Harms, who reported that the question was already being raised as to whether, on the basis of this "Declaration" of the Congregation for the Doctrine of the Faith, "the Church of Rome" was not on the way to becoming a megasect. With specific reference to the sentences just quoted, he said that, in view of them, "one could see with concern that the churches of the Reformation had obviously not succeeded in making clear their understanding of the Church of Christ".[101] These comments are based on an inexact reading of the text, which does not claim that the sentences describe the Protestant understanding of the Church but takes issue, rather, with a trend within

---

[100] Cf. the commentary on section 8 especially of the "Dogmatic Constitution on the Church" by that document's principal author, Gérard Philips, L'Église et son mystère au II Concile du Vatican (Paris: Desclée, 1967), 1:114–19. See also Aloys Grillmeier, Das Zweite Vatikanische Konzil. Konstitutionen, Dekrete und Erklärungen, LTK, Supplement, ed. Heinrich Suso Brechter et al. (Freiburg: Herder, 1966), 170–76.

[101] Bishop Hans Heinrich Harms, "Dreht Rom das Rad zurück?" First published in Publik-Forum, October 16, 1973; quoted here from a reprint in Una Sancta 28 (1973): 189–91. The quotation will be found on 189–90.

the Catholic Church herself, the existence of which no one who reads the modern literature about the Church can seriously deny. I believe we can say that a similar trend exists also in the Protestant sphere with no particular reference to the Protestant understanding of the Church, which, in any event, does not exist in the singular.

As to the matter of the megasect, the same formula was also used after the demise of *Publik*,[102] which fact alone shows with what verbal hyperbole we are dealing here. At that time, some theologians seemed to divide salvation history itself into the time before and the time after the end of *Publik*—and anyone who regards this sentence as an exaggeration need only read the inquiry conducted in 1972 by the journal *Wort und Wahrheit* about the state of the Roman Catholic Church in order to find abundant evidence in support of it. The same opinion was also voiced by relatively temperate theologians in connection with the preparatory texts for the Bishops' Synod of 1971; at the same time, however, it was apparent to the somewhat neutral observer that, by contrast, a text of the Commissio Theologica Internationalis was greeted with notable forbearance since, apparently, no one had noticed that it stemmed from the same authors as the so sharply criticized Roman text, whose principal fault must, therefore, have been the fact that it came from Rome. Obviously, then, the charge of being on the way to becoming a megasect belongs to a fund of stock phrases that are always ready at hand whenever unwelcome decisions are announced, especially by Rome. Whatever we may think of word games in which a word is chosen for its political connotations rather than for its relevance to the context in which it is used, they do seem out of place in the present instance, because the censure is directed to the repetition of sentences that, at the end of Vatican Council II, were regarded as the genuinely ecclesiological breakthrough of the Council: with the formulas that are now so harshly criticized, the Council actually succeeded, without detriment to Catholic identity, in finding a formula within the logic of Catholicism for the ecclesial character of non-Catholic communities. Should precisely that which was then regarded as an ecumenical breakthrough really be regarded after eight years as marking the way to becoming a sect? We can, I think, draw two conclusions from such a contradiction:

a. It is obvious how completely the factual content of Vatican Council II has been forgotten today and what a changed awareness has come to exist in Christianity.

b. With this, the danger of a lightly conceived ecumenism becomes clear, for an ecumenism that is superficial, that forgets the foundations,

---

[102] See below, pages 383 and 389.

can be but an insignificant alliance. In this respect, the consternation about the Roman "Declaration" should be salutary: if the text makes us aware of the fragmentary character of foundations that are not foundations, then it will have served us well.

Let us turn our attention now to the other two themes addressed in the document. The first, the question of infallibility, occupies by far the largest part of the text. It is almost impossible to do it justice in a brief summary. I shall attempt, however, to outline its principal arguments. To begin with, the text addresses the infallibility of the Church as a whole. Again, it is Vatican Council II, which, in its "Dogmatic Constitution on Divine Revelation", had found very beautiful expressions for describing the relationship of Church and word, which sets the tone: the word lives and grows in the Church in a harmony of proclamation, prayerful acceptance and daily living and suffering of the word. We come to know what it means, what it is in reality, as ever new situations of human life and human history are steeped in this word; as we place the material of our lives at its disposal; as we ruminate on it in prayer, in struggle, in love, in suffering, and so rediscover it again and again.[103] Without this living of the word, the proclamation of it would be an empty heaping-up of words; it exists so that the leaven can penetrate and show its power. On the other hand, God's word always precedes and confronts us: however often and however deeply it permeates us, it is never simply our own; even when it is in us, it is above us. The proclamation of the word constitutes this encounter with it, and the text states here the special task of the ministry of shepherds: the pro-clamation [Vor-legen] of the word, the authorized and authentic attestation of it, is their particular role, which is something quite different from the expertise of specialists. Here the text touches upon a critical point. In an age that puts so much credence in knowledge, the specialist takes the place of the priest. Nevertheless, it has long since become clear in the realm of politics and economics that the world cannot be built by specialists alone. The decision of one who bears responsibility and is called to responsibility cannot be distilled from some special knowledge; it is necessary precisely as a responsible decision. The same is said here, from a theological perspective, with regard to the Church, and anyone who remembers how sharply the young Barth ridiculed the attempt to build the certainty of faith on the certainty of specialists will consider the diminution of the role of the expert in the Church as at least appropriate.

There follows a second "hot iron": Although the teaching ministry lives

---

[103] On article 8 of the "Dogmatic Constitution on Divine Revelation" (which is basic to this discussion), cf. my commentary in LTK, Supplement, 2:518–23.

by the fruits that accrue to the service of the word from the mediation, experience and research of the faithful, it is, nevertheless, not only an interpreter of understandings already reached but can be useful also in bringing about such understandings where they have not been reached. Mario von Galli, who kindly reported on the whole document, believed this passage reflected on unsuccessful *ex post facto* justification of the encyclical on birth control and concluded that the evidence cited could not be reconciled with what was said.[104] I am obliged, unfortunately, to disagree with him. What is offered in evidence is a particularly controversial text of Vatican Council I—perhaps the major stumbling block in orthodox Christianity. Vatican Council I had said that the pope can make definitive decisions not only with the consent of the Church but also in his own right (*"ex sese"*). Although many efforts were made during Vatican Council II to interpret this harsh and very ambiguous formula in such a way that its real meaning would be more readily apparent, they were not successful at that time because of disagreement among those concerned. It is my opinion that what was then only a wish is again being attempted in this section of the "Declaration". It is no longer simply stated that the teaching ministry can make decisions on its own—*ex sese*. Now it is more accurately stated that, while the teaching ministry always acts against the background of the faith and prayer of the whole Church, ". . . its office is not reduced merely to ratifying the assent already expressed by the latter; indeed, in the interpretation and explanation of the written or transmitted word of God, the Magisterium can anticipate or demand their assent"; in the confusion of a Church where consensus is lacking, it must present the word that can demand the consent of all. Consequently, there resides in the teaching ministry, under certain conditions, the possibility of authentically and therefore bindingly distinguishing true faith from false—again in close reliance on the two Vatican Councils. Thus the inner certainty of faith is decisively emphasized: a Church that cannot assume responsibility for the content of her faith has no right to teach. The fifth chapter of the text, which follows here, has been the most kindly received because, indeed, it goes far beyond Vatican Council II in discussing the linguistic aspect of the faith and its historical character, that is, the distance that always exists between the historical words of man and truth. Unfortunately, I cannot pursue this aspect of the question here because it is not the positive elements of the text but only what was regarded as ecumenically problematical that is the subject of discussion. It can be said, however, that here, for the first time, there

---

[104] Mario von Galli, "Eine Verurteilung oder Ansatz zum Gespräch?" First published in *Orientierung*, nos. 13–14 (July 15 and 31, 1973); quoted here from a reprint in *Una Sancta* 28 (1973): 185–89. Quotation will be found on 186.

was composed something in the nature of an official ecclesial theory of dogmatic history that actually takes, as its central conviction, the notion that, even in the mutability of history, identity of faith, including identity of content, is possible and real.[105]

The last section of the document, which bears the title "The Church Associated with the Priesthood of Christ", has stirred up a lot of dust. The reason may be, partly at least, that the text has been measured by a false standard. Anyone who hopes to find in it a comprehensive teaching about the priesthood will inevitably be disappointed. But this was obviously not what was intended here; for one thing, the Bishops' Synod in Rome had presented such a document only two years previously,[106] and mention should also be made of the letter of the German bishops[107] and of the book on the same subject published by the Commissio Theologica Internationalis.[108] Here the sole intention was simply to protect without any particular systematization two particularly threatened statements that are indispensable to the Catholic understanding of the spiritual ministry. Nevertheless, a fatal isolation was avoided by first emphasizing the priestly character of the entire Church and only against this background setting forth the real nature of the priestly ministry. Those who do not read with a priori anti-Roman spectacles—a practice which, unfortunately, has meanwhile become fashionable in Germany—will also be able to find here very beautiful and ecumenically valuable formulations about sacraments and word in the priestly service, about the trinitarian character of the Eucharist and about the Eucharist as the fulfillment of the ecclesial community. Umbrage has been taken with regard to these key statements: the priesthood is linked to the apostolic succession as it is represented in the chain of bishops united with the priests. Jurisdiction with regard to the Eucharist and, therefore, the commission to speak the holy words of the sacrament, are inseparably and exclusively linked to the priestly ministry. The sacramental gift of this ministry is for life. The document touches here upon a sensitive point, perhaps *the* sensitive point, in the present ecumenical dialogue, which the ecumenical memorandum of six German universities tried to banish with a bold stroke. But their action strikes one as more and more curious the longer one contemplates it. For how can anyone say that there is no longer anything that separates the churches if he

---

[105] Cf. also ITK, *Die Einheit des Glaubens und der theologische Pluralismus* (Einsiedeln: Johannes Verlag, 1973), 17–67, esp. 61–67.

[106] Synod of Bishops, 1971: *Das Priesteramt,* intro. by Joseph Cardinal Höffner; commentary by Hans Urs von Balthasar (Einsiedeln, 1972).

[107] *Schreiben der deutschen Bischöfe über das priesterliche Amt. Eine biblisch-dogmatische Handreichung* (Trier: Paulinus, 1969).

[108] ITK, *Priesterdienst* (Einsiedeln, 1972).

does not, at some point, bother to cite the teaching of the Church?[109] The "Declaration" from Rome presents this teaching of the Church, and no one who takes the trouble to read the evidence, or who has any knowledge at all of what the Church teaches, can deny that the Catholic Church does indeed so teach and, at least in the first two points, is in full agreement not only with the Orthodox Church but also with the non-Chalcedonian churches, whose separation from Rome dates back to the fifth century. Nothing new is being taught here. Why, then, the consternation? Anyone who interprets the text narrowly could conclude from it that the priesthood and, consequently, the Eucharist are being denied to Protestant churches. But the question of priesthood is contested on both sides, since Protestant Christianity is, for the most part, inclined to fear, in the Catholic version thereof, a lapse from the gospel. If the Catholic Church sees a "too little" in the Protestant churches, they, for their part, find a "too much" in the Catholic Church. There is a lack of unity here that does not have to be regarded as irremediable and that shows signs of hope again and again in individual areas of misunderstanding. On the whole, however, the dissension is there, though it can hardly be said to have originated with the present text. As regards the Eucharist, it is quite certain, not least because of the disagreement over the question of ministry, that here, too, there are many questions to be asked on both sides; that here, too, there will be the same complaints about too much and too little. But the Catholic teaching here recalled to memory does not in any way deny that Protestant Christians who believe in the presence of the Lord also share in that presence. In this instance, the authors have obviously been too little aware of the fact that it is impossible today to speak internally without being heard externally; but external misunderstanding can very easily destroy internal effectiveness.

What does all this tell us about the state of ecumenism? Although I would oppose almost *in toto* Bishop Harms' comments on the contents of the "Declaration" from Rome, I believe he has found exactly the right words with which to characterize the basic task. If dialogue is to be genuine, he wrote, then "questions must be asked more exactingly and more obstinately. No partner in the dialogue must cast thoughtless aspersions against any other. All participants are concerned with truth, which suffers no compromises."[110] Truth alone provides a firm ground for our feet. If that is the case, then the frank words of the Congregation for the Doctrine of the Faith have rendered ecumenism a service. As to its own

---

[109] *Reform und Anerkennung kirchlicher Ämter. Ein Memorandum der Arbeitsgemeinschaft ökumenischer Universitätsinstitute* (Munich-Mainz, 1973), 11–25. See also Karl Lehmann in IKZ 2 (1973): 284–88.

[110] Bishop Harms, 189.

purpose, the Congregation states that it does not aim at research or at the development of new knowledge or proofs but seeks only to recall Catholic dogma to mind in order to create clarity where there is mist—in other words, an act of recollection, nothing more. And that is also the way the Bible envisions the service of the servants of the word: to remember; for this they are called. At first glance, recollection can seem burdensome, truth a hindrance. But progress that is based on forgetting is deceptive; unity that finds embarrassment in truth is transitory. The Roman text can be criticized in many particulars, but, as a whole, it is a necessary service— necessary in the often unpleasant but useful way of a clamorous alarm clock that rouses from the web of dreams and summons to the tasks of another day.

CHAPTER 2

THE KEY QUESTION IN THE
CATHOLIC-PROTESTANT DISPUTE: TRADITION
AND *SUCCESSIO APOSTOLICA*

A. Holy Orders (Ordo) as the Sacramental Expression of the Principle of Tradition

Prefatory remarks

This article was originally written for an ecumenical symposium of Orthodox and Catholic theologians. Its purpose was not to introduce new points of view into the discussion about the priesthood but, rather, to inform our partners in the discussion—in this case, Greek Orthodox theologians—as exactly and as thoroughly as possible about the doctrinal position of the Catholic Church on this subject.[1] As we saw in the previous chapter, this is also a central question in the dispute with the Protestant churches and in the related intra-Catholic dispute—both of which suffer from a lack of accurate information. I thought it would be helpful, therefore, to place this text, which was written for the express purpose of supplying such information, at the beginning of the section that proposes to describe the ecumenical problems associated with a statement of theological principles.

Anyone who inquires about the Church's teaching with regard to holy orders finds at his disposal a relatively rich supply of source materials; three councils have spoken extensively on the subject: Florence, Trent and Vatican II.[2] Mention should also be made of the important apostolic constitution of Pius XII (*Sacramentum ordinis*) of the year 1947. Since the more recent texts—the constitution of Pius XII and the pronouncements of Vatican II—also incorporate the earlier statements, it will be practical to begin our study with them in order first to discover the current doctrinal

---

[1] The limited purpose of this article will also justify the omission of any critique of the vast literature on the subject. The fundamental and accurate study by Karl J. Becker, *Der priesterliche Dienst II: Wesen und Vollmachten des Priestertums nach dem Lehramt,* Quaestiones disputatae 47 (Freiburg: Herder, 1970), deals directly with this topic. It is also to be recommended for its account of the related historical problem.

[2] I omit the *Professio fidei Waldensibus praescripta* (DS 794) and *Lateranense* 4 (DS 802), since they treat holy orders only *in obliquo* in connection with the Eucharist, not *in recto*.

239

position of the Catholic Church before turning our attention to the earlier texts.

1. Pius XII's rectification of the Middle Ages

Pius XII's apostolic constitution (DS 3857–3861) deals with an apparently external question in relation to holy orders; it clarifies the essential elements in the administration of the sacrament and responds, above all, to the need for positive definitions, for clarity and for certainty. To that extent, its mentality is Western. It continues that development that, in all things, seeks accurately to establish what is important and what is less important in order to reduce scrupulosity—which, in point of fact, is often increased by such means. Nevertheless, the text takes an important step forward: it states clearly that the proper sacramental sign of holy orders is the imposition of hands, nothing else. By this text, the Catholic Church was liberated from her entanglement with Germanic legal forms, the strongest expression of which was the corresponding passage in the Decree for the Armenians, issued in Florence in 1439: there, the handing over of the chalice with the wine and of the paten with the bread was defined as the central action in the conferral of holy orders. This supplanting of the original form was recognized by Pius XII for what it was and was suppressed. His action meant a deliberate return to the tradition of the early Church and, consequently, to the Churches of the East. The text itself expresses this clearly by emphasizing the fact that the Roman Church never wished to force this peculiarly Western form upon the universal Church but expressly desired that (as decreed by the Council of Florence) the Greek Church should confer holy orders even in Rome in accordance with her own rite. The gesture that had been obligatory in Rome for centuries was thereby eliminated from the universal Church as a special Western custom and explicitly dismissed as secondary. This fact seems to me to have great significance in a general ecclesiological sense as well as for the particular question of the sacrament of holy orders. It is important ecclesiologically because a form traditional in the West was explicitly changed to conform with the standard of the universal Church; because the problem of peculiarly medieval developments was recognized; and because the practice of the early Church was specifically acknowledged as normative. The process is important for holy orders itself because the gesture of the imposition of hands points to a different traditional context than does that of the handing over of the instruments and so offers a different and more comprehensive meaning than is conveyed by the Germanic gesture. That is also immediately apparent when we consider the words that were decreed in 1439 and in 1947. The text of 1439 says that the crucial sacramental formula is as follows: "Receive the fullness of power to offer sacrifice in the Church for the living and the dead in the Name of the Father and of the Son and of the Holy Spirit" (DS 1326). Following the ancient tradition, the text of 1947, by contrast, declares that the actual sacramental formula is the consecratory Preface, the ordination prayer modeled on the High Prayer of the Mass, that also bears the character of an *epiclesis*; Pius XII defines as the central words those spoken at the consecration by the bishop: "Send forth upon him, O Lord, we beseech thee, the Holy Spirit, by whom may he (the ordained) be strengthened to perform faithfully the work of thy service with the help of thy sevenfold gift" (DS 3860). Three things are important here:

a. While the medieval text prescribed a so-called indicative sacramental formula and saw the ordination as resulting from the indicative of the conferral of power, ordination is accomplished according to the 1947 text in a supplicatory form, in the manner of a petition, of a prayer. Thus it is apparent even in the external form that the true conferrer of power is the Holy Spirit, to whom the sacramental prayer is addressed, not the human consecrator.

b. The medieval rite is formed on the pattern of investiture in a secular office. Its key word is *potestas*. The rite that Pius XII decrees represents a return to the form used in the early Church. It is pneumatologically oriented in terms of both gesture (since the imposition of hands signifies the conferral of the Holy Spirit) and word: the Preface is a petition for the Holy Spirit. Accordingly, the key word is now *ministerium* or *munus*: service and gift; hence the words of priestly ordination speak also of the duty of good example and moral discipline.

c. Finally, we can see that, in the text of Pius XII, consecration by the bishop, as the full form of the sacrament of holy orders, is more strongly emphasized, whereas Florence mentions the bishop only as the conferrer of the priestly ordination. On this point, it must be admitted, no further decisive action occurred until Vatican Council II.

Let us summarize. Whereas the Middle Ages patterned ordination on the model of a conferral of power (*potestas*), Pius XII returned to the pneumatologically oriented form of the early Church, which, in the imposition of hands and in the consecration, is the expression of the confident prayer of the Church of Jesus Christ. Precisely this form, in contrast to the strongly secular character of the medieval rite, is typically sacramental. For it expresses the fact that the Church does not confer the fullness of power in her own right, as secular institutions do, but is, rather, the creation of the Holy Spirit, by whose gifts she continually lives. She must beseech him to enable human beings to serve him, for only he can do so. As a ministry bestowed only by the Holy Spirit at the prayer of the Church, the priesthood is a sacrament. The interrelationship of imposition of hands and prayer is a meaningful expression of what the Church means by "sacrament". This thought becomes stronger and clearer when we realize that the Church does not derive from herself even this gesture of sacramental prayer: she enters thereby into the apostolic form, into the tradition of the apostles; and it is precisely this that constitutes the sacrament: that it is a question, not of what the Church has devised for herself, but of what she has received—which, precisely because it has been received, is the certain point of contact with the power of the Holy Spirit that comes from the Lord.

2. *On the contribution of Vatican Council II*

Vatican Council II developed theologically the beginnings that, in the apostolic constitution of Pius XII, were concealed in what seemed at first to be an orientation toward the rite of the sacrament: in chapter 3 of the "Dogmatic Constitution on the Church" (*Lumen gentium*), these beginnings form the central theme whose content is later developed even further in the "Decree on the Ministry and Life of Priests" (*Presbyterorum ordinis*).[3] Two points of view are crucial for determining the mind of the Council in this matter:

a. There is a turning to the episcopate as the fundamental form of the sacrament of holy orders.

b. From this there follows, as a matter of course, the link with the concept of apostolic succession and the association with the concept of tradition.

We shall discuss each of these in turn.

a. Presbyterate and episcopate

Whereas the early Church had regarded holy orders as fundamentally related to the episcopate, in the Middle Ages a shifting of emphasis occurred that had its origin in St. Jerome, who represented a kind of presbyterianism that was later adopted and enlarged upon by the *Statuta ecclesiae antiquae*, a text that originated in Gaul in the fifth century. The Middle Ages distinguished likewise between fullness of power over the

---

[3] On this subject, see especially Paul Josef Cordes, *Sendung zum Dienst. Exegetisch-historische und systematische Studien zum Konzilsdekret "Vom Dienst und Leben der Priester"* (Frankfurt: Knecht, 1972). See also the extensive bibliography provided there.

corpus Christi verum and fullness of power over the *corpus Christi mysticum*, which distinction was linked to that between *sacramentum* and *iurisdictio*. Only the power to change bread and wine into the *corpus Christi verum* was recognized as the truly sacramental power, while the administrative power over the *corpus mysticum*, the Church, was considered a juridical power that was fundamentally distinct from the sacrament. Power over the *corpus verum* was fully bestowed at ordination to the priesthood; what the bishop held over and above this was power over the *corpus mysticum*, that is, juridical—and, ipso facto, not sacramental—power. According to this view, consecration of a bishop did not have sacramental character; this was apparent externally in the fact that the concept of *sacerdos*, which, in the early Church, had been used predominantly of the bishop, now became the equivalent of the word *presbyter*.[4] Whereas the bishop was formerly looked upon as priest in the full sense of the word, this was now true only of the *presbyter*. The widespread consequences of this view are readily discernible: *potestas*, power, fullness of power, became everywhere the crucial issue. The priesthood was seen as directly ordered only to the power of transubstantiation and was so defined—a fact which, as we have seen, then appeared in the sacramental rite. Pastoral care was divorced from it and was limited to juridical power over the Mystical Body. Above all, however, there followed an individualization of the priestly ministry, which thereby completely lost its character as *communio*. For Vatican Council II, on the contrary, the crucial point of departure, from which it developed its teaching on the sacrament of holy orders, is the sentence: "That divine mission, which was committed by Christ to the apostles, is destined to last until the end of the world (cf. Mt 28:20), since the gospel which they were charged to hand on is, for the Church, the principle of all her life for all time."[5] The basic concepts are, then: mission of the apostles—gospel—tradition—life of the Church. The point of departure is the mission of the apostles, but this mission is the handing on of the gospel. Apostolate and the handing on of the gospel are two sides of one and the same thing, the personal and the factual aspects, which belong inseparably together.

If we look first at the personal aspect, it means this: the apostles appoint successors; it is the bishops who, in the words of Tertullian, are, by right of succession, "the ones who pass on the apostolic seed".[6] Here the

---

[4] Cf. J. Guyot, *Das apostolische Amt* (Mainz, 1961); Ludwig Hödl, *Die Geschichte der scholastischen Literatur und der Theologie der Schlüsselgewalt* 1 (Münster: Aschendorff, 1961); Joseph Ratzinger, *Das neue Volk Gottes*, 216ff.

[5] *Lumen gentium*, chap. 3:20.

[6] Tertullian, "De praescriptione haereticorum", in CChr I, Series Latina, caput 32, 3, lines 12–13.

relationship with the concept of tradition is again immediately clear. Taking the apostles as the point of departure for a consideration of the sacrament of holy orders, which then led to a viewing of the sacrament in terms of the episcopacy, had two important results: Catholicity and apostolicity are revealed as the two fundamental characteristics of the priestly office. How is this so?

The sacrament of holy orders is realized primarily in the bishop. But one becomes bishop by being consecrated by bishops and entering into the already existing context of the apostolic tradition and the apostolic succession. One is not alone as bishop; becoming a bishop means, at the same time, entering into the basic context of the *successio*. In the early Church, this was shown by the fact that the bishop received the *litterae communionis* of his fellow bishops. One is bishop only by reason of the apostolic context and the Catholic community. Botte has demonstrated this fact impressively by a number of texts from the early Church. In the disagreement about Paul of Samosata, for instance, the bishops appealed to the Emperor Aurelian, who decided that the church building belonged to the person who was recognized by the bishop of Rome. In other words, the Emperor knew, even as one outside the Church, that bishops did not exist alone but were "Catholic"; that there was a Catholic Church and that this context was the surety for their office. Within the Church, the surety of the *Domnus* was the fact that he received the *litterae communionis* of other principal sees: Alexandria, Constantinople, Rome.[7] Thus the sacrament of holy orders is the expression and, at the same time, the guarantee that the bishops are faithful to what has been handed on from the beginning. It incorporates the unity of the Church and her fidelity to her original form. This Catholicity of the episcopate, which is, in turn, its apostolicity, is continued in the communal character of the presbyterate: becoming a priest means entering into the *presbyterium* of a bishop. One is not alone as priest; one is in the *presbyterium* of a bishop. In this sense, ordination to the priesthood is reception into the mission of the apostles by inclusion in the community of witnesses. It would undoubtedly be dangerous if this view were allowed to obscure the directly pneumatological and, consequently, sacramental character of every individual ordination and destroy it by a kind of mystique of community. The community can do nothing of itself. It can be pneumatological only if each member of it is imbued with the Spirit. On the other hand, however, the community of the whole Church, the community of the visible form of her link with her beginning, is, for the individual, the place of the Spirit and the guarantee of union with the Spirit.

[7] B. Botte, in Guyot, 82–83.

b. The *successio apostolica*

The apostolic succession is not a purely formal power; it is part of the mission for the gospel. That is why the concepts of succession and tradition were not separated in the early Church and why Vatican Council II is justified in linking the two closely together. The *successio*-structure is the expression both of the link with tradition and of the concept of tradition in the Catholic Church. On this question, there is, so far as I can see, no essential difference between the Catholic Churches of East and West. The pneumatological rite of the imposition of hands and prayer points, in the imposition of hands, to the unbroken content of ecclesial tradition as the *situs* of the Spirit. As the International Theological Commission states in its report on the priesthood, the rite gives expression to the connection between Christology and pneumatology and, thus, to the Catholic form of ecclesiology: "The constant working of the Holy Spirit and the unique event of the Incarnation are inwardly linked: the Spirit is the highest gift that the glorified Christ bestows on those who were with him 'from the beginning' (Jn 15:26–27) and on those who carry out a ministry in his Church (Eph 4:8–12). The mission of the Spirit brings the salvific work of Christ near to men of all times but never replaces it."[8] The necessity of the apostolic succession and the impossibility of denying its sacramental form emanate from the "impossibility of thinking of a 'Church of Christ' here below that is not closely linked to his Incarnation and his whole historical activity."[9]

The high-church movement that was introduced into some forms of Protestantism in the nineteenth century was unable fully to understand this Catholic concept of holy orders and the related symbolism of the imposition of hands but rather obfuscated it in many respects. This movement undoubtedly stems from a nostalgia for the sacrament and from the feeling that the service of the Spirit in the Church cannot be regulated in a purely organizational way but only in a spiritual—and that means "sacramental"—manner. In addition, there was the longing for a link with the origins of Christianity; a feeling of dissatisfaction with communities that cannot, as such, be traced back to these origins; and a need to demonstrate, in a visible way, their membership in the Church of all ages. These sentiments are, in themselves, perfectly legitimate and helped to break down many barriers even while being, at the same time, responsible for the fact that those who held ministries in these churches

---

[8] ITK, *Priesteramt* (Einsiedeln, 1972), 93.
[9] Ibid., 94.

managed somehow to arrange an imposition of hands by bishops who could demonstrate a connection with the imposition of hands in the Catholic Church and were thus able to claim a formal legitimacy of apostolic succession. As a result, there are, today, a number of persons holding such ministries whose succession is, if I may so phrase it, apocryphal. Wherever such "high-church" ordinations are conferred or received thus "apocryphally", the fundamental nature of the imposition of hands has been totally misunderstood. Regardless of the positive reasons that occasion it, it expresses, in such cases, either a liturgical romanticism or a canonical tutiorism. These churches want a formally assured legitimacy and tend toward an archaizing liturgical model (often, too, toward an equally archaizing dogmatic model), but they accomplish all this without venturing to revise the ecclesial context in anything but rite. Where this occurs, however, the sacrament is, in fact, restricted to a liturgical-juridical formalism. The more genuine rite and the more genuine genealogy appear as automatic guarantors of sacramentality and apostolicity. The inevitable result is that this formalism is regarded with irony by the other side and is countered by the genuineness of the word independent of the rite.

In truth, the imposition of hands with the accompanying prayer for the Holy Spirit is not a rite that can be separated from the Church or by which one can bypass the rest of the Church and dig one's own private channel to the apostles. It is, rather, an expression of the continuity of the Church, which, in the communion of the bishops, is the *locus* of tradition, of the gospel of Jesus Christ. Catholic theology places great emphasis on the unbroken identity of the tradition of the apostles, which is firmly held in the unity of the concrete Church and is expressed in the ecclesial gesture of the imposition of hands. There is, in other words, no separation of the material from the formal aspect (succession in respect to the word, succession in respect to the imposition of hands); rather, its inner unity is a sign of the unity of the Church herself: the imposition of hands takes place in and lives from the Church. It is nothing without the Church—an imposition of hands that is not an entering into the existential and traditional context of the Church is not an ecclesial imposition of hands. The sacrament is the sacrament of the Church, not a private way to the beginnings of Christianity. The question raised here between Catholic churches and Protestant congregations touches, therefore, not only the problem of the sacrament and of sacramentality but the even deeper problem of Scripture and tradition. It might be phrased in this way: Can the essential character of the word and the essential character of the Church be present where there is a break with the concrete continuity of the Church that celebrates the Eucharist with the bishops? Can the gospel be found in an isolated approach to Scripture, in *sola Scriptura*? Or is validity to be found only in *Scriptura in communione traditionis*?

Let us summarize what has been said. As an ecclesial sacrament, the sacrament of the imposition of hands is, at the same time, an expression of the traditional structure of the Church. It binds apostolicity and Catholicity together in the unity of Christ and the Spirit, which is represented and completed in the eucharistic community.

3. The Council of Trent

Just a brief comment on the Council of Trent: the Tridentine *Doctrina de sacramento ordinis* (July 15, 1563; DS 1763–1778) is a polemical text that must be read together with the Tridentine Reform Decrees if the direction of the Council as a whole is to be apparent. If one considers these decrees as well, it is obvious that some crucial weaknesses of the medieval system are being attacked: the obligation of the bishop to reside in his diocese—that is, his link with the *ecclesia localis* over which he presides—is strengthened. This strengthening is but the canonical expression of the fact that the bishop is regarded as pastor: responsible for the sacraments, responsible for the homily. There is also the corresponding duty of visitations and regular synods. It could be said, then, that the Reform Decrees of Trent make the episcopal character of the sacrament of holy orders and the community of *presbyterium* and bishop the key point in its view of the sacrament of holy orders, from which follows ipso facto the pastoral concept of the priestly ministry.[10]

The *doctrina* itself is directly associated with a key problem in the Catholic-Protestant debate: the connection between *sacerdotium* and *sacrificium*. The nature of the questions that originated with Luther and pointed the course for the Council of Trent cannot be studied in detail here. Suffice it to say that Luther saw in the link between *sacerdos* and *sacrificium* a denial of grace and a return to the law. Since he also saw in this link the reason why the Catholic Church designated *ordo* as a sacrament, he had to reject this sacramentality, which he believed to be based upon a central and destructive error. This position, which, with its passionate concern for the purity of Christian doctrine, points to the heart of Luther's urge to reform, had far-reaching consequences for the whole structure of the traditional Church. Rejection of the sacramentality of the priestly ministry led Luther, by a kind of inner necessity, to regard the ministry of

---

[10] Cf. Becker, 56–109. See Part Two, Chapter 2B in the present work: "Sacrifice, Sacrament and Priesthood in the Development of the Church".

the priest as strongly concentrated on the word: he is the preacher of grace, nothing else; even in the celebration of the Eucharist and in confession he is speaking, in a special way, of the grace of forgiveness; even in these actions, the priest does not transcend his role as preacher. The consequent restriction to the word alone had, as its logical outcome, the pure functionality of the priesthood: it consisted exclusively in a particular activity; if that activity was missing, the ministry itself ceased to exist. Consequently, this functionality, in turn, included the strict equality of Christians. In principle, all Christians may preach; for reasons of order, and only for such reasons, restrictions are put upon their doing so. This equality led to secularity. There was purposely no further mention of priesthood but only of "office"; the assignment of this office was, in itself, a secular act; this, in turn, made possible, in the course of further development, a far-reaching fusion of political and ecclesial forms. The head of state was also head of the local church, which thus became a civic church, a "state church".

The Council of Trent did not attempt here a comprehensive treatment of the problem as a whole. Therein lies the weakness of the text it promulgated, the effect of which was all the more disastrous since the Reform Decrees, with their broad theological range, were not fully incorporated into the theology of the schools. The uneasiness about the Catholic doctrine of the priesthood as proclaimed by Trent that was recognizable even before Vatican Council II and that grew into an avalanche as a result of the bold ecumenical stance taken by that Council has its historical foundation in the limited range of the Tridentine statement. For, in contrast to the biblically motivated force of Luther's attitude, the Tridentine statement seemed too positivistic and ecclesiological. The issue cannot be treated further in these pages;[11] nevertheless, what has been said should suffice to clarify, to some extent, the scope of the problem and thus to show the course to be followed: we must read Trent in the context of the whole ecclesial tradition and, in this way, recognize the magnitude of the question, which is by no means limited to the problem of sacrifice. If we do that, the Tridentine statement will not, of course, be nullified, but its context will, to a certain extent, change its perspective and so give Luther's questioning the weight it deserves. To this extent, a purifying and deepening of our own witness can and must result from our attention to the concerns of the Protestant churches, and it was along these

[11] See Peter Bläser, Suso Frank, Peter Manns, Gerhard Fahrnberger and Hans-Joachim Schulz, *Amt und Eucharistie* (Paderborn: Bonifatius Druckerei, 1973), for an important contribution to this theme, especially P. Manns, "Amt und Eucharistie in der Theologie Martin Luthers", 68–173. Vinzenz Pfnür, "Kirche und Amt", in *Catholica*, Supplement 1 (1975), offers an extensive bibliography.

lines that Vatican Council II sought to develop the Tridentine position. Certainly, we must not expect a full resolution of differences from such a deepening. The question we raised earlier with regard to Vatican Council II about the relationship of Scripture and tradition, of Church and tradition, and which we recognized as the real center of the sacramentality of holy orders, still remains and can ultimately be answered only by a Yes or No. In any event, the development has been varied even within the Protestant communities. Where it has relied heavily on the Augsburg Confession, it has come very close, structurally, to the Catholic model; it remains different from that model especially in those churches that emphasize, above all, the position Luther took in De captivitate Babylonica and, despite many changes of attitude in the matter, obviously never abandoned.

It follows that the Tridentine text can be correctly understood only if we read it, not as an exhaustive and positive presentation of the Catholic understanding of the priesthood, but as a polemical statement, the sole purpose of which was to formulate antitheses to Luther's main theses. The anchoring of the text in the totality of tradition and the inevitability of its logic can best be understood if we read it, as it were, backward; that is, if we keep in mind the position it took with regard to the consequences of Luther's denial of the sacramentality of holy orders; from that perspective, we can more easily see why the Council could not be satisfied with merely negating these consequences but felt compelled to contest their starting point—to defend the sacramentality and, with it, the special eucharistic mission of the priestly ministry. In fact, this is the logical precondition for the Council's rejection of Luther's exclusive theology of the word (can. 3, DS 1773); it plays a part also in its upholding of the irrevocability of the priestly ministry against Luther's purely functional view of it (can. 4, DS 1774; cf. can. 4, DS 1767). To express this definitive and unequivocal quality, the Council employed the concept of "character" that the Middle Ages had inherited from Augustine:[12] one who becomes a priest is always a priest, just as one who has been validly baptized is always a Christian. With this teaching, the Council of Trent rejected the concept of reordination of one who has been validly ordained just as it rejected the concept of rebaptism.

Against egalitarianism and the notion of a state church, the Council declared that there are ministries in the Church that cannot be changed (can. 6, DS 1776; cf. can. 3, DS 1768—the concept of "hierarchy" occurs in this context). At the same time, the Council forcefully rejected the idea

---

[12] Cf. Ernst Dassmann, *Character indelebilis. Anmassung oder Verlegenheit* (Cologne: Presseamt des Erzbistums, 1973), where Augustine's so often falsely described role in the development of this question is precisely determined and the theological motives of the formula are elucidated from all sides.

that the office of priest can be validly conferred by the community, the civil arm or a secular administrative body alone. It stated explicitly that there is only one way of becoming a priest: ordination by an authorized bishop (can. 7, DS 1777; cf. can. 3, DS 1769).

Vatican Council II was fortunately able to transcend the polemical level and delineate a positive whole of ecclesial tradition in which the concerns of the Reformation are also included. Its weakness seems to be the exact opposite of that of Trent: since it completely renounced confrontation and described itself as a theological tract rather than an authoritative formulation of tradition, it seemed to many to belong to the category of those treatises that are constantly being superseded, that are measured solely by the exactness of their exegetical foundation. In the last analysis, consequently, the whole text raises the question of the fullness of power of the teaching Magisterium of the Church, of the form of tradition in the Church. How closely this fundamental question of contemporary theology is related to the specific question of holy orders should be obvious by now. To that extent, holy orders is not only a single material issue; rather, it is indissolubly linked to the fundamental problem of the form Christianity takes in time. To pursue the question further is outside the scope of these remarks, which are intended only to present the actual doctrinal decisions of the Church in their inner context and to clarify their meaning.

B. Sacrifice, Sacrament and Priesthood in the Development of the Church

Introductory reflections on the state of the question

In answer to the question of how the relationship of sacrifice, sacrament and priesthood developed in the Church, there exists today an explanation that is as simple as it is enlightening and that has met with wide acceptance. The New Testament, it holds, represents the end of sacral taboos and, consequently, of sacrificial priesthood and even of sacrifice. But, it is argued, the freedom thereby achieved was short-lived; attempts at resacralization are to be found even in the New Testament itself. The concept of sacrifice was reintroduced allegorically at first, but, through the paralleling of New Testament functions with the Old Testament orders of high priest, priest and levite in what is probably the oldest of post-New Testament writings, the first letter of Clement, the revival of pre-

Christian concepts became all but total;[13] it spread rapidly and was ultimately affirmed as dogma by the Council of Trent. In consequence, it is said, there is an urgent need for firm action to counteract the dogmatization of this error in order that desacralization may finally be accomplished; that the sacramental ministry may be replaced by a functional one; that the still flourishing remnants of the former magic— sacrifice—may be banished; and that a nonmagical, rationally structured, "efficient" office [*Amt*] that will at last achieve what Jesus intended may be established in the spirit of Jesus.

Anyone who has learned to think, however haltingly, in terms of sources will readily see that this vision was constructed, not on the basis of texts, but in terms of current goals, for the justification of which a canon within the canon was constructed in the test tube of "enlightened" reason to serve as a basis for what is fundamentally an antihistorical vision. Its real goal—often scarcely recognized even by itself—is to free itself from the burden of history in order thus, as it were, to be able to begin again at the hour zero without the oppressive burden of history. The serious problem posed by this attitude and the strength with which it has established itself are due, not to its historical insights (which are nonexistent), but to its antihistorical protest and the gesture of liberation that is observable in it. Are we still able to bear the burden of *history,* or should we secede from it and pay allegiance only to the matter *at hand*? But the counterquestion arises immediately: *Can* we actually secede from history? What forces stand behind rationality, functionality, efficiency? Why this tarnishing of history?

A study of the development of the relationship of sacrifice, priesthood and sacrament in the history of dogma reveals an exceptionally compli- cated constellation that cannot be adequately described, even in broad out- line, in a single chapter. It is even less possible because we are dealing, not with an individual regional problem, but with the basic element in the concept of the Church and with the central element of Christology: Where is the nucleus of Christology? In the Cross? If so, is the Cross a sacrifice? And how is it present to the Church? How does the Church relate to Christ? Is she a practical necessity revealed to the disciples after Easter? a pragmatic instrument that the disciples created after Easter in order to pro- long Jesus' work? an external apparatus to be judged solely by whether or not it serves a purpose? Or does she come, as such, from the Lord, freed, in her basic characteristics, from her own manipulation, so that, precisely in her concreteness, she is nevertheless more than just an organization—she

[13] Jean Colson, *Ministre de Jésus-Christ ou le sacerdoce de l'évangile* (Paris: Beauchesne, 1966), 225–56, shows in some detail that this reflects a misinterpretation of 1 Clem 40–41.

is the "Body"-organism of Christ? Only when the basic distinctions are kept clearly in mind can we see the matter as it really is. I propose first to describe the essential form of the ancient Church from this broader horizon in order then to review, against this background (and always, of course, with reference to the subject at hand), the specific development of the Latin Middle Ages and the Reformation protest and, in conclusion, to offer some comments on the position taken by the Council of Trent.

The basic form of the primitive Church as a lasting norm

The most important characteristic of the primitive Church[14] is, I think, the fact that it was *ecclesia in ecclesiis*. The one Church existed in many (local) churches; the many local churches existed as the one Church (in which connection it should be noted that the "plurality" of local churches is not to be equated with the plurality of denominational churches that exists today).[15] But this unique interaction of singular and plural would have been impossible if there had not been preserved in the Church the original meaning of the word "ecclesia"—that is, a "coming together". The real *locus* of the Church is not some kind of bureaucracy or the activity of a group that considers itself "basic" but a "coming together". *This* is the Church in action, in terms of which the interaction of singular and plural becomes clear, for her form is the incarnate Word of God that is made flesh again and again by the word of faith and, as flesh, deigns again and again to become word. Or, more exactly, the content of the "coming together" is the receiving of the word of God, which reaches its climax in the remembrance of the death of Jesus, in a remembrance that creates presence and signifies mission.[16] It follows from this that *every* coming together is wholly Church, for the Body of the Lord is always whole. Consequently, the individual "coming together", the individual community, can be Church only if she is so in the whole, in union with all other "comings together". For the Body of the Lord, which is whole in every community,

[14] Because of the necessarily limited space at my disposal, I can only repeat here in summary what I have said in earlier works (where references are also given) about the ecclesiology of the primitive Church. Cf., especially, *Volk und Haus Gottes in Augustins Lehre von der Kirche* [henceforth *Volk und Haus Gottes*] (Munich: Zink, 1954); *Das neue Volk Gottes*, 11–224; Joseph Ratzinger and Hans Maier, *Demokratie in der Kirche. Möglichkeiten, Grenzen, Gefahren* (Limburg: Lahn, 1970), 24–44. See also Louis Bouyer's presentation in *L'Église de Dieu. Corps du Christ et Temple de l'Esprit* (Paris: Cerf, 1970), 17–65.

[15] On this subject, see my book *Das Konzil auf dem Weg* (Cologne, 1964), 60–67.

[16] Cf. Heinz Schürmann, *Ursprung und Gestalt. Erörterungen und Besinnungen zum Neuen Testament* (Düsseldorf: Patmos, 1970), 77–150; Jean-Jacques Allmen, Ökumene in Herrenmahl (Kassel, 1968), esp. 25–29; 120–26.

is, nevertheless, one Body in the whole Church, and this is true also of the word of God; we can possess it only if we possess it with others. If, as Church, a community isolates itself from the whole, it immediately ceases to exist as Church.

The concept of "office" [*Amt*] developed out of this context, which contains the driving forces of that development in which, from the intermingling of missionary and local, Jewish-Christian and pagan-Christian structures, a recognizable basic form for the whole Church finally crystallized in broad outlines; but only the total process of crystallization, not just an isolated part of it, can tell us about "office" as it is in the New Testament.[17] The classic model, which, it must be acknowledged, is expressed in the history of the Church with considerable variation, is that described by Ignatius of Antioch: the individual community led by an *episkopos,* who is assisted by two "councils": one of presbyters, the other of deacons. In this combination of ultimate responsibility and subsidiary councils, which are, in turn, ordered to the assembly of the whole, the interaction of singular and plural is expressed even within the community—by the fact that, on the one hand, the whole community is the assembly and, consequently, the Church, while, on the other hand, only the one assembly can be the Church. For Ignatius, the figure of the bishop is the expression at once of the unity and of the public character of the Eucharist. The social structure in which the Church exists is not a club, not a circle of friends, but the "people of God" in contrast to the people of the word—for which reason the Eucharist is not a private celebration for special groups; it continues to be Eucharist only when it is a public assembly of the whole in which the whole community is one with the Lord and thus one among themselves.[18]

At this point, we see the inner openness of this apparently closed communal structure. The Eucharist of the community must be public in character and one in itself; it must also be public—that is, open—to the Church as a whole so that every Christian is equally at home at every eucharistic table throughout the world. The bishop guarantees not only the unity of each individual community but also the unity of the individual community with the one Church of God in this world. Just as the community continues to be a community only by being so in reference to the bishop, so the bishop continues to be a bishop only by being so in reference to other bishops who, together, form a public unity, which, in turn, is ordered to a primacy; the body of bishops is not simply a

---

[17] Cf. my comments in *Das neue Volk Gottes, 105–20; cf. also Heinz Schürmann, Traditionsgeschichtliche Untersuchungen zu den synoptischen Evangelien* (Düsseldorf: Patmos, 1968), 310–40.

[18] *Das neue Volk Gottes,* 123.

"collegium"; it is structured in primacies, which, in turn, are structured among themselves to the all-embracing primacy of the successor of St. Peter.[19]

By way of summary, we can say that the center of the oldest ecclesiology is the eucharistic assembly—the Church is *communio*. Not only is the very specific structure of the interrelationship of unity and plurality evident from this perspective, but the unity of Christ and Church is also established—the impossibility of separating the visible Church from the spiritual Church, the Church as organization from the Church as *mysterium*: the concrete *communio is* the Church, which is to be sought nowhere else—the very thought is out of place when we think of *communio* as the center of the concept of Church. This means, likewise, that the concept of Church is concentrated in the divine service: the Church is Church in the divine service, but this divine service is called *agape, eirene, koinonia,* thus signifying an all-embracing human responsibility. This *cultus* is always unlimited and unlimitable. In the last analysis, the whole, if we may so express it, signifies a eucharistic concept of "office": if the Church *is* Eucharist, then the ecclesial office of overseer (*episkopos*) is essentially responsibility for the "coming together" that is identical with the Church—but this process of coming together encompasses all of life.

Development in the Middle Ages

What changes occurred during the Middle Ages? The question is extraordinarily complex. We can attempt to unravel only a few strands. The most crucial event in the development of the Latin West was, I think, the increasing distinction between sacrament and jurisdiction, between liturgy and administration as such. Several factors were at work here. In the early Church, the form of the (local) churches was appropriate to the urban structure of ancient society, but this form was impossible in the essentially agrarian structure of the new nations.[20] Consequently, changes occurred not only in the function of the bishop but also in that of his *presbyterium.* There existed likewise a combination of missionary and local structures in various forms. The Church of the Irish monks had no episcopal authority. Fullness of power for the celebration of the Eucharist

---

[19] Ibid., 122ff.; cf. H. Grotz, *Die Hauptkirchen des Ostens. Von den Anfängen bis zum Konzil von Nikaia (325)* (Rome: Pont. Instit. orientalium studiorum, 1964); M. J. Le Guillou, "L'Expérience orientale de la collégialité épiscopale et ses requêtes", in *Istina* 10 (1964): 111–24.

[20] Cf. the comments in Raymund Kottje and H. Th. Risse. *Wahlrecht für das Gottesvolk?* (Düsseldorf, 1969), 17ff.

was no longer combined with that for administration. The individual Church entity that developed according to the legal forms of the Germanic realm led in the same direction. The priest became a cult-minister in the retinue of a feudal lord.[21] The Ottonian combination of *imperium* and *sacerdotium*—the employment of the *sacerdotium* in the service of the *imperium*—only seems to point in a different direction: the Church became, as it were, the proprietary Church of the German Empire; as a functionary of the Empire, the bishop was concerned only secondarily with the ecclesial assembly and, of necessity, allowed its concrete functions to be carried out by others. In the late Middle Ages and far into the Baroque era, the separation of prebend and spiritual ministry developed even further, thus bringing the separation of sacrament and legal jurisdiction, of sacramental function and the power of administration, to its most distressful form. The office, as a legal entity to which certain revenues were due, was bestowed on some important personage, often not even ordained, who relegated the performance of liturgical services to an ill-paid Mass-priest, who had no responsibility for administration and none in his own position either. He was not trained to proclaim the word and often restricted himself to the *cultus* alone, which, in practice, lost its real meaning because of this.

From a theological standpoint, the critical effect of this separation of sacrament and jurisdiction seems to me to have been the resultant isolation of the concept of sacrament. The essential identity of Church and liturgical assembly, of Church and *communio,* was no longer evident. Like any other society, the Church was now, in a certain sense, a juridical instrument, a complex of laws, ordinances, claims. In addition, of course, she had also what was peculiarly her own: the fact that she was the *situs* of cultic acts—of the sacraments. But the Eucharist was just one of these—one liturgical act among others, no longer the encompassing orbit and dynamic center of ecclesial existence per se. In consequence, the Eucharist itself was fragmented into a variety of loosely related rites: sacrifice, worship, cultic meal. With the isolation of the sacrament there was linked a naturalization. The pneumatic character of the remembrance that produced presence was dimmed; the linking of the whole sacramental event to the oneness of the one crucified and risen Lord was overshadowed by the emergence of a plurality of separate sacrificial rites—this, too, indubitably a product more of concrete situations than of theological considerations. The doctrine of the fruits of the Mass gave meaning to the stipend and led to the greatest possible emphasis on the unique fruits of each separate Mass, in which

---

[21] Cf. Friedrich Kempf, in Hubert Jedin, *Handbuch der Kirchengeschichte* 3:1 (Freiburg: Herder, 1966), 296–309 and elsewhere.

special fruits were granted that would not otherwise exist. The whole seems more like the ideological superstructure of a particular economic situation than like a genuine theological consideration that corrects and transforms human situations.[22] I think we should be honest enough to admit the temptation of mammon in the history of the Church and to recognize to what extent it was a real power that worked to the distortion and corruption of both Church and theology, even to their inmost core. The separation of office as jurisdiction from office as rite was continued for reasons of prestige and financial benefits; the isolation of the Mass, its separation from the unity of *memoria* and, therefore, its privatization were products of the amalgamation of Masses and stipends. What Ignatius of Antioch strove to combat returned here with full force: the Mass became the private possession of the pious (and the impious) by which they hoped to effect their private reconciliation with God.

In this way, the legitimate concentration of the office of priest on the Eucharist acquired a completely different meaning: ordination, which, as a separate sacrament, was also forced out of the larger context of the ecclesial assembly, was considered necessary to ensure the sacramental rites prescribed by the Church. Here, once again, personal Christianity was considered in isolation from the Church: Christian existence was associated with rites, while the Church consisted of legal prescriptions and positions that seemed to have no point of contact with the Christian existence of the individual. The place of the word was, to a large extent, empty. To a large extent, also, it was regarded as a special academic doctrine that, on the one hand, legitimized existing conditions and, on the other hand, negated what existed by evaluating it as a positivistic arrangement that, by comparison with the *potestas absoluta* of God, was regarded as pure arbitrariness. God could, if he wished, bestow salvation under conditions that were diametrically opposite; there was no inner relationship between ecclesiological reality and reality per se.[23] In its mixture of ecclesiological positivism and metaphysical speculation, the theology of the late Middle Ages was, to a large extent, an ironic reflection of the spiritual reality of the Church behind which was barely concealed the fact that the Church had lost her meaningful context.

Granted, this was not the whole impact of the Middle Ages. If we are honest, we must admit that the separation of sacrament and law, however dire its consequences, also answered a fundamental inner necessity. For it

[22] On the theory of the fruits of the sacrifice, see Karl Rahner and A. Häussling, *Die vielen Messen und das eine Opfer* (Freiburg: Herder, 1966), 45–73. What has been said here should not be construed as a denial of the fact that a positive interpretation as well as a positive use of the Mass stipend is not only possible but has actually been realized.

[23] Cf. the basic discussion in Pfnür, *Einig in der Rechtfertigungslehre?*, 29–88.

shed light on the role of the human element in the Church and revealed the gulf between what was unalterably given and what had always to be done. Even more importantly, there always went hand in hand with the movement toward dissolution, toward the "more probable state" of emphasis on the human, a movement against verisimilitude and toward what was genuine. However unfortunate the centralism of the Gregorian reform may have been in many respects, there can be no denying its basic accomplishment: liberation of the Church from the control of the *imperium* and restoration of the unity of the spiritual office and its spiritual character. Here, too, there was a regrettable side-effect, which did not, however, alter the fundamental necessity of the action: the problem of the laity, which arose at this time and still haunts us today. From this time on, there existed the problem of breaking that "domination of the laity" in the Church that arose from the separation of juridical officeholder from sacramental priest and of ensuring that he who holds the office actually exercises his office—his whole and undivided sacramental office—in terms of the sacrament and not for money or any similar purpose.[24]

Thus far, we have been discussing the unity of sacrament and jurisdiction; consideration of the second great reform movement of the Middle Ages, that of the mendicant orders, raises the question of the unity of sacrament and word, of liturgical service and proclamation of the word. In addition, these orders struggled to emancipate the Church from feudal structures and to free the gospel from the material structures of the medieval order.[25] In the hunger for the word that had arisen in a Church without the proclamation of the word, Dominic sought to establish a movement of preachers and Francis a simple popular catechesis. From both movements there arose a new type of priestly office, not linked to the episcopacy, but defined essentially by its missionary element, by moving from place to place in the service of the word.

Luther's protest

To understand Luther's protest, we must go beyond what has already been said and examine another thread in the relationship of sacrifice, sacrament and priesthood in the development of the Church—a thread that reaches back to the reflections of Augustine, the explosive power of

---

[24] On the Gregorian reform, see Kempf, 401–61; Yves Congar, *L'Église. De saint Augustin a l'époque moderne* (Paris: Cerf, 1970), 89–122.

[25] On the "evangelical" character of the movement toward mendicant orders, cf. the exemplary comments of Marie Dominique Chenu in *St. Thomas d'Aquin et la théologie* (Paris: Seuil, 1959) and *La Théologie au douzième siècle* (Paris: Vrin, 1957), 221–73.

which had long been concealed but which came now to their full power. Augustine experienced a split in the Church of his native Africa that was unparalleled in the rest of the ancient Church. In every city, altar stood against altar, episcopacy against episcopacy; Donatists and Catholics were found everywhere in almost equal numbers. Conversions went back and forth from one Church to the other, often for very superficial reasons. As a result, the ecclesial community was thrown into confusion. Against this background we can understand why Augustine could not immediately see the true Church in those who came together for the eucharistic celebration—quite possibly by tomorrow they would belong to a different Church. For him, consequently, the true Church consisted of those who would ultimately be brought together by God's final call—the number of the elect. One who was presently within the Church could actually be outside her when that call came, and vice versa. The immediate result of this combination of ecclesiology and speculations about predestination was to create a distinction between the concrete community that came together to celebrate the Eucharist and a purely spiritual concept of the Church that would one day reveal the external assembly as secondary. The true Church was composed of the elect. In contrast to this "being", the assembled community was only "appearance". Granted, Augustine himself did not make this distinction absolutely. Appearance and being continued to be intertwined in his thought. Even if the always changing state of the assembly did not reflect the community that would exist at the end of time, the ecclesial *communio* was, nevertheless, an indispensable prelude to the community that was to come. Final membership in the Church that celebrates the Eucharist is the sign of election.[26]

A notion was thus generated that, under other circumstances, would and did lead to a complete devaluation of the Church as a liturgical *communio*. These circumstances arose from the increasing politicizing of excommunication after Gregory VII, which, by the age of the great schisms, had become the central problem of the Church of the West. The crisis was most evident in the teachings of Wyclif and Hus, although it did not, at first, have any widespread historical impact.[27] It achieved this impact on the occasion of Luther's own excommunication: with the burning of the bull of excommunication, a definite practice of excommu-

---

[26] Cf. Ratzinger, *Volk und Haus Gottes*, 136–58 (esp. 145ff.) and 205–18. For a criticism of my views, see Walter Simonis, *Ecclesia visibilis et invisibilis* (Frankfurt: Knecht, 1970); see also the review of Simonis' book by A. de Veer in *Revue des Études Augustiniennes* 17 (1971): 396ff.

[27] On the concept of *communio* in Hus' theology, see Bonaventura Duda, *J. Stojković de Ragusio, doctrina de cognoscibilitate ecclesiae* (Rome: Pont. Athenaeum Antonianum, 1958), 60 and 134ff. Georg May offers typical examples of the corruption of the practice of excommunication in *Die geistliche Gerichtsbarkeit des Erzbischofs von Mainz im Thüringen des Spätmittelalters* (Leipzig: St. Benno, 1956).

nication was also destroyed, but the idea of *communio*, which had been adversely affected by this practice, likewise received a severe blow. Even Hus' followers had pointed out that church communities existed that were larger than that of the bishop of Rome, from which they concluded that what was important was not the institutional organization but membership in the hidden community of true Christians. Even Luther looked to the Greek Church, which had remained a true church without being submissive to the pope, [28] and he, too, concluded that what was important was not the concrete, structured *communio* but the community behind the institutional one. In this way a problematical position arose that could in fact not be resolved by appealing to the *communio*-structure of the early Church, for the discrediting of *communio* by the politicizing of excommunication had led, at the same time, to the dissolution of the identification of Church and *communio* and thus to the destruction of the primitive model. The concrete Church thereby became just an institution and, as such, more or less a *quantité négligeable* from a spiritual point of view.

Linked with this was Luther's protest against the form of eucharistic piety inherited from the Middle Ages. Just as he saw in the practice of worship the abandonment of what the Lord had instituted in favor of an autocracy not rooted in Scripture, so he saw in the concept of sacrifice a transformation of the gospel into law and hence the conversion of Christianity into its opposite. Law was for him the attempt to appease God by one's own effort, which could lead only to self-justification and so to perdition; gospel, on the other hand, was a grace-filled gift of God that bestowed on us what we could not earn for ourselves—the Eucharist was, consequently, the meal of those who were redeemed, not the sacrifice of those in need of redemption; not the atonement of the Church, but the gift of reconciliation from the God who reconciles. The Augsburg Confession expresses it thus: ". . . the holy sacrament, then, was instituted . . . so that our faith might be awakened and our consciences consoled. . . ."[29]

Here we see the restricted character of the protest, which, while it unmasked the domination of money and power that stood behind the practice of stipends and prebends and the theology oriented toward this, could not encompass the whole legacy of the early Church. The narrowing focus of Luther's *Babylonian Captivity* is portentous: "The

[28] *Der authentische Text der Leipziger Disputation*, ed. O. Seitz (Berlin, 1903), 83: "an non longe sit impudentissimae iniquitatis, tot milia martyrum et sanctorum per annos mille et quadringentos in Graeca ecclesia habitos extra ecclesiam eiicere. . . . Graeca ecclesia usque ad nostra tempora nunquam accepit episcopos suos confirmatos ex Roma. Ideo si fuisset ius divinum per tantum tempus omnes episcopi Alexandriae, Constantinopolis aliquot sanctissimi, ut Gregor. Nazian et ceteri quam plurimi essent damnati, haeretici et Bohemici, qua blasphemia nihil potest detestabilius dici."

[29] CA XXIV, 33, *Bekenntnisschriften*, 94.

Mass is, therefore, . . . nothing more than the above-quoted words of Christ: Take and eat, etc., as if he would say: See, you sinful and condemned man, . . . with these words I promise you the forgiveness of all your sins."[30] Similarly, in another passage: "I have, therefore, correctly ascertained that the whole power of the Mass lies in the words of Christ, which testify that the forgiveness of sins is guaranteed to all who believe."[31] The continuation of this passage is even more pointed: "It is certain, then, that the Mass is not a work that can be transferred to others, but an object . . . of each one's own belief, which can be nourished and strengthened by it."[32]

It should be noted that what we encounter in this early work of Luther, the reformer, is an extreme example of an impassioned protest seeking a suitable outlet; much of what he said here was later expressed more calmly and brought into harmony with the legacy of the primitive Church. Nevertheless, this stage of his protest must not be treated too lightly, for it continues to exert an influence. Many protests of the present day are surprisingly reminiscent of these beginnings in the questions they raise. Let us try, therefore, to diagnose more exactly what happened here. We cannot fail to see that the Eucharist was reduced to the only aspect that was for Luther the core and content of the Christian faith: the reliable, uncommunicable assurance to the individual's troubled conscience that his sins have been forgiven. The medieval limitation of the essential element of the Mass to the account of the institution of the Eucharist achieved here its ultimate radicality. The all-embracing early Christian context of the "beraka"—the table-prayer inherited from the synagogue and retained by Jesus and the apostles, which as remembrance was united with the liturgy of the word and as praise represented both the reception of what was remembered and the thanksgiving for it—was completely destroyed and, like the concrete form of the Latin canon, condemned as the "work of man".[33] The result was not only the banishing from the liturgy of the

---

[30] This and the following quotations are from *Luthers Werke in Auswahl*, 4 vols., ed. Otto Clemen (Bonn: A Marcus and E. Weber, 1912): "Est igitur Missa . . . nihil aliud, quam verba Christi praedicta: Accipite et manducate etc. ac si dicat: Ecce o homo peccator et damnatus . . . his uerbis promitto tibi . . . remissionem omnium peccatorum tuorum", 1:446, lines 31–36.

[31] "Recte itaque dixi, totam uirtutem Missae consistere in uerbis Christi, quibus testatur, remissionem peccatorum donari omnibus, qui credunt", 1:449, 18–21.

[32] "Est ergo certum, Missam non esse opus aliis communicabile, sed obiectum . . . fidei, propriae cuiusque alendae et roborandae", 1:455, 21–23.

[33] The *Formula missae et communionis* of 1523 (Clemen, 2:427–41) still preserves a remnant, however abbreviated, of the Canon of the Mass: the introductory responses to the Preface and the unchanging nucleus of the Preface, to which is immediately attached the account of the institution of the Eucharist (sung or silent). While the choir then sings the *Sanctus* and the *Benedictus*, the elevation of the host and chalice follow as in the old rite; then the *Pater Noster*

context of *communio,* the constitutive element of the Church, but also the obfuscation of the two-sidedness of Chalcedonian Christology, which not only knew Christ as the God who descended to earth and in whom God emptied himself even unto the abyss of death but also included God's acceptance of man, who, in the God-man, became capable of responding to God precisely as man and, in Christ, could again become sacrifice. For Jesus Christ, in whom are united the law and the gospel, is not just the promise of forgiveness; he is also the gathering together of the dispersed Adam into the *communio* of *agape.*[34] The Mass is more than the certainty that I have been forgiven: it is the highest degree of communicability, truly embracing the living and the dead. . . .

It is against this background that we must understand Luther's initially comprehensive negation of the spiritual office, about which he spoke vehemently in the *Babylonian Captivity:* "The Church of Christ does not know this sacrament, it was invented by the pope's Church."[35] All the bitterness of the young reformer against the existing priesthood finds expression in such shocking exclamations as the following: "O you princes, not of the Catholic Church, but of the synagogue of Satan, yes, of darkness. . . ."[36] "Like the . . . priests of Cybele, they have castrated themselves and burdened themselves with a celibacy that is completely hypocritical."[37]

---

and *Libera nos* (without the embolism), and the *Pax Domini* as "a kind of public absolution of the sins of the communicants"; the Communion follows. In the German Mass of 1526 (3:294–309), the Canon has completely disappeared. The sermon is followed here by "an official paraphrase of the Our Father and an admonition to those who want to approach the sacrament" (3:304). The account of the institution of the Eucharist follows at once without any prayer context; the hosts are distributed immediately after they have been consecrated. This is followed by the consecration of the wine and its distribution. During the distribution of the hosts, the *Sanctus* is sung; during the distribution of the chalice, the *Agnus Dei* (305). Thus nothing remains of the structure of the original Mass. On this development, see H. B. Meyer, *Luther und die Messe* (Paderborn, 1965); on the primitive Christian structure of the Mass and its origin in the prayer life of Israel, see Louis Bouyer, *Eucharistie. Théologie et spiritualité de la prière eucharistique* (Tournai: Desclée, 1968); Joseph Ratzinger, *Das Fest des Glaubens. Versuche zur Theologie des Gottesdienstes* (Einsiedeln: Johannes, 1981). [For an English translation, see Joseph Cardinal Ratzinger, *The Feast of Faith, Approaches to a Theology of the Liturgy* (San Francisco: Ignatius Press, 1986), (Trans.).]

[34] Cf. the material in Joseph Ratzinger, *Die Einheit der Nationen. Eine Vision der Kirchenväter* (Salzburg-Munich, 1971), esp. 31–37; Henri de Lubac, "Credo . . . Sanctorum Communionem", in IKZ 1 (1972): 18–32.

[35] "Hoc sacramentum Ecclesia Christi ignorat, inuentumque est ab Ecclesia Papae" (Clemen, 1:497, lines 21–22). The quotations in nn. 36–41 are also from this source.

[36] "O principes, non catholicarum Ecclesiarum, sed Satanicarum synagogarum, immo tenebrarum!", 1:503, 9–10.

[37] "Se ipsos, sicut Galli, Cybelis sacerdotes, castrauerunt, et celibatu onerarunt simula-tissimo", 1:502, 28–29. Cf. also "Itaque, horales et Missales sunt sacerdotes, id est,

It is interesting to observe, however, that Luther's criticism was never directed primarily against the notion of sacrifice or the relationship of priest and Mass, of *sacerdotium* and *sacrificium*: that is never the object of his attack, from which we may well conclude that this relationship was by no means as exclusive as we might have thought or as overemphasized as we might have imagined. What Luther was saying was this: the principal occupation of priests today is "reading the breviary"; therefore, they should look for their ordination formula, not in the words of the Last Supper, but where Christ commands us to pray always[38]—unintentionally not so negative a comment, perhaps, on the contemporary priesthood and, in any event, a correction of the notion that it was exclusively or even primarily a priesthood restricted to the saying of Mass, an office interpreted solely in terms of sacrifice. The reason for his rejection of the office as sacrament stems from the same objection that we met before: it contains no promise.[39] At this time, Luther's own definition of office was couched solely in terms of preaching: "One who does not preach . . . is in no way a priest. The sacrament of holy orders can, therefore, be no more than a rite by which to choose a speaker in the Church."[40] From this follows logically the purely functional interpretation of the office: "He [the priest] is distinguished from the layman only by what he does."[41] Behind this radical "desacralization" and "functionalizing" which reduces the priest to preacher, lurked the ominous reduction of the *sacramentum christianum,* of the whole Christian reality, to a statement of the forgiveness of sins. The moral quality of this protest against the domination of power and money in the Church is lessened here not only by the formless passion but even more by the minimizing of what is essentially Christian,

---

Idola quaedam uiua, nomen sacerdotii habentia, cum sint nihil minus, quales sacerdotes Hieroboam in Bethauen ordinauit de infima fece plebis, non de genere Leuitico", 1:502, 28f.

[38] "Deinde, cum hodie sacerdotis ad primarium opus sit . . . legere horas Canonicas, cur non ibi ordinis sacramentum conceperunt, ubi Christus orare praecipit", 1:500, 37–39. In 1:501, 4, reference is made to a *sacerdotium orationale.*

[39] "Christus hic nihil promittit, sed tantum praecipit", 1:500, 31–32. In this formula (Christ promises nothing here, but only commands), we hear the distinction between *evangelium* (promise) and law (command); where there is question only of command, not of promise, there can be no sacrament (as a form of *evangelium*).

[40] "Ex quibus fit, ut is, qui non praedicat uerbum, ad hoc ipsum per Ecclesiam uocatus, nequaquam sit sacerdos. Et sacramentum ordinis aliud esse non possit, quam ritus quidam eligendi Concionatoris in Ecclesia", 1:501, 34–37. Cf. also: "Quare, eos, qui tantum ad horas Canonicas legendas, et Missas offerendas ordinantur, esse quidem papisticos, sed non Christianos sacerdotes, quia non modo non praedicant, sed nec uocantur ad praedicandum; immo, hoc ipsum agitur, ut sit sacerdotium eiusmodi alius quidam status ab officio praedicandi", 1:502, 4–8. See also: "Sacerdotis munus est praedicare, quod nisi fecerit, sic est sacerdos, sicut homo pictus est homo", 1:503, 22–24.

[41] "Cum a laico nihil differat, nisi ministerio", 1:505, 4.

which seems to be viewed from a single perspective: the affliction of a conscience crying for forgiveness. No attention is paid to the fact that the pneumatic character of the Church (which is all but overlooked) expresses itself in the pneumatic character of her ministries. In consequence, the whole context of *communio* is abolished and only the "speakers" are left. As we have noted above, Luther very quickly saw the fatal consequences of these decisions in the movement of the "fanatics", against whom he took stringent measures that made possible the development of a new ecclesial life.[42] It is, consequently, all the more regrettable, I think, that the debate about office that is being carried on in the Church today relies, to a large extent, on the early Luther (this is by no means a thought that is expressed here for the first time) without recognizing the religious center that was most important to him: the call to forgiveness. That which in Luther makes all else bearable because of the greatness of his spiritual fervor, that which orders it to a Christian center—precisely that is being ignored.

The response of Trent

How did Trent respond? Its *Doctrine of the Sacrament of Holy Orders* (DS 1733–1778) was confined to a rejection of the most important theses in Luther's *Babylonian Captivity*. It countered the thesis that the priesthood is just an office of preaching by declaring that it is endowed with the specifically sacramental power of celebrating the Eucharist and of forgiving sins. Luther's functional concept of office was countered by the sacramental concept, in terms of which it was concluded that the conferral of office had also to be sacramental, not political. The remaining statements are in a similar vein. It is clear from the nature of the text and made even clearer by the Acts of the Council that a complete conciliar doctrine of the priestly office cannot be constructed on the basis of these negations. The only attempt to compose a positive outline of the doctrine was abandoned because of the complexity of the undertaking. The Council limited itself deliberately to a rebuttal of Luther's negations in order to prepare the ground for theological discussion.[43] The *Doctrina de sacramento ordinis* must, therefore, be read in the double context of the Acts that delimit it and of Luther's theses. Only in this context can its nature, its pronouncements and the intended limits of its statements be rightly

---

[42] Cf. Erwin Iserloh, in Konrad Algermissen, *Konfessionskunde* (Paderborn, 1969), 317–38; Pfnür, in ibid., 381–82.

[43] Cf. W. Breuning, "Amt und geschichtliche Kirche, Probleme der lehramtlichen Aussagen über das Priestertum", in *Catholica* 24 (1970): 37–50; Karl J. Becker, *Der priesterliche Dienst* 2:92–109.

understood. But the *Doctrina* has also a third context, which, though it is in my opinion the most important one, is almost never mentioned or considered: the Tridentine *Decreta super reformatione*. It would greatly exceed the bounds of this study to analyze these Decrees individually. I should like, however, to refer to some aspects of two of them: that of July 15, 1563, and that of November 11 of the same year.

The first document, which follows immediately after the *Doctrina de sacramento ordinis,* begins by stating that all those who have the care of souls are commissioned by the words of the Lord "to know their sheep, to offer the holy sacrifice for them, to nourish them by the proclamation of God's word, by the administration of the sacraments and by the example of good works; they are to care, like a father, for the poor and for all needy persons and to take upon themselves all the other duties of a shepherd".[44] *Canon 14* decrees that only he can be admitted to the priestly office who has spent one year in the diaconate and has shown himself capable of teaching the people and administering the sacraments and who can be expected to live a life that can itself serve as an example to others.[45] *Canon 16* prescribes a kind of relative ordination. No one may henceforth be ordained unless, in the judgment of the bishop, he is needed by and can be useful to a particular (local) church. Let us turn now to a much richer text—the Decree of November 11, 1563. This is not the place to analyze in detail all the Decree's circumspect and open regulations (which can vary according to local circumstances) for choosing a bishop. I shall mention only a few that are important for a complete overview of the priestly office. *Canon 1* points to the great responsibility of him who has the care of souls, since the Lord Jesus Christ will ask him about the sheep that were entrusted to him and will demand of him the "blood" of those who were lost through his fault. *Canon 2* requires that synods be held regularly. *Canon 3* regulates visitations and declares that the "principal purpose of all these visitations shall be to introduce . . . sound and right doctrine, to protect good morals, . . . and to lead the people to religion, peace and innocence." *Canon 4* states, finally, without any counterreformation embarrassment,

---

[44] *Conciliorum oecumenicorum decreta,* ed. Josepho Alberigo et al., 3d ed. (Bologna: Istituto per le Scienze Religiose, 1973), 744, lines 24–28. Becker also refers to this text, 107ff.

[45] Ibid., 749. *Canon 18* (750–53), which orders and provides regulations for the erection of seminaries, is especially important for Trent's concept of the priesthood. We should note what is said after the naming of the general conditions for admission to the seminary: "It (= the Synod) wills that preference be given to the children of the poor" (750, lines 40–41). After specifying the secular subjects to be studied, the text then names the theological ones in this order: sacram Scripturam, libros ecclesiasticos, homilias sanctorum atque sacramentorum tradendorum, maxime quae ad confessiones audiendas videbuntur opportuna, et rituum ac caeremoniarum formas ediscent (751, lines 6–9). Understandably enough, Holy Scripture is first on the list while questions of ceremony and ritual come at the end.

that "Preaching is the prime duty of the bishop." Consequently, this Canon requires the bishop to preach on all Sundays and holydays and daily during Lent and Advent. "The bishop shall earnestly admonish the people that each one is obliged . . . to hear the word of God." *Canon 7* states the corresponding obligations of pastors: catechesis, preaching and administering the sacraments.[46]

The great advantage of the Reform Decrees over the dogmatic pronouncements is that they sought, without counterreformation concern, to bring about a positive renewal. Unfortunately, precisely this important part of the accomplishments of Trent has practically disappeared from later theological manuals. Sad to relate, the ideals they contained were only gradually adopted. The weight of custom and of institutions was too strong. Nevertheless, the Decrees were not totally without effect. In Italy, to cite only one great example, St. Charles Borromeo modeled his life on this heritage and built on it an ecclesial way of life that persisted even into the twentieth century. Alessandro Manzoni erected a great monument to him in *I Promessi Sposi,* thus disseminating far and wide the reputation his efforts had earned for him as a bishop in the spirit of the conciliar reform. It might be said, indeed, that this novel paints a most typical picture of what occurred after Trent in its contrasting of the venal, cowardly and greedy local pastor with the altruistic Padre Christoforo, who, in the misery of an age shattered by sickness and war, became for the young a selfless helper and the epitome of the highest meaning of the word "priest": a shepherd who in the end gave himself; on whose unselfish readiness to help they could rely unconditionally and always. In our century, we have seen a last impressive echo of St. Charles Borromeo's reform in the person of Pope John XXIII, whose edition of the great bishop's protocol for visitations is a legacy in which his own way is reflected. In his view, the Council he called had no other purpose than to renew the same impetus to reform that had burned in St. Charles Borromeo, in whom he found truly embodied the words of the Council of Trent.[47] I am convinced that we will make pro-

---

[46] For regulations for choosing a bishop, see the following: *Canon i* (735f.): for the text quoted (et bonos maxime atque idoneos pastores singulis ecclesiis praeficiat; idque eo magis, quod ovium Christi sanguinem, quae ex malo neglegentium et sui officii immemorum pastorum regimine peribunt, dominus noster Jesus Christus de manibus eius sit requisiturus), see 761, lines 8–12; *Canon 2* (761): the regulation that diocesan synods be held every year is especially important (lines 29–31); *Canon 3*: the text quoted will be found on 762, lines 16–20; *Canon 4* (763): this is an important text; *Canon 7* (764): imposes the obligation of catechetical instruction for the people and of explaining the sacraments and the meaning of the Mass in the mother tongue.

[47] On the importance of Charles Borromeo for the spiritual development and attitude of John XXIII, see F. M. William, *Vom jungen Angelo Roncalli zum Papst Johannes XXIII* (Innsbruck, 1967), 122ff.

gress today, not by turning away from Trent, but only by a radicalization of what is to be found there.

A final thought

To develop that thesis would be to exceed the purpose and, consequently, the limits of the present work. I have chosen, instead, to conclude this chapter with an episode from Solzhenitsyn's *The First Circle*. No one, I think, can be left untouched by what is said there if he wonders today about the meaning of the priesthood and, in doing so, does not join the rebellion of yesterday but chooses to heed the challenge of today. I refer to the following scene. The Marxist idealist Rubin is enduring a difficult night, the night of Christmas, 1949. Although he is a bitter opponent of Stalin's police system, he has, nevertheless, undertaken to identify the voice of a man who had warned another man that he was to be imprisoned. The fact that the crime of both the one and the other lay in their humanity need not not concern us here. Rubin struggles with his guilt. A quarrel with one of his friends had disturbed him deeply because, despite all his intellectual resistance, the conversation had made him suspect that his basic orientation, however much he might deny it, was forcing him along the way set by Stalin: "When you realize that it's a dreadful thing to do, that you'd never do it again and that you have already paid for it as much as possible—how can you say that it never happened? to whom can you suggest that it be ignored? whom can you ask to 'unhappen' it? What strange thoughts force themselves, in a sleepless night, from the despairing soul of a sinner?"[48]

During this night, Rubin remembers a plan he had written for the future of Communist Russia. "Perhaps, at the present moment, a certain realization of the moral needs of the people would be more important for the Soviet State than the building of the Volga-Don Canal or the Angara Dam?"[49] This thought awakened in him the idea that what Marxist society needed was secular cathedrals with solemn rites for the fundamental moments of human life. "The architectural structure of the cathedrals should spread over everything a breath of greatness and eternity." Everything depended, of course, on there being "persons to serve the cathedrals" who, "supported by the love and confidence of the people, would be willing to lead spotless, altruistic and worthy lives."[50]

[48] Aleksandr Solzhenitsyn, *Der erste Kreis der Hölle* (S. Fischer, 1970), 483.
[49] Ibid., 485.
[50] Ibid., 487.

Man needs forgiveness. He needs the challenge that supports and preserves his soul. He needs room for his soul. All this is symbolized by the cathedral. And it is clear that the cathedral would have no meaning if it were just a building—a museum or a block of offices; it becomes a cathedral by reason of those human beings who build room for their souls and by this means perpetuate the unending challenge to mankind without which man cannot be man. It is too easy, I think, to say that this is just a philosophical, a completely unbiblical concept—impressive from a human standpoint but irrelevant from a Christian one. The thought is Christian precisely because it is so human.[51]

C. The Priest as Mediator and Minister of Christ in the Light of the Message of the New Testament

We have gradually grown weary of discussing the nature of the priesthood. All the arguments are familiar to us, and for each of them there is a counterargument, so that the quarrel has long since become a trench warfare in which each side merely strengthens its own position. Only from a distance do we glimpse the fact that the dispute cannot be decided by argument but only by the experiment of a life lived and a ministry fulfilled. Regardless of appearances, it does not owe its origin primarily to some new scholarly insight. The fact that new pages were suddenly discovered in the Bible and that old ones could no longer be found there was due, in the first place, to an upheaval of existence that, in the context of new experiences, made it no longer possible to accept what had been handed down as a meaningful force for today and tomorrow; hence arose a new alertness for something that had been overlooked in the past, and the old frequency beamed increasingly over emptiness. From this perspective, we can say with some reason that new arguments will, in fact, be just newly lived and suffered experiences by which the ideas of today must be either affirmed or negated. In recent years, we have assuredly had some experiences of this kind that we would not like to see perpetuated; but the positive—that which makes life possible and full—needs more time to

---

[51] I am more and more convinced that the isolation of the New Testament office from the whole realm of man's religious needs that has become customary today—and is attributable, no doubt, in large part to Karl Barth's emphasis on the absolute paradox of faith—is an unwarranted absolutization of a single aspect that causes us to overlook the whole tenor of the biblical development. Unfortunately, we can here only indicate, but not treat further, this problem that is related to the preliminary aspects of the question. Cf. the important work by G. Goldbrunner, *Seelsorge—vergessene Aufgabe* (Freiburg, 1971).

create a convincing form for itself. For that reason, we must bring patience
to this problem whose time is not to be shortened by theological acuity—
lived experience cannot be replaced by a philosophical construction, however important it may be.

From what has been said, the scope of these remarks will already be
apparent: they remain within the realm of argument and, consequently,
within the bounds that are already established. But this does not make the
effort of arguing superfluous. For however true it is that man cannot live
by reflection alone, it is just as true that his life cannot do without
reflection. Ultimately, it is only by truth that man can be satisfied. By it,
he becomes one with what is essentially himself, with what is, at the same
time, always outside himself. The inquiry of thought and the preservation
of life are linked in a reciprocity for which neither side is dispensable.

Another limiting and precautionary remark is necessary here. The
priesthood is a broad subject. It is treated in this section only to the extent
necessary for our purpose, which is to clarify the formal structures of
Church and theology. That is why we began with a question about
whether and how the reality of the priesthood fits into the basic form of a
Church for which the interrelationship of Scripture and tradition, of word
and sacrament, as a way of making Christ's words and deeds present is, for
all time, the definitive mark. We have already seen that the word requires
the communal *form* of tradition and the communal *fullness of power* that
come from the Lord. We have also seen that this structure of the word
must, by its nature, be sacramental: the priesthood, we said, is the
sacramental link with tradition; it transcends both the individual and the
community. In a second step, we determined that the liturgical context of
the priestly office also stems from this fact, for the Eucharist is an entering
into the daily prayer of Jesus Christ, in which he commits himself—
sacrifices himself—to the Father and so forms the Church. In this way, the
Eucharist becomes comprehensible as the unity of word, sacrament and
obligation to lead a Christian life. From this perspective, the all-embracing
task of the priestly ministry becomes visible and, with it, the purpose of
the ecclesial structure. Since these two reflections on the heritage of the
New Testament were introductory rather than exploratory, it is fitting to
offer here a few thoughts that will both deepen and broaden what has been
said.

As we know, there has been, in recent years, an intensive discussion of
this subject. Our approach here will be, therefore, to examine some
aspects of the question from a single, arbitrarily chosen perspective. I
choosing this perspective, I have been guided by the topic assigned to me
in 1969 at the Summer School in Maynooth, Ireland, where I was asked to
speak about the priest as mediator and minister of Jesus Christ. In view of

the fact that the most recent debate on the subject is particularly critical of the concept of "mediator" in connection with the priesthood, it was not easy for me to address this topic. It cannot be denied, however, that, especially in the last century, the concept of mediation has had great significance, particularly in Catholic circles, for the development of the concept of priesthood. It seemed right, therefore, to accept the proposed topic and to examine first the meaning of "mediator" and then the concrete reality of Christian ministries. The results of this inquiry are outlined in a few short paragraphs at the end of these reflections.[52]

I. *The concept of mediator in the New Testament*

The word "mediator" appears only six times in the New Testament. Our first conclusion must be, then, that the concept is peripheral, that it never became a central theme in the New Testament interpretation of Christian reality. Nor did the concept ever appear as an actual title of Christ or find a place in the language of the creeds. Where it appeared, it belonged, rather, to theological reflection—to the attempt to make the key doctrines of faith accessible to thought. To that extent it must be regarded as a secondary concept within the New Testament, not a part of the central content of tradition, but belonging already to the sphere of interpretation, albeit of an interpretation within the biblical tradition itself. A glance at the texts leads immediately to a second conclusion. Within the New Testament, the word "mediator" is used, not with a single meaning, but rather with antithetical meanings: in the epistle to the Galatians, it is used negatively; in the epistle to the Hebrews, positively.

Let us look first at the epistle to the Galatians. Arguing with a community disposed to Judaism, Paul attempted to explain how inferior and merely temporary the law is in comparison with the promise made to Abraham, which was fulfilled in Christ, thus abolishing the law. He sees the law as secondary because it was "promulgated by angels assisted by an

---

[52] The following remarks have been revised and the New Testament texts reviewed against the background of and inspired by the current discussion. It seemed pointless to me to obfuscate this characteristic of the text by a superfluity of bibliographical material. As representative of many texts, therefore, I cite the following: Alfons Deissler, Heinrich Schlier, Jean-Paul Audet, *Der priesterliche Dienst,* vol. 1, Quaestiones disputatae 46 (Freiburg: Herder, 1970). Further literature on the subject is suggested by Johann Auer, *Kleine katholische Dogmatik* 7 (Regensburg: Pustet, 1979): 296–97. Attention should also be called to three other recent texts of a more or less official nature which present the current debate in some detail: the publications of the German bishops on the subject of the priestly office; ITK, *Priesterdienst* (Einsiedeln, 1972); Synod of Bishops, 1971, *Das Priesteramt* (Einsiedeln, 1972), which has an important commentary by Hans Urs von Balthasar.

intermediary. Now there can only be an intermediary between two parties, yet God is one" (Gal 3:19–20). The fact that the law has need of a mediator is here an indication of its inadequacy. In the New Covenant, God acts alone: he himself fulfills the promise; there is no need for a mediator. In this text, then, Paul understands mediation as being ultimately that-which-separates from the goal, from God and his saving power. I am reminded of Kafka's *The Trial,* in which an accused person is referred to one intermediary after another and so realizes with increasing hopelessness the unapproachability and inaccessibility of the real judges— of the incomprehensible power in the background, which he cannot approach because he must always deal with intermediaries. By contrast, Christ is for Paul the experience of God's immediacy, the restoration of man's direct relationship with God and, hence, the end of a mediatorship that seemed to be helpful but in reality led ever farther from the goal. Christ is not mediator but immediacy, the very presence of God's dealing with us, which is fulfilled in us through him, the one son of Abraham, so that we become "one" in him (Gal 3:28). Thus there is, on the one side, the one God; on the other, Christ, together with whom we, too, are "one"; whatever stood between has been abolished. There is a certain similarity to this thought in the passage in the epistle to the Ephesians that sees salvation in the destruction of the barrier between Jews and pagans, in the fact that they will all be one in Christ's body stretched on the Cross (Eph 2:11–22), which embraces the dimensions of height and depth, of length and breadth, and unites all in the power of love, which is higher and broader than any *gnosis* (Eph 3:18–19).

Although the epistle to the Hebrews has a similar historical background, the concept it develops is quite different. It, too, regards the Jewish religion as promulgated by angels, who play a decisive role in it; it, too, sees the distinctiveness of Christianity in the fact that, instead of angels, it is the Son who comes, who points the way from image to reality. But this new and immediate relationship to God, which this author also proclaims, does not lead him to reject the notion of mediator; rather, he expressly designates Jesus as mediator (Heb 8:6; 9:15; 12:24), thus pursuing a line of thought that occurs again in 1 Timothy 2:5, where it is said: ". . . There is only one God, and there is only one mediator between God and mankind, himself a man, Christ Jesus". What do these texts intend when they apply to Jesus the concept of mediator? The gist of the Epistle to the Hebrews can be expressed briefly as follows: the whole cult of the Old Testament remained in the realm of σάρξ, that is, of the reality of this world; it did not extend to the properly divine realm, the realm of πνεῦμα. To that extent, it did not exceed the order of images (Heb 10:1) and never arrived at reality itself. The whole cult was, as it were, unable to pierce the barrier of images; it could represent, but it could not bring to perfection. Only Christ, who gave himself on the Cross by dying the real death of a condemned person, has no need of images. He does not rend a metaphorical veil in order to enter a metaphorical Holy of Holies; he rends the real curtain, the σάρξ, the dividing barrier that constrains our earthly existence, and passes through it to the other world to stand before the divine majesty of the living God. For the author of the epistle to the Hebrews, this realism of the Cross is the essential answer to the shadow-cult of the Old Covenant; it is a real priesthood and a real mediation with God. The first epistle to Timothy explains the word "mediator" by adding: "Who sacrificed himself as a ransom for all"; it, too, sees a close relationship between mediator and Cross, between mediator and priesthood.

We have now reached the crucial statement: the epistle to the Hebrews understands its theology of Christ as mediator as a theology of the priesthood. That Christ is, in the full sense of the word, the mediator who rent the curtain of creaturehood, the boundary of this world, and stood before God himself means, at the same time, that he is the true and only real priest. In the epistle to the Hebrews, the concepts of priest and mediator are ultimately inseparable. The more crucial and comprehensive concept is that of priest; the word "mediator" is a clarification of just one aspect of it. When the epistle to the Hebrews places special emphasis on the uniqueness of Christ's priesthood, this includes also his role as mediator, although the reference to the "one mediator" actually occurs in the first epistle to Timothy. If, on the basis of these reflections, we inquire about the most important marks of Christ's mediatorship as it is presented in Hebrews and in the first epistle to Timothy, we can name two in particular:

1. This mediatorship is exclusive, but—to speak paradoxically—it is exclusive because it is inclusive. Or, to express it more clearly: Jesus' mediation between God and man is not just one of a number of possible mediations; on the contrary, it is the only true mediation between the creature man and God, so that, beside this name, all other mediations are of no avail. Jesus excludes every further mediation with God because he is able to include all things in himself, because his mediation is valid for all times and for all places. Its uniqueness lies in its universality, and its universality is the source of its uniqueness.

2. The uniqueness of Christ's mediation is grounded, above all, in its realism, which transcends that of all other mediations, which are but processes within the image-world of creatures. Hence the realism of the Cross is the real foundation of Christ's mediation. The meaning of the Cross depends, in turn, on the fact that God himself appointed Christ, as "Son", to the dignity of high priest and made him capable of the cosmic

liturgy that no one can perform of himself (Heb 5:5, 9:11). In this sense, the real root of Christ's mediatorship is the action of God himself: only the Son can be mediator in this way. The man Jesus can be mediator of man to God only because, in him, God has already mediated himself to man. A comparison is now possible with the passage we have discussed in the epistle to the Galatians. This epistle, as we saw, contrasts mediation with immediacy. We may well say that, in their inherent direction, the epistle to the Hebrews and the first epistle to Timothy are not far removed from this concept. They, too, regard as crucial the fact that Christ transcends the region of mediatorship, the shadow-play of religions. Perhaps we can best define what they mean as "mediated immediacy". In Christ the mediator, God is immediately present to us. Christ reveals himself as the true mediator precisely by the fact that he leads to immediacy, or, rather, that he is himself that immediacy.

Let us add one further comment on the historical impact of this text. This seems important to me, as opposed to any mere biblicism, because the text has a reality capable of shaping history only because of its own history, because of its acceptance into the faith, life, prayer and reflection of the Church; we cannot properly understand it without this history that depicts its course. Patristic commentary, if I interpret it correctly, developed in particular two trains of thought that were indicated in the Bible but had not yet been more closely explored. Although the epistle to the Hebrews depicted the Cross as the concrete fulfillment of Christ's mediatorship and plainly mentioned the Sonship of Jesus, that is, his investiture by the Father with the office of priest, as the precondition of his function as mediator, the theology of the Fathers concentrated even more closely on this basic presupposition. The mediation of Christ was, to a large extent, identified with his Incarnation, which was therefore recognized as the true mediation, accomplished by God himself, between the nature of God and the nature of man in which there took place the *sacrum commercium*: *innovantur naturae*—both natures experienced something new—*Deus homo factus est; id quod fuit permansit, et quod non erat assumpsit* (Roman Breviary: antiphon of the Benedictus for the octave of Christmas).

Nor should we overlook the link with the concept of the Body of Christ that we encounter in Galatians 3:28. There Paul expresses the exclusive inclusivity of Christ in the formula: ". . . You are one in Christ Jesus", thus rendering superfluous the notion of a mediator, since there is question only of God and Christ. From this perspective, Christ no longer appears as an individual distinct from the rest of mankind but as the one in whom all things are contained, who established the Church as his Body and who, together with her, is one whole Christ. In consequence, the Church, insofar as she is "one in Christ Jesus", shares in his mediatorship. She is mediation with God because she is the form in which Christ remains present in history. The inner interpenetration of Christology and ecclesiology makes it possible thus to extend the concept of mediation without affecting the uniqueness of Christ's mediatorship. This is, of course, where the dangers begin. Before investigating this question more closely, we must turn again to the New Testament and ask what is said or omitted there about the servants of Christ, about their priesthood and about their role as mediators.

II. *Ministerial offices in the New Testament*

1. The office of apostle

We must first state a basic fact: the New Testament speaks of no ἱερεύς within the ἐκκλησία, the community of Jesus, but it does speak of ἀπόστολοι and, incidentally, of a variety of ministries in the individual local churches that grew out of the work of the missionaries (the apostles). The question of the extent to which the absence of ἱερεύς was due less to reasons of principle than to reasons of history—since the Jewish temple still existed and its ἱερεύς were recognized as such—need not be investigated here. Our purpose is simply to analyze the data that exist, beginning with the concept of apostle. The only question that has importance for us at this point is this: What was the relationship of the apostles to Christ? What kind of power is inherent in their office? To begin with, we can say that the New Testament consistently traces apostleship to a specified institution by the Lord and defines it as an act of calling (cf. Mk 3:13–19). To this should be added that apostleship is a sharing in the mission of Jesus Christ: like Christ, the apostle proclaims the nearness of the kingdom of God, and, from Christ, he has the power to make the coming visible by signs of power (Mk 3:14–19; Mt 10:7–9). The close relationship of Christ's mission and that of the apostle is summarized in two statements: "Anyone who listens to you listens to me; anyone who rejects you rejects me, and those who reject me reject the one who sent me" (Lk 10:16; cf. Mt 10:40). Closely related to this formulation in the synoptic Gospels are the words of the resurrected Lord in John's Gospel: "As the Father sent me, so I am sending you" (Jn 20:21). In both instances, Christ himself is represented as the Apostle of the Father so that those whom he sends as apostles represent what he is himself.

This thought, which is relatively peripheral in the synoptic Gospels, is fully developed in John's Gospel, in which the notion of mission becomes the key christological concept. Christ is, by nature, the One sent by the

Father, whose whole Being consists in being sent and who, as pure Mediator, has no other relationship to the Father than that of being his complete *repraesentatio* among men; the concept of mission in John's Gospel is basically a variation on the theme of mediator, the significance of which in the New Testament is thus once more revealed. With the interpretation of Jesus as "Apostle", apostleship becomes a central concept of Christology; by it, the Lord shares the origin and *raison d'être* of his own earthly existence. Apostleship is thus revealed to be a christologically instituted office. If mission means representation of him who sends and is, consequently, a mediation to him who sends it, it cannot then be doubted that this central office of the evolving Church qualifies as a ministry of mediation. It is important to note, however, that John does not use the word "mediator"; that the mission of the apostle is inseparable from the parallel "as the Father sent me, so I am sending you"; that it is inseparable from Christ as the axis; and, finally, that the concept of mediation, if we consider it, has a different emphasis here from what it has in the epistle to the Hebrews and the first epistle to Timothy. Mediation consists here in the selflessness of him who is sent, who is completely subsidiary to the message and to him who sends him; who does not give himself but mediates the other. Mediation involves here the self-emptying of the individual and his receptivity to another. It involves, not the individual's own action, but his investiture by the other, his being at the disposal of the other, his being subsidiary to the other. The particular ethos of the New Testament minister begins to emerge here as something quite different from the self-concept of priests who belong to other spiritual contexts. How is this expressed in Paul's writings? It is well known that for Paul, too, the immediate calling by Christ is the constitutive element of the apostolic ministry (for example, Gal 1:10–17); that for him, too, apostleship is a specific office, not just something that belongs in like measure to every Christian, to all the faithful (1 Cor 12:29). The two following observations are, I think, of particular significance for the question we are discussing:

a. In the second epistle to the Corinthians, against opponents who deny that he is an apostle, Paul develops a comprehensive theology of apostleship. In this context, he defines the apostle as the pneumatic enhancement and transcendence of the figure of Moses and assumes a pneumatic identification between the office of Moses and that of the apostle, but with the understanding that the office of Moses remains within the world of stone and letter while the apostolic office is the same office on the level of pneuma, of the living divine reality that has been revealed. Consequently, the office of Moses is designated as an office of death and condemnation (διακονία τοῦ θανάτου, τῆς κατακρίσεως); the office of apostle, on the other hand, as an office of pneuma and justification (διακονία τοῦ πνεύματος, τῆς δικαιοσύνης) (2 Cor 3:7–9). The fact is important for our inquiry because, in modeling apostleship on the figure of Moses, Paul has recourse to the central mediator of the Old Testament. Here, too, apostleship is conceived christologically, although the concept of Christology seems different and more complicated than in the synoptic concept of mission as developed by John. Christ mediates the pneumatic understanding of the figure of Moses—an understanding that he also makes possible since he is himself the Pneuma, that is, the reality of which Moses is but the type. Nevertheless, the apostle, who is mediated by Christ as axis, is interpreted in terms of Moses; his ministry is explained as the pneumatic antithesis— made possible by the Lord—of the ministry of Moses. The Lord encompasses both: the type and the reality. This is perhaps the first time in early Christian literature that the thought is definitively stated that, in comparison with that of Moses, the community of Jesus is a new and unique order which, therefore, includes a new ministry that corresponds, on the one hand, to that of Moses and is, on the other hand, fundamentally different from it. Paul takes up this notion again in the fifth chapter of this epistle. By calling apostleship a ministry of "reconciliation", he brings it very close to the ministry of the high priest in the Old Testament, whose most important duty was the liturgy of the Feast of the Atonement—here, too, the pneumatic christological reinterpretation of the idea of reconciliation is as much antithesis as parallel. Starting from this premise, Paul refers quite plainly to the mediating character of the apostolic ministry when he says: "So we are ambassadors for Christ; it is as though God were appealing through us, and the appeal that we make in Christ's name is: be reconciled to God" (2 Cor 5:20). In the background is clearly distinguishable the figure of Moses, who brought the voice of God to the people, who won the people for God and God for the people, who sought to mediate between them and was ready to let himself be crushed in the process, to spend himself between the two. Significantly, this quality is also reflected at the end of the second epistle to the Corinthians: "I am perfectly willing to spend what I have, and to be expended, in the interests of your souls" (2 Cor 12:15). Again, the whole is reflected through the figure of Christ, who is himself our reconciliation.

All in all, we can say, then, that the text we have before us is the one that establishes most clearly the relationship between the bearer of a New Testament office and the concept of mediator. As we have seen, the interpretation of the minister of the New Covenant as mediator stems, not directly from Christology, but from a christological interpretation of the Old Testament. It is derived from the figure of Moses as it appears in Exodus 34 and in Deuteronomy; that is, it is not based on cult but on the image of Moses who, as messenger of the word, stands between God and the people, between the cloud on the mountain and the people in the desert at the foot of the mountain, who are concerned only with their own needs. In the last analysis and despite their quite different orientation, this conception is closely related in content to what we saw in the synoptic Gospels and in John. The apostle's ministry of mediation is intimately associated with his readiness to let himself be spent for the gospel.

One further observation should be made here. It must be obvious that the same Paul who, in the epistle to the Galatians, rejects the concept of mediation even in reference to Christ here depicts the apostle in formulas that belong to the same train of thought as the concept of mediator. This fact shows plainly, I think, how wrong it is to attempt to draw final conclusions from isolated texts of the New Testament. Neither the New Testament as a whole nor its individual authors follow a strict system of terminology. They grasp a thought from a particular perspective, but they do not systematize it. They speak in examples and with the binding force of the exemplary but also with the limitations inherent in the example, which can always be expanded by other examples and by other trains of thought. This means, of course, that its statements are not all equally pertinent. The formula in the first epistle to Timothy, in which Christ is described as the one Mediator, is taken from the realm of New Testament belief and is, for our discussion, more relevant than the formula in the epistle to the Galatians, which is taken from the realm of Torah speculation, according to which there is no mediator at all in the New Covenant. Nevertheless, we must regard with reservations any too-literal dogmatization even in the case of the formula used in the first epistle to Timothy.

b. In the epistle to the Romans, Paul discusses apostolic ministry in the context of the cosmic liturgy that is to develop from Christ as the real *cultus* that will replace the shadow-play of the past. In the epistle to the Philippians, he includes the apostle in that realism of the Cross and of the liturgy of the Cross that for Christians ushered in the end of the temple by causing the curtain of the Holy of Holies to be rent as a sign that the end had come. In both epistles, we find thoughts that are not unlike those we encounter in the epistle to the Hebrews, except that what, in that epistle, is said of Christ alone is here repeated in the context of the apostolic ministry. In the epistle to the Romans, Paul describes himself as the "priest of Jesus Christ . . . [appointed] . . . to carry out my priestly duty by bringing the good news from God to the pagans and so make them acceptable as an offering, made holy by the Holy Spirit" (Rom 15:16). The whole sentence is permeated with cultic terminology; all its fundamental concepts belong to the realm of the temple and its sacrifice. But the whole has been transported to a new level. The gift that is to be made blameless, cultically perfect, "holy", is not a sacrificial animal but the nations of the earth; the means by which they are to be consecrated to God and made a living host is the message of the gospel, which will convert them to God—hence the "priestly duty" of the apostle is identical with his duty as a missionary of the gospel. In the epistle to the Philippians, Paul uses the sacrificial terminology of the temple to speak in the same vein of his being "poured as a libation" upon the "sacrificial offering of [their] faith"—that is, he speaks of his martyrdom, which is, for him, the crown and ultimate perfection of the liturgy of faith (Phil 2:17). In other words, the liturgy of the missionary is likewise that of the apostle: as the ministry of Christ, which consists first of all in the proclamation of the good news, this liturgy achieves its fulfillment only in the Cross, in the minister's spending of himself for the word. It is obvious that we have here, too, a very close intermingling of the terminology of apostleship and of Christology—something that, for Paul, was self-evident and needed no special comment. The concept of mediator does not appear here; but, although the context of the thought is completely different from that of the second epistle to the Corinthians, its theme is, nonetheless, the same so that elements of the concept of mediator actually are present here as well. The theme we have already discovered—that the mediator must, of necessity, become "sacrifice", that this is demanded of him by the real liturgy of the Crucified One—is confirmed even more strongly here by the fact that it culminates in a theology of martyrdom.

2. The other ecclesial ministries

By comparison with this developing theology of apostleship, the ministries of the local churches remain, for the most part, obscure. Even the terminology is not fixed from the beginning. In the epistle to the Hebrews, those who hold these ministries are called ἡγούμενοι (Heb 13:7, 17, 24), an expression that also occurs once in the Acts of the Apostles (Acts 15:22). In the first epistle to the Thessalonians (1 Th 5:12) and in the epistle to the Romans (Rom 12:8), they are called προϊστάμενοι, a word that appears once in the first epistle to Timothy, where, however, it is linked to the designation πρεσβύτεροι (1 Tim 5:17), which appears also in the Acts of the Apostles and in the Catholic and pastoral epistles as the usual designation of one who holds office within the community. In the epistle to the Philippians, finally, they are called ἐπίσκοποι καὶ διάκονοι (Phil 1:1). We find the word ἐπίσκοπος in the singular in 1 Timothy 3:2 and in Titus 1:7; in the Acts of the Apostles, it is not used as an actual title but is applied to the presbyter as a designation of function (Acts 20:28); the first epistle of Peter applies it to Christ as an honorary title but with a clear reference to those who hold office in the community (1 Pet 2:25). Paul developed a theology of these ministries only indirectly by describing them as parts of the numerous charisms of the organism of the Body of Christ, in which the Pneuma confers many gifts and duties and, ipso facto, also these ministries (Rom 12:6–8; 1 Cor 12:28–31). The epistle to the Ephesians takes up this point of view but names among the gifts of the Pneuma that come to the Church by the glorification of the Lord only those ministries that are explicitly associated with an office: apostles, prophets, evangelists, pastors, teachers (Eph 4:11). There is, consequently, an essential difference between what is said here and what is said in the great epistles: it is no longer the pneumatically constituted plurality of the Body of Christ that is described; rather, the ministerial offices within this Body are represented as gifts of the Pneuma from the glorified Lord. The theological development that is more presumed than explicit in this text is somewhat more clearly expressed in the Acts of the Apostles and in the Catholic and pastoral epistles. In Paul's farewell address to the presbyters of the Church of Ephesus, the Acts of the Apostles (20:18–35) has already developed an astonishingly comprehensive theology of the presbyterate that is characterized by three themes in particular:

a. As a whole, the address is basically an outline of the concept of apostolic succession. It is conceived as a kind of testament in which Paul confides the community to the faithful hands of the priests and, in words of exhortation, transfers his responsibility to them. It is apparent from the whole text in the Acts of the Apostles that Luke regards this address as exemplary and intends to represent in it the apostle's relationship to the presbyters. He is attempting to demonstrate the bond between the apostolic and postapostolic Church by depicting the transfer of pastoral responsibility from apostle to presbyters, who thus become, in practice, the "successors of the apostles".

b. The office of presbyter is understood as the institution of the Holy Spirit: it is not Paul who institutes the priesthood but the Pneuma (Acts 20:28).

c. The concept of ἐπίσκοπος is still understood here in a quite functional sense: presbyters are "overseers" of the flock; the concept interacts with the image of shepherd. The interpretation of the office of presbyter in terms of shepherd and flock is, we might say, the third important characteristic of this text. By it, the priestly office is incorporated into a great tradition of Israel, which, on the one hand, depicts Yahweh as the only true Shepherd of the people but, on the other hand, also understands the kings and priests as shepherds who will be judged according to their ministerial and faithful relationship to Yahweh. We need not determine, here, the extent to which the development of the image of shepherd—

which we find in 1 Peter 2:25, in Hebrews 13:20 and in John 10, and which is suggested also in Mark 6:34 and in Mark 14:27—is christological, although we cannot fail to be struck by the relationship of the text in the Acts of the Apostles to the corresponding passage in the first epistle of Peter (1 Pet 5:1–4). What is certain is that the office of priest is in this way incorporated into the traditional line of sacral ministries among the ancient people of God, Israel, and, at the same time, made susceptible of a christological interpretation. By the image of shepherd and flock, moreover, which includes a relationship that is to be neither changed nor dissolved, it is placed in clear contrast to the community, which, as a whole, is not "shepherd" (for that would be meaningless) but is guided by the shepherd given it by the Pneuma.

Within the group of Catholic epistles, the first epistle of Peter offers two guidelines. The passage in 1 Peter 5:1–4 is, as we have seen, a vivid reminder of the address to the presbyters in the Acts of the Apostles that is discussed above; it might, in fact, be called a kind of presbyteral mirror. It is particularly important because the Apostle designates himself there as a συμπρεσβύτερος of the presbyters. The question of whether the text actually originated with the Apostle has no real significance for our discussion. For, in any event, it cannot be denied that the epistle depicts the Apostle as the speaker and that, by its designation of him as a fellow presbyter, the two offices—apostle and presbyter—are identified with each other. By this formula, the apostolic office is interpreted as identical with the presbyteral office. This, in my opinion, is the strongest linking of the two offices to be found in the New Testament. In practice, it means a transfer of the theology of apostleship to the presbyterate.

The same text, moreover, applies the idea of shepherd to the interpretation of the presbyteral ministry, the scope of which it expressly enlarges on the basis of Old Testament admonitions, thus incorporating it even more plainly into the traditional context we have been discussing. At the same time, it establishes a link with another passage of this epistle in which Christ himself is designated the "Shepherd and Guardian of your souls" (1 Pet 2:25). Precisely in this context, it cannot be doubted, I think, that this designation of Christ is a reference to the ecclesial bearer of that office, that it binds him to Christ as the true Shepherd. In that case, the christological roots of the episcopal ministry are expressed here with complete clarity.

The pastoral epistles add nothing essential. The imposition of hands as a rite of pneumatic investiture in office is explicitly stated (2 Tim 1:6; but cf. Acts 6:6); a sharper contrast is made between the one bishop and the group of presbyters; the bishop has the duty of installing presbyters in the different localities (Titus 1:5), although, on the other hand, his office is not as yet strictly distinguished from the office of presbyter (1 Tim 3:2–7; Titus 1:7–10). Nevertheless, the transfer of apostolic responsibility to Timothy and Titus is clear enough, since there is repeated there that inclusive formulation of the concept of succession that we have already found in the Acts of the Apostles in the address to the presbyters of Ephesus. For evaluating the relationship of the pastoral epistles to the great Pauline epistles, a brief passage in the first epistle to the Corinthians seems important to me and can, perhaps, be considered the stimulus for the great epistles of the early period. In it, Paul admonishes the Corinthians to "copy" him and continues: "[That is] why I have sent you Timothy, my dear and faithful son in the Lord: he will remind you of the way that I live in Christ as I teach it everywhere in all the churches" (1 Cor 4:17). The pastoral epistles attempt, as it were, to extend and confirm this commission; but Timothy's responsibility remains unchanged: he is to be the emissary of the Apostle, who, in turn, is the emissary of Christ, just as Christ is the emissary of the Father. As emissary, his task is to remind men of the Apostle's way as a way in Christ, reminding them to keep present the Apostle's teaching to the whole Church as the one message of faith. If we take this text seriously, we must acknowledge that, whoever may have composed them, the pastoral epistles are "Pauline in origin".

At the conclusion of these reflections, we can say that the New Testament has itself established the link between the office of apostle and that of presbyter, so that the constitutive elements of the one belong also to the other. Above all, the presbyter is involved in the mediating ministry of Jesus Christ in the same way that the apostle is; like the apostle, he is the servant of Jesus Christ.

III. *Conclusions*

I propose now to summarize what has been said under four points and to apply them, by way of conclusion, to the question of a correct understanding of the existence of the priesthood in the Church. Let us begin by stating what we have discovered thus far:

1. The ecclesial office of priest can be understood only in relation to the at once exclusive and inclusive office of Jesus Christ as Mediator. It cannot be understood in terms of any universal cultic theology but originates in, is made possible by and receives its character from the figure of Jesus Christ.

2. The office of Jesus Christ as Priest and Mediator reaches its fulfillment in the Cross; its precondition and foundation are in the Incarnation, by which Christ is constituted Son and, consequently, "high priest of all the blessings . . . to come" (Heb 9:11).

3. Apostleship is the immediate measure and starting point of the office of presbyter. As a continuation of the mission of Jesus Christ, it is, in the first place, an office of evangelization. But the ministry of the word, which it thus represents, is to be understood against the background of the incarnate and crucified Word. It includes the duty of an authorized use of signs as well as a claim to credibility in the Cross of the witness; the precondition for both is the fullness of power established by the Father in the Incarnation.

4. The Pauline theology of apostleship finds its understanding of the priest's role as mediator principally in the extent to which the mediatorship of Christ is concretized and represented in the actions and sufferings of the apostle. The priest, accordingly, is "mediator" only as the servant of Christ. That is the principal concept; to avoid ambiguity, the concept of mediator should be understood as subordinate to it. The great problem of theology will always be to preserve the exclusive inclusivity of Christ not only verbally on the margin of its thinking but in the entire breadth of that thinking. The great problem of ecclesial and, above all, priestly life will always be to devote itself entirely to the actual performance of the ecclesial ministries, to inclusion in Christ; to build and to be, not near him, but only in him and thus, by making him the all-inclusive center, to let his necessary exclusivity—which, by its inclusivity, does not destroy but liberates all things—become reality. The success of this way of thinking depends ultimately, as we have said, on whether the experiment of a life of ministry lived is successful. The failure of thought as well as its more or less great advances are always an indication of the nature of a particular period of Church history. When we hear the whole, we will not only understand but will ourselves be overcome by the alarm the disciples experienced when they first learned all that was entailed in the discipleship to which they had committed themselves. Jesus' words to the rich young man let them see the extent to which they had to become "poor" if they wanted to be included in the "exclusivity" of Jesus Christ. Astonished, they inquired, "Who can be saved?" (Mk 10:21). Only when we have been overcome by this fear of what Jesus calls the "impossible" (Mk 10:27) are we even close to what discipleship requires.

The question that concerns us—let us repeat it here—finds its answer first as the experiment of a life lived. Every theological formulation has here the character of an afterthought. Nevertheless, we cannot do without this reflection. An examination of the experiences and sufferings of the Church in her effort to understand this office reveals above all, I think, two complementary aspects of priestly existence.

1. Augustine made the first aspect clear in his quarrel with the Donatists about the absolute requirements of holiness. The Donatist Bishop

Parmenian had advanced a number of Old Testament texts about the qualities of a Christian bishop, as, for example, the sentence from the Latin version of Leviticus: "Any one of your descendants . . . who in a state of uncleanness approaches the holy offerings . . . shall be outlawed from my presence" (Lev 22:3). In his counterargument, Augustine emphasized the fact that the holiness of the Church depends, not on the holiness of her bishops, but on the holiness of Jesus Christ, the true priest. On this premise, he rejected Parmenian's thesis that the bishop is the mediator between God and the people,[53] which he regarded as the fundamental error of Parmenian's theology. He quoted instead John's teaching: "If anyone should sin, we have our advocate with the Father, Jesus Christ, who is just" (1 Jn 2:1). John, Augustine pointed out, does not say: If anyone sins, you have me as mediator with the Father; I shall pray for you. If he had said this—as Parmenian does—everyone would have known that it was no longer the Apostle of Jesus Christ who was speaking but the Antichrist, who had put himself in the place of Christ instead of being his apostle. By this Augustine was not advocating laxity; he was concerned that there be many holy bishops in the Catholic Church, but he wanted to make clear where the cornerstone of Christian hope and true Christian cult—Christian sacrifice—is to be found: in the Lord who intercedes for us with the Father. The absolute claim of Jesus Christ means that the types of the Old Testament are to be interpreted in reference to him, not to the minister who is the temporary incumbent of an office. It means that salvation is mediated by Christ, not by men. It means that the salvation of Christ can be mediated by ministers who are themselves not holy, because it comes not from them but from him. The primacy of Christology means, therefore, an objectification of the Church's prerogative of holiness, which is not dependent on the subjective worthiness of her ministers. That relativizes the status of the holder of a spiritual office; it clarifies his subsidiary position vis-à-vis the absolute primacy of Christ; it also relieves him of a burden, because he knows that, like all the faithful, he, too, can rely on the saving advocacy of the Lord, even though it is his duty, in his official sacramental capacity, to represent the Shepherd Jesus Christ and to mediate his presence. This insight should warn us about overexaggerated claims to holiness. Augustine called this a Pharisaical trait: "The Pharisee and the Publican prayed in the same temple. The Lord tells us that the sinner who confessed his sins received more justification than the Pharisee who praised his own merits: they (the Donatists) resemble him."[54]

2. We have said that the primacy of Christ makes the priest humble even while it frees him. We must add: it also points us in the right direction. It

[53] St. Augustine, "Contra epistulam Parmeniani", Liber 2, caput 8, 15, PL 43:60ff.
[54] Ibid., 17, PL 43:63.

means that the priest must know in his heart that his place is on the side of the Church, of the people who stand outside before the Holy of Holies and rely on the intercession of him who alone can pass beyond the curtain. It means that the priest cannot say: You have me; but only: You have Christ, as your mediator with God. The objectivity of salvation, of which we have spoken, must make the priest, too, objective. He preaches, not himself, but the faith of the Church and, in that faith, the Lord Jesus Christ. This matter of objectivity, of the elimination of the "I" to make room for that other whom one represents, is the true ascetic formula that exists in the Church as a result of the christological orientation of the *sacerdotium*. The holiness of the priest consists in this process of becoming spiritually poor, of decreasing before the other, of losing himself for the other: for Christ—and, in Christ, for others: for those whom the Lord has entrusted to him.

I venture to close these reflections with a personal comment that will shed another light on the whole. At the end of a lecture on the historical character of dogma, a student priest remarked to me that, however one may twist and turn it, dogma is still the principal obstacle to every kind of proclamation. This remark seems to me to be symptomatic of the misunderstanding of the priestly function that is so prevalent today. For, in reality, the opposite is true. Today, many Christians, myself included, experience a quiet uneasiness about attending divine services in a strange church; they are appalled at the thought of the half-understood theories, the amazing and tasteless personal opinions of this or that priest that they will have to endure during the homily—to say nothing of the personal liturgical inventions to which they will be subjected. No one goes to church to hear someone else's personal opinions. I am simply not interested in what fantasies this or that individual priest may have spun for himself regarding questions of Christian faith. They may be appropriate for an evening's conversation but not for that obligation that brings me to church Sunday after Sunday. Anyone who preaches himself in this way overrates himself and attributes to himself an importance he does not have. When I go to church, it is not to find there my own or anyone else's innovations but what we have all received as the faith of the Church—the faith that spans the centuries and can support us all.

To express that faith gives the words of even the poorest preacher the weight of centuries; to celebrate it in the liturgy of the Church makes it worthwhile to attend even the externally most unlikely liturgical service. Hence the substitution of one's own invention for the faith of the Church will always prove to be too superficial, however intellectually or technically (seldom aesthetically) impressive this substitution may be.

Certainly, if it is to remain vital, the objective content of the Church's faith needs the flesh and blood of human beings, the gift of our thinking and willing. But it must be a gift, not just the sacrifice of a moment. The priest always fails in his duty when he wants to stop being a servant: an emissary who knows that it does not depend on him but on what he himself can only receive. Only by letting himself become unimportant can he become truly important, because, in that way, he becomes the gateway of the Lord into this world—of him who is the true Mediator into the immediacy of everlasting Love.

CHAPTER 3

CATHOLICITY AS THE FORMAL
PRINCIPLE OF CHRISTIANITY

A. The Community's Right to the Eucharist? The "Community" and the Catholicity of the Church

I. *The new debate about the community's right to the Eucharist*

In recent years, the discussion about the priestly office that has been energetically pursued in the Catholic Church since the end of Vatican Council II has acquired a new label: it is now subsumed in large part under the heading: "the community's right to the Eucharist". In many respects, this new version of the problem shows that progress has been made. For one thing, it recognizes the fact that the ecclesial community is centered around the Eucharist and, consequently, understands the Church herself in terms of her original liturgical context, thus apparently accepting anew the indispensability of the priestly office. After all the talk of desacralization, of the end of a professional priesthood, and the like, there seems to be a renewed insight into the basic indispensability of the priest whose function it is to lead the community solely in terms of its eucharistic center. Often a criticism of the new proxy offices (as the new lay ministries are designated) and of Sunday services without a priest is added to the thesis of the community's right to the Eucharist: regular eucharistic celebrations, it is said, cannot be dispensed with even during a period of crisis. "There is a justifiable fear", as J. Blank puts it, "that, when this period of crisis has come to an end, there will be no community. Anyone who cares about the future of Christianity and the Church is urged to do something about it."[1] It seems, then, to be an obvious sequel when this plea is followed by a demand that—for the sake of those values that are most important: the Eucharist, which forms the community and requires a priest—a value that is not so indispensably necessary, the universal celibacy of the priesthood, be renounced. If we look more closely, however, we shall see that the simple and apparently straightforward formula: "the community's right to the

---

[1] J. Blank, P. Hünermann, P. M. Zulehner, *Das Recht der Gemeinde auf Eucharistie* (Trier, 1978), 26. The best introduction to the theme of "community" is that offered by Karl Lehmann, "Was ist eine christliche Gemeinde? Theologische Grundstrukturen", in IKZ 1 (1972): 481–97; Karl Lehmann, "Chancen und Grenzen der neuen Gemeindetheologie", in ibid., 6 (1977): 111–27.

Eucharist", has many levels of meaning and contains implications that are not so self-evident as they may at first seem to be. It must be admitted that this formula harbors a variety of perspectives. The most radical is that of J. Blank, who, on the basis of his interpretation of the New Testament legacy, traces the right of the community "directly to the command of Jesus" that they appoint "one of their number to preside". "The celebration of the Eucharist takes precedence over the 'office'. From this it is clear that the organizational forms of the office must be constituted in such a way that the eucharistic celebration is guaranteed forever its place as the center of the community. The office cannot absolutize itself and make the eucharistic celebration dependent on its continued existence. . . ."[2] If we note also that Blank defines the Eucharist as "remembrance by means of an analogous practice"[3] and expressly emphasizes that we should speak, not of "words of transubstantiation", but of "words of interpretation",[4] then it is clear that we have here a quite different understanding of Church and Eucharist. For that reason, even Schillebeeckx has dissociated himself from Blank,[5] although, I must admit, I find no significant difference between Blank's ideas and Schillebeeckx's. Nevertheless, we find in Schillebeeckx the most fundamental attempt to date to base the thesis of the community's right to the Eucharist not only on a particular interpretation of the New Testament but also on an analysis of tradition as a whole.

Schillebeeckx also links this thesis to a thoroughgoing criticism of the dogmatic tradition of the second millennium as formulated by the Councils of the Middle Ages and of Trent. He sees a fundamental distinction between the first Christian millennium and the second. It was the second millennium, he says, that produced the ontological and sacerdotalizing image of the priest, with its concept of the sacramental character of the priesthood. Against this image, he wants to reestablish an understanding of the office that is sacramental but not sacral.[6] The key point in his nonsacral concept of the sacrament is that holy orders is to be understood as "ordinatio", while this, in turn, is to be understood quite literally and exclusively as "orientation" to a community. But, for this "orientation" that is the whole content of ordination, the action of the community as a whole assumes primary importance.[7] Schillebeeckx, it is true, seeks to

---

[2] Blank, 25.

[3] Ibid., 16.

[4] Ibid., 14.

[5] Eduard Schillebeeckx, "Das christliche Gemeinde und ihre Amsträger", in *Concilium* 16 (1980): 205–27. See 212: "This certainly does not mean to imply, however, that the celebration of the Eucharist should not be associated with an 'office'." In n. 25 (225), which refers to this passage, Schillebeeckx ascribes this error to Blank "and others" and affirms: "The statement cannot be accepted in this form."

[6] Schillebeeckx, 218.

[7] Ibid., 219.

avoid giving complete autonomy to the community by arguing that unity with other communities is indispensable,[8] but, in practice, the dominant thought is of the strong communal character of the office, which, as such, is an "orientation" to which the community has a right and which, in case of necessity, it can even establish. With respect to a series of reports from all over the world about various kinds of "alternative ways of exercising the office", he says: "As a Christian theologian, I must emphasize that the variety of practices in Christian communities . . . is a dogmatic and apostolic possibility. . . . It is foolish and blind to use terms like 'heretical' and 'heterodox' here only because . . . there is a question of a practice that differs from that of the universal Church."[9] "Even Vatican Council II had difficulty in determining the boundaries of membership in the Church. There must, of course, be such boundaries, but who will consider himself qualified to state with certainty where they are drawn."[10] I find it somewhat strange that Schillebeeckx goes on to state: "My opinion here is not the audacious opinion of one individual but the consensual opinion of contemporary theologians"—anyone who does not agree is just "a subservient instrument of the ecclesial Magisterium".[11] This method of gaining consensus by disqualifying all who hold differing opinions is, I think, hardly likely to benefit the theological discussion.

Let us pause here for a moment. We have seen that the apparently straightforward thesis of "the community's right to the Eucharist", which is then immediately defined as "the community's right to a priest", tends at least by its juridical claim to change the concept of both Eucharist and priesthood.[12] Where the Eucharist is claimed as the right of the community, there quickly follows the notion that the community can, in fact, confer it on itself, in which case it no longer needs a priesthood that can be bestowed only by ordination in the *successio apostolica,* that is, from within the "Catholic" context, the Church as a whole and her sacramental power.

At this point, a problem arises with respect to the concepts "right" and "community" that requires closer examination. Actually, it is the basic structure of the Church that is being debated here, that is, the question of the extent to which Catholicity is inherently essential to the Church in the

---

[8] Ibid., 217 and 219.

[9] Ibid., 223.

[10] Ibid.

[11] Ibid., 206. In general, Schillebeeckx's text offers valuable material and important points of view but shifts back and forth between a historical presentation and systematic postulates. This is even more pronounced in the introduction (*Concilium* 16 [1980]: 155–56).

[12] This is not necessarily the case, as we see from the excellent contributions by Hünermann and Zulehner in the volume cited above in n. 1. The course of the debate until now makes it clear, however, that the theme tends to this conclusion by a kind of inner logic.

deepest recesses of her life. Any discussion of this central question must be preceded by an analysis of the concepts "right" and "community". The crucial concept here is that of "community", which gives the concept of "right" its particular character; everything depends, therefore, on how it is interpreted. Nevertheless, I shall begin with a brief preliminary remark about the question of "right". There exists in the *Corpus Iuris Canonici*— the official legal code of the Latin Church—a norm that is analogous to the postulate of the community's right to the Eucharist, namely, Canon 682, which addresses the right of the laity to receive [from the Church] spiritual goods and, in particular, those helps that are necessary for salvation. In the Canon, in other words, the Church specifically acknowledges that Christians have a right to receive from her the sacraments that have been given solely for their benefit. There are, however, two differences that seem to me to be particularly worthy of note between the norm found in canon law and the topic we are discussing. The Code of Canon Law does not speak of the right of communities but of the right of laymen, that is, of those who have been baptized. Moreover, it links this right to the *norma ecclesiasticae disciplinae*—to the norm of ecclesiastical discipline. Both points are important, I think. On the one hand, there is question of the Church as a whole; on the other hand, when the way of salvation is at issue, the emphasis is on the individual. Precisely these two differences between the Code and the modern thesis raise again the question of community, which contemporary thought seems to regard as the proper subject of rights—which is said, even, to bear within itself the right to establish both sacrament and office.

II. *Definition of terms*

1. The language of Vatican Council II

What are, then, the rights of the community? Who or what is it actually? Before Vatican Council II, Catholic theology did not employ the concept of community [*Gemeinde*]. Under the heading "Community", the second edition of the *Lexikon für Theologie und Kirche*, edited by Karl Rahner, first speaks of the biblical concept of Church and then treats of community as a Protestant concept. The Council itself did not use the concept. It designated the following three levels in the concept of Church:

> *Ecclesia universalis* ("the universal Church"), that is, the whole Catholic Church, which includes those Churches having different rites, thus spanning East and West and all possible rites—in other words, the "Catholic Church" as such;

Ecclesia localis ("the local church"), that is, the "patriarchate", or those communities that preserve specific traditions and rites;

Ecclesia particularis ("the particular church"), that is, the community of the faithful that is subject to a bishop; a "diocese".[13]

What strikes us about this terminology, which, though not completely uniform, is, nevertheless, used with great consistency, is the fact that the expression "local church" encompasses a larger radius—namely, the communities with different rites—than does the expression "particular church". We are struck also by the fact that the lowest level that is here precisely defined and theologically designated as a specific realization of the concept "Church" is the episcopal church—what we are accustomed to call today a "bishopric" or "diocese". This terminological system is not discarded even in the famous text of the third chapter of the *Dogmatic Constitution on the Church* (*Lumen gentium*), which is often cited as a countertext: "This Church of Christ is truly present in all legitimate local congregations (*legitimis fidelium congregationibus localibus*), which, united with their pastors, are themselves called Churches in the New Testament. . . . In any community existing around an altar, under the sacred ministry of the bishop, there is manifested a symbol of that charity and 'unity of the Mystical Body, without which there can be no salvation' " (Art. 26). Two aspects of this text are important for our discussion:

a. Beyond doubt, the Council was primarily concerned here with the local celebration of the Eucharist; by the word "legitimate", however, the local assembly is placed in the context of the apostolic succession and so of the universal Church. If the assembly lacks this inner Catholicity, it is not a "legitimate" assembly, that is, it does not exist as a real eucharistic assembly and, consequently, as a "community". That fact is underscored again by the reference to union with pastors.

b. In the second sentence quoted above, the altar congregation is defined as a community under a bishop; it is only by virtue of this community, which transcends place, that it is what it is. By this fact, the text is very plainly incorporated into the general schema of the Council.[14]

[13] See "Decree on the Catholic Eastern Churches" [Orientalium ecclesiarum], esp. sec. 2; "Decree on the Church's Missionary Activity" [Ad gentes divinitus], esp. chap. 3; and "Dogmatic Constitution on the Church" [Lumen gentium], chap. 3, 26, in *Vatican Council II. The Conciliar and Post Conciliar Documents,* Austin Flannery, O. P., gen. ed. (Northport, N. Y.: Costello Publishing Co., 1975). [Trans.] Cf. the thorough analysis of the conciliar text in Henri de Lubac, *Les Églises particulières et l'Église universelle* (Rome: Città cattolica, 1971). [For an English translation, see Henri de Lubac, *Motherhood of the Church,* pt. 2 (San Francisco: Ignatius Press, 1982). (Trans.)]

[14] Gérard Philips, *L'Église et son mystère,* 337–43. This authentic commentary by the principal author of *Lumen gentium* should always be consulted in any interpretation of art. 26.

It must be admitted that there is a stronger accent on the local assembly in this text than in most of the other texts of the Council. It should perhaps also be mentioned that the archaizing language seems to imply a situation such as existed at the time of the New Testament and the early Fathers, when the local assembly and the church of the bishop were, for the most part, identical. To that extent, the text offers points of departure for the development of a concept of community. Nevertheless, it is clear that the total view of the Council as it is quoted above has by no means been relinquished in *Lumen gentium* III, 26. Here, too, the place, the geographical element, is less constitutive of the local church, of the "community", than is communion with the bishop—that is, the theological element; this theological element, in turn, is seen in conjunction with the reality of the "apostolic succession", which the bishop guarantees.

In some of the later Council texts, there does appear the concept of a *communitas christiana,* which is best translated "Christian community". It can be regarded as another point of departure for the development of the concept of community. But it is just a point of departure. For, if we compare the various texts, we see that this word has no single, consistent meaning; in chapter 2, article 3, of the "Decree on the Church's Missionary Activity" [*Ad gentes divinitus*], for example, it refers to the community of Christians living in a missionary country—the Church in the process of formation. It is by no means possible, therefore, to speak of a fixed meaning—or even of a concept of "community" as we understand it today.

2. The roots of the modern concept of community

In the last part of these remarks, we shall ask ourselves again what the terminological and theological subdividing of the concept of Church in the thought and language of Vatican Council II means for the current discussion of the concept of community. The fact that the Council itself, despite some intimations and beginnings, did not develop such a concept, did not speak of "community" as we understand the term, does not necessarily mean that such a concept is not admissible. But the fact is, nonetheless, indicative of the small importance the Council attached to the concept, and, by the same token, the Council's silence also sets guidelines that are essential to any new consideration of it. First, however, we must ask: If the concept of community does not stem from Catholic tradition,

---

Cf. also, Karl Lehmann, "Was ist eine christliche Gemeinde?" (see n. 1 above), 497 and 487–88.

by what roots is it nourished? What constitutive features are associated with it? How can it be accepted—even purified—if need be? I distinguish three essential sources.

a. The crucial source must be sought in the Reformation of the sixteenth century. For Luther, the word "Church" expressed all that he wanted to reject—the *catholica* of tradition. Consequently, he never used the word for what we call Church but instead regularly made use of the word "community". In his translation of the Old Testament, the word "Church" usually designates a pagan shrine.[15] G. Gloege can say without fear of correction, therefore, that we must regard the "community as the central situs of the basic doctrines and philosophical structures of the Reformation".[16]

In fact, the terminological shift from "Church" to "community" reveals more convincingly, perhaps, than is revealed anywhere else the inner process of the Reformation's transposition of the structure of faith. For Luther, Church means community, whereas the Church as *successio,* as the unity of binding tradition in a sacramental and personal form, loses for him her theological content. At best, she becomes an instrument, an organization; at worst, she is the Antichrist, the organized and sacrally clothed obstacle to the "gospel" (by which he means, not the four Gospels or the Bible as such, but the message of justification as the central concept of Holy Scripture).[17] According to this gospel, all that is valid theologically is the individual community that comes together and places itself under the word. From this perspective, Gloege and Brunner regard the community as the crisis of the Church as an institution. Karl Barth, on the one hand, remains entirely within the context of the Reformation when he interprets community as an actual presence; Brunner, on the other hand, interprets it in a way that is strongly personalistic (and, therefore, anti-institutional).[18]

The notion that it is actually only the community that is "Church" in the true sense (that is, the place of the "gospel") and that the other—the universal—Church is, by contrast, just an instrument, an organization with no spiritual status—this notion is accepted as self-evident today by

---

[15] Gerhard Gloege, "Gemeinde", in RGG 2 (1958): 1328.

[16] Ibid., 2:1329.

[17] It should be noted that the concept of "gospel" is as obscure as the concept of "community" in recent Catholic publications. The fact that it is most frequently used in texts that are critical of the Church shows something of its Reformation character, although it is not clear (as Luther's doctrine of justification is clear) precisely in what this consists. Instead of the great religious earnestness that Luther's criticism of the Church manifests precisely because of this doctrine of justification, vague attitudes frequently appear that regard the "gospel" all too often from the banal perspective of something "happy" (the "good news"). Cf., on this subject, Part One, Chapter 1, Section 2C of the present work: "Faith as Trust and Joy—Evangelium".

[18] RGG 2:1328–29.

the average [Protestant] Christian and exerts a more or less recognized influence also in Catholic circles. Under the motto "local ecumenism", it offers itself even as the solution of the ecumenical problem.[19]

b. Luther conceived the notion of community largely in terms of the word (the gospel). Gloege is thus well within the Lutheran tradition when he names as the two essential ingredients of the concept "Church" God's call to assembly and the answer by which that call is realized.[20] This pronounced predominance of the word does not generally exist for us today; the expression "the community's right to the Eucharist" has, by contrast, a stronger sacramental—a eucharistic—accent and, consequently, a specifically "Catholic" quality that has been added to its Reformation origin. We thus meet a second and more complex root of the concept of community, for we find combined here the legacy of Reformation tradition, the theses of modern exegesis and—touched by both—the ideas of the Churches of the East. In particular, the more recent exile literature of the Orthodox Churches has produced new views by intermingling (for the most part by way of French theology) the traditions of the Orthodox Churches of the East with the influences of the West. I am thinking of theologians like Afanasieff and others who, in opposition to a juridical concept of the Church in the West and her juridical notion of unity, have expressly developed a eucharistic ecclesiology that is, at the same time, an ecclesiology of the local church, of the community: the Church is formed by the Eucharist. Where the Eucharist is present—that is, in whatever place; in the congregation celebrating the Eucharist in one place—there the whole Lord and thus the whole Church are present with the whole mystery of the sacrament. A congregation that celebrates the eucharist needs nothing more. It has the whole Lord; in the sacrament, it thus has also the whole Church and *is* the whole Church. The Church is wholly present in the eucharistic assembly, that is, in every local assembly; to this, the "universal Church" can add nothing more, for there *is* nothing "more" than the eucharistic assembly. For such a view, the unity of the universal Church is a pleromatic enhancement but not a complement, not an augmentation of ecclesiality.[21]

Terminologically, it is true, we have been speaking here less of the community than of the local church; the themes are different, but they are related. The point of departure for the Churches of the East lies on the one hand in a sacramental way of thinking, on the other hand, in a rejection of the Roman claim to unity. For this very reason, however, this theology

[19] Cf., in the present work, Part Two, Chapter 3B: "Local Ecumenism".

[20] RGG 2:1325.

[21] Cf. Nicolas Afanasieff et al., *La Primauté de Pierre dans l'Église orthodoxe* (Neuchâtel: Delachaux et Niestlé, 1960).

goes beyond the proper content of Orthodox tradition. For one thing, it certainly seems incontrovertible to say that with the Eucharist all else is given—that is, the Lord himself, who leads men together in the Church—and that, consequently, nothing more can be added. But the question of addition is not the question that should be raised here. Of course nothing can be added to the eucharistic mystery, but we must, nonetheless, ask what its conditions are; how it comes into being. The community cannot bestow it on itself. The Lord does not arise, as it were, from the midst of the communal assembly. He can come to it only from "without"—as one who bestows himself. And this Lord is always one, always undivided not only in one place but in the whole world. To receive him means, therefore, to be united with all others. Where this does not take place, the door is closed to the Lord himself. But that means that unity with all other communities is not just something that may or may not be added to the Eucharist at some later time; rather, it is a inner constitutive element of the eucharistic celebration. Being one with others is the inner foundation of the Eucharist without which it does not come into being. To celebrate the Eucharist means to enter into union with the universal Church—that is, with the one Lord and his one Body. That is why there belongs to the Eucharist not only the anamnesis of the whole of sacred history but also the anamnesis of the whole community of the saints, of those who have died and of all living believers throughout the world. The outward sign that one cannot manipulate the Eucharist at will and that it belongs to the universal Church is the *successio apostolica*: it means that no group can constitute itself a church but *becomes* a church only by being received as such by the universal Church. It means, too, that the Church cannot organize herself according to her own design but can *become* herself again and again only by the gift of the Holy Spirit requested in the name of Jesus Christ, that is, through the sacrament.[22]

The link between every eucharistic celebration and a bearer of this *successio* is the necessary link with the sacrament of unity (with unity *and* with the sacrament!), with the self-transcendence of the community, which can be church only from and in the whole Church. This linking of Eucharist with office is not a formalization of office; it is simply the inherently necessary expression of the fact that the Lord is one and hence is to be found only in unity; it is the expression of the fact that the Church can receive what she cannot give herself, can become Eucharist, and hence Church, only by her confident prayer for the gift of the Holy Spirit, that is,

---

[22] Cf. Part Two, Chapter 2A in the present work: "Holy Orders (Ordo) as the Sacramental Expression of the Principle of Tradition". The theses of the papal Commissio Theologica Internationalis on the subject of *successio* are also important: see IKT 4 (1975): 112–24.

through the sacrament. That is why Vatican Council II always stresses the episcopal character of the Eucharist and the local church [Ortskirche]. In doing so, it is in full accord with the authentic tradition of the Eastern Church.

In other words, Catholicity is not just a pleromatic redundance and even less an external means of organizing the whole; it is a central inner dimension of the very mystery of the Eucharist. Nor is it to be separated from the apostolicity of the Church.[23] The condition of the Church's apostolicity is her Catholicity; the content of her Catholicity is her apostolicity.

It is not surprising, when we reflect on these interrelationships, that the concept of Eucharist is always modified when the dimension of Catholicity is either removed from or reduced in the concept of Church. For the essential sacramentality of the Eucharist is identical with its unity and its unsusceptibility to change from without. When this fact is not recognized, the Eucharist becomes just a meal in common, a self-fulfill-ment of the community, which finds in it the symbols of the interaction of its members. Its theological meaning is then sought primarily in the meals Jesus took with sinners, which deprives these meals of their great symbolic function as the expression of Jesus' divine power to forgive sins and of the coming of the kingdom.[24] When sacramentality is attacked, sacrality is also attacked; when that occurs, sacramental ministry is replaced by an or-ganization that determines itself and has, consequently, only functions to offer; it is no longer a state to which one is called. The danger that the com-munity will become just a recreational center is then perilously near.

c. Finally, modern ideas of "base" democracy, of the antithesis between top and bottom, of a new society built on this "base", also play a role here—not seldom laden with the utopias of modern social criticism: the community is to be the *locus* of "the highest concord and radical equality of opinions" where all differences will be demolished and a society free from dominance will be realized both as the model and as the revolution-ary ferment of a new universal society.[25]

---

[23] Cf. also Schillebeeckx: "No local Church [Ortskirche] has a monopoly on the gospel or on apostolicity" (210). "Secondly, we have always known that no Christian community is autonomous and itself the ultimate source of the powers and authority of its ministers" (217). Unfortunately, it cannot be said that these insights are characteristic of Schillebeeckx's whole text. Otherwise he could not have written: "However, this structure includes the right of the community to be able and permitted to do everything that is really necessary to make it a 'community' of Jesus" (221).

[24] Cf. Joseph Ratzinger, *Das Fest des Glaubens* (Einsiedeln: Johannes, 1981). [English translation: *Feast of Faith* (San Francisco: Ignatius Press, 1986). (Trans.)]

[25] Cf. here Karl Lehmann, "Was ist eine christliche Gemeinde?", 482 and 494–95. On 483, Lehmann points out that H. R. Schlette based on just such a utopian concept of the

3. Conclusions

From this we may conclude not only that many varied and significant motifs find expression in the new concept of community but also that it includes motifs and concepts that cannot fail to distort the concept "Church". This distortion consists precisely in the reduction of the divine gift of the Eucharist to a group right, thus making it a means of self-fulfillment and self-support for the group rather than a means of incorporating the group into the great company of all those who believe. One conclusion at least should thus be made clear: the concept of "community" must be purified if it is to be truly useful for Catholic theology. This positive approach is only now beginning to make itself felt.[26] We need not develop it here but only approach it closely enough to find in it an answer to the problems raised by the slogan: "the community's right to the Eucharist".

A positive concept of community might well begin with Luther's notion that "community" is constituted by the call of God's word. But it must then be added that the word of God is not vacillating, not a thing of the present moment only, not an always new experience with no recognizable continuity with what has gone before. Rather, it exists as something that is itself bound and that is, therefore, binding; that is, it exists in a personal, historical and social manner and leads to a history that is likewise bound—that the Lord himself holds in his hands. As we have seen, the word finds its sacramental meaning in the *successio apostolica,* which is the personal and sacramental mode of "tradition". In the *successio apostolica,* it is itself the sacrament of unity, and, vice versa, the sacrament has the character of word. Its meaning is the guarantee of the communal presence of the one word: "What matters is that I preach what they [the apostles] preach, and this is what you all believed" (I Cor 15:11).[27] "To be called to enter into the word" always means to be called into the bound and binding historical and existential context of the society brought into being by the word—into the context of "Catholicity". From this perspective, we can again affirm what was said above: the "hierarchical" office is not a later organizational addition to the word; it belongs, rather, to the Catholic, sacramental essence of the word that is one and remains one in history. If we link these reflections with what was said earlier about the

---

notion of community his dictum: "There is no Christian community." We can speak of such a community, Schlette says, only in the optative or the subjunctive, as, for example: "The Christian community, if it existed, would be a zone of humanity."

[26] See especially the above-mentioned works by Karl Lehmann.

[27] Cf. Heinrich Schlier, *Der Geist und die Kirche* (Freiburg: Herder, 1980), 179–200; 225–40.

structure of the word and the "Catholic" structure of the Eucharist, we see
that the structure of the word and the structure of the Eucharist are identical, the one Catholic structure without which neither the Church nor the
community can exist in a theological sense. We understand thus the point
of view adopted by the Council, that is, that a community does not set
itself up in opposition to the office (in order then itself to create offices or to
demand that there be such); *ecclesia* becomes real at every level only when
she is sacramental in structure, when she is woven into the context of the
apostolic succession. Therefore, the opposition between, on the one hand,
a community's relationship to the office and, on the other hand, the office
itself and the Eucharist, as is presumed in the slogan "the community's
right to the Eucharist", is based on a fundamental misunderstanding. Believing individuals become community only when they exist in the context of the ministry of *successio,* however loosely this context may at first
be construed either on the local or the personal level.

III. *The right form of the question and the real task*

Our questions have thus become concrete. How loose may this context
be? To answer properly, we must refer again to the conciliar text
considered earlier, in which, as we saw, the "episcopal church" is the
lowest entity to be given a clear terminological and theological identity.
The circle of individuals and places that are under a bishop is determined
by the concept of the unity of the *presbyterium* that is active in each place. In
other words, by placing the concept "local church" [*Ortskirche*] on the
episcopal level, the necessary "Catholic" and "successional" (that is,
sacramental and apostolic) character of every Christian "community" is
definitively established. The question of the local subdivisions of this
lowest entity[28]—that of the episcopal community—thus continues to be
broad and capable of adaptation; it is not infringed either theologically or
juridically. No particular place or group is identified with the "local
church" [*Ortskirche*] and thus theologized. The various local and personal
forms of community have meaning as "place", or "part" or "cell" only in

---

[28] A word of caution is appropriate here. In referring earlier in this chapter to the ecclesial
level designated by Vatican Council II as the *ecclesia localis,* Ratzinger used the German word
Ortskirche to translate the Latin expression. I have consistently used the English equivalent
"local church" to translate both the German and the Latin term. In this paragraph, however,
and throughout Part Two, Chapter 3B below, the term *Ortskirche* in the German text and,
consequently, the translation "local church" refer, not to the *ecclesia localis,* but to what the
Council called the *ecclesia particularis,* that is, the lowest ecclesial level, the church under the
leadership of the bishop. (Trans.)

relation to the bishop. The way in which individual places and persons are understood and brought into the living context of the faith is a matter that must always be regulated in terms of presently existing conditions.

The individual assembly, the congregation of persons that has grown together in individual places or out of particular groups, will certainly receive henceforth stronger theological emphasis and can form here a pastorally and theologically fruitful concept of community. My suggestion, then, would be to define community as the concrete form in which the faith is "at home" in any given place and which, in the best case, will—but by no means has to and, unfortunately, often does not—coincide with the parish. It would then be regarded, not as an immediately theological concept, but rather as an anthropological unity and would have for theology the value and necessity that are appropriate to anthropology in matters of theology.

With this we approach the possibility of correcting the false premise that lies at the root of the expression "the community's right to the Eucharist" and replacing it with the question that is really at issue here. To do so, we must return to one of the reflections with which we started. We saw that canon law speaks of the laity's right to the sacraments. In one respect, this may express a too-individualistic view of the sacraments. In another respect, however, it is an important reminder of the meaning the faith assigns to the individual as a person before God. The question of salvation is a personal one. Certainly, the Eucharist builds community; it unites the individual with Christ and thus with others who receive the same Body of Christ and in so doing should become the Body of Christ. But it builds community precisely by establishing itself in, by reaching into, the innermost core of the individual. Only by the most intense involvement of the person can true community come into existence. We sometimes encounter romantic interpretations of community among those who overemphasize this aspect of the question and expect to be freed by the community from the burden of self. Granted, real community can, in fact, become a basic support for the person who finds in it the "you" and "we" that he needs. But it can be so only if the person is capable of giving himself in the process and, in giving, learns to receive himself anew.

Now, at last, we are able to formulate positively the question that is our basic concern. It should read somewhat as follows: What must the Church—those who bear office and the laity, each in his own fashion—do to respond to the right every individual has to the signs of salvation and to enable every individual actually to experience the universal community of the Church as a supporting community, as the homeland of his soul? We shall speak first of the obligations of office. The ecclesial office must so form and equip the episcopal communities (*ecclesiae particulares*) that they are able, in their sphere, to build the life of faith in the Church with the necessary adaptability and openness, to create believing communities and to meet the individual's right to word and sacrament.

But that is only one side of the picture. A solution that comes only from "the top" will not suffice here—certainly not if, to reach its goal, it requires a lessening of belief in the Eucharist and in the sacramental context of the Church—that is, a diminution or falsification of God's word. Spiritual fruitfulness cannot be manufactured. But where the Church is insufficiently able to generate priestly vocations or to inspire individuals to an undivided, even celibate, service of God's kingdom, there cannot fail to be doubts also about her eucharistic efficacy. We should note, too, that there is a correspondence between the capacity for sacramental marriage in accordance with the gospel and an openness to virginity. Where the latter decreases, the former also grows weak—that is, a state of spiritual emergency becomes everywhere evident, the challenge of which will not be overcome by laxity or by more or less external manipulation. Indeed, the celibacy of the priest is the historical way, anchored in the gospel, in which the Church reminds herself of the fact that she cannot manipulate spiritual vocations and binds herself in a way that makes it impossible for her to meet spiritual crises by organizational manipulation, which only apparently solves them and makes them even more difficult to overcome.

In this respect, I think, the Church of Latin America, which, after centuries of a lack of priests due essentially to a lack of inner dependence, is now on the way to a resurgence, offers us a good example in many of her base communities. She has found it necessary to form living cells that have deliberately moved out of the constraints of modern living in order to live together the "alternative" of the gospel, thus forming a milieu of faith. In such cells, which are built around the double commandment of love of God and love of neighbor and are thus shaped by a culture of prayer and Christian service, the Church can find new growth, vocations can ripen in which the never-failing fruitfulness of God's word can again be fulfilled. In them it can be demonstrated anew that the "Catholic" principle does not mean rigidity or anonymity in mega-organizations but a call to life. Certainly, such a way is much more demanding than simply granting "communities" already in existence the power to provide for their own spiritual needs. But the way to the joy of the gospel and to its great fruit leads only through the door of conversion. The greatness of the gift is always in proportion to the greatness of the gift of self.[29]

---

[29] For these concrete perspectives, see the carefully weighed and richly substantiated reflections of Karl Lehmann, "Chancen und Grenzen der neuen Gemeindetheologie" (see n. 1 above). On the one hand, Lehmann has provided us there with a well-conceived statement of what should be retained from the already existing order; on the other hand, he has realistically assessed the range of new possibilities.

B. Local Ecumenism

The subject of "local ecumenism" is being raised more and more frequently today. Until recently, it seemed to be just a question of how the ecumenical knowledge and experience of the universal Church could be realized in the individual local church. It seemed to be just a question of the practical application of something already possessed. It became increasingly clear, however, that application is never just application: ultimately the progression from thought to practice is, at the same time, a means of con-firming [be-währen] thought, of testing its feasibility. Thus it also affects—retroactively modifies, criticizes, limits or extends—the form of thought. If we carry this insight, to which we shall return later, to its logical conclusion, we must say that practice does not follow the discovery of truth as something that is simply secondary to it; on the contrary, it is part of the process of truth. This explains the new importance enjoyed today by the subject of "local ecumenism". It no longer seems to be just a practical addendum to but a distinct aspect of the problem of ecumenism. To this new evaluation of the praxis is also linked a new evaluation of the local church that began with Vatican II. The following conclusion suggests itself: if the local church is not just the lowest level of the universal Church but is herself an immediate and actual realization of Church per se, then local ecumenism is not just an instrument of ecumenism "from the top"; it is the original form of ecumenism and a separate source of theological knowledge.

This conclusion, which at first seems to be entirely theoretical, has been widely accepted because it is supported by the historical experience of the struggle for Christian unity during the last decades. In the Catholic realm (but not only there), ecumenism clearly began "at the bottom": charismatic individuals or small groups prepared the way. To give just a few examples, which could, however, be multiplied: Abbé Couturier, Yves Congar, the monks of Chevetogne in the French-speaking area; in Germany, Max Josef Metzger, Robert Grosche and the Paderborn group, which found an ecclesiastical leader in Archbishop Jaeger and thus had early access to the hierarchy of the Church. Conditions in local churches also prepared the ground for ecumenical encounters. Congar tells how the destruction of the Catholic church in his native Sedan by German soldiers in 1914 led to a *rapprochement* with Protestants and the remedying of a situation in which proximity had hitherto failed to foster friendly relations;[30] in Germany, the attack against practicing Christians of all

---

[30] Unfortunately, I can no longer locate the autobiographical sketch in which Yves Congar relates this incident.

denominations by leaders of the Third Reich brought about a better understanding.

With the Council and with the formation of the Secretariat for the Promotion of the Unity of Christians, everything seemed changed. In the Catholic Church, ecumenism emerged from its hitherto mostly local and more or less "charismatic" form; it became the concern of the universal Church—and it became official: to such an extent, in fact, that official statements were made prematurely in advance of the living and comprehensible reality that existed in the local communities and seemed to give the impression that the problem of unity would, in the foreseeable future, be solved step by step from above. In contrast to the earlier situation, resistance came now from below—perhaps least of all in the Catholic Church, but noticeably in the Orthodox Churches and in many parts of world Protestantism. For this reason, the question had to be transferred again—and even more emphatically—to the level of the local church. But not for this reason alone. With the question of interconfessional communion, there arose also a question concerning the apostolicity of the Church and of the indispensable components of unity per se. When is unity really unity and when does it become an empty fiction that eventually disappears of its own accord because it no longer has any content? Pragmatic solutions were of no avail here, for what was at stake was the core of the ecclesial interpretation of faith itself. That is why the hitherto speedy progress of ecumenism "from the top" came to a halt; Church authority, which had been leading the way, found itself relegated to the task of evaluating and restraining. This was a disappointment for all those who had meanwhile begun to think that there were no longer any unsolvable problems, that good will or political tact on the part of the Church was all that was needed. In this way, too, a call was generated for the return of ecumenical activity to the level of the local church; the intention, for related problems as well, was to establish, as it were, a new era of pioneers—modeled on the pioneer efforts of the years 1920–1962 and their inclusion by the Council in the plan for the universal Church—in which what was tried first at the local level could then become universal. It is significant in this context that the Synod of German Bishops, in the first drafts of the Commission, discussed the problem of interconfessional communion under the title "local ecumenism" and obviously hoped to make it possible to find a solution by placing the question on this level.

With this we are in a better position to understand the new way of posing the question. But the subject of "local ecumenism" cannot be satisfactorily treated today by simply considering all that the local church is able to do in the area of ecumenism; we must, rather, investigate the meaning of the question itself and the motives that prompt it. Only in this way can we really perceive the hopes and dangers of the new orientation. It seems to me that there are at work in the background three concepts that are by no means everywhere recognized and obvious but that contribute, nevertheless, to the general contour of the theme and to its vitality in the Church today.

I. *The notion of the "base"—construction from "above" or from "below"*

We must first call attention to an increasing scepticism toward institutional ecumenism that seems to be a rejection of already established forces. This brings us to a factor we have not yet mentioned: the involvement of ecumenism itself in the worldwide phenomenon of protest. The accusations in this context against institutional ecumenism cannot be simply dismissed as directed against what we might call "immobilism"; despite the hitherto inviolable restrictions under which ecumenism has labored, such a concept would be seriously out of place here. Nevertheless, influential forces in the World Council of Churches, the one supreme organization of ecumenism, are advocating a council of all churches, thus raising a stimulating challenge, the consequences of which have not yet been fully considered.[31] On the other hand, it is possible to point to the partial establishment of interconfessional communion between Catholic and Orthodox Churches. The full implications of this step, too, have yet to be sufficiently explored. Although the break between the eucharistic communities of East and West was never total, there is question here of a step that can introduce a really new third millennium of Church history and give the text *Lumen gentium*, for the first time, a concrete historical meaning.[32]

Let us return to our subject. The accusations, we have said, do not speak

---

[31] Cf. E. Lange, *Die ökumenische Utopie* (Stuttgart-Berlin, 1972), 204–7. Under the title *Die Konziliarität und die Zukunft der ökumenischen Bewegung*, this text was published by Faith and Order-Plenum (Louvain, 1971). Cf. also, L. Vischer, "Die Zeit der Entscheidung ist gekommen", in *Ökumenische Rundschau* 20 (1971): 158–65, esp. 164–65.

[32] Cf. "Decree on the Catholic Eastern Churches" [*Orientalium ecclesiarum*], in *Vatican Council II. The Conciliar and Post Conciliar Documents,* Austin Flannery, O. P., gen. ed. (Northport, N. Y.: Costello Publishing Co., 1975), 441–51. Cf. also the commentary on this decree by Johannes Hoeck in LTK, *Das Zweite Vatikanische Konzil* 1:362–63; Τόμος Ἀγάπης, *Vatican-Phanar (1958–1970)* (Rome-Istanbul: Typis Polyglottis Vaticanis, 1971); Ernst Christoph Suttner, ed., *Eucharistische Zeichen der Einheit* (Regensburg, 1970); R. Graber, "Im Gedenken an Patriarch Athenagoras", in *Una Sancta* 27 (1972): 121–23. On the historical aspect of the question: W. de Vries, "Communicatio in sacris. Gottesdienstliche Gemeinschaft mit den von Rom getrennten Ostkirchen im Licht der Geschichte", in *Concilium* 1 (1965): 270–81.

primarily of immobilism; they are directed, rather, against the institutions as such. Lengsfeld, for instance, has stated explicitly that reunion on an institutional level is not desirable in the near future because it would result in a consolidation of efforts by the establishments that would threaten to suppress the "progressive" forces that are now at work.[33] This statement is not to be understood against a background of general hostility to institutions such as could be observed in the early stages of Marxism—the goal is to salvage the institutions. But one can observe a hostility toward existing official organs, which are regarded as instruments of repressive and reactionary forces that will impede future development. From a certain sociological concept, therefore, an ecumenism from "below", an ecumenism of the "base", inevitably arose against ecumenism from "above", against the ecumenism of institutions.

The ease with which the word "base" has, in the meantime, insinuated itself into the vocabulary of high Church officials is one of the oddities in the development of the Church in recent years. The word implies a system of values that is far from self-evident. It suggests that the action groups that are everywhere making their appearance and that regard themselves as the "base" of a changed society (or Church) of the future are also, in reality, the base against which the Church of today must be measured. Especially dangerous is the ambiguity with which the word "base" shifts between the meanings "lowest ecclesial unit" (local church) and "groups formed spontaneously by their own initiative", usually clearly identified with a particular issue—the protest against existing societies as organs of oppression. The structuring in terms of a "base" is intended to give the oppressed an opportunity to speak for themselves and so finally to convert the heretofore false structure of society into a new and sound one. Naturally, these implications of the concept "base" are not always equally prominent and are frequently totally unintentional. For that reason, we must be careful to avoid false accusations and global recriminations. It is true, nonetheless, that there is a change in ecumenical activity that transfers the problem, not from the universal Church to the local church, but from the traditional Church to the "base" groups of the Church of the future, the contours of which are derived essentially from the program of a sociology inspired by neo-Marxism. Shifting the problem "below" is here, in essence, a shifting "forward"—liberation from the past, a Church to be constructed for a history to be constructed.[34] The goal is not just the

---

[33] P. Lengsfeld, "Sind heute die traditionellen Konfessionsdifferenzen noch von Bedeutung?", in *Una Sancta* 26 (1971): 27–36. The reference here is to 34.

[34] In *Die Grundlagen des Glaubens,* 2 vols. (Einsiedeln, 1971), L. Dewart offers an original attempt to provide a philosophical basis for such a change: "The intention of the progressivists to launch a deliberately controlled new development of Christian belief

unity of the Church as such but first of all the consolidation of the "progressivists", who will then, they believe, become the Church of the future.

The more strongly this tendency establishes itself in various places, the wider will be the division in ecumenism: it is no longer just a question of institutional ecumenism against "base" ecumenism but of the ecumenism of a Church man can construct against that of a Church founded and given by the Holy Spirit. Suddenly, precisely those persons who were until then unconcerned about ecumenism and thought they were happily settled in their own Church now discover that they are fundamentally one in comparison with that new "Church", the contours of which they can discern in her now visible base. In the face of such a comparison, denominational differences are secondary. As a "base", the *credo* creates its own ecumenism. The paradox of the situation lies in the fact that precisely this ecumenism of a unity experienced in terms of the creed is sceptical with regard to institutions—is, in certain respects, even farther removed from them than is base ecumenism with its predilection for action. Apart from occasional pronouncements, it continues to be, for the most part, silent and, consequently, ineffective, if not actually useless.

It is here, I think, that both the problem and the hope of the situation appear most clearly. The unity at the center of the *credo*, which reveals its binding force in the confrontation of the present, must also be explicitly stated. Those who discover it must have the courage to relinquish their distrust of institutions and to take advantage of the forms and the possibilities that they offer and develop. Only in this way can be formed alternatives to a slipping into self-constructed unities that lack a sufficient foundation in the faith; only in this way can ecumenism be prevented from lapsing into mutually antipathetic ecumenisms. Institutions are, in fact,

---

implies the judgment that the traditional forms of Christianity are not only without relationship to experience but are even inadequate for this experience. . . . Therefore, progressivism means, by implication, a conscious or unconscious criticism—either philosophical or based on everyday experience—of the most basic principles of all traditional Christian philosophical thought" (1:34). "The deepest root of the negative reaction of traditionalists against the historical situation, which forces Christianity to be creative in furthering its own evolution, lies in the traditional concept of truth" (1:27). Despite the abstract language and the nebulous arguments, Dewart's book is, by reason of its thoroughness and sincerity, an important self-reflection of contemporary "progressivism". It is certainly correct in identifying the concept of truth as the core of the current crisis in the Church. The new concept of truth, which, in what I judge to be Dewart's correct diagnosis, forms the foundation of "progressivism", rests on a rejection of the old equation *ens = verum*. The new formula reads *being = fact*. Things are first of all pure facts; meaning is bestowed on them later by man himself. That means not only the radically historical character of truth (new meaning displaces old) but also its total "facticity".

ordered to the spontaneous forces that are alive in communities. Without the presence of these forces, they degenerate into empty formalism. It is not properly their task to create new forms by mandates from above; it is their task, rather, to be aware of the good, wherever it may appear, to foster it, to distinguish it from what is not appropriate and to make its potential available to the whole. Institutions have the task of inspiring, of distinguishing, of purifying, of mediating. They must help those who hesitate to seize the positive that exists; they must remind the too-hasty of their responsibility to the whole and thus serve the unity of all. This means, certainly, that communities or other bearers of ecumenical life on the local level must be prepared to render such mediation to the whole. They are by no means obliged, in what they do, to wait for mandates from above. But they must do what they do out of a sense of responsibility to the whole and out of openness to the whole; they must not risk the unity of the whole for the sake of local unities.

The meanings of these general characteristics can be made clear only by way of examples. For more than a decade, Taizé has been, without a doubt, the leading example of an ecumenical inspiration, emanating from a local center inspired by a particular "charism". Similar communities of faith and of shared living should be formed elsewhere in which the foregoing of a communal reception of the Eucharist would, without ceasing to be a hardship, become comprehensible and in which its necessity would be understood by a prayer community that cannot answer its own prayer but is, nevertheless, calmly certain it will be answered. It should be the task of those forces that seek actively for unity to find positive alternatives to interconfessional communion—perhaps on the model of the penitential and catechumenal liturgies of the ancient Church.[35] Origen has a wonderful interpretation of Jesus' words of renunciation at the Last Supper: "I shall not drink any more wine until the day I drink the new wine in the kingdom of God" (Mk 14:25). Origen comments: Jesus cannot drink alone the chalice that he wanted to drink with all his disciples. His festive drink is postponed until he can drink it with *all* of them.[36] Is it not a meaningful form of liturgical action if separated Christians, when they come together, consciously emulate this renunciation of Jesus—if they communicate with him and with one

[35] Outstanding examples of such an ecumenical liturgy, which respects the boundaries yet makes visible the deep oneness in the Lord, are offered in the three forms of common liturgical celebrations between Pope Paul VI and Patriarch Athenagoras I that are to be found in the appendix of the volume Τόμος Ἀγάπης, 630–71. They should be widely disseminated as models of common liturgical services.

[36] Origen, "Homiliae in Leviticum", Homilia 7:2, in PG 12: 478–82; translated into French in Henri de Lubac, *Catholicisme*, 355–61.

another precisely by means of this renunciation; if, as penitents, they unite themselves with the penance Jesus performed as their representative and thus receive the "Eucharist" of hope?[37] Would this not emphasize the fact that reconciliation must precede the shared meal; that we must first learn to be penitents together, to celebrate the penitential liturgy together, before we can venture the next step? In view of these questions, we can perhaps say that, despite signs to the contrary, the tendency of ecumenism today is to do away with the passion and imagination necessary for responsible action on the local level and to regard each church as a universal Church, so that there is no longer a distinction between the local and the universal aspects.

2. "Local church" and universal Church

These reflections bring us directly to the second significant tendency in the development of the theme "local ecumenism": the shifting of ecclesiological emphasis from the universal Church to the local church as we so frequently experience it today. To a certain degree, this tendency corresponds to a similar tendency of Vatican Council II, but it is developing with increasing rapidity into a new one-sidedness in which problematical, and even dangerous, aspects of the Reformation are unknowingly adopted along with its more correct insights. Until now, one might have said more or less correctly that, by comparison, Protestant ecclesiology places too little emphasis on the universal Church and too much on the community, whereas Catholic ecclesiology places too little emphasis on the local church and too much on the universal Church. From a historical perspec-

---

[37] This thought would find further confirmation if we could accept Jeremias' exegesis of Lk 22:15–18, and the parallel verse in Mk 14:25, according to which Jesus fasted at the Last Supper and, by this self-excommunication from Israel's eschatological joy, took upon himself the fate of the servant of God, thus making intercession for his people: *Die Abendmahlsworte Jesu*, 3d ed. (Göttingen: Vandenhoeck, 1960), 199–210. Nevertheless, it is certain that it was the custom for Christians to fast at the quartodeciman Easter celebration in the Passover night at the time of the Jewish festive meal and that the Eucharist was not celebrated until three o'clock in the morning. Despite all the differences of opinion about the meaning of quartodecimanism, this much is clear: that the fasting was related to the thought of standing proxy for Israel and that the primary emphasis of the festival was on the expectation of the parousia—the motif of hope. Cf. Jeremias, 166–67; Bernhard Lohse, *Das Passafest der Quartadecimaner* (Gütersloh: Bertelsmann, 1953); Josef Blank's translation, *Melito von Sardes, Vom Passa* (Freiburg: Lambertus, 1963), 26–41. There is, of course, no question here of an archaizing revival of past forms but, rather, of making fruitful the whole wealth of tradition and thus of gaining the possibility of coming to terms with a situation that, in many respects, resembles that of the early Christians.

tive, there exists between these divergent positions a mutual conditioning about which I should like to make a brief comment. *Sermo 15 de sanctis* of pseudo-Augustine, which the Roman Breviary so long prescribed for the feast of St. Peter's Chair in Rome, obviously because of its explicit formulation of the doctrine of primacy, states plainly that Peter received the primacy "for the good of the churches" (*pro ecclesiarum salute*).[38] In the Middle Ages, the plural ("churches") gradually disappeared so that little by little, the expression *ecclesia Romana* acquired the meaning of *ecclesia catholica*. That means, on the one hand, that there was a question of only one local church and, on the other hand, that this one local church was identified with the universal Church so that, in consequence, the notion of a multiplicity of local churches was, for the most part, obliterated.

The reverse movement in the case of Protestant communities is well known: the creation of established churches, especially in the domain of the *Sacrum Imperium*, destroyed the universal—"catholic"—context as a concrete reality. But even the established "churches" could not claim to be churches in the sense of the theological entity *ecclesia*; they were incidental political structures that had no relationship with the source and hence did not have the spiritual character by which alone they could be constituted *ecclesia*. They provided an institutional and administrative framework, nothing more. It is a simplification, but one still true to the facts, to say that after she had lost communion with the universal Church, all that remained of the church was the local community. From Luther's point of view, that was, certainly, not just an accident resulting from adverse

---

[38] The text will be found in PL 39:2100–2101, under the title *Sermo 190*, "*In cathedra Sancti Petri*". A comparison with the authentic *Sermones* of St. Augustine for this feast will clearly reveal their different theological perspective. In contrast to the text quoted, Leo the Great emphasizes the singular *ecclesia* (also *ecclesia universalis*), but without entirely suppressing the plural. Particularly noteworthy is his Epistle 156, PL 54:1127–32 (translated in Hugo Rahner, *Kirche und Staat im frühen Christentum* [Munich: Kösel, 1961], 241–45), where the word *ecclesia* is used four times in the singular to signify the universal Church; *ecclesia universalis* is used twice; *Alexandrina ecclesia* is used three times; and the plural *ecclesiae* is used once, but then with a negative connotation: a journey to the East proposed by the Emperor for the purpose of settling disputes that had flared up again after the Council of Chalcedon is rejected by the Pope with the explanation that such an action would give the impression that new questions were being raised about those statements *quas Ecclesia universalis amplexa est— atque ita nullum collidendis Ecclesiis modum ponere, sed data licentia rebellandi dilatare magis quam sopire certamina*. In *Die Lehre von der Kirche von Augustinus bis zum abendländischen Schisma*, in Michael Schmaus, Aloys Grillmeier and Leo Scheffczyk, *Handbuch der Dogmengeschichte*, vol. 3, 3c (Freiburg: Herder, 1971): 177, Yves Congar points to a particularly advanced example of medieval linguistic development in *Aegidius Romanus, De ecclesiastica potestate* 3, ed. R. Scholz, 109, where it is said that the pope *tenet apicem ecclesiae et potest dici ecclesia*. Cf., on the whole question, Joseph Ratzinger, *Das neue Volk Gottes*, 2d ed. (Düsseldorf: Patmos, 1970), 121–46, esp. 136–37.

political conditions; it was also the expression of a theological concept. The universal Church, as he knew her in her Roman and papal garb, did not seem to him to be the Church. More precisely: he could not acknowledge an institutionally concrete universal Church as a spiritual entity that should be retained. This fact is revealed linguistically, for instance, in the almost total elimination of the word "church" from his translation of the Bible.

In the Catholic sphere, Vatican Council II, with its turning to the theology of the Fathers and to Christian ecumenism as a whole, brought about a rediscovery of the relationship between plurality and unity that had as its effect a new emphasis on the ecclesial significance of "local churches" in the universal Church. In doing so, it defined "local church", as the Fathers had defined it, in terms of the bishop, not in terms of a geographical oneness of "place", although it cannot be denied that there is a certain lack of clarity in many texts.[39] In countries with a strong Protestant background, this patristic theological definition of the concept "local church" has continued to be alien to members of the Church, who have automatically interpreted it in terms of what is familiar to them, that is, in the sense of an established church (using the language of the country) or in the sense of a "community", in which case a conversion is occurring more and more frequently from local community to "base" group—that is, to a designation that is not local but ideological. This process of adapting the Council teachings to other types of tradition has, in the meantime, affected in many ways the official self-understanding of the Church. I mention two examples from the German scene. In the German translation of the *Missale Romanum*—that is, in the official liturgical texts of the Catholic Church in German-speaking countries—the word "church" has all but disappeared.[40] It has been replaced by the word "community", which is all the more prevalent because, for some incomprehensible reason, it has also supplanted other expressions, such as the beautiful word "family", with its rich traditional meaning. In consequence, the variegated shades of meaning in the concept "church" have been lost in the homogeneous gray of the word that alone makes holy: the "community".

The new baptismal rite offers a second example. The act of signing with the sign of the Cross, which was so meaningful in the early Church, is

[39] On the Council's concept of "local church", see Gérard Philips, *L'Église et son mystère au IIe Concile du Vatican* (Paris: Desclée, 1967), 1:337–43; Karl Rahner in LTK, *Das Zweite Vatikanische Konzil,* 1:242–46; Joseph Ratzinger, in *Church,* ed. Foote, Hill et al. (New York, 1969), 57. Cf. also Part Two, Chapter 3A of the present work.

[40] This is not changed by the fact that the word "church" is still to be found with some frequency in the texts of the Eucharistic prayers. It is valid if we concentrate on the new liturgical texts as a whole, including the readings.

presented in the Latin text in the following colorless formula: *NN magno gaudio communitas christiana vos excipit. In cuius nomine ego signo vos signo crucis. . . .* In the German text, the bland and unhistorical expression *communitas christiana,* which at least had the merit of suggesting the *communio,* is translated by the words *"Die christliche Gemeinde* or, in an alternate version, *Die Pfarrgemeinde* receives you." According to this ritual, the catechumen is not baptized into the one Church that transcends time and space but is made a member of a parochial congregation and is signed with the sign of the Cross in *its*—and only in its—name.

We must keep this change in the concept of Church firmly in mind if we would not misjudge the seriousness of the question about "local ecumenism". If baptism has only the community as its object, then communion is also the affair of the community, and the question of interconfessional communion will be solved there according to the ecumenical maturity of the individual community, rather than in terms of the problem of succession, of the *communio* of the universal Church, of the faith professed by the universal Church.

It is by no means, and should not be, the intention of these reflections to throw suspicion on the concept "local church" or to do away with it in the name of a centralistic concept of a unified Church. It is a question, rather, of seeing the proportions and stating the problem correctly. The first task must be to provide a more exact clarification of the concept "local church". It will be clear from what has been said that the word itself is misleading: no one thinks of the local church primarily in terms of a geographical criterion, whichever of the three principal concepts he may have in mind: the conciliar, which conceives it in terms of the theological criterion "bishop"; the post-Reformational, which conceives it politically, linguistically and socially; or the modern ("community"), which is based on ideological stimuli. How can the three starting points be reconciled? How can they support and fructify one another? Rightly understood, all three can assuredly contribute to the living realization of the concept "local church",[41] but the measure and proper order of their contributions is crucial, while the separation of the nontheological factors from that which actually forms the church (the office of bishop) destroys the *ecclesia localis* and rends the *ecclesia universalis.*

---

[41] My intention is not to legitimize "ideology" in its modern sense. If the third element is accepted here as a possible factor in the concept of community, it is because the elements of community that stem from a given spiritual and social situation can also properly be the starting points of intraecclesial groupings in which the phenomenon "community" has been made concrete. On the other hand, the formation of communities will the more fully realize the concept of "church" the more fully they transcend political, linguistic and ideological boundaries—this could be a definitive criterion of their ecclesiality.

It is of primary importance, precisely in our situation, that there be concrete "communities" that can and do provide an environment in which the individual can experience the *communio ecclesiae* as a real *communio*. The collapse of the natural social groupings that formerly served this purpose and the resultant anonymity of a technical civilization makes it all the more important that there be such visible embodiments of the faith. The fraternities and clubs of an earlier generation served much the same purpose, but the benefits that accrued at that time have lost their appeal for modern man and must be replaced or augmented by the formation of "communities" that can be "home" to the seeking individual of today. But the formation of such communities must be accomplished in conjunction with the bishop and thus in conjunction with the universal Church, into which the community must be integrated and which it must not replace but only reveal. It must be "Catholic", that is, the life that is from and for the whole must be the principle on which it is constructed— that is true on all levels. This statement leads automatically to a further insight: to the extent that the "Catholic" dimension, rightly understood, requires also the "ecumenical" dimension, every "community" and every group of communities united to form a "local church" must live its faith ecumenically. It cannot, as a "community", attempt to explain away those problems that can be solved only on the universal level. But it must be all the more aware of the tasks that can be accomplished on the local level. It must fructify the universal Church by its experience of faith, its patience and its creative imagination. The universal Church, for her part, must be open to this enrichment, must disseminate it to the whole Church through the communion of bishops with the pope and, where necessary, must purify and deepen it in terms of the whole.

3. *Theory and praxis*

This leads to a final comment. As we intimated at the beginning, the new view of the relationship between theory and practice that is widely accepted today under the influence of neo-Marxist thought undoubtedly shares the responsibility for the emphasis that is being placed on the subject of "local ecumenism". In its most radical form, this view holds that truth is not the measure but the product of practice; change produces truth by turning future potential into reality and freeing mankind from the past. Even in its less radical form, this view destroys faith in a truth that constantly bears witness to itself and in terms of which facts can be measured in a binding way. The impression continues to grow that facts must be created that compel one to recognize and vindicate retrospectively the theory on which they are based. In our context, that means that we would no longer expect to solve a question such as that of interconfessional communion by a clarification of the theoretical and theological problems that will then be accepted by whatever institutions are currently "at the top". Facts—or so it is thought—must come first; and they are not to be found at the top but only at the "base", whose character as "base" rests precisely on the fact that it is the sole source from which new facts can be generated.

What response can we make? To find a suitable answer, we would have to discuss the whole problem of theory and praxis as well as the question of truth and being, of truth and word.[42] But this is not the place to do so. We must content ourselves with the following remark. The more clearsighted and liberal among Marxist thinkers are well aware today that Marx made things too easy for himself with this dictum that man was not to interpret the world but to change it. Voices are now being raised to say that the time has come for interpreting anew a world that was changed in haste so that man can once again lead a meaningful life in it. Logos and ethos are inseparable. One who neither acts nor suffers learns nothing. But one who neither thinks nor learns can produce no facts in which knowledge and meaning have their dwelling. It is certain, therefore, that nothing fruitful can be expected where the question of the ecclesial community is separated from the question of a community of truth and is replaced by the autonomous production of facts.

Let us try now to draw a conclusion. The topic "local ecumenism" points to two vital areas of contemporary theological and human inquiry. It raises the question of the relationship of "facts" and "truth"; it contains the problem that makes itself heard in words like "community" and "base", that is, the question about what constitutes the smallest units of the ecclesial community and about their role in the discovery of truth and the shaping of the future. This is not the place for uncritical enthusiasm; the "discernment of spirits" is indispensable here. Ultimately, however, we are certain of this: it is not permissible to make truth a product of fact. But it is equally impermissible to reduce "praxis"—to reduce life in the concrete units that form the Church—to simple application. Rather, the "local church" is to be regarded as a place of learning by experience, of the real testing of faith, as a place of suffering but, at the same time, as a place of knowledge that derives from suffering. From that perspective, it is not

---

[42] On the problem of theory and praxis, see Werner Post in *Sacramentum Mundi* 4 (Freiburg: Herder, 1969): 894–901 (with bibliography). The following work is very important for the biblical view of the problem: J. de la Potterie, "La Notion biblique de la vérité et sa rencontre avec la notion hellénistique dans l'Église ancienne", in *Fede e cultura alla luce della Biblia. Atti della sessione plenaria della Pont. Comm. Biblica* (Torino, 1981), 307–40. Cf. also, in the present work, Part Three, Chapter 1A: "What is Theology?"

surprising that the time since 1962—since the onset of a turbulent development of ecumenism "from above"—has today entered a phase of retardation, at least in what concerns the relationship between Catholicism and
Protestantism. What was once the property of a particular unit has become, to a large extent, the property of all; new developments lack the
support of experience tested at the local level. That certainly does not
mean that the meetings of active ecumenists have become superfluous as
places for transmitting, testing, encouraging and recognizing those measures that have already been attempted. That is not what we are saying.
But it does mean that the "local churches" and the experiences that they
alone can make possible are being called forth anew. Rightly understood,
it can be said without reservation that we are again in need of pioneers of
the future—but it is not just by doing something different that one becomes a pioneer; it is by doing what is meaningful and right, a constitutive
element of which is an innermost oneness with the universal Church as she
is revealed in her fundamental traditions.

We cannot say today where these pioneers will appear—pioneers, not of
a unity that is arbitrarily manipulated and by that fact doomed to failure,
but of a unity that touches upon these most interior depths of faith in
which the true call of the Lord becomes audible to both sides. We cannot
say what paths they must travel in order to make new unities possible. We
can say only that they will achieve their goal, not by mitigation and
destruction, but by a deeper penetration into the truth of Jesus Christ. We
can say also that it is not by ordinance but by the ardor of a love that
springs from faith that they will gain that effectiveness that, if God so
wills, will in its turn lead to new ordinances, decrees and instructions. To
make a reality of "local ecumenism" means, therefore, to work in the
spirit of pioneers for the unity of faith and to hope that God will send it
when he knows that its hour has come.

PART THREE

THE FORMAL PRINCIPLES
OF CHRISTIANITY
AND THE METHOD OF THEOLOGY

CHAPTER I

QUESTIONS ABOUT THE
STRUCTURE OF THEOLOGY

A. What is Theology?

Address for the seventy-fifth birthday of Hermann Cardinal Volk

Anyone who has known Cardinal Volk in the context of Vatican Council
II, in the commissions of the postconciliar era or in the synods of the
German bishops or who has had the privilege of working with him in the
German Bishops' Conference knows his characteristic way of posing a
question. His thinking does not stop short at peripheral arguments, nor is
it content to belabor the obvious. It leads always to the heart of the matter.
With inimitable perspicacity, it penetrates to the real alternatives that are
hidden behind the tactical and strategical considerations. When opinions
differ as to what should be done or when it should be done, he sweeps all
this to one side with a firm gesture and asks: What is the truth? What is the
interior motive that leads to such alternatives? What hidden forces are at
work here? He makes plain the insufficiency of mere pragmatism and
reveals the problems that are genuinely pressing and often suppressed.
The call to return to the matter at hand is typical of him; and that may
justify the fact that this address on the occasion of his seventy-fifth
birthday is not to be a *laudatio* of him and his achievements but a
consideration of the matter that has been and is of primary importance to
him.

Any attempt to interpret this matter reveals, however, just how
unsatisfactory the word "matter" is in this case. For Cardinal Volk's
"matter", the matter he has zealously pursued, is the person—both divine
and human. But this orientation toward the person has, on the other hand,
its own objectivity. For Cardinal Volk, its medium is theology. In view of
Cardinal Volk's own endeavors, I should like, therefore, to offer on this
occasion a few reflections on the always pressing question: What is
theology? When I attempt to address this question in the context of
Cardinal Volk's efforts, two thoughts immediately present themselves.
On the one hand, I think of the motto on his coat of arms (which is also the
title of one of his books): "God Is All In All", and of the spiritual program
it implies; on the other hand, there comes to my mind something I have
already mentioned: a mode of questioning that is entirely philosophical,

that does not stop with apparent or real historical facts, with sociological diagnoses or with pastoral techniques but insists inexorably on the search for causes.

Two themes suggest themselves, therefore, as guides for our inquiry into the nature of theology:

1. Theology has to do with God.
2. Theological speculation is linked to philosophical inquiry as its basic methodology.

The two themes will seem contradictory if, on the one hand, we include under philosophy a way of thinking that, by its nature, belongs—and must belong—to revelation and if, on the other hand, we adopt the view that God can be known only by way of revelation and that the question of God is actually not a problem of reason as reason. I am convinced that such a position, which, in recent times, has become more and more a kind of *sententia communis* for philosophers and theologians, will in the end prove crippling to both philosophy and theology. But if it is true that the search for truth and the openness to it that are the subject matter of both philosophy and theology are indispensable to the humanity of man, then we have arrived here at a very central point. I am convinced, in fact, that the crisis we are experiencing in the Church and in humanity is closely allied to the exclusion of God as a topic with which reason can properly be concerned—an exclusion that has led to the degeneration of theology first into historicism, then into sociologism and, at the same time, to the impoverishment of philosophy. Against initial appearances, I maintain, therefore, that precisely the opposite is true: the two theses we have named condition each other. If theology has to do primarily with God, if its ultimate and proper theme is not salvation history or Church or community but simply God, then it must think in philosophical terms. On the other hand, it cannot be denied that philosophy precedes theology and, even after revelation has taken place, is never subsumed by theology but continues to be an independent path of the human spirit, in such a way, however, that philosophical speculation can enter into theological speculation without thereby being destroyed as philosophy.

Theology has to do with God, and, in that way, it also fulfills the ultimate task of philosophical speculation. I would like now to develop this thesis positively in two steps, both of which are derived from fundamental insights of medieval theology, since they both touch upon one of the controversial points in the crisis of the thirteenth century, which was soon formalized as a Scholastic antithesis but continues to be raised as an actual problem of theology. If I am correct, Thomas Aquinas was the first to draw, with any emphasis, from the concept *theo-logy* the conclusion that the object—he even says "the subject"—of this science is

God.[1] With that conclusion, he was at odds with a number of contrary concepts. First of all, and in the foreground of medieval thought, was the definition to be found in the theological manual that was authoritative throughout the Middle Ages—the *Sententiae* of Peter Lombard. Taking as his point of departure a comment of St. Augustine's, Lombard named *res et signa* as the object of theology—the doctrine of reality and signs.[2] This somewhat peripheral schema nevertheless raises a very basic question when we realize that what we have there is a variation of the earlier division into theology and economy and that the question of the relationship between the two still remains: Is economy, which is the doctrine of salvation history and the elucidation of signs—that is, of the sacramental realm and, therefore, of the doctrine of the Church—is economy to be called "theology"? Or are the two to be kept always separate? If the first alternative is correct, then there is danger that "economy" will solidify into either a salvation-historical or an ecclesiological positivism, or that it will become mythology and perhaps even mythological pragmatism. From this perspective, the new designations of the object of theology by the Victorines and by early Franciscan theology did not really offer new alternatives when they named as the object of theology the *opera reparationis,* for these could be equally well designated as salvation history or as the "whole Christ". In the theology of the period between the two world wars, the last concept was enthusiastically promoted as a call—in which there was likewise concealed a criticism of the metaphysical redundance of Neo-Scholasticism[3]—for a christocentric theology. Such a christocentric theology, as a theology of *Christus totus,* considers itself also an ecclesiology. In contrast to Neo-Scholasticism, it can be very positive because, in its thinking, it does not go beyond what has been positively established but rather finds in what is positive, in the Church, the reflection of God's nature and being. We can hardly fail to notice that, in its basic assumptions, Vatican Council II was strongly characterized by this way of thinking. The statement that the Council's whole content can be subsumed

---

[1] ST I q 1 a 7.

[2] Peter Lombard, *Magistri Sententiarum Libri IIII* [henceforth *Sent.*], (Lyons: apud Antonium Tardif., 1581), liber I, dist 1, c 1, 1, 2. Lombard is referring here to St. Augustine's *De doctrina christiana libri IV,* 1:22 (see CChr 32 [1962]: 7).

[3] On the decidedly salvation-historical conception of Hugo of St. Victor, cf. esp. "Libri prioris de Sacramentis", prologus, c 2, PL 176:183–84, and "Commentarium in Hierarchiam Coelestem S. Dionysii Areopagitae", cap. 1, PL 175:923–28. Note the modification of the formula to be found in Alexander of Hales, *Summa theologica* 1 (Florence: Ad claras aquas, 1924), *Tractatus introductorius,* q 1 c 3 resp, 6: "Theologia est scientia de substantia divina cognoscenda per Christum in opere reparationis." Representative of the revival of such views in the interval between the two world wars is Emile Mersch, *Le Corps mystique du Christ,* Études de théologie historique (Louvain: Museum Lessianum, 1933).

under the division "the Church *ad intra*" and "the Church *ad extra*" has, it is true, never become an official component of conciliar doctrine, but the concept did, nevertheless, have a decisive influence on the selection and arrangement of materials.[4]

Before taking a position, we must, however, shed some light on the problem as a whole. These differences with regard to the object of theology are linked, of necessity, to a variety of methodological orientations and to different concepts of the goal to be attained. Both differences are most concisely characterized by the corresponding key words of the thirteenth-century controversy. According to one—the Thomistic—view, theology is to be regarded as a *scientia speculativa*; according to the other—the Franciscan—view, it is to be regarded as a *scientia practica*.[5] Without need of lengthy proof, we can see again how current this question is when we recall the key words "orthodoxy" and "orthopraxis" that came into use after the Council to describe the attempt to reorient theology. In the meantime, however, a controversy has broken out, the like of which would have been inconceivable in the Middle Ages. For if the word "orthopraxis" is pushed to its most radical meaning, it presumes that no truth exists that is antecedent to praxis but rather that truth can be established only on the basis of correct praxis, which has the task of creating meaning out of and in the face of meaninglessness.[6] Theology becomes then no more than a guide to action, which, by reflecting on praxis, continually develops new modes of praxis. If not only redemption but truth as well is regarded as "*post hoc*", then truth becomes the product of man. At the same time, man, who is no longer measured against truth but produces it, becomes himself a product. Granted, the most extreme positions occur but rarely. But less militant—what we might call Western bourgeois—forms of the undivided sovereignty of *scientia practica* are ultimately marked by the same loss of truth. When it is claimed positivistically that truth is, in any event, inconceivable and that to believe otherwise is tantamount to an attack on tolerance and pluralism, there the method produces

---

[4] Cf. Guilherme Baraúna, *De Ecclesia. Beiträge zur Konstitution "Über die Kirche" des Zweiten Vatikanischen Konzils* I (Freiburg: Herder, 1966); Gérard Philips, *L'Église et son mystère* I. Cf. also the texts of Pope Paul VI in Yves Congar, Hans Küng and D. O'Hanlon, *Konzilsreden* (Einsiedeln, 1964), 15ff.

[5] Cf. Thomas Aquinas, ST I q I a 4: "Sed contra: omnis scientia practica est de rebus operabilibus ab homine. . . . Sacra autem doctrina est principaliter de Deo". St. Bonaventure, *Opera omnia* I, "Commentaria in quatuor libros sententiarum Magistri Petri Lombardi", prooem q I resp, 7: "hic (sc. habitus) est contemplationis gratia et ut boni fiamus, principaliter tamen ut boni fiamus."

[6] Cf. D. Berdesinski, *Die Praxis—Kriterium für die Wahrheit des Glaubens? Untersuchungen zu einem Aspekt politischer Theologie* (Munich, 1973). Cf. also Part Two, Chapter 3b of the present work and the bibliographical references listed there in n. 42.

its own truth, that is, the decision about *what* to communicate is decreed in terms of *how* it is to be communicated; there is no longer any attempt to decide *how* a message is to be communicated in terms of *what* is to be communicated. The fundamental rejection of a catechism that we have witnessed in the last ten years is perhaps the plainest example of an attitude that lets the question of communication be determined by methodological praxis rather than by seeking a means of communication that is appropriate to the matter. I have the impression that, even in the realm of spiritual exercises and pastoral counseling, the formal psychomontage replaces, more often than not, an objective content that is no longer trusted; but, because the purely formal treatment of man and his being is just as little possible as the pure self-reflection of praxis, new content slips in unnoticed, the justification of which is just the expected "functioning" of man—who, deprived of truth, can no longer be anything more than the functioning of a system of no particular finality.

In the early 1920s, Romano Guardini spoke of the primacy of *logos* over *ethos*,[7] intending thereby to defend the Thomistic position of *scientia speculativa*: a view of theology in which the meaning of christocentrism consists in transcending oneself and, through the *history* of God's dealings with mankind, making possible the encounter with the *being* of God himself. I admit that it has become clear to me only through the developments of recent years how fundamental this question actually is. For Thomas Aquinas had, in fact, only reflected anew on an answer already formulated by Irenaeus of Lyons, the real founder of Catholic theology, in his controversies with Gnosticism: The new message of Jesus Christ, he said, consists in the fact that he opened the way to a meeting with him who had until then been the Untouchable, the Unreachable, with the Father himself, and destroyed the insurmountable wall that had separated mankind from the *being* and truth of God.[8] This means that we fail to understand the meaning of Christology precisely when it remains locked in a historico-anthropological circle and does not become a real theo-logy, in which the metaphysical reality of God is what is discussed. On the other hand, this means that, in the last analysis, it is only theology that can guarantee the continuing possibility of metaphysical inquiry;

[7] Cf. Josef Pieper's report of his first meeting with Romano Guardini, in which he became aware of the superiority of being over duty and so found the topic of his dissertation: *Die ontische Grundlage des Sittlichen nach Thomas von Aquin*, in Josef Pieper, *Noch wusste es niemand. Autobiographische Aufzeichnungen 1904–1945* (Munich, 1976), 69ff. [English trans.: *No One Could Have Known . . . , an Autobiographical Sketch* (San Francisco: Ignatius Press, 1987). (Trans.)]

[8] Cf. L. Tremblay, *La Manifestation et la vision de Dieu selon St. Irénée de Lyon* (Münster: Aschendorff, 1978).

where theology does so, the way is also cleared for philosophy to pursue the question of cause to its ultimate radicality.

We have thus returned to the point from which we started: theology has to do with God, and it conducts its inquiry in the manner of philosophy. The challenge and the difficulty of such a concept will have become clear by now. Such a metaphysical (ontological) alignment of theology is not, as we have long feared, a betrayal of salvation history. On the contrary, if theology will remain true to its historical beginnings, to the salvation event in Christ to which the Bible bears witness, it must transcend history and speak ultimately of God himself. If it will remain true to the *practical* content of the gospel, which is the salvation of mankind, it must first be a *scientia speculativa*; it cannot start by being a *scientia practica*. It must preserve the primacy of that truth that is self-subsistent and that must be discovered in its self-ness before it can be measured in terms of its usefulness to mankind.

If we thus agree with Thomas Aquinas' basic alignment, that is not to say that the direction taken by St. Bonaventure—who, incidentally, was in total accord with Thomas' central thesis—has no meaning for us. He, too, states explicitly that the subject of theology, to which all else is referred, is God himself.[9] But he links this thought, which received its definitive form from Thomas Aquinas, to a very different concept of human reason. Bonaventure knows a *violentia rationis*—a violence of reason—that is not to be measured by personal reality.[10] He argues that the concept "Christ died for us" has an impact on the human intellect that is different from that made by a mathematical theorem: "Fides sic est in intellectu", he says, "ut . . . nata sit movere affectum."[11] Later, the notion that God is the subject of theology acquires, in his thought, a new depth in which this specific challenge to the human intellect finds its ultimate foundation. After the *Itinerarium mentis in Deum,* that is, after the year 1259, a gradual change of meaning becomes apparent in his concept of theology as a result of his reading of the works of the pseudo-Dionysius. Dionysius still accepted the ancient Greek use of the word θεολογία to designate, not a human science, but the divine discourse itself, for which reason the Greeks logically designated as "theologians" only those who

---

[9] I *Sent.,* prooem q 1 resp, 7: "Nam subiectum, ad quod omnia reducuntur ut ad principium, est ipse Deus. Subiectum . . . , ad quod omnia reducuntur . . . ut ad totum integrum, est Christus. . . . Subiectum . . . , ad quod omnia reducuntur sicut ad totum universale . . . est res et signum."

[10] I *Sent.,* prooem q 2 ad 6, 11: "in anima hominis dominantur violentia rationis. Sed quando fides non assentit propter rationem, sed propter amorem eius, cui assentit, desiderat habere rationes".

[11] I *Sent.,* prooem q 2 resp, 13.

could be regarded as the voice of the deity himself, as instruments of the divine discourse—for example, Orpheus and Hesiod.[12] Hence Aristotle draws a distinction between θεολογία and θεολογική—between theology and the study of theology. By the first, he distinguishes the divine discourse; by the second, human effort to understand the divine.[13] On the basis of this linguistic tradition, pseudo-Dionysius used the word "theology" to designate Holy Scripture; for him, *it* is what the ancients meant by the word—the discourse of God rendered in human words. In his later years, Bonaventure made this mode of speech his own and, on the basis of it, rethought his understanding of theology as a whole.[14] Properly speaking, God himself must be the subject of theology. Therefore, Scripture alone is theology in the fullest sense of the word because it truly has God as its subject; it does not just speak of him but *is* his own speech. It lets God himself speak. But Bonaventure does not thereby overlook the fact that this speaking on the part of God is, nevertheless, a human speaking. The writers of Holy Scripture speak as themselves, as men, and yet, precisely in doing so, they are "theologoi", those through whom God as subject, as the word that speaks itself, enters into history. What distinguishes Holy Scripture from all later theology is thus completely safeguarded, but, at the same time, the Bible becomes the model of all theology, and those who are the bearers of it become the norm of the theologian, who accomplishes his task properly only to the extent that he makes God himself his subject. In this way, Bonaventure achieved in his later works the synthesis he had sought in his earlier ones, where he had affirmed the ontological character of theology and thus the proper rank of the theoretical and yet had spoken, at the same time, of the necessary self-transcendence of contemplation into the practice of the faith. What we have said can now be formulated as the third and final thesis of these remarks: theology is a spiritual science. The normative theologians are the authors of Holy Scripture. This statement is valid not only with reference to the objective written document they left behind but also with reference to their manner of speaking, in which it is God himself who speaks.

---

[12] Cf., for example, B. F. Kattenbusch, *Die Entstehung einer christlichen Theologie*, new printing (Darmstadt, 1962; first published, 1930), 4, n. 2.

[13] θεολογία appears only once in Aristotle: in Meteorologica, B 1, line 35, *Aristotelis opera, ex recensione Immanuelis Bekkeris* (Berlin: Gruyter, 1960), 353. θεολογική appears frequently, e.g., in τὰ μετὰ τὰ φυσικά 5:1, line 19, in ibid., 2:1026.

[14] The following passage from the prologue to the "Breviloquium" (St. Bonaventure, *Opera omnia*, 5:201) is typical of Bonaventure's later linguistic usage: "sacrae scripturae, quae theologia dicitur". Cf. Jacques Guy Bougerol, *Breviloquium I, Prologue* (Paris, 1966), 76ff. On the relationship between Bonaventure's usage and that of pseudo-Dionysius, cf. Joseph Ratzinger, *Die Geschichtstheologie des heiligen Bonaventura*, 92, n. 18.

I think this fact has great significance for our present situation. It was an unprecedented turn of events when Abélard moved theology out of the monastery and into the classroom—and so into the neutrality of academe. [15] Nevertheless, it remained clear in the following centuries that theology could be studied only in the context of a corresponding spiritual praxis and of a readiness to understand it, at the same time, as a requirement that must be lived. It seems to me that it was only after World War II and completely only after Vatican Council II that we came to think that theology, like any exotic subject, can be studied from a purely academic perspective from which one acquires knowledge that can be useful in life. But just as we cannot learn to swim without water, so we cannot learn theology without the spiritual praxis in which it lives. This is by no means intended as an attack on lay theologians, whose spiritual life often enough puts us priests to shame, but, rather, as a very basic question about how the study of theology can be meaningfully structured so that it does not succumb to academic neutralization in which theology becomes ultimately a contradiction of itself.

With that, I have reached the end of my remarks. It will not have escaped the attentive reader that everything I have said, while it has referred directly to the question about the nature of theology, has been, nevertheless, an implicit *laudatio* of Cardinal Volk. With admirable steadfastness, he has held continually before us the primacy of *logos* over *pragma*; he has opened to us the philosophical depth of theological questions; and, last but not least, he has given us the example of a truly spiritual theologian. For all this, it is fitting that all of us express to him now our heartfelt thanks.

B. The Church and Scientific Theology

With the topic "The Church and Scientific Theology" we encounter a sensitive area of contemporary consciousness. Anyone who approaches it enters upon a battlefield where strong emotions are in conflict. On the one hand, it is the point of crystallization for attacks against the official Church, which, from Galileo to Küng, has been accused of being hostile to science and—without having learned anything in the process or even being embarrassed by her past errors—of continuing her stubborn resistance to progress and of preventing the victory of better insights as long as she was able to do so. From the perspective of the logic of modern

---

[15] On the characteristics of monastic vs. Scholastic theology, cf. Jean Leclerq, *Wissenschaft und Gottverlangen. Zur Mönchstheologie des Mittelalters* (Düsseldorf, 1963). On the distinction between cloister and school, see esp. 223ff. and 237 (Bernard and Abélard).

science, which obeys the inner demand of enlightened reason, the problem is even more fundamental: science can find its norm only in itself. It is regulated and criticized only by the scientific process of forming hypotheses which it then shows to be either true or false. It is against the very nature of modern science to allow any external court of appeals to share in this process. If a science allows this to happen, it ceases to be a science in the contemporary sense of the word because it no longer follows the one law of its own being, its own methodology, but, by submitting to a power outside itself, betrays its own fundamental law.

For such a concept of science, it is absurd that the ecclesial Magisterium should claim to be the highest court for the interpretation of Holy Scripture or should hold fast to dogma as the binding interpretation of the Bible. Such an action is regarded as a clinging to medieval conditions in which the intellectual step of the Enlightenment, of the transition to the modern era, has not yet been taken. The claim that a theology open to such a mode of thinking and believing is a science, as the word is understood in academic circles today, is categorically denied; conversely, a theology that claims to be a science will, for that very reason, feel itself obliged to protest against the possibility of such incursions into its domain. It will not be able to understand from what source the Magisterium receives its normative judgment in matters of biblical exegesis since such historical insight is to be found only in the historical method, which resides in the sciences—and nowhere else. The Church comes thus to be regarded as an extrascientific organization that can serve as a vehicle for scientific undertakings but may not share in the scientific process itself.

When we have pursued the matter thus far, questions arise that lead beyond emotions and differences of opinion to a more basic form of reflection. Is a theology for which the Church is no longer meaningful really a theology in the proper sense of the word? Let us omit, for the moment, the specifically Christian aspect of the question and concentrate, instead, on the questionable aspects of modern science itself. Is the strict self-determination of science really as unlimited as it seems to be? Is it not clearly marked, in the questions it poses as well as in the methods it employs, by a multiplicity of preexisting values and interests? At the end of the sixties, neo-Marxist criticism claimed with caricature-like exaggeration that the apparent disinterestedness of science was but a camouflage for the anonymous interest of the capitalistic world and a cloak for its claim to power. Today it is hardly necessary to show that this criticism was itself a bid for power or to describe the kind of power to which it aspired. The real point of these remarks is that all questioning is accompanied by premises and that mere technical ability can never be the sole criterion of science. All too often, the proof of error comes too late.

Today we know that many a specialization leads only to a bypath and that reconsideration of the whole is imperative even in the case of individuals. The portals are beginning to open, however, cautiously, to a self-criticism of enlightened reason. If, then, the coordination of Church and theology is described as medieval, that fact should raise the basic question of whether it is not precisely here that enlightened reason finds its limits.

Before pursuing this line of thought any further, we must look at the opposing criticism of the relationship between the Church and scientific theology, which also has strong supporters today. Whenever theology begins to play a role in the Catholic Church similar to that which it has long played in the Protestant domain, there appears among us, too, that reaction that, in the Protestant churches, goes by the name of fundamentalism. Against the complication and conditioning of Christianity that occurs in the academic world the protest is raised for a simple faith that opposes to the "ifs" and "buts" of the scholar the plain Yes and No of faith. The shepherds of the Church not only find themselves exposed today to the accusation that they still hold fast to the methods of the Inquisition and try to strangle the Spirit by the repressive power of their office; they are, at the same time, attacked by the voice of the faithful, who accuse them more and more loudly of being mute and cowardly watchdogs that stand idly by under the pressure of liberal publicity while the faith is being sold piecemeal for the dish of pottage of being recognized as "modern". An important scholar, who is likewise a thoughtful and intelligent Christian, recently reduced this protest to an unforgettable formula. He writes: "A more or less lengthy visit to a Catholic bookstore does not encourage one to pray with the psalmist: 'You will reveal the path of life to me.' Not only does one quickly discover there that Jesus did not turn water into wine but one also gains insight into the art of turning wine into water. This new magic bears the name 'aggiornamento'."[16] Under this new aspect, the shepherd of the Church is offered the opportunity of giving his teaching ministry a democratic form: of becoming the advocate of the faithful, of the people, against the elitist power of the intellectuals. Actually, absolutism is an invention, an inner consequence, of the Enlightenment. Advised by enlightened minds and himself at the pinnacle of the Enlightenment, the king knew the needs of the unenlightened people better than they did themselves. Therefore, he canceled their freedoms and the rights of the social classes that limited *his* powers in order thus to give full sway to the demands of that reason of which he was the representative. The absolutist

---

[16] Robert Spaemann, *Einsprüche. Christliche Reden* (Einsiedeln, 1977), 7. To avoid misunderstanding: Spaemann's book has nothing to do with "fundamentalism". It is a model of responsible philosophical participation in the inquiry into the present status of the faith.

claim to power is not, as it were, a relic of the Middle Ages; it is a product of the Enlightenment and is represented symbolically by the Sun King. Only the inner conviction that reason, which was the sole norm, was also something that could be administered made absolutism possible.[17] Some of this absolutism of the Enlightenment is still to be found among intellectuals today, and many an ecclesial reform would surely have been carried out more prudently if the triumphant enthusiasm of being right had not set the tempo. To that extent, we are correct in seeing in the function of the ecclesial Magisterium a democratic element that derives from its Christian origin. But we must, at the same time, be mindful of the fact that the protest against modern theology is always meaningless if it is based only on the rejection of what is new or on a fundamental hostility to science and its contributions: a mere negation cannot support faith, and democratic representation is equally useless if it has no spiritual basis. Quantity can never replace truth—that insight does not apply only to the Church; the fact that it is hardly reflected in our political theory is one of the causes of the present loss of confidence in democracies.

But let us return to our topic. From the opposing views regarding it, some facts have emerged that can, perhaps, be summarized as follows. Faith is not to be placed in opposition to reason, but neither must it fall under the absolute power of enlightened reason and its methods. This insight, which, I think, expresses the central concept of what I have to say, must now be substantiated and developed. It has always been clear from its very structure that Christian faith is not to be divorced from reason. In his book about the two kinds of faith, Martin Buber has pointed out that, for Christian faith, the act of conversion and, with it, the act of "holding as true" are fundamental.[18] However much we may criticize his reflections in other respects, he is undoubtedly right when he says that affirmation—saying Yes—is a constant element of Christian faith; that it is true that Christian faith, in its most basic form, has never been a formless trust but always a trust in a particular Someone and in his word—that is, an encounter with truth that must be affirmed in its content. Precisely this marks its unique position in the history of religion.

[17] Cf. H. Staudinger and W. Behler, *Chance und Risiko der Gegenwart* (Paderborn, 1976), 49–96.

[18] Cf. Martin Buber, *Zwei Glaubensweisen,* in Martin Buber, *Werke* 1 (Munich-Heidelberg: Kösel, 1962): 651–782. [For an English translation, see Martin Buber, *Two Types of Faith* (New York: Harper Torchbooks, 1961). (Trans.)] Cf. also, Hans Urs von Balthasar, *Spiritus Creator. Skizzen zur Theologie* 3 (Einsiedeln: Johannes, 1967): 51–91. The excellent article "πιστεύω" by Bultmann and Weiser, in ThWNT 6:193–230, esp. 216ff., is important and illuminating for our subject.

Some forty years ago, Hendrik Kraemer formulated the distinction between Hinduism and Christianity in these terms: Hinduism, he said, knows no orthodoxy but only orthopraxis.[19] In other words, the Hindu religions are characterized by no binding common belief but only by common forms of cultic *praxis* that vary in the degree to which they are binding, while, for Christianity, a common belief—orthodoxy—is both characteristic and indispensable. From this follows something of great importance: whereas the religious philosophy of Buddhism—and, for a long time now, of Hinduism as well—regards all religious knowledge as merely symbolical, Christian belief has always insisted on the reality of that knowledge in which truth reveals itself in a form for which other symbols cannot be substituted. Hinduism, for instance, preserves very impressive myths about the descent of the god Krishna. But because, in the last analysis, they are for it only images of the infinite that can never be confined in words, these histories can be extended, rewritten, enlarged by borrowings and varied in a number of other ways; there is, therefore, no problem about adopting the history of Jesus Christ as one of the descents of Krishna.[20] Christian faith, on the other hand, holds firmly that, in Jesus, God really came into the world in a way that is historical, not symbolical. This does not mean that the Krishna-myths have no value. But the way in which a Christian can understand them is different from the fusion with Christ that occurs in Hinduism. For the Christian, Krishna is a dramatic symbol of Christ, who is reality, and this relationship is not reversible.

What does this mean in relation to our question? It means that Christian faith affirms truths, the contents of which are not subject to a totally free symbolic interpretation but are to be understood as statements that are valid and true as they stand. This holds good in the realm of history as well as in that of philosophy. Christian faith maintains that this Jesus lived, died and rose again from the dead at a particular time. It maintains that the same God who became man in Jesus Christ is the Creator of the world. By such statements, Christian faith goes beyond the domain of merely symbolical knowledge and enters the realm of historical and philosophical reason; its intention is to say only what is in accordance with reason and so to address reason itself, to make it an instrument in the act of conversion. The fact that Christian faith has, from the beginning, had a missionary character is

---

[19] H. Kraemer, *Die christliche Botschaft in einer nichtchristlichen Welt* (1940). [For an English translation, see *The Christian Message in a Non-Christian World* (London: Edinburgh House, 1938). (Trans.)] See also, H. Kraemer, *Religion und christlicher Glaube* (Göttingen, 1959). Cf. Helmuth von Glasenapp, *Die fünf grossen Religionen* (Düsseldorf-Cologne, 1952), 1:7–25; H. W. Gensichen, RGG 3:349–52.

[20] Cf. J. Neuner, "Das Christus-Mysterium und die indische Lehre von den Avatáras", in Grillmeier and Bacht, *Das Konzil von Chalkedon*, 3:785–824.

due to its structure. Its purpose is to lead out of the past and to guide to new knowledge. Because it proposes both truths and facts, it is not just the preserver of tradition in a limited circle; from the beginning, it has existed as the recipient of facts and the revealer of truths that forced its first confessors to leave the place where they were and to call others into the new community. That is why theology is a peculiarly Christian phenomenon: the Eastern religions produced religious philosophies in which religious symbols were explained and interpreted intellectually. By contrast, theology is something quite different: a rationality that remains within faith itself and that develops the appropriate context of faith. This fact explains also the peculiar phenomenon that the Christian faith, in its early days, found its ally, not in other religions, but in the great philosophy of the Greeks. The Christian mission borrowed the criticism of the mythical religions from Greek enlightenment and thus continued the line of Old Testament prophets and wisdom teachers who, in their criticism of the pagan gods and their cults, spoke the language of the enlightenment. The Christian mission sought to persuade men to abandon false religions and turn to the true one. It saw the greatest evil of the mythical religions in the fact that they led people to worship as real what could be, at best, only a symbol and so to become untrue themselves because they treated the symbol as reality. In this sense, the Christian mission participated energetically in the demythologizing of the world and in furthering the action of *logos* against *mythos*. In the struggle for the human soul, it regarded, not the existing religions, but rational philosophy as its partner, and, in the constant disputes among the various groups, it aligned itself with philosophy. The synthesis with Greek philosophy is already discernible in the sermons of the earliest Christian missionaries, which, in their turn, had been strongly influenced by the intellectual efforts of the Jewish diaspora.[21]

We can say, then, that it is characteristic of Christian belief to seek to reveal true knowledge, which, as such, is also immediately meaningful to reason. That is why it pertains to the nature of faith to develop theology; any fundamental rejection of theology would be a denial of its own inner starting point. Granted, theology in this original Christian sense of reason that exists in and from faith is seriously threatened by the intellectual climate of our time; this crisis of theology reveals, at the same time, the deep-rooted crisis of faith itself. The contemporary scientific approach has a tendency to reduce to two disciplines what was once regarded as theology. On the one hand, theology becomes the philosophy of religion,

---

[21] Cf. my article, "Der christliche Glaube und die Weltreligionen", in Johannes Baptist Metz, Walter Kern, Adolf Darlapp and Herbert Vorgrimler, *Gott in Welt*, Festgabe für Karl Rahner, 2 vols. (Freiburg: Herder, 1964), 287–305.

respecting Christianity as symbolic knowledge but attempting at the same time, to place it on a par with world religions—exactly where it does not itself want to be placed. Christianity is thus totally downgraded from the level of a spiritual reform of values to that of symbol, even though, in its fundamental statements, it has itself always claimed to be the real and the true. On the other hand, all that then remains of the whole heritage of theology is the strictly historical analysis of relevant historical texts, but this process, if it is not secretly garnished with a variety of religio-historical statements, represents the complete reversion of Christianity to the general domain of the historical sciences. Basically, this means that faith itself has abdicated its rational responsibility; that the Christian cult either treats symbols as realities or, as a whole, becomes simply a charade. In any event, the truly Christian element is destroyed in the process; it is submerged in the general deposit of the history of religion.

Certainly, things have not yet come to such a pass. But the mere suggestion lets us see how inseparably faith and theology are bound together and the extent to which the Christian faith itself is threatened by the dangers to which theology is exposed from many sides. What, then, should be the nature of scientific theology today? That is the very practical question to which we must now turn our attention.

Our question will be more easily answered if we try first to ascertain the precise cause of the crisis in which theology finds itself. Even among believing Christians, the notion is widespread today that Christian faith rests on God's revelation but that this revelation as a whole is contained in a single book, the Bible. If, then, we want to discover what God has revealed, we must read and interpret the Bible. But modern science has evolved the only instruments that are still possible and useful today for communicating what a book really says: the historico-critical method and the scientific method of literary criticism. If this is so, theology, too, must use these methods for a scientific interpretation of the Bible. Any other approach is to be rejected as medieval. But the notion that God's revelation is identical with literature and that the dissecting knife of the literary critic is the only correct way of disclosing God's secrets misconstrues both the nature of God and the nature of literary criticism. Enlightenment is here transformed into naiveté. The Bible itself does not think in this way. It certainly does not teach that the act of faith by which an individual receives revelation is located in the encounter between a book and that person's analytical reason. The act of faith is rather a process that frees both the reason and the existence of the individual from the bonds that restrict them; it is the introduction of the isolated and fragmented reason of the individual into the realm of him who is the *logos*, the reason and the rational ground of all things and of all persons.[22] Anyone who construes the essence of the act of faith as the encounter between a book and the thinking of an individual has failed to understand the act of faith. For it is essentially an act of union; it leads into that spiritual realm where unity with the ground of all things and, hence, the understanding of that ground are present in a living community. Intrinsic to the basic structure of the act of faith, in other words, is incorporation into the Church, the common situs of that which binds together and that which is bound. In Romans 6:17, for instance, this act of faith is defined as the process by which an individual submits himself to one particular creed and, in doing so, performs an act of obedience that comes from his heart, that is, from the center of his whole being.[23] This presumes that, in her catechesis, the Church proclaims and lives a particular creed which, on the one hand, is the essential foundation of her community and, on the other, is sustained by this community. To become a Christian is to enter into this one particular creed, into the communal form of faith. The inner bond between the community itself and this creed is expressed by the fact that acceptance into the community has the form of a sacrament: baptism and catechesis are inseparable. Entering into the community of faith means entering into a community of life and vice versa. As part of the sacrament, this basic catechesis is not subject to the will of the Church. It is the mark of her identity, without which she is nothing, but which can, nevertheless, exist only in her communal life.[24]

In other words: the reality that is the Church transcends any literary formulation of it. Of course, what she believes and lives can be, and is, contained in books. But it is not totally assimilated by these books. On the contrary, the books fulfill their function as books only when they point to the community in which the word is to be found. This living community cannot be replaced or surpassed by historical exegesis; it is inherently superior to any book. By its very nature, the word of faith presupposes the

---

[22] Henri de Lubac, *Credo. Gestalt und Lebendigkeit unseres Glaubensbekenntnisses* (Einsiedeln, 1975), 29–56. [English trans.: *The Christian Faith, an Essay on the Structure of the Apostles' Creed* (San Francisco: Ignatius Press, 1986). (Trans.)]

[23] Cf. Ernst Käsemann, *An die Römer* (Tübingen: Mohr, 1973), 171: "The baptismal hymns of the New Testament, the catechetical tradition preserved in 1 Cor 13:3–8 and the later development of Roman symbolism . . . testify to the fact that a summary of the gospel . . . was given at Baptism. . . . From this we may logically conclude that it is not the deliverance of tradition to the catechumen that is being ascertained but the deliverance of the catechumen to tradition". Cf. also, Heinrich Schlier, *Der Römerbrief* (Freiburg: Herder, 1977), 208ff.; Otto Kuss, *Der Römerbrief* (Regensburg: Pustet, 1959), 388–89.

[24] Cf. Part One, Chapter 1, Section 1B ("Baptism, Faith and Membership in the Church— the Unity of Structure and Content") in the present work and the literature indicated there.

community that lives it, that is bound to it and that adheres to it in its very
power to bind mankind. Just as revelation transcends literature, so it also
transcends the limits of the pure scientism of historical reason. In this
sense, it can be said that the inner nature of faith justifies the Church's
claim to be the primary interpreter of the word and that this claim cannot
be abdicated in favor of enlightened reason without rendering
questionable the very structure of faith as a possibility for mankind.[25]
Community of faith is the situs of understanding. It cannot be replaced by
the science of history.

But in what does this transcendence of communal understanding over
the mere exegesis of texts consist? The germ of an answer can be found in
the first epistle of John. It was composed at a time when the emergence of a
new group of intellectuals, the so-called Gnostics, raised problems that are
not unlike those we are facing today. They interpreted the Christianity of
the Church as a Christianity of the naive in comparison with the "real"
Christianity, in which the letter of faith, which Christians had thus far
accepted, could be manipulated by sophisticated methods of interpretation to accord with one's own views. Simple Christians felt themselves
deceived and, at the same time, more or less helplessly victimized by the
intellectual superiority of the Gnostics and their inventions. In his response (1 Jn 2:18–27), John says: You have all received the anointing that
instructed you; you have no need of further instruction. The Apostle opposed to the arrogance of an intellectual elite the unsurpassability of simple
faith and of the insight it bestows. By the word "anointing", he recalls the
baptismal catechesis and its central content: that is, Christ, the Son of God,
who was anointed by the Holy Spirit, and the consequently trinitarian
character of faith. This common knowledge, which comes from baptism,
is not subject to a higher interpretation; it is itself the measure of every
interpretation. It is the source of life for the Church, which, in the sacrament and in the catechesis that is part of the sacrament, is the real bearer of
the word.[26]

We come thus to understand the duty of bishops as representatives of the
Church with regard to theology. Their obligation as bishops is not to seek
to play an instrument in the concert of specialists but, rather, to embody
the voice of simple faith and its simple primitive instincts, which precede

---

[25] This is the substance of Tertullian's clearsighted comments in *De praescriptione
haereticorum* (see Part Two, Chapter 2A, n. 6, for bibliographical information). For a
discussion of this fundamental text by the great African ecclesiologist, see Otto Kuss, "Zur
Hermeneutik Tertullians", in Josef Blinzler, Otto Kuss, Franz Mussner, *Neutestamentliche
Aufsätze*, Festschrift für Josef Schmid (Regensburg: Pustet, 1963), 138–60.

[26] For a commentary on the biblical text, cf. Rudolf Schnackenburg, *Die Johannesbriefe*
(Freiburg: Herder, 1953), 124–43.

science and threaten to disappear where science makes itself absolute. In this sense, they serve, in fact, a completely democratic function that rests, not on statistics, but on the common gift of baptism. We might, perhaps, say here in passing that even modern society should seek something of this kind—a council of the wise as it were—to remind it of values that are basic and immutable. For these values do not constrain science; they challenge it and set its tasks. But let us return to the specific structure of the Church and her faith, which can certainly not be imitated by the state. The common ground of baptismal faith, which the Magisterium must protect, does not fetter a theology that properly understands itself but rather issues to it that challenge that has proved fruitful again and again throughout the centuries. The model of enlightened reason cannot assimilate the structure of faith. That is our problem today. But faith, for its part, is comprehensive enough to assimilate the intellectual offer of the Enlightenment and give it a task that is meaningful also for faith. That is our opportunity. We must make the effort to accept it.[27]

[27] The relationship between this topic and the universal political and intellectual problems of our age has been impressively analyzed by M. Kriele, *Befreiung und politische Aufklärung* (Freiburg, 1980), 239–55.

CHAPTER 2

THE ANTHROPOLOGICAL ELEMENT
IN THEOLOGY

A. Faith and Education

Later historians will rank *education* among the most distinctive forces of postwar German history and, even, of the worldwide intellectual and political evolution that marks the second half of our century. It has become an explosive topic that reaches far beyond the realm of theoreticians and the educational centers of former days and into world history itself. Karl Erlinghagen's diagnosis of the deficiencies of Catholic education caused a stir in postwar Catholic Germany.[1] Gradually, the theme was incorporated into a more general complaint about the serious state of education in Germany as a whole, which seemed to be entering a world that had become technical and scientific without the requisite number of academicians—which was afraid of being relegated to the status of a developing country; of being excluded from the driving forces of history and included among those countries whose only role was to be the objects of patronage by developed and wealthy nations.[2]

This nightmare very quickly changed the intellectual and political landscape of Germany. New universities sprang from the ground, and, because of their steadily growing overpopulation, both old and new became places of lively ferment that echoed as frequently with cries for ever greater knowledge as with protests against the intensity of the effort required to attain it. As the movement progressed, the concept of "enlightenment" became a conspicuous mark of the present. A decade earlier, the phenomenon known to intellectual history as the Enlightenment had been greeted with more or less visible reservations. Today, on the other hand, radical enlightenment—the completion of what had been only insufficiently begun—has become, together with emancipation, both the stated goal of education and the aegis under which the spirit of the times deliberately chooses to present itself.

The area in which this is most widely recognized—namely, the attempt to do away with the problem of sex and eros in the name of enlightenment, to turn it into a nonproblem by means of a knowledge devoid of taboos—

---

[1] K. Erlinghagen, *Katholisches Bildungsdefizit in Deutschland* (Freiburg: Herder, 1965). It goes without saying that the value of this warning is by no means belittled here.

[2] The impetus given by Georg Picht, *Hier und Jetzt. Philosophieren nach Auschwitz und Hiroshima* (Stuttgart: Klett, 1980), should be especially recalled in this connection.

is only one (admittedly characteristic) symptom of an optimistic enlightenment that has, as its ultimate goal, liberation through knowledge. This
explains the urgency of the drive for progress; the fact that liberation, the
emancipation of mankind, has yet to be achieved is attributed to the other
fact that science itself has yet to achieve its goal, that it is still faced with
unanswered questions. The good of mankind, or so it seems, is inextricably linked to the speed with which science progresses—but what hinders
"progress" is an attack against man himself, the new form of guilt.

In the Catholic domain, Vatican Council II fostered participation in this
general movement. Even earlier, the reawakening of theology and all it
meant in terms of a new understanding of Holy Scripture and of the
Fathers, of liturgy and of openness toward separated Christians had
created a new enthusiasm for learning and had, for a time, even banished
the traditional pragmatism of many theology students: theological
knowledge seemed to promise a new possibility of faith, new ways for the
Church. The impetus given by Teilhard de Chardin exerted a wide
influence. With daring vision it incorporated the historical movement of
Christianity into the great cosmic process of evolution from Alpha to
Omega: since the noogenesis, since the formation of consciousness in the
event by which man became man, this process of evolution has continued
to unfold as the building of the noosphere above the biosphere.

That means that evolution takes place now in the form of technical and
scientific development in which, ultimately, matter and spirit, individual
and society, will produce a comprehensive whole, a divine world. The
Council's "Pastoral Constitution on the Church in the Modern World"
took the cue; Teilhard's slogan "Christianity means more progress, more
technology" became a stimulus in which the Council Fathers from rich
and poor countries alike found a concrete hope that was easier to interpret
and disseminate than was the meaning of the complicated discussions
about the collegiality of the bishops, the primacy of the pope, Scripture
and tradition, priest and laity.[3]

The components of the problem

a. Faith and simplicity

Although this line of thought conveys the predominant orientation of the
development, some moments of retardation, nonetheless, occurred. In the
predictable world of science, a nostalgia for the unpredictable arose; in the

---

[3] On the subject of Teilhard's influence on Vatican Council II, cf. the study by Wolfgang
Klein, *Teilhard de Chardin und das Zweite Vatikanische Konzil* (Paderborn: Schöningh, 1975).

Church, a longing for what had once been. But the greatest obstacle to the union between faith and enlightened culture was a more profound one: it cannot be reduced to a romantic nostalgia but, rather, finds its nourishment in the roots of faith itself and is as old as the first encounter between faith and enlightened culture. On the threshold of the modern age, the *Imitation of Christ* voices a dramatic protest against the disintegration of faith into a theology that had become empty learning and the determined option for a Christianity of the unlearned: "Let it be our highest study to become absorbed in meditation on the life of Jesus Christ."[4] "Even if you knew by heart the whole Bible and the sayings of all the philosophers, what would it profit you without the love of God and his grace?"[5] "Everyone has a natural craving for knowledge, but of what avail is knowledge without the fear of God?"[6] "An unlearned person who serves God is surely better than a learned one who proudly searches the heavens while neglecting himself."[7] "Give up your excessive desire for learning. Therein are to be found only illusion and inner emptiness."[8]

If we step backward in history, we find something similar in one who is perhaps the greatest saint in the history of the Church: St. Francis of Assisi. Again and again, he emphatically referred to himself as "simple and ignorant, without knowledge and ignorant" (*simplex et ydiota, ignorans et ydiota*).[9] In the so-called First Rule we find, for instance, these sentences: "Let us be on our guard against the wisdom of this world and the prudence of the flesh; for the fleshly spirit tries by all means to have the word but is little concerned with carrying it out; it seeks not for inner religion and sanctity, but for that which will be seen by men."[10] E. Gilson makes the following pertinent evaluation: "If we examine more closely the various utterances of St. Francis, we find that he never condemned learning as such but that he never wanted to see it develop in his order. It was not in itself evil in his eyes, but the pursuit of knowledge seemed to him useless and dangerous."[11]

---

[4] *De imitatione Christi*, I, 1, 3.

[5] Ibid., I, 1, 10.

[6] Ibid., I, 2, 1.

[7] Ibid., I, 2, 2.

[8] Ibid., I, 2, 5.

[9] Cf. especially his *Testament*, 4. For a German translation, see Kajetan Esser and L. Hardick, *Die Schriften des heiligen Franziskus von Assisi*, 3d ed. (Werl: Franziskus Verlag, 1963), 95. Sophronius Clasen, *Franziskus Engel des sechsten Siegels* (Werl: Franziskus Verlag, 1962), provides abundant material on the subject. Consult index under "Einfachheit" and "Einfalt".

[10] No. 17 in Esser-Hardick, 67 (newly translated from Latin into German for the present work).

[11] Étienne Gilson, *Die Philosophie des heiligen Bonaventura*, 2d ed. (Darmstadt, 1960), 64. The whole section, which is devoted to the topic "Bonaventura—The Franciscan", is relevant here (59–83).

Finally, there is also the witness of Holy Scripture itself. We might recall, for instance, the biting scorn with which Paul, in the first epistle to the Corinthians, describes the wisdom of the Greeks and contrasts it with the simplicity of the Christian message. The Cross of the carpenter's son of Nazareth is, for the believer, the wisdom of God, which men, for all their wisdom, have not known (1 Cor 1:21–25).[12] At the beginning of the whole movement stands its most profound formulation—Jesus' praise of the simple: "I bless you, Father, Lord of heaven and earth, for hiding these things from the learned and the clever and revealing them to mere children. Yes, Father, for that is what it pleased you to do" (Mt 11:25). In these words, we find the root of that reserve with regard to culture and learning that appears again and again throughout the history of the Church; they also explain the profound seriousness of the question we are discussing, which no believing Christians engaged in the work of education can afford to ignore if they want to do justice to its most essential task. If we examine the way in which disciples were called in the Old and New Testaments, we find there the same emphasis: in Hosea, the procedure takes this form: "Go, take . . . ! So he went and he took . . ." (Hos 1:2–3). In Mark 1:17–18, we find much the same structure: "Follow me . . . ! And at once they left. . . ." The call of God requires immediate compliance, an answer that seems to admit of no delay, no reflection: Yes or No, not "Yes, but. . . ."

b. The rational basis of faith

Is that all? Anyone who is aware of the profound theological reflection in the Pauline epistles and the Gospel of John cannot fail to realize that something else is at work here. But what? How does Paul reconcile his scorn for the wisdom of the Greeks with his own spiritual struggle to comprehend the content of faith—a struggle that would have been unthinkable without the legacy of Hebrew and Greek learning? How are the two combined in the history of faith—the constant reference to the unlearned and the steady development of scholarly theological knowledge? The question is of prime importance because it reflects the debate that is still in progress, despite the lapse of time, about the foundation, the possibility and the direction of a coexistence of faith and learning.

To begin with, we can say that it is a postulate of Christian faith that one called by God is always likewise called (though admittedly in a variety of ways) to his fellowmen. The missionary element is of the essence of the

---

[12] On this text, cf. the study by Rolf Baumann, *Mitte und Norm des Christlichen. Eine Auslegung von 1 Kor 1, 1–3, 4* (Münster: Aschendorff, 1968).

Christian faith, which is there to be proclaimed. It is meant for all because "God . . . wants everyone to be saved and reach full knowledge of the truth" (1 Tim 2:4). The love that is required by faith and that belongs to its innermost nature does not exclude the other's need for truth. If it did, it would refuse to respond to his most urgent need. The faith that reaches out to the other reaches out of necessity to his questioning as well, to his need for truth; it enters into this need, shares in it, for it is only by sharing in the question that word becomes answer. If it seemed at first that faith excluded reflection, the bending back upon itself, we must now say that, for that reason, it includes even more surely the reaching out to the other's need; in such a reaching out, one necessarily turns the questioning also upon oneself and, in the metamorphosis of word into answer, one learns oneself to know the faith more deeply and under a new aspect. To mold others, one must first let oneself be molded.[13]

This first step points the way for our next one. We have seen that the rationality of faith develops of necessity from the love that is intrinsic to it: the love that comes from faith must be a prudent love that is not content with providing the other with bread but also teaches him to see. A love that gives less or that is unwilling on principle to extend itself to the other's need for truth fails to attain a genuinely human level and is consequently not love in the full sense of the word. But when faith, as love, gives the ability to see, as is so beautifully portrayed in the story of the healing of the man born blind (Jn 9), this tells us something about faith itself. Such a faith is not just a blind gesture, an empty confidence, an adherence to a secret doctrine or the like. On the contrary, it wants to open men's eyes, to open their eyes to truth. On a purely linguistic level, this is demonstrated in the New Testament by the fact that faith is almost always expressed there by the formula πιστεύειν ὅτι: to believe *that* such and such is so. Precisely therein lies the difference between the faith of the New Testament and that of the Old;[14] Martin Buber, as we know, made this "rationalizing" of faith an object of reproach.[15] Faith, as the New Testament understands it, is more than a fundamental trust; it is my Yes to a content that compels my belief. The existence of this content is a structural constituent of Christian faith, because he whom we believe is not just any man but the Logos, the Word of God, in whom is contained the meaning of the world—its truth.

[13] For a further discussion of the attempt to base theology on the missionary dimension of the word and hence on the interrelationship of faith and love, cf. the careful analyses by Hansjürgen Verweyen, *Ontologische Voraussetzungen des Glaubensaktes. Zur transcendentalen Frage nach der Möglichkeit von Offenbarung* (Düsseldorf, 1969), 23–42.

[14] Cf. R. Bultmann, πιστεύω κτλ., in ThWNT 6, esp. 209–18.

[15] Cf. especially his book *Zwei Glaubensweisen* (see Part Three, Chapter 1A, n. 18, for bibliographical details), 651–782.

Christian faith is word-oriented. In this it differs from the opinion held by many Gnostics that what is final is, not the word, but silence—that there is no access to what is last and deepest. The confession of Jesus Christ as Logos (Word) means that in him God himself is revealed, the truth of all things.[16] Christian faith is thus at once more optimistic and more radical not only than the intellectual world of antiquity but precisely also than the intellectual world of the modern era, which regards the question of truth as something almost improper and, in any event, as highly unscientific and unintellectual. Only those systems that are "right" in themselves, that are "in tune", can be affirmed, but truth—it remains hidden. The only thing we must ask about or that can be of interest to us is the effect, the advantage or disadvantage, of a particular piece of knowledge. All that counts is praxis; it alone is the "truth" that is fitting for man. I believe that the meaning of Christian naiveté and its foundation are to be found here—in the fact that it is not hostile to learning but oriented to it. Christian naiveté consists in holding fast to the question of truth and referring learning to truth. If it fails to do so, it becomes indeed soulless and dangerous—we all know this and have experienced it.

Three theses about the unity of faith, simplicity and reason

Now that we have shed light on the antitheses that obscure the contemporary discussion of education, we are, I think, in a position to answer—briefly at least—in three theses the question about the relationship of faith and reason in our time.

First thesis

Christian faith is open to learning and has some things in common with the Enlightenment

After what we have just said, this thesis will not come as a surprise, but it is in need of some elaboration. In the intellectual development of mankind, the Enlightenment is not a unique phenomenon, nor is it a phenomenon reserved for the modern era. It appears, by a kind of inner necessity, at a particular stage of development and leads to a crisis of traditional values that, on the one hand, has the nature of a liberation, of an opening to new possibilities, but, on the other hand, brings about the downfall of a society if no new stable system of values has been discovered—if the enlighten-

---

[16] This is most evident in the debate between Irenaeus and the Gnostics; cf. R. Tremblay, *La Manifestation et la vision de Dieu selon St. Irénée de Lyon* (Münster: Aschendorff, 1978).

ment is not accompanied and appropriated by a new and deeper religious experience.

Starting in the fifth century, B.C., the Mediterranean world became the scene of a slow but steadily advancing enlightenment that, having originated in Greece and reached its zenith at the beginning of the Christian era, led first to the destruction of the ancient Greek social structure and ultimately to the collapse of the Graeco-Roman culture and its world. In this intellectual climate, Israel had a position that was at once particular and unique. It set itself in opposition to this world that found its security in the mystery religions, rejecting it with ever sharper criticism. It criticized the gods—what the Gentiles held as sacred and they themselves held as sacred—in forms that were close to those of the Enlightenment and became ever more so. Criticism of the pagan gods by the prophets and in wisdom literature is clearly expressed in the philosophical and linguistic mode of the Enlightenment. As representative of many such texts, let us recall the well-known passage in Psalm 115:4–6: ". . . their idols . . . have . . . eyes but never see, ears but never hear, noses but never smell. . . ." In other words, they are not existing, living beings but only images of wood or stone that man has made for himself and now worships as though they had the power to hear him, although they are but products of his own making. Elijah's mockery of Baal is in the same vein: Perhaps your god does not answer because he is wrapped in thought, "or he has gone on a journey; perhaps he is asleep and will wake up" (1 Kings 18:27).

The philosopher of religion cannot fail to be shocked by this callous treatment of a strange religion; from today's standpoint, he would say instead: Should we not respect what is sacred to man? Can we simply dismiss the worship of other gods with the argument that their images have been made by human artists? But, for the faith of Israel, there was question here of something quite different: of the destruction of concepts that were contrary to truth and that therefore made man unfree or led him to hypocrisy. Belief in the one God who created the world by his word cannot tolerate the pious illusion of myths; it enlightens the world. It believes that reason is justified in recognizing no other limits than its own origin in the creative will and word of God.

It is from this standpoint that we are to understand the drama of the establishment of Christianity in the pagan world. Christian faith was regarded as an attack on the world of religion as such, as a partner of the enlightenment that was destroying not only religion but the very foundations of the world; Christians were therefore accused and condemned as "atheists". In fact, however, the advancing process of reason had long since deprived these religions of their value and had made them weak; the spiritual collapse was in full progress and could be halted only by a deeper religious power such as it found in the encounter with God in the Person of Jesus Christ, which would outlast antiquity.[17] It belongs to the religio-historical nature of Christian belief to put man in the way of truth, to give him stability, not in customs, but in truth and thus to lay claim to the truth. It would be untrue to itself if it hid itself from reason. The struggle against ignorance, the banishment of sham piety, is its proper task. The search for learning is innate in it. It wants to free man from his apathy because it knows that he is a creature of God and an image of him who is the Logos, the truth. Man glorifies his Creator by letting the riches of the Creator shine forth in him.

Second thesis

Christian faith rejects the equating of learning and Enlightenment as well as the notion of Enlightenment as a way of salvation

Christian faith has, it is true, some elements in common with the Enlightenment and partly interchangeable with it, as is demonstrated by the criticism of myths in the prophetic and wisdom books of the Bible. Nevertheless, its identification with the Enlightenment and the consequent interpretation of Christianity as atheism was an error and not, as the God-is-dead theology would have us believe, the beginning of a better understanding of Christianity. For Christian faith has its source in a totally different fundamental option.

Plato, who, in the crisis of the first wave of Greek enlightenment, engaged in a struggle with its destructive forces precisely by adopting what was necessary in it, has described with great accuracy, especially in the *Gorgias,* the various exponents of the Enlightenment.[18] First, he presents Gorgias himself, the literary connoisseur, successful and firmly established in his bourgeois respectability—but without foundation and, in the last analysis, a nihilist. His assistant, Polos, is more radical by a generation; he abandons what is left of those customs that were once supportive but have become irrational and thus pitilessly reveals what they formerly concealed—the fundamental illogic of such thinking. The third figure on this scene that is so relevant for us today is Callicles, the political

[17] On this subject, cf. my article "Christentum", in *Meyers Enzyklopädisches Lexikon* 5 (1972): 669–71.

[18] I base these remarks on the analysis by Josef Pieper in his book *Kümmert euch nicht um Sokrates* (Munich, 1966), 11–80 under the title "Gorgias oder: Wortmissbrauch und Macht". Also relevant is M. Kriele, *Befreiung und politische Aufklärung* (Freiburg, 1980), in which the various kinds of enlightenment are distinguished from one another against the background of the historical situation and the present crisis. See esp., 72–82 and 187–206.

pragmatist, for whom the question of truth and the realization of goals "are two completely different things: 'The search for truth is an obstacle to him who wants to accomplish something practical'."[19] Enlightenment in this sense is illogical reason, for which only the knowable is valid and which, therefore, loses itself more and more in the makable. Culture is equated with the extent of one's knowledge; only the empirical has value. But this means ruin for man. The new remedy that has made its appearance seems at first to be full of promise: the ruthless, scientific dissection of oneself, psychoanalysis, the "enlightenment" referred now to man himself and thus becomes total. Left to itself, however, this remedy cannot fail to be disappointing, cannot fail to intensify the sickness to its utmost; for precisely this deliverance to pure knowledge with no measure of truth is a sickness unto death.

For the Christian, the learned person is not the one who knows and can do the most but the one who has become most and most purely man. But one can neither become nor be that without letting oneself be touched by him who is the ground and measure of man and of all being. That is why a very simple person who bears within himself a sense of values and, thus, a sensitivity toward others, toward what is right and beautiful and true, is immeasurably more learned than the most experienced technocrat with his computer brain. Augustine experienced this in the case of his mother: while he, with his friends, all of whom came from the academic world, struggled helplessly with the basic problems of humanity, he was struck again and again by the interior certainty of this simple woman. With astonishment and emotion, he wrote of her: "She stands at the pinnacle of philosophy."[20]

Anyone who has ever met such a simple person—a person who lets himself be inwardly permeated by the strength of the Christian faith—has experienced the same thing and will be unable to think of that person without the greatest respect. Consequently, Catholic educational activity will never equate the learning of a people with the number of its academicians; will never equate diploma with learning; will never make enlightenment its only goal; but will always press for those accompanying factors without which the increase of learning becomes, at the same time, the destruction of culture.

[19] Pieper, 14–15.

[20] St. Augustine, *De ordine*, I, 11, 32 in PL 32:994. On this subject, see Hans Urs von Balthasar's beautiful comments on the faith of the simple of heart in *Spiritus Creator. Skizzen zur Theologie* 3 (Einsiedeln: Johannes Verlag, 1967), 51–75, esp. 69–75. See also K. Krenn, ed., *Der einfache Mensch in Kirche und Theologie* (Linz, 1974).

Third thesis

Faith educates the individual. It requires different modes of education according to the situation of each and establishes for every mode the points of reference it needs to become more than just knowledge.

The nucleus of culture is faith itself. Faith does not take its place, as it were, alongside learning and cultural knowledge as an area of darkness cut off from enlightenment. The early Church applied to faith, and claimed for herself, the fundamental concept of the ancient cultural world: *paideia*.[21] Faith is *eruditio*, the civilizing of man, his development in openness and depth. An indifferent faith that is juxtaposed to life as something unassimilated and quasi-magic would not be Christian faith.

From this it is evident that the equality anchored in the doctrine of creation cannot mean uniformity—for which reason, the notion that the equality of man must find expression in, for instance, nondifferentiated schools must seem questionable to the Christian, who, on the contrary, will be moved to defend a plurality of educational models. Christian faith, which acts on the conviction that every human being has a particular vocation, will be more inclined to point to the equality of the various models and to recognize, in the symphony of many vocations, the unity and equal value of all. Granted, Christian consciousness is not yet fully formed to this way of thinking and has many errors to combat. A philosophy of life built on envy could not have become so powerful if there had been no categorizing for it to feed on.

On the other hand, a society and a humanity will not long endure in which persons in service careers—in hospitals, for instance—no longer find meaning in their service, and universal irritation, mutual suspicion, destroy life in common. God's revelation was to the simple—not out of resentment against the great, as Nietzsche would have it, but because they possess that precious naiveté that is open to truth and not subject to the intellectual temptation of nihilism. This should be the foundation of the great respect the Christian should always feel for those who are simple of heart. Christian education must be many-leveled, differentiated, but nevertheless one in the fact that it is an education for reverence, for the overcoming of prejudice and for the search for true equality in the midst of diversity. That is how it serves peace; that is how it serves humanity. That is how it is truly conformable to the faith.

[21] Cf. P. Stockmeier, "Glaube und Paideia. Zur Begegnung von Christentum und Antike", in *Theologische Quartalschrift* 147 (1967): 432–52.

B. Faith and Experience

The question of experience and faith has acquired more and more urgency in the theological dialogue of recent years; a number of studies have touched upon it and produced important insights, but many problems have, of necessity, been left unsolved. The purpose of this chapter is not to offer something new or even to give a more or less comprehensive survey of the discussion to date but simply to clarify some of the basic concepts that suggest themselves. Above all, it will not attempt a clear definition of what has still not been satisfactorily explained—namely, the concept of "experience" itself, which Gadamer has numbered among "those concepts that have yet to be elucidated".[22] Nor will it attempt to clarify the concept of "faith". With these two questions, it is ultimately the structure of the human spirit and of human knowledge as such that is being broached—the question of how God can enter into the human spirit. But this question, whether it is approached from the concept of God or from the nature of man, leads us to the most profound depths of our understanding of reality per se.

Let us leave it at that, then. In view of the limited purpose of this chapter in the totality of our reflections, I should like, without more ado, to present and expound upon four basic themes in which are expressed the main aspects of the relationship between experience and faith.

1. Experience as the basis of all knowledge

We shall begin with an Aristotelian axiom that Thomas Aquinas reduced to the formula: *Nihil est in intellectu quod non prius fuerit in sensu* ("There is nothing in the intellect that was not first in the senses")—sensory perception is the indispensable gateway to all knowledge as such. This basic concept of the doctrine of cognition was so significant for Thomas that he applied only to the realm of cognition the basic anthropological formula that defines man as a spirit contained in a body in such a way that the two are inseparably intertwined. His formula *Anima forma corporis* ("The soul is the form of the body") regards body and soul as so fused that together they form but one existential entity. If this is so—if, on the one

---

[22] Hans Georg Gadamer, *Wahrheit und Methode*, 2nd ed. (Tübingen: Mohr, 1965), 329, quoted here from Leo Scheffczyk, "Die Erfahrbarkeit der göttlichen Gnade", in Heribert Rossmann and Joseph Ratzinger, eds., *Mysterium der Gnade. Festschrift für Johann Auer zum 65. Geburtstag* (Regensburg: Pustet, 1975), 146–59; quotation is on 154.

hand, it pertains to the nature of the human spirit to be able to exist only as the form of the body, and if, on the other hand, it pertains to the nature of human corporality to be the expression of spirit—then it follows that the way of human cognition always requires the combination of corporal instrument and spiritual appropriation. Of necessity, then, all human knowledge must have a sensory structure; it must have its beginning in experience, in the perception of the senses. Thomas extended this view (which was shocking from the point of view of the then reigning Augustinian-Platonic tradition) to the knowledge of God as well. In fact, he had no choice but to do so. For if it is correct to say that in man spirit exists only as incarnate, then this epistemological theory cannot be limited to a particular realm of thought: it is valid for every kind of human knowledge.

Thus it was clear to Thomas that we cannot know God except through the senses and that even our way of thinking about God is dependent on and mediated by sense perception. If this is so, it means that every introduction to the faith—catechesis, catechumenate—must be by way of the senses. Here, too, it is necessary to find the way to faith by means of experiences made possible by the senses.

What we have discovered first from a philosophical view of mankind is confirmed when we examine the pedagogical method of Holy Scripture and especially of Jesus himself. Jesus taught consistently in the form of parables—and the parable was obviously not, in this case, just a pedagogical trick that could be eliminated without loss. In his farewell words, Jesus states explicitly that the parable is the way in which knowledge of the faith is to be realized in this world (Jn 16:25); in the Synoptics, too, the parable appears as the structure by which access is to be had to the mystery of the kingdom of God (Mk 4:10–11).

If we look more closely, we see that the parables have two principal functions. On the one hand, they transcend the realm of creation in order, by this transcendence, to draw it above itself to the Creator. On the other hand, they accept the past historical experience of faith, that is, they prolong the parables that have grown up with the history of Israel. We should, perhaps, add here a third point: they also interpret the simple world of everyday life in order to show how a transcendence to what is more than just human stereotype occurs in it. On the one hand, the content of faith reveals itself only in parables, but, on the other hand, the parable makes clear the core of reality itself. This is possible because reality itself is a parable. Hence, it is only by way of parable that the nature of the world and of man himself is made known to us.

In summary, we can say that the parable has a twofold structure: the content of faith is made transparent in the reality of the senses, and this knowledge of the faith has, in its turn, a reciprocal effect on the world of the senses, making it comprehensible as a movement that transcends itself. There is no question here of an ex post facto grafting onto a content that is in itself neutral with respect to God of a religious application that, in the last analysis, is alien to the earthly content and remains exterior to it; rather, there appears in the parable precisely that which is essential to sensory reality itself. The parable does not approach our experience of the world from without; on the contrary, it is the parable that gives this experience its proper depth and reveals what is hidden in things themselves. Reality is self-transcendence, and when man is led to transcend it, he not only comprehends God but, for the first time, also understands reality and enables himself and creation to be what they were meant to be. Only because creation *is* parable can it *become* the *word* of parable. That is why the material of daily living can always lead beyond itself; that is why a history can take place in it that both transcends it and is profoundly conformable to it.

Let us conclude by repeating in different words what we have said above: the way to faith begins in sensory experience, and sensory experience as such is a sine qua non of faith and is capable of transcendence.

From this, we can, I think, draw some very important conclusions. For, from this perspective, it is possible to arrive at an answer to the question of whether and how we ourselves can compose parables. Essential to such an undertaking is an awareness of *what* should be portrayed: namely, Christian reality; on the other hand, it is clear that the material of creation, the material of history and the material of daily living are the sources in which this reality can and always will be portrayed. We might add that, from this perspective, faith has the added task—in a time when creation has been forgotten, in which we live, to a large extent, in a secondary world of the self-made—of putting man once again in the way of creation in order to let him see it again and thus learn to know himself.

2. *Limits of experience*

I owe the wording of my second thesis to St. Ignatius Loyola. In it, I propose to turn my attention to that part of the Platonic-Augustinian tradition that continues to have enduring value and that Thomas Aquinas also recognized as self-evident. I refer to the sentence: *Deus semper maius*— "God is always greater." Whatever is discovered to exist, God always transcends it. In other words, precisely when we are most aware of the potentiality of the sensory world for revealing God, we must, at the same time, hold fast to the knowledge that God alone is divine; that he can be seen only when I do not stand still but regard experience as a road and set out upon it. R. Brague offers the following trenchant formulation of this concept: "God alone is divine. Anyone who makes the experience of God his final goal is interested only in his own psychology. . . . Left to itself, experience is satisfied with too little."[23] On the one hand, no doubt, the search for one who is greater can proceed only from the experience one has had and the question it poses. On the other hand, we must likewise be aware that man, of his own accord, poses too few questions and that the answer that comes from faith neutralizes all his questions and brings about a permanent widening of his inquiry. The reality of God is greater than all our experiences, even our experience of God. That is why faith cannot be transmitted simply as a matter of supply and demand; why it cannot be satisfied with what man is content to ask. So limited, it would no longer be able to let its own radiance shine forth but would constrict man and dull his sensibilities. For, as we have said, man asks too little of his own accord—and even that little he does not ask rightly.

From this perspective, we can now broaden and deepen our earlier insights. Faith starts with experience, but it cannot be limited by any experience that happens to present itself. On the contrary, it gives rise to a whole dynamics of experience and itself creates new experiences. The always greater God can be known only in the transcendence of the always "more", in the constant revision of our experiences. Thus faith and experience form the continuum of a road that must go farther and farther. Only by keeping step with the always new transcendence of faith can we come at last to the true "experience of faith".

3. Stages of experience

Having considered the relationship between faith and experience, we are ready now to examine and differentiate more precisely the various stages in the concept of experience itself. Our thesis should, therefore, read simply: experience is a multi-dimensional concept. Throughout this section, I adhere closely to the ideas presented by Jean Mouroux, which were adopted and developed further by W. Beinert.[24]

a. Mouroux calls the first stage empirical experience. Empirical experi-

---

[23] R. Brague, "Was heisst christliche Erfahrung?", in IKZ 5 (1976): 481–82; quotation is on 482.

[24] Jean Mouroux, L'Expérience chrétienne. Introduction à une théologie (Paris: Aubier, 1952). [For an English translation, see The Christian Experience. An Introduction to a Theology, trans. George Lamb (London: Sheed and Ward, 1955). (Trans.)] W. Beinert, "Die Erfahrbarkeit der Glaubenswirklichkeit", in Mysterium der Gnade (see n. 22 above), 134–45.

ence—in other words, that immediate and uncritical perception by the
senses that is common to all of us. We see the sun rise; we see it set. We see
a train pass. We see colors; and so forth. This manner of experience is, certainly, the beginning of all knowledge, but it is always superficial and inexact. And therein lies its danger. Because of its immediate certainty, it can
be an obstacle to deeper knowledge; because of the superficial empiricism
of what it seems to have perceived without ambiguity, it leads to falsity if
the impression is accepted as final and definitive. There is no need to
confine these observations to the region of faith alone, for the insight into
the possibility and the necessity of criticizing "empirical experience" is the
starting point of the natural sciences. In fact, the natural sciences came into
existence precisely because man had learned to criticize and exceed the impressions received by his senses. The dispute that centered around Galileo
was, in part, also a dispute about the meaning and limitation of sensory
experience, about the relationship between perception and understanding.
The real substance of the dispute was actually something quite different
from what we usually imagine it to have been. Galileo's opponents were
Aristotelian empiricists, whereas Galileo himself was a Platonist who,
therefore, put more emphasis on understanding than on sensory experience. As empiricists, his Aristotelian opponents defended sensory perception, which clearly saw the sun rise and set and, therefore, encircle the
earth. In his thesis, Galileo rejected what everyone can see. The same is
true of the laws of gravity, which never actually occur in reality as Galileo
formulated them but are a mathematical abstraction and, for that reason,
also contrary to our immediate experience.[25] Modern natural science is
built on the rejection of pure empiricism, on the superiority of thinking
over seeing. In his fundamental exposition of the theory of evolution, Jacques Monod has offered a most stimulating proof that modern natural science is ultimately Platonism, that it is based on the superiority of thought
over experience, of the ideal over the empirical, and that it has its source in
the fundamental notion that reality is composed of intellectual structures
and can, consequently, be known more exactly by thought than by mere
perception.[26] Hence it is valid not only in the realm of faith but quite generally to say that, while "empirical experience" is the necessary starting

[25] Cf. H. Staudinger and W. Behler, *Chance und Risiko der Gegenwart* (Paderborn, 1976),
56–63. See there the following quotation from Carl Friedrich Weizsäcker, *Die Tragweite der
Wissenschaft* 1, 2d ed. (Stuttgart, 1966), 107: "Galileo took a great step forward in daring to
describe the world as we do not experience it". Werner Heisenberg offers good examples of
Galileo's fundamentally Platonic (non-Aristotelian) orientation in *Das Naturbild der heutigen
Physik* (Reinbek, 1955), 59–78; cf. also Norbert Schiffers, *Fragen der Physik an die Theologie*
(Düsseldorf: Patmos, 1968), 25–39.

[26] J. Monod, *Zufall und Notwendigkeit. Philosophische Fragen der modernen Biologie* (Munich,
1973), esp. 127ff. and 139.

point of all human knowledge, it becomes false if it does not let itself be criticized in terms of knowledge already acquired and so open the door to new experiences.

b. With this we come to the second stage of experience, which Jean Mourroux calls "experimental", as opposed to empirical, experience. We can safely say that this second stage, to which belong all the modern natural sciences, is based on the juxtaposition of the Aristotelian axiom: *Nihil in intellectu nisi in sensu* ("There is nothing in the intellect that was not first in the senses") and the Platonic corrective: *Nihil in sensu nisi per intellectum* ("There is nothing in the senses without the prior action of the intellect"). The senses experience nothing if no question has been raised, if there is no preceding command from the intellect without which sensory experience cannot take place. Experimentation is possible only if natural science has elaborated an intellectual presupposition in terms of which it controls nature and on the basis of which it can bring about new experiences. In other words, it is only when the intellect sheds light on sensory experience that this sensory experience has any value as knowledge and that experiences thus become possible.

The progress of modern science is produced by a history of experiences that is made possible by the repeated critical interaction and reciprocal prolongation of these experiences and by the inner bond of the whole. The question that raised the possibility of constructing, let us say, a computer could not even have been asked in the beginning but became possible only in the continuum of an experiential history of experiences newly generated by thought. Up to this point, the structure of the experience of faith is completely analogous to that of the natural sciences; both have their source in the dynamic link between intellect and senses from which there is constructed a path to deeper knowledge. But we must point, here, also to a crucial difference. In a scientific experiment, the object of experience is not free. The experiment depends, rather, on the fact that nature is controlled (which is why Heidegger labeled the technique *Ge-stell*: a "set-up"). R. Brague expresses it this way: "Because we have removed from it everything that might be a freedom (vagueness, contingency, etc.), it can become the object of science."[27] It is, of course, also possible to experiment with a person. One attempts to control the person in terms of what is tangible, of what does not depend on his freedom. We know from the modern human sciences how much we can actually learn about man in this way. It is, in fact, possible to learn so much that it is easy to imagine there is nothing more to be learned; that one has "controlled" the whole person by this "set-up". "However, what is personal" in man cannot be controlled

[27] Brague, 492.

in this way but "reveals itself voluntarily through speech".[28] In this connection, L. Kolakowski has made the interesting observation that the way in which the natural sciences deal with nature is actually a form of necrophilia. They dissect it as though it were a dead object and, in this form, are able to control it.[29] If we apply this thought also to the human sciences, we might conclude that their way of dealing with human beings is likewise a kind of necrophilia. The fact that a similar way of dealing with faith and with God must of necessity lead to a God-is-dead theology need hardly be elaborated here. Thus, in this second sphere—that is, in the sphere of experimental experience—we encounter a higher stage in which experiences are modified and new ones are revealed by the intellect. But this stage is not appropriate to what is truly divine or truly human because the condition of experience at this level is, as it were, a putting to death of the object. We see here the danger to which modern science is subjected, for all its greatness, by the Platonism that is—in a certain sense rightly—so shocking to Aristotelians.

c. We have arrived now at the third type of experience, which Mouroux calls "experiential" and Beinert translates as "existential" experience.[30] It is an experience that accepts the intellectual principle we have discussed above but, at the same time, permits the freedom that is its own specific characteristic.

1. It has its source in the already described bond between intellectual assimilation and a constantly renewed influx of experience. However, it is not a closed circuit of supply and demand but the openness of a road that is never barred.

2. Moreover, it gives free play to the experience itself and lets itself be led "where it would rather not go" (cf. Jn 21:18). Granted, in scientific experience, too, knowledge leads man beyond his intended goal. We are gradually becoming aware of this at a time when we cannot help feeling threatened by the nightmarish thought that such a course may well be leading to our own destruction and to that of nature as well. Nevertheless, it is always man who acts with violence, who treats an object in terms of necrophilia. In "existential experience", on the contrary, the decisive factor is not control but letting oneself be controlled and the new way of "going where one would rather not go" that is thus made possible. An integral part of this latter process is acceptance of the experience of nonexperience, which is the only way one can reach a higher level. Let us quote Hans Urs von Balthasar on this subject: "It can be said with

---

[28] Ibid.

[29] Leszek Kolakowski, *Die Gegenwärtigkeit des Mythos* (Munich, 1973), 95–96.

[30] Beinert, 137.

certainty that there is no Christian experience that is not the fruit of the overcoming of one's own self-will or, at least, the determination to overcome it. And with this self-will we must include also all our willful efforts to evoke religious experiences on the basis of our own initiative and by our own methods and techniques."[31] "It is only when we renounce all partial experiences that the wholeness of being will be bestowed upon us. God requires unselfish vessels into which to pour his own essential unselfishness."[32]

I regard the last point as essential. To say that God is trinitarian means, in fact, to confess that he is self-transcendence, "unselfishness", and, consequently, that he can be known only in what reflects his own nature. From this there follows an important catechetical conclusion: the being-led to a religious experience, which must start in the place where man finds himself, can yield no fruit if it is not, from the beginning, directed to the acquisition of a readiness for renunciation. The moral training that, in a certain sense, belongs to the natural sciences, as does the asceticism of transcendence, becomes more radical here because of the meeting of the two freedoms. In any event, it is inseparable from training in the acquisition of religious knowledge. From this perspective, we can understand why the Fathers of the Church regarded the basic formulation of religious knowledge as such this teaching from the Sermon on the Mount: "Happy are the pure in heart: they shall see God" (Mt 5:8). Here it is a question of "seeing". The possibility of "seeing" God, that is, of knowing him at all, depends on one's purity of heart, which means a comprehensive process in which man becomes transparent, in which he does not remain locked in upon himself, in which he learns to give himself and, in doing so, becomes able to see. From the perspective of Christian faith, we might say that religious experience in its most exalted Christian form bears the mark of the Cross. It embraces the basic model of human existence, the transcendence of self. The Cross redeems, it enables us to see. And now we discover that the structure of which we are speaking is not just structure; it reveals content as well.

4. Christian experience

After this general analysis of experience, I propose, by way of conclusion, to present a fourth thesis about the specific nature of Christian experience. Christian experience begins in the ordinary course of communal

---

[31] Hans Urs von Balthasar, "Gotteserfahrung biblisch und patristisch", in IKZ 5 (1976): 497–509; quotation is on 500.

[32] Ibid., 508.

experience, but it relies, for its future course, on the extent and richness of the experiences already accumulated throughout history by the world of faith. We are made capable of this transcendence of the place where we find ourselves and of the things we would ask of our own accord because we see before us the transcendence that has already occurred in the world of faith, which, as it were, lets itself be contemplated there and invites our participation. Doubtless, this contact with already existing Christian experience was more obvious to man in the past than it is today; man lived then in a world that bore the stamp of faith. Today, the Church as a place of accumulated experience is for many an alien world. Nevertheless, this world continues to be a possibility, and it will be the task of religious education to open the door to this place of experience that is the Church and thus to encourage participation in the experience she has to offer. We might say, in fact, that the Church as a place of experience is, in a threefold way, the source of new personal experience:

a. The communal life of faith and liturgical worship in the Church offers what might be called experiential support ("experiential", that is, in Mouroux's sense of the term). In mutual faith, in praying, celebrating, rejoicing, suffering and living together, the Church becomes a "community" and thus a genuine living space for man where faith can be experienced as a force that sustains him both in his daily routine and in the crises of his existence. This explains the value of forming specific communities, substructures of various kinds, in which that becomes possible which can no longer be offered in the larger framework of the parish: the experience of a community grounded in faith through which the Church becomes the place of concrete revelation, the place of "spirit and life".

b. One who truly believes, who lets himself be matured by faith, begins to become a light for others; he becomes a source of support to whom others can turn for help. It is quite normal in the early stages of faith for one for whom the logic of faith is not yet wholly apparent to say to himself: this or that person is better informed and has more experience than I; if he believes, then there must be something in this faith, and I shall believe as he does. It is at first, as it were, a kind of borrowed faith in which one does not yet comprehend the content of what one believes but has confidence in a convincing living embodiment of it and thus opens the way to one's own growth. It is at first a secondhand faith that is, at the same time, an access to faith "at firsthand", to a personal encounter with the Lord. For all that, we shall always experience faith to some extent at "second hand", for it is our human portion to need one another even where there is question of ultimate realities.

c. A higher form of this daily phenomenon that is one of the essential functions of the Church may be found in the person of the saint. The saints, as the living personifications of a faith actually experienced and tested, of a transcendence actually experienced and confirmed, are themselves, we might say, places into which one can enter, in which faith as experience has been, as it were, stored, anthropologically seasoned and brought near to our own lives. In the last analysis, it is by the gradually ripening and deepening participation in these experiences that there grows in us that experience that is specifically Christian in the most integral sense of the word—which is called in the Psalms and in the New Testament "the tasting of God" (Ps 34:8; 1 Pet 2:3; Heb 6:4). Here one rests in reality itself; one no longer believes "at secondhand". Certainly, we must say with Bernard of Clairvaux and the great mystical teachers of all times that such an experience can be but a "brief moment, a rare *experimentum*".[33] In this life, it can be no more than an initial foretaste[34] that must not become an end in itself. For, if it did, faith would become self-satisfaction instead of self-transcendence and would thus betray its own nature. Such moments are governed by the law that governed the experiences on Mt. Tabor: they are not places where we can linger but are intended to encourage and strengthen us to go out, with the word of Jesus Christ, into the routine of daily living and to know that the radiance of the divine nearness is always present wherever anyone goes in the strength of that word.

In summary, we can say that there are three kinds of *Christian* experience:

a. The experience of creation and history, which offers itself to man not only in the range of possibilities that are open to him for transcending the superficial but also as a road leading him to a meeting with the ground of being.

b. The experience of the Christian community and of Christian individuals, in which the ways of transcending creation and history are opened to man, that is, in which the first type of experience is made ready, intensified and cast in a Christian mold.

c. From a combination of types one and two, there develops, then, a very personal experience with God in Christ and, finally, the genuinely supernatural experience that we have just described.

For catechesis, it will normally be only the first two types that come into

---

[33] Scheffczyk, 151.

[34] Cf. the penetrating description of the anticipatory experience of the divine in S. *Aureli Augustini Confessionum Libri XIII*, esp. 7:10, 16 and 7:17, 23–21, 27; for the vision at Ostia, see 9:10, 23–26, in *Corpus scriptorum ecclesiasticorum latinorum* 33, ex recensione Pii Knöll (Vindobonae: Tempsky, 1896). Cf. also André Mandouze, "L'Extase d'Ostie", in *Augustinus Magister* 1 (Paris: Études Augustiniennes, 1954): 67–84; and Henrique de Noronha Galvao, *Die existentielle Gotteserkenntnis bei Augustinus. Eine hermeneutische Lektüre der Confessiones* (Einsiedeln: Johannes Verlag, 1981).

consideration. It is crucial that the forward-pressing dynamics of faith never be sacrificed to a circle of mere supply and demand that would enclose man in the status quo instead of freeing him and leading him into the open.

Appendix. A biblical example

In a brief appendix, I should like, now, to exemplify what has been said by means of a biblical text—the account of Jesus' meeting with the Samaritan woman at Jacob's well (Jn 4).

This pericope seems to me to be a beautiful and concrete illustration of what we have just been saying. It opens with the meeting of Jesus and the Samaritan woman in the context of a normal, human, everyday experience—the experience of thirst, which is surely one of man's most primordial experiences. In the course of the conversation, the subject shifts to that thirst that is a thirst for life, and the point is made that one must drink again and again, must come again and again to the source. In this way, the woman is made aware of what in actuality she, like every human being, has always known but to which she has not always adverted: that she thirsts for life itself and that all the assuaging that she seeks and finds cannot slake this living, elemental thirst. The superficial "empirical" experience has been transcended.

But what has been revealed is still of this world. It is succeeded, therefore, by one of those conversations on two levels that are so characteristic of John's technique of recording dialogue, the Johannine "misunderstanding", as it is called by the exegetes. From the fact that Jesus and the Samaritan woman, though they use the same words, have in mind two very different levels of meaning and, separated thus by the ambiguity of human speech, are speaking at cross-purposes, there is manifested the lasting incommensurability of faith and human experience however extensive that experience may be. For the woman understands by "water" that of which the fairy tales speak: the elixir of life by virtue of which man will not die and his thirst for life will be entirely satisfied. She remains in the sphere of *bios,* of the empirical life that is familiar to her, whereas Jesus wants to reveal to her the true life, the *zoe.*

In the next stage, the woman's full attention has been attracted to the subject of a thirst for life. She no longer asks for *something,* for water or for any other single thing, but for life, for herself. This explains the apparently totally unmotivated interpolation by Jesus: "Go and call your husband!" (Jn 4:16). It is both intentional and necessary, for her life as a whole, with all its thirst, is the true subject here. As a result, there comes to light the real dilemma, the deep-seated waywardness, of her existence: she is brought face to face with herself. In general, we can reduce what is happening to the formula: one must know oneself as one really is if one is to know God. The real medium, the primordial experience of all experiences, is that man himself is the place in which and through which he experiences God. Admittedly, the circle could also be closed in the opposite direction: it could be said that it is only by first knowing God that one can properly know oneself.

But we anticipate. As we have said, the woman must come first to the knowledge of herself, to the *acknowledgment* of herself. For what she makes now is a kind of confession: a confession in which, at last, she reveals herself unsparingly. Thus a new transition has occurred—to preserve our earlier terminology, a transition from empirical and experimental to "experiential" experience, to "existential experience". The woman stands face to face with herself. It is no longer a question now of *something* but of the depths of the *I* itself and, consequently, of the radical poverty that *is* man's I-myself, the place where this *I* is ultimately revealed behind the superficiality of the *something*. From this perspective, we might regard the conversation between Jesus and the Samaritan woman as the prototype of catechesis. It must lead from the *something* to the *I*. Beyond every *something* it must ensure the involvement of man himself, of *this* particular man. It must produce self-knowledge, and self-acknowledgment so that the indigence and need of man's being will be evident.

But let us return to the biblical text! The Samaritan woman has achieved this radical confrontation with her own self. In the moment in which this occurs, the question of all questions arises always and of necessity: the question about oneself becomes a question about God. It is only apparently without motivation but in reality inevitable that the woman should ask now: How do things stand with regard to adoration, that is, with regard to God and my relationship to him? (cf. Jn 4:20). The question about foundation and goal makes itself heard. Only at this point does the offering of Jesus' true gift become possible. For the "gift of God" is God himself, God precisely as gift—that is, the Holy Spirit (cf. verses 10 and 24). At the beginning of the conversation, there seemed no likelihood that this woman, with her obviously superficial way of life, would have any interest in the Holy Spirit. But once she was led to the depths of her own being, the question arose that must always arise if one is to ask the question that burns in one's soul. Now the woman is aware of the real thirst by which she is driven. Hence she can at last learn what it is for which this thirst thirsts.

It is the purpose and meaning of all catechesis to lead to this thirst. For one who knows neither that there is a Holy Spirit nor that one can thirst for him, it cannot begin otherwise than with sensory perception. Catechesis must lead to self-knowledge, to the exposing of the *I*, so that it lets the masks fall and moves out of the realm of *something* into that of being. Its goal is *conversio*, that conversion of man that results in his standing face to face with himself. *Conversio* ("conversion", metanoia) is identical with self-knowledge, and self-knowledge is the nucleus of all knowledge. *Conversio* is the way in which man finds himself and thus knows the question of all questions: How can I worship God? It is the question that means his salvation; it is the *raison d'être* of catechesis.

C. The Gift of Wisdom

Like virtue and sin, for example, the word wisdom belongs to those words that have no precise connotation in modern linguistic usage. Words like these create a kind of antiquarian impression and easily come close to irony, to a supercilious mockery of what seems old-fashioned and out of date. One may boast, for instance, that one has advanced in age but has not grown "any the wiser". In other words, that one still has so much vitality that one does not have to become virtuous and that one still enjoys, as it were, the full vigor of unexhausted youth. Naturally, a general shift of values also takes place. What was once called wisdom may, perhaps, stir quietly in the conscience, but its admonitions are disdainfully silenced because such a way of thinking is considered a sign of weakness. Although it is in terms of the spirit that the universal should be conceived and the particular should be reincorporated into the whole, the élan vital, because it is the stronger, appropriates to itself the responsibility of the spirit.

Before pursuing these thoughts further, it is imperative that we ask: What, actually, is wisdom? And what do we mean when we call it a "gift of the Holy Spirit"? To begin with, the word wisdom has a long history behind it. It has appropriated to itself man's centuries-long struggle with and about himself, about the proper realization of what it means to be human, and thus it puts us, as it were, in contact with man's wrestling with his own identity. Its content cannot be understood, therefore, unless we have before us at least some broad outline of this historical struggle. In the Old Testament, as well as throughout the Near East and in the early Greek world, wisdom had, at first, the meaning of ability and skill. It designated the proficiency of the artisan who knew his craft; it meant, above all, competent judgment, sure eye, dexterity of the individual—his ability to say and do the right thing at the right time. In this early view, wisdom was the mark of a successful person. It was accepted that such wisdom, as an essentially spiritual quality, was of more value than mere physical strength, which, in the long run, did not establish the superiority of man.[35]

In this form, the concept represented a first step in the conquest of a shallow vaunting of physical strength; it referred now to man's real strength, which lies in the realm of the spiritual. But present success in life was still the determining factor. This concept of wisdom has existed for longer or shorter periods in all cultures as the question of success became increasingly clear. In the world of the Old Testament, a decisive step in the breakthrough to a new insight is recognizable in Isaiah 11:1-5, that is, in the prophetic text on which rests the Christian tradition of the seven gifts of the Holy Spirit.[36] The prophet had, at first, threatened the corrupt Davidic kingdom with the judgment of God: God would strike the kingdom of David as a woodcutter strikes the trees with his axe. But, after the fall of this king who thinks now only of power and success, the prophet sees coming a ruler who is sent by God himself. Of him, who will spring like a shoot from the root of Jesse, it is said that the Spirit of God rests upon him: the spirit of wisdom and of understanding, the spirit of counsel and of fortitude, the spirit of knowledge and of the fear of the Lord. Thus wisdom is, here, one of the words used by the prophet to describe the difference between human spirituality and the nature of the Spirit of God, which, as the common denominator that is named before all six or seven gifts, must be understood to apply to each of them.

What is distinctive about the new king is that he does not act just in his own interest or in his own name, as do the absolute monarchs of all times. He does not act for himself or for his own success but aligns himself with God's way of thinking. Action that is properly and truly royal arises from the fact that man is, first of all, one who receives, who lets himself be drawn into God's way of thinking, to which he has submitted his own will.

We discover what this means, how it can be put into practice, when we examine the context in which this text occurs. The king's wisdom will be seen in the fact that he protects the rights of the poor and the needy. His wisdom is integrity, which makes right powerful even when—especially when—it has no visible power.[37] But it is evidenced just as surely by the fact that he punishes the evildoer and avenges injustice with severity.[38]

---

[35] Cf. V. Hamp, "Weisheit I", in Heinrich Fries, ed., *Handbuch theologischer Grundbegriffe* 2 (Munich: Kösel, 1963), 800–805, esp. 800–801.

[36] On what follows, cf. Otto Kaiser, *Der Prophet Jesaja, Kapitel 1–12* (Göttingen: Vandenhoeck and Ruprecht, 1963), 125–28.

[37] Ibid., 127.

[38] Ibid., 128.

Here, too, wisdom reveals itself as the ability to judge correctly, but it is understood in a more radical sense: it is a sharing in God's ability to see and judge things as they really are. God reveals himself as God by his just judgments; as God, he sees things without disguise, as they really are, and deals with each according to his truth. Wisdom is a sharing in God's way of seeing reality. But there are, obviously, certain preconditions to this knowing from God's perspective. We cannot possess it unless we are united with God. This, in turn, means that this last and deepest mode of knowledge is not just an intellectual experience. In all that is essential, knowledge and life are inseparable. If something of the incorruptibility of God himself belongs to this deepest kind of knowledge, then there belongs to it also that purity of the "I" without which man is not incorruptible. From this, the meaning of the concepts "gifts of God" and "sharing in God's way of thinking" also becomes clear. Only if we let ourselves be cleansed of the corruptibility of the "I" and come thus gradually to live by God, to be united with God, do we come to a true inner freedom of judgment, to a fearless independence of thinking and deciding, that no longer cares about the approval or disapproval of others but clings only to truth. Such a purification is always a process of opening oneself and, at the same time, of receiving oneself. It cannot take place without the suffering of the vine that is pruned. But it makes possible the only form of power that leads, not to slavery, but to freedom. Incidentally, it is possible, from this perspective, to understand also why very simple persons are often so wise and able to judge so correctly in matters that are essential and why, on the other hand, there is often observable in intellectuals such an incredible blindness.

With these reflections, we are already well into what is essential. But we must return once more to the historical aspects. The kings who reigned in the years after Isaiah's prophecy did not fulfill the expectation that the prophet's words had aroused. In the long line of kings that brought the Davidic dynasty to an end, there was not one who conformed to this expectation. Thus the words of the prophet remained empty, as it were, like a garment that had not yet found its wearer. Christians recognized in Jesus of Nazareth the humble shoot that had sprung from the ancient lineage of Jesse. In him they saw the son of David in whom the spirit of wisdom moved unhindered. Thus wisdom and the Cross entered into that close relationship that Paul would later make the focus of his preaching. The notion of success had, to all intents and purposes, been transformed into its opposite. He who was truly wise ended his life on the Cross; those who would measure him against the standards of success would put him aside, as they do even today, as lacking all intelligence and wisdom. But he appears to faith as that integrity that accepts even the Cross, as the triumph of the truly human through the triumph of God over merely human self-sufficiency.[39] It is through reflections such as these that Isaiah 11 has become a fundamental text of Christology and, at the same time, the central text from which the doctrine of the Holy Spirit has been developed. Even today, these words of the prophet are retained in the ritual for confirmation, the Christian sacrament of the spirit. In this way, they define not just Christ and the Spirit but also the ideal of Christian living. It follows, therefore, that wisdom presumes, above all, a Christian community. It can make its appearance only when an individual walks with Jesus and thus gradually learns to see as he sees. At the same time, we come to see more clearly the close relationship that exists between the doctrine about Christ and the doctrine about the Holy Spirit. Christ is what he is precisely because the Holy Spirit dwells within him. Conversely, we can know what the Holy Spirit is by contemplating the attributes of Jesus Christ. The concept of the seven gifts is preserved in the book of Revelation in the reference to the seven spirits before the throne of God and in the concept of the seven lamps. In ancient number-symbolism, the number seven, like the number three, was considered a reinforcement of the number one: it was a way of expressing the—for us incomprehensible—multiplicity of oneness. In this context, it tells us that, unlike the Father and the Son, the Holy Spirit, in particular, can never be comprehended in a single form. His special property is revealed precisely in this multiplicity of forms; we learn to know who he is by contemplating at one time all the royal attributes of wisdom, understanding, counsel, fortitude, and the rest, and thinking of them in the interlacement of their mutual relationships.

In what has been said, we have indicated the biblical root of the concept of the gift of wisdom. But the Church received her definitive form in the transition from Jewish to pagan—that is, to Graeco-Roman—culture, hence we must now cast a glance at the intellectual current that flowed into Christianity from this source. Even among the Greeks, wisdom was at first, as we have seen, identified with efficiency in this life; here, too, arose, as in Israel and from the same inner necessity, a crisis in the way of thinking about success and a search for something deeper. The mysteriously great figures who are known in the history of philosophy as the pre-Socratics plumbed the depths in their search for the "invisible harmony"[40] that was stronger than the visible harmony. It was Heraclitus,

[39] Cf. Ulrich Wilckens, *Weisheit und Torheit. Eine exegetisch-religionsgeschichtliche Untersuchung zu 1 Kor 1 und 2* (Tübingen: Mohr, 1959); R. Baumann, *Mitte und Norm des Christlichen. Eine Auslegung von 1 Kor 1, 1–3, 4* (Münster: Aschendorff, 1968).

[40] Fragment 54, in Hermann Diels, *Die Fragmente der Vorsokratiker* 1 (Berlin: Weidmann, 1956): 162; cf. Johannes Baptist Metz, "Weisheit II", in Fries, 805–13; quotation is on 807.

with whom the expression originated, who undertook to awaken and point the way to the many who "act and talk as though they are asleep".[41]

It was only with Plato, however, that the Greek concept of wisdom acquired the form in which it has left its mark on history. This man saw himself embroiled in a crisis of the Greek state that was all the more radical because it included also a crisis of the soul, a crisis of humanity itself, which, in many respects, resembled that deep inner restlessness that today affects our whole existence to its very core.[42] For that reason, it is still meaningful today—and, precisely today, again meaningful—to listen to this unique thinker who, it is true, was not in the end able to stave off the crisis but who, nevertheless, was the first to formulate those insights that, in union with Christianity, were able to shape a new world. Like his teacher Socrates before him, Plato encountered a radical enlightenment, the keen rationality of which had led to the conviction that, strictly speaking, truth as such is in no way accessible to man. Whenever such a rejection of truth occurs, humanity experiences an extreme crisis because conscience becomes meaningless and the only standard that endures in the end is naked power. Such situations occur whenever a sophisticated form of technical knowledge becomes the standard of knowledge as such. Granted, with regard to the ultimate questions of who God is or what good is, we can never achieve the degree of certainty we can achieve in the realm of mathematics and technology. But when all knowledge that does not take the form of technical knowledge is declared to be nonknowledge, then we are cut off from the truth. We cannot, for instance, decide whether what Jesus said is true but can only dispute whether or not he said it. But that is ultimately an idle question. Our defenselessness before the spiritual demands of dictators and our own inner strife are due to the situation in which we find ourselves today: wisdom—that is, knowledge of truth itself—cannot become scientific in the real sense of the word; but if only scientific knowledge counts as knowledge, it seems to be an unenlightened naiveté even to speak about truth. But if that is the case, then there are no universal values that are binding on all of us. And if that is the case, then there is no law except that which is called law at any given moment—the order imposed by those who have put themselves in power. There is then no qualitative difference between the power exercised in the name of the law and that exercised by him who breaks the law; the concept of a constitutional state becomes empty. That is our situation. It was also the

[41] Fragment 73, in Diels, 167.

[42] Cf. Josef Pieper, "Missbrauch der Sprache—Missbrauch der Macht", in *Über die Schwierigkeit heute zu glauben* (Munich: Kösel, 1974), 255–82; idem, *Kümmert euch nicht um Sokrates* (Munich, 1966).

situation created by the "enlightened" Sophists of Plato's Greece. We might describe it in these words: by its exactness, exact knowledge bars the way to wisdom, which asks about the most profound depths of our existence.

Plato accepted the scepticism of the enlightenment, which considered man incapable of truth, only to the extent of saying that truth, in its proper meaning, is an attribute of God alone. But because, despite the prevailing scepticism, he judged man capable of receiving God, he judged him also to be open to truth. According to Plato, man cannot, it is true, actually possess truth, but he can love it and search for it. In Greek, that means: he can be a philosopher.[43] It is there that the limitation and the greatness of man lie: he is not wise, but he is in loving search of wisdom. In this way, Plato gave the word "philosophy" the noble content that enabled it to become likewise the goal of all those who thought and lived as Christians throughout the ages. As a philosopher, man's place, according to Plato, is between wisdom and the absence of truth. But the content of wisdom is being itself, or even more—the Good and the Beautiful that are beyond being. For man, then, philosophy is a great reaching out for eternal Being, a learning to contemplate truth, a rational effort of the Spirit to find true meaning.[44] Its strength is Eros, that openness of man that compels him to transcend again and again the limits of the merely knowable and to move toward the eternal.

It is not difficult, I think, to discover here, despite all the differences of language and living conditions, a close relationship to the spiritual movement of the Old Testament. Unlike knowledge, wisdom reveals itself as man's constant openness to the whole. It is identical with man's pilgrim character; for it is precisely that unrest that makes him always a pilgrim en route to the eternal and that prevents him from being satisfied with anything less. From science it will learn sobriety, exactitude, methodical carefulness, but it will also be critical of science; it will criticize the self-satisfaction of science, will disclose its limitations and uncertainties and will firmly oppose to it the logic of the eternal, of the divine. Admittedly, it cannot develop its full potential in the realm of the merely intellectual, for where Eros is not directed to what is eternal, it cannot produce the knowledge that is proper to it. Without experience, there is no understanding: that is true also in the human sphere. Only experience of God can yield knowledge of God. The wisdom that teaches us this is not, therefore, arational or even antirational; rather, it establishes the unity of man. Where rationality is limited to the exact sciences, everything that

---

[43] Ulrich Wilckens, σοφία, in ThWNT 7:407–8.

[44] For an excellent summary of Platonic teachings, see Ulrich Wilckens, "Definitiones", 414b, in ThWNT 7:471.

cannot be so designated is consigned to irrationality—and that means man
in particular. There evolves, then, above all in a totally rationalized world,
a frightening dictatorship of uncontrolled irrationality. But where knowledge and love are united in an Eros ordered to the eternal, there the sobriety of the rational illumines love; there the rational receives fecundity and
warmth from the depths of the Spirit in whom truth and love are one.

Once again, a historical question has led directly to a discussion of the
subject itself. In conclusion, we must make a third excursion into the
realms of history in order to come to as complete an understanding as
possible of the meaning of the word wisdom. Summarizing what we have
said thus far, we can now pose the question: How are the biblical heritage
and the Christian heritage fused in the history of Christianity? To what
conclusions has this fusion led? In view of the wealth of Christian tradition
amassed over the last two thousand years, this problem cannot be reviewed in a few pages. We shall do no more here than offer several comments chosen at random.

Our starting point can be the fact that in Rabbinic Judaism, in other
words, more or less in the time of Jesus, there was a unique narrowing of
the concept of wisdom that had as its effect to make the whole very
practical, very realistic. The following maxim of Rabbi Hillel has been
handed down to us: ". . . the more Torah, the more life; the more school,
the more wisdom; the more counsel, the more insight; the more
beneficence, the more peace."[45] It is presumed here that in the Torah, that
is, in the law of the Old Testament, wisdom has taken the form of the
word. Wisdom is, therefore, identical with the knowledge and practice of
the Torah. "The 'wise man' is the finished and recognized Torah scholar,
the ordained Rabbi."[46] In this last sentence there is a careful narrowing of
perspective: the Torah is ordered, not to knowing, but to doing. Thus it is
not the recognized Torah expert who is considered wise but he in whom
knowing and doing have become one. The transformation of these
beginnings into Christian concepts readily suggested itself because, in a
very ancient tradition, the so-called "Logia", words of wisdom had
already been put into Jesus' mouth by the notion that he was the wisdom
of God speaking among men.[47] The way was prepared for this per-
sonalizing of wisdom in the Person of Jesus by the fact that in the later
books of the Old Testament, in imitation of Egyptian models, the wisdom
of God is depicted as a self-subsistent person.[48] What must have seemed, in

[45] Ibid., 505.
[46] Ibid., 505–6.
[47] Ibid., 516.
[48] G. Fohrer, σοφία, in ThWNT 7:490ff.; Gerhard von Rad, *Weisheit in Israel* (Neukirchen-
Vluyn: Neukirchener Verlag, 1970), esp. 189–228.

the Old Testament, to be but a fanciful figure of speech gains unexpected and profound reality in the context of the Person who is Jesus. The wisdom of God is a Person and, therefore, is God. In the man Jesus, we encounter, in person, the pure and undiminished wisdom of God. If this is so, then it is not just the complicated way of philosophical reason that Plato developed in his disputes with the Sophists that leads to wisdom. No; wisdom loses here its eliteness and becomes quite simple. For the faith that binds me to Jesus is the wisdom that is open to all and even more especially to the simple. The rabbinical concept of the Torah as wisdom that has become word is adopted here and, by its union with the Person of Jesus Christ, freed of all national or pedantic limitations: whoever believes in Jesus has, as it were, entered into the thinking and judging of wisdom; he no longer acts in the superficial twilight-zone of the moment, like one who is asleep, but has awakened and lives from the depths of this wisdom, however simple his life may otherwise be.

For Augustine, this was the crucial discovery of his life. The philosophy of Plato was elite and, in the last analysis, hypothetical even in its loftiest pronouncements; faith in him who had become man opened the royal way of the philosopher to all men and made it a real way.[49] In the same vein, Bonaventure, on seeing an elderly woman of deep faith, once exclaimed to his astonished brethren that this woman actually possessed more wisdom than the greatest scholars. He thus repeated in his own way the experience of Augustine, who, in the last months of his struggle against accepting Christianity, discovered to his deep amazement that his mother, that simple and unlearned woman, had reached the pinnacle of philosophy by virtue of her discernment and the simplicity of a life rooted within.[50] Thomas Aquinas' comment that love becomes the eye by which man sees belongs also in this context.[51]

Although the concepts of faith and wisdom are thus closely intertwined, they are not completely equated. Faith is the door to wisdom and can, in a broad sense, be designated as wisdom; but there are, as one would expect, stages in the development of one's familiarity with faith and one's insight into its truth. That is why wisdom, in the narrower sense, can be called a gift of faith; that is why there is also both a wisdom that is non-Christian and a Christian wisdom that is different from ordinary faith. What, then, is distinctive about wisdom from the Christian standpoint? In the course of

[49] Cf. Joseph Ratzinger, *Volk und Haus Gottes*, 1–12.

[50] *De ordine* I, 11, 32 PL 32:994. On Bonaventure, see Gilson, *Die Philosophie des heiligen Bonaventura*, 105–36.

[51] St. Thomas Aquinas, *Opera omnia* (Parma: Typis Petri Fiaccadori, 1857), "Commentum in Quatuor Libros Sententiarum Magistri Petri Lombardi", vol. 2, col. 404, III Sent, dist. 35 q 1 a 2; cf. Johannes Baptist Metz, in Fries, 809.

history, there have been many attempts to answer this question, but I shall mention here only one of them. Augustine attempted, from a New Testament perspective, to shed more light on the Old Testament concept of the gifts of the Spirit, which had meanwhile been associated with the Person of Jesus Christ, the true king of the house of David, by linking it with the eight beatitudes, which, incidentally, numbered only seven in this arrangement. He saw an inner correspondence between the beatitudes of Jesus and the gifts of the Spirit; they are mutually illuminating and, in their interrelationship, make the life of the Holy Spirit more clearly comprehensible in its effects and forms. Even if we cannot today regard this correspondence as a scientifically acceptable interpretation of the Bible, the basic concept is, nonetheless, right: the spiritual life has an inner unity, and the words of the Lord can ultimately project no other design of existence than that contained in the description of the inner fullness conferred by the Holy Spirit. The correspondence discovered by Augustine shed light, first of all, on his own understanding of the unity and plurality of Christian life. But, as the fruit of a preoccupation with the words of the Bible that manifested itself not only in his thought but also in his life, love and suffering, they are also lasting reflections of spiritual reality. Which of the eight beatitudes did Augustine select as the counterpart of the gift of wisdom? For him, it was the words: "Happy are the peacemakers; they shall be called sons of God" (Mt 5:9).[52] At first glance, it may seem surprising that wisdom is not linked to the vision of God, to the promise that the pure of heart shall see God. Instead, it is very practical in its orientation, very earthbound: the work of wisdom is peace. But it is precisely because wisdom is a penetrating of the depths, an entering into God's own perspective, into his Spirit, that it is not something merely private and interior but a sharing in the work of the Messiah: My peace I give you. Wholly in the spirit of Augustine, Thomas Aquinas accounted for this fact by saying that only the integrity of the wise can comprehend the true order of things and so give to each its due: in the last analysis, peace can be generated only by actions appropriate to it, and this presumes a prior purification of the heart—which is the wisdom that is, as we learned from Isaiah, a sharing in God's way of looking at things and people.[53]

This closes the circle of our reflections. The longing for wisdom found its most profound expression in Israel and Greece at a time of unbridled

---

[52] Augustinus, *De sermone Domini in monte* I, 1, c 4, PL 34:1235. For Augustine's teaching about wisdom, see esp. *De Trinitate* XIII, 19, 24 in *Oeuvres de St. Augustin* 16 (Paris: Desclée de Brouwer, 1955): 332–36. Cf. Gottlieb Söhngen, "Wissenschaft und Weisheit im augustinischen Gedankengefüge", in *Die Einheit in der Theologie* (Munich: Zink, 1952), 101–6.

[53] ST II-II q 45 a 6.

domination that destroyed peace and made human coexistence impossible. It is precisely the practical, the ordinary, conduct of daily life that calls for what is most profound, for a seeing and acting from God's perspective. That is why peace is a messianic gift that can be given ultimately only by him who bears God's spirit in all its fullness. That is why wisdom is not the private luxury of a few pampered spirits but the messianic gift for which man must always struggle and pray so that at least some of that peace that will come at the end of time may be realized in this world and man's life can be made truly livable. That is what is meant when the Church beseeches God to grant, among the seven gifts of the Holy Spirit, the gift of wisdom.

EPILOGUE

ON THE STATUS OF CHURCH
AND THEOLOGY TODAY

A. Review of the Postconciliar Era—Failures, Tasks, Hopes

In 1975, when I was asked by many persons to prepare a review of the ten years that have passed since Vatican Council II, my thoughts went back, first of all, to the days when the Council began. On October 10, 1962, that is, on the eve of the first session, Cardinal Frings had invited me to describe for the German-speaking bishops the theological problems they would be called to work upon during the Council. In searching for a suitable introduction, I came across a text by Eusebius of Caesarea, who, in the year 325, had participated in the first ecumenical council in the history of the Church—the Council of Nicaea—and had formulated his impressions of this ecclesial assembly in the following words: "The foremost servants of God had assembled from all the churches in the whole of Europe, Africa and Asia. And the *one* Church, become, as it were, worldwide by God's grace, embraced Syrians, Cilicians, Phoenicians, Arabs and Palestinians as well as Egyptians, Thebans, Africans and Mesopotamians. There was even a Persian bishop at the synod. Not even the Scythians were missing. Pontus and Galatia, Cappadocia and Asia, Phrygia and Pamphilia sent their best representatives. Thracians and Macedonians, Achaeans and Epirotes came, too—and persons from even further away. . . . Even a well-known Spaniard was among the numerous participants in the assembly."[1] In these enthusiastic words we hear an echo of the description of the feast of Pentecost given by St. Luke in the Acts of the Apostles; there can be no doubt, therefore, about the theological statement that Eusebius intended by his report: Nicaea was a new Pentecost, the true fulfillment of the Pentecostal sign, for now the Church was actually speaking in all languages and confessing in them the one faith, thus proving herself the Church of the Holy Spirit.

The Council is a Pentecost—that was a thought that corresponded to our own experiences at that time; not only because Pope John had formulated it as a wish, as a prayer, but because it reflected what we experienced on our arrival in the city of the Council: meetings with bishops of all countries, all tongues, far beyond what Luke or Eusebius could have imagined and, thus, a lived experience of real Catholicity with its Pentecostal hope—that was the promising *signum* of those first days of Vatican II.

That is the way it was then. But such a "triumphalist" text is no longer thinkable as an introduction to my present remarks. I happened, however,

---

[1] Über das Leben Constantius" III, 7, in *Eusebius Werke* I, ed. Ivar A. Heikel (Leipzig: J. Hinrich'sche Buchhandlung, 1902), 80; quoted here from H. Dallmayr, *Die grossen vier Konzilien* (Munich, 1961), 33–34.

to see a text written some fifty years later by another Father of the Church that reflects the change of perspective that we also have experienced. The author is Gregory of Nazianzus, one of the great inheritors of Nicaea and himself a participant in the Council of Constantinople in 381, which added to the Nicaean formula the explicit statement of the divinity of the Holy Spirit. In 381, the deliberations had not yet come to an end when, through the official Procopius, the Emperor invited Gregory, an important bishop and theologian, to attend a kind of second session at Constantinople in the year 382. Gregory's answer was laconic—a refusal with the following explanation: "To tell the truth, I am convinced that every assembly of bishops is to be avoided, for I have never experienced a happy ending to any council; not even the abolition of abuses . . . , but only ambition or wrangling about what was taking place."[2] Martin Luther, who at first called urgently for a free general council, adopted this text in 1539 in his writing "On Councils and Churches", in which he expressed his later opinion about the advantages and disadvantages of councils. For this change from an earlier enthusiasm to a later scepticism with regard to councils, Luther had reasons of his own that a Catholic will certainly not share: he had realized that a Church council must confirm Church doctrine and that he could not look for approval from such a source because he had placed himself in opposition, not just to abuses, but even to Church doctrine itself. He fought, therefore, to establish the superiority of the secular court, which seemed to offer him a better chance of a favorable hearing.[3] But if we cannot, therefore, put too high a value on Luther's negative judgment in the meaning it had for him, the judgment of one of the great Fathers who helped to formulate ecclesial orthodoxy in the councils of the fourth century will still have its own value. Admittedly, it can be argued that, however great Gregory may have been as a theologian, as a person he was a hypochondriac and possessed of an oversensitive artistic nature.[4] It is all the more impressive, therefore, that the judgment of someone who, also as a person, was one of the most prominent figures of the century of the great councils, Gregory's friend Basil, was actually

[2] Gregory of Nazianzus, Epistle 130, "Ad Procopium", in Gregor von Nazianz, Briefe, in GCS 53, ed. Paul Gallay (Berlin: Akademie Verlag, 1969), 59f. On the historical classification of the text, see Gallay XXVIII. On the Councils of Constantinople in 381 and 382, the most important information is in Conciliorum Oecumenicorum Decreta, 21–35, which also provides a bibliography.

[3] Martin Luther, Von den Konziliis und Kirchen, WA 50: 509–653; quotation is on 604. For the place of this work in Luther's thinking, see the introduction on 488–509. Hans Küng called attention before the Council to this text from Gregory and its use by Luther: "Das theologische Verständnis des ökumenischen Konzils", in ThQu 141 (1961): 65.

[4] See A. Hamman, Die Kirchenväter (Herder, 1967), 104–13, for an excellent description of Gregory, in which the real greatness of this sensitive individual comes clearly to the fore.

even more sharp in his criticism. Basil speaks of the "shocking disorder and confusion" of the conciliar disputes, of the "incessant chatter" that filled the whole Church.[5]

From the kind of macroscopic view of history with which we can look back today on the happenings of that time, we must contest the views of both these bishops: it is precisely the councils of the fourth and fifth centuries that have become beacons for the Church, that point the way to the heart of Sacred Scripture and, by the stamp they have left on its interpretation, have, at the same time, assured the unity of faith in the passage of time. But if the judgment of history is, on the whole, a different one, if only the great accomplishments have proved lasting and, vice versa, only what has lasted has been proved great, their immediate contemporaries were, obviously, repeatedly exposed to the experiences described by these two witnesses of the century of great decisions. To the macroscopic view there is opposed, as it were, the microscopic one, the view from close by. And it cannot be denied that, from close by, nearly all councils have seemed to destroy equilibrium, to create crisis. The Council of Nicaea, which formulated the definitive statement of the divine Sonship of Jesus, was followed by a crushing dispute that brought about the first great heresy in the Church, that of Arianism, and, for a decade, rent the Church to her very core. The same thing happened after the Council of Chalcedon, which defined not only the true divinity but also the true humanity of Christ. The wound inflicted at that time is not closed even today: the loyal heirs of the great Bishop Cyril of Alexandria felt that they had been betrayed by formulas opposed to the tradition they held sacred. As Monophysite Christians, they form even today a significant minority in the East who, by the very fact of their existence, let us suspect something of the harshness of the disputes of that time. Closer to the present time, we have the memory of Vatican Council I, which caused the breakup of many departments of theology in Germany. The wounds did not heal for decades.

Thus the critical development that followed Vatican Council II is part of a long history; it is surprising only because, in the enthusiasm generated by the beginning of the Council, these historical experiences were largely forgotten; perhaps also because there was a feeling that everything had been done in a way that was different and better. It seemed safe to suppose that a council that refrained from dogmatization and excluded no one would also offend no one and would be repugnant to no one but would

[5] Basil, *De Spiritu Sancto* XXX, 76 C and 77 C, ed. Benoît Pruche in *Sources chrétiennes*, no. 17, 2d ed. (Paris: Éditions du Cerf, 1968), 522, 28f. and 524, 42f. German text: *Über den Heiligen Geist*, ed. M. Blum (Freiburg, 1967), 113 (65 b) and 115 (66 c). On the person of Basil, see Hamman, 94–103.

rather meet with the approval of everyone. Actually, it met with the same fate as the councils that had preceded it; no one can seriously deny the critical manifestations to which it led. Certainly, there are also unambiguously positive effects that must not be minimized. To mention only the more important theological results: the Council reinserted into the Church as a whole a doctrine of primacy that was dangerously isolated; it integrated into the one *mysterium* of the Body of Christ a too-isolated conception of the hierarchy; it restored to the ordered unity of the faith an isolated Mariology; it gave the biblical word its full due; it made the liturgy once more accessible; and, in addition, it made a courageous step forward toward the unity of all Christians. Perhaps, from a later macroscopic perspective, it will be only these results that will be counted, and there may, even now, be those who, as it were, live and judge from this macroperspective. But, for anyone who feels responsible for his own age, that which may, perhaps, at some future date be the decisive factor cannot be the only criterion; it is precisely the small happenings of daily life that he must face and with regard to which he must struggle to make the right decisions. From such a close view, in fact, there are weighty and very disturbing negative factors that cannot be denied—again, to name just a few: anyone who has not discovered it for himself can learn from the statisticians that our churches, our seminaries, our convents have become more and more empty during the past ten years; it does not require extensive proof to show that the climate in the Church is at times not just frigid but even acrimonious and aggressive; it is one of the daily experiences that threaten to destroy the joy of Christianity that all kinds of divisions are disrupting community. Anyone who says all this is quickly accused of pessimism and excluded from the discussion. But there is question here of empirical facts. To feel obliged to deny them is to betray not just pessimism but despair. No, to see facts is not pessimism; it is objectivity. Only when we face them can we ask what these facts mean, whence they come and how they are to be met. Two questions present themselves, therefore, for our further discussion: first, the question of the reasons for this development and, secondly, the question of how we are to respond to it.

1. *How did the postconciliar development arise?*

To explain what happened, I shall limit myself to just a few points. First, we must be aware that the postconciliar crisis in the Catholic Church coincided with a global spiritual crisis of humanity itself or, at least, of the Western world; not everything that distressed the Church in those years can be attributed to the Council. The human conscience bore the stamp not just of the voluntary decisions of the individual but also, to a large extent, of those external circumstances that were produced by economic or political factors. Jesus' comment that it is easier for a camel to go through the eye of a needle than for a rich man to enter heaven describes the situation in words that cannot be ignored. I offer just one example from our own history. The collapse of the old Europe during the First World War directly and fundamentally altered the spiritual landscape and, in particular, the panorama of theology. Liberalism, which had previously flourished as the product of a sated and self-assured world, suddenly became meaningless, although its great representatives were still living and teaching. Young people were attracted no longer to Harnack but to Karl Barth: a theology based on a strong faith in revelation, a theology that was quite intentionally ecclesial, was formed amid the troubles of a changed world. The return of the old prosperity in the sixties brought with it a similar change in thinking. The new wealth and the bad conscience that accompanied it fostered that remarkable mixture of liberalism and Marxist dogmatism that we have all experienced. We should not, therefore, exaggerate the part played by Vatican Council II in the most recent developments; Protestant Christianity underwent a similar crisis without any council, and political parties have also had to deal with a phenomenon of like origin.[6] Nevertheless, the Council was one of the factors that shared in the development of world history. When an institution as deeply rooted in souls as is the Catholic Church is shaken to its very roots, the earthquake extends to all mankind. What are, then, the critical factors that stemmed from the Council?

Involved here, I think, are two concepts that acquired increasing significance in the consciousness of the Council Fathers, the periti and those who reported on the Council. The Council understood itself as a great examination of conscience by the Catholic Church; it wanted ultimately to be an act of penance, of conversion. This is apparent in the confessions of guilt, in the intensity of the self-accusations that were not only directed to the more sensitive areas, such as the Reformation and the trial of Galileo, but were also heightened into the concept of a Church that was sinful in a general and fundamental way and that feared as triumphalism whatever might be interpreted as satisfaction with what she had become or what she still was. Linked with this excruciating plumbing of her own depths was an almost painful willingness to take seriously the whole arsenal of complaints against the Church, to omit none of them. That implied as well a careful effort not to incur new guilt with respect to

---

[6] I have attempted to present these relationships more clearly in my book *Dogma und Verkündigung* (Munich: Wewel, 1973), 439–447.

the other, to learn from him wherever possible and to seek and to see only
the good that was in him. Such a radical interpretation of the fundamental
biblical call for conversion and love of neighbor led not only to uncertainty
about the Church's own identity, which is always being questioned, but
especially to a deep rift in her relationship to her own history, which
seemed to be everywhere sullied. In consequence, a radically new beginning was considered a pressing obligation. The second point to which I
referred stems from this fact: something of the Kennedy era pervaded the
Council, something of the naive optimism of the concept of the great society. We can do everything we want to do if only we employ the right
means.[7] It was precisely the break in historical consciousness, the self-
tormenting rejection of the past, that produced the concept of a zero hour
in which everything would begin again and all those things that had formerly been done badly would now be done well. The dream of liberation,
the dream of something totally different, which, a little later, had an increasingly potent impact on the student revolts, was, in a certain sense,
also attributable to the Council; it was the Council that first urged man on
and then disappointed him, just as the public examination of conscience at
first enlightened and then alienated him.

For a psychologist, this mutation of the conciliar spirit would provide an
excellent example of the way in which exaggeration turns virtues into
their opposites. Penance is a necessity for both the individual and the
community. But Christian penance means, not self-rejection, but self-
discovery. The ancient Acts of the Saints emphasize the fact that no word
of complaint about creation ever crossed the lips of the Christian martyrs.[8]
In this, they differed from the Gnostics, who turned Christian penance
into a hatred of mankind, a hatred of their own lives, a hatred of reality.
The inner precondition for penance is precisely the affirmation of oneself,
of reality as such. Its contemporary antitype is to be found in statements
like that of the great painter Max Beckmann: "My religion is arrogance
before God, revolt against God. Revolt because he created us, because we
cannot love ourselves. In my paintings, I reproach God for everything he
has done badly."[9] Something very essential becomes evident here: radical
irreconcilability with oneself that rages against the self and is no longer
satisfied with creation either in oneself or in others is no longer penance; it
is arrogance. Wherever the fundamental Yes to being, to life, to oneself,
ceases to exist, penance disappears and turns into arrogance. For penance

[7] Cf. Hans Küng, *Christ sein* (Munich, 1974), 30ff.

[8] See Erik Peterson, *Theologische Traktate* (Munich: Kösel, 1951), 203 and 222; cf. also
Josef Pieper, *Zustimmung zur Welt. Eine Theorie des Festes*, 2d ed. (Munich: Kösel, 1964), 48.

[9] Quoted from P. Hübner, *Vom ersten Menschen wird erzählt* (Düsseldorf-Vienna, 1969),
between 156 and 157.

presumes that man is permitted to affirm himself. By its very nature, it is a penetration to the Yes in the hidden places of whatever obscures the Yes. That is why true penance leads to the gospel, that is, to joy—even to joy in oneself. The kind of self-accusation at which the Council arrived with respect to the Church's own history was not sufficiently aware of this fact and so expressed itself in ways that can only be called neurotic. It was both necessary and good for the Council to put an end to the false forms of the Church's glorification of self on earth and, by suppressing her compulsive tendency to defend her past history, to eliminate her false justification of self. But it is time now to reawaken our joy in the reality of an unbroken community of faith in Jesus Christ. We must rediscover that luminous trail that is the history of the saints and of the beautiful—a history in which the joy of the gospel has been irrefutably expressed throughout the centuries. Anyone who remembers only the Inquisition when he thinks of the Middle Ages should be asked where his eyes are. Could such cathedrals, such images of the eternal, full of light and quiet dignity, have been created if faith had been just an affliction for mankind? In a word, it must become clear again that penance requires, not the destruction of one's own identity, but the finding of it. Wherever a positive relationship to history once again becomes manifest, there that utopianism will come automatically to an end that believes that, hitherto, everything has been done badly and only now will begin to be done properly. In any event, the end of the Kennedy era showed us plainly enough the limits of the makable, and a part of that spiritual peacefulness that we seem to observe today is undoubtedly due to the fact that making and receiving, planning and reflecting, appear to have found again a better balance.

2. What should be done?

It is even more difficult to answer this second question than it was to answer the first one: what we are discussing here is the whole problem of contemporary pastoral ministry. In this connection, I propose to touch upon two points that seem important to me: first, I shall say a few words about the real role of councils; then, by way of conclusion, I should like, in terms of the two basic tendencies of Vatican Council II, to venture a comment on the proper reception of it.

a. Meaning and limits of councils

What significance does a council actually have in the Church? With this question, we return to the point from which we started our reflections.

Gregory of Nazianzus and Basil, both of whom spoke from experience, were right in saying that, with the coming together and the inevitable disagreements of many individuals, a council gives rise to unpleasant effects—ambition, strife and the wounds that accompany them. Sometimes, however, such secondary effects must be endured for the sake of removing longstanding evils, just as we take medicine, despite many side-effects, for the sake of combating a greater evil. From time to time, councils are a necessity, but they always point to an extraordinary situation in the Church and are not to be regarded as a model for her life in general or even as the ideal content of her existence. They are medicine, not nourishment. Medicine must be assimilated and its immunizing effect must be retained by the body, but, in general, it achieves its effect precisely by becoming superfluous, by continuing to be an extraordinary measure. In plain language: the council is an organ of consultation and decision. As such, it is not an end in itself but an instrument in the service of the life of the Church.[10]

The real content of Christianity is not the discussion of its Christian content and of ways of realizing it: the content of Christianity is the community of word, sacrament and love of neighbor to which justice and truth bear a fundamental relationship. The dream of making one's whole life a series of discussions, which, for a time, brought even our universities to the brink of paralysis, also exercised an influence on the Church under the label of the conciliar idea. If a council becomes the model of Christianity per se, then the constant discussion of Christian themes comes to be considered the content of Christianity itself; but precisely there lies the failure to recognize the true meaning of Christianity.

b. The question of the proper reception of Vatican Council II

An analysis of the later history of the "Constitution on the Church in the Modern World" led me, in 1975, to the conclusion that the reception of the Council has yet to begin.[11] But what kind of reception should it be? As I have indicated above, I shall attempt to exemplify it in terms of two basic tendencies of the Council; in the process, it may become clear, to some extent, that, while the Council formulated its pronouncements with the

[10] I have demonstrated this with multiple examples from the conciliar language and theology of the ancient Church in my book *Das neue Volk Gottes*, 147–70, esp. 151–63. (This section is unfortunately missing from the Taschenbuchausgabe of 1972.) As I have shown in terms of the sources, the opposing thesis of Hans Küng, *Strukturen der Kirche* (Freiburg: Herder, 1962), rests on philosophical errors that point the remaining interpretation in the wrong direction.

[11] Cf. Section B, below, in the present work.

fullness of power that resides in it, its historical significance will be determined by the process of clarification and elimination that takes place subsequently in the life of the Church. In this way, the whole Church participates in the Council; it does not come to an end in the assembly of bishops.

One of the key words of Vatican II was collegiality. Its immediate meaning was that the episcopal ministry is a ministry with others. It is not that a particular bishop succeeds a particular apostle, but rather that the college of bishops is the continuation of the college of apostles. Thus one is not alone as bishop but essentially with others. That is true also of the priest. One is not alone as a priest; to become a priest means to enter into the priestly community that is united to the bishop. Ultimately, a basic principle of Christianity itself is evident here: it is only in the community of all the brothers and sisters of Jesus Christ that one is a Christian, not otherwise. The Council tried to convert this basic principle into a practical reality by forming organizations by means of which the insertion of the individual into the whole became the basic rule of all ecclesial action. In place of the informal meetings of bishops that had taken place up to that time, for instance, a strictly juridical and carefully organized bureaucracy, the episcopal conference, was created. The synod of bishops, a kind of council with regular meetings, was created to express the solidarity of all episcopal conferences. The national synods met and declared their intention of developing into permanent organizations of the Church in their respective countries. Councils of priests and pastoral counselors were formed in the dioceses and community councils in the parishes. No one will deny that the basic concept was a good one and that community realization of the Church's mission is necessary. Nor will anyone deny that much good was accomplished as a result of these organizations. But neither will anyone doubt that their uncoordinated multiplication led to an excess of duplication, to a senseless mountain of paper work and to much wasted time during which the best efforts were consumed in endless discussions that no one wanted but that seemed inevitable in view of the new forms. The limitations of this paper-dominated Christianity and of the reform of the church by paper have meanwhile become clear. It has become obvious that collegiality is one thing but that personal responsibility and personal intuition are something quite different—that they cannot be replaced and may not be suppressed. Collegiality is one principle of what is genuinely Christian and ecclesial; personality is the other. It is one of the lessons of this decade that only a proper balance of the two can create freedom and fecundity.

Let us turn now to another basic concept of the Council: that of simplicity. "Simplicity" is one of the fundamental words in the "Constitution on the Sacred Liturgy", where it is always to be interpreted as a transparency and openness to human understanding. We must say, then, that a properly understood rationality is one of the main ideas of the Council. Today it is being said with increasing frequency that the Council thereby placed itself under the aegis of the European Enlightenment.[12] But the Council Fathers had a different motive for their orientation; they derived it from the theology of the Fathers of the Church, where St. Augustine, for example, strongly emphasized the difference between Christian simplicity and the empty pomp of pagan liturgies.[13] But we can also say that, after the largely unsuccessful attempts to achieve such an outcome in the disputes of the nineteenth century, an entrance was provided here for the spirit of the times. In this matter, too, we are better able now to assess gain and loss. In the course of history, new growth must be repeatedly pruned and attempts must be made to reach the simplicity that lies at the heart of things; for a missionary religion, the struggle for comprehensibility is indispensable. But we had more or less forgotten that man understands not only with his reason but also with his senses and his heart; and we are only now gradually beginning to learn that, in pruning, we must distinguish between the wheat and the cockle; that we must not take the embryo as our norm but must allow ourselves to be guided by the law of life.

With this, we have begun to address the process of reception by which the word is tested in life itself and, by tedious effort, is given a clarity of meaning that it cannot possess simply as word. This process of discernment is in full course with all the sufferings and pains of childbearing, in which it is always the human person who is involved. On the one hand, there are unquestionably signs of disintegration that we must not minimize. For some, it is an exclusive and, consequently, blind rationality that diminishes and pales the mystery; for others, it is political or social zeal that reduces faith to the role of a catalyst of revolutionary activity. I have no wish to impugn the noble impulses that are at work here. A Christian faith that takes seriously the Sermon on the Mount cannot be content to accept calmly as an economic necessity the differences that exist between rich and poor; it cannot, with a shrug of the shoulders, dismiss wars and oppression as the statistically inevitable byproducts of progress. But where faith is converted into an earthly messianism that justifies the senselessness of destruction and limits man's hope to what is makable, there we find also a betrayal of Christianity and a betrayal of mankind. On the other hand, we are witnesses today of a new integralism that may seem to sup-

---

[12] Cf., for example, Elmar Klinger, *Ekklesiologie der Neuzeit. Grundlegung bei Melchior Cano und Entwicklung bis zum Zweiten Vatikanische Konzil* (Freiburg: Herder, 1978), 241–54.

[13] Cf. the excellent presentation by F. van der Meer, *Augustinus der Seelsorger* (Cologne, 1951), 329–70, esp. 375–83 ("Der puritanische Zug").

port what is strictly Catholic but in reality corrupts it to the core. It produces a passion of suspicions, the animosity of which is far from the spirit of the gospel. There is an obsession with the letter that regards the liturgy of the Church as invalid and thus puts itself outside the Church. It is forgotten here that the validity of the liturgy depends primarily, not on specific words, but on the community of the Church; under the pretext of Catholicism, the very principle of Catholicism is denied, and, to a large extent, custom is substituted for truth. In an intermediate space that is full of uncertainty, but, at the same time, full of honest effort and full of hope, are to be found those movements in which are expressed the indestructible longing for what is genuinely religious, for the nearness of the Divine: the movements toward meditation and the pentecostal movements, both of which are laden with ambiguities and dangers, but both of which are also full of possibilities for good. Finally, there are a number of specifically ecclesial movements that promise new possibilities: Focolare, Cursillo, Communione e liberazione, catechumenate movements and new forms of communities. Here there is apparent a search for a center that will give the lie to the diagnosis that religion is dead and that will open ways of living a new life built on faith that will testify anew to the inexhaustible fruitfulness of the faith of the Church.

Let us attempt here a comprehensive summary. At the end of the Council, Karl Rahner offered the following comparison: huge amounts of pitchblende are needed to produce a small quantity of radium, which is the sole object of the process. In like manner, he said, the tremendous exertion of the Council was, in the last analysis, worthwhile because of the small increase of faith, hope and charity it produced. At the time, perhaps, we could not properly appreciate to its full extent the frightening gravity of this comparison. After all, there is a necessary relationship between radium and pitchblende. Where there is pitchblende, there is radium, even if the relative amounts are discouraging. But there is no such equation between the pitchblende of words and paper that was the Council and the living Christian reality. Whether or not the Council becomes a positive force in the history of the Church depends only indirectly on texts and organizations; the crucial question is whether there are individuals—saints—who, by their personal willingness, which cannot be forced, are ready to effect something new and living. The ultimate decision about the historical significance of Vatican Council II depends on whether or not there are individuals prepared to experience in themselves the drama of the separation of the wheat from the cockle and thus to give to the whole a singleness of meaning that it cannot gain from words alone. What we are thus far able to say is that the Council has, on the one hand, opened ways that lead from all kinds of byways and one-way streets to the real center of

Christianity. On the other hand, however, we must be self-critical enough to acknowledge that the naive optimism of the Council and the self-esteem of many of its supporters justify, in a disturbing way, the gloomy diagnoses of early churchmen about the danger of councils. Not every valid council in the history of the Church has been a fruitful one; in the last analysis, many of them have been just a waste of time.[14] Despite all the good to be found in the texts it produced, the last word about the historical value of Vatican Council II has yet to be spoken. If, in the end, it will be numbered among the highlights of Church history depends on those who will transform its words into the life of the Church.

B. Church and World: An Inquiry into the Reception of Vatican Council II

Of all the texts of Vatican Council II, the "Pastoral Constitution on the Church in the Modern World" (Gaudium et spes) was undoubtedly the most difficult and, with the "Constitution on the Sacred Liturgy" and the "Decree on Ecumenism", also the most successful. In its form and in the direction of its pronouncements, it is most closely related to the history of former councils and, more than any of the other texts, allows us to see the physiognomy of the last council. Since Vatican Council II, it has come, therefore, to be increasingly regarded as the true legacy in which, after three years of fermentation, the real intention of the Council seems to have been incorporated. The lack of clarity that persists even today about the real meaning of Vatican Council II is closely associated with such diagnoses and, consequently, with this document. Are we, then, to interpret the whole Council as a progressive movement that led step by step from a beginning that, in the "Dogmatic Constitution on the Church", was only just emerging from traditionalism to the "Pastoral Constitution" and its complementary texts on religious liberty and openness to other world religions—an interpretation that makes these texts, too, become signposts pointing to an extended evolution that will permit no dallying but requires a tenacious pursuit of the direction the Council has finally discovered? Or are we to regard the Council texts as a whole in which the documents of the last phase, which are directed to the Church's relationships ad extra, are, nevertheless, oriented toward the true center of faith that is expressed in the dogmatic constitutions on the Church and on divine revelation? Are

[14] In this connection, reference is repeatedly made, and with justification, to the Fifth Lateran Council, which met from 1512 to 1517 without doing anything effective to prevent the crisis that was developing.

we to read the dogmatic constitutions as the guiding principle of the pastoral constitution, or have even the dogmatic pronouncements been turned in a new direction?

I. *Diagnosis of the text and its tendencies*

Such considerations introduce us directly to the history of the effect of the Council and of the text we are discussing. Before attempting to shed further light on the subject, however, we must ask ourselves again what exactly was the new and special character of the "Pastoral Constitution". Obviously, it will be impossible to sketch here in a few strokes the content of this document, which is, in fact, a kind of *summa* of Christian anthropology and of the central problems of the Christian ethos. Despite its many shortcomings, the text has, on the whole, succeeded in so purifying and deepening the heritage of tradition that, with no curtailment in what is essential, it has new value precisely for the problems that face us today. But what was most effective was not its content, which was entirely in keeping with the tradition of the Church and exploited its latent possibilities; rather, it was the general intention—most apparent in the preface—of introducing a fundamental change. Consequently, I shall limit my remarks here to an analysis of the most characteristic features of this preface. Not, I repeat, as though I could in that way fully explain the text itself, but because, as we shall see, the history of its influence is not to be separated from the spirit of this preface and is, to a large extent, stamped with its ambiguity.

A first characteristic seems to me to reside in the concept of "world", which, despite many attempts to clarify it in section two of the document, continues to be used in a pretheological stage but which, in that very form, has exercised its special influence. By "world" the Council means the counterpart of the Church. The purpose of the text is to bring the two into a relationship of cooperation, the goal of which is the reconstruction of the "world". The Church cooperates with the world in order to build up the world—it is thus that we might characterize the vision that informs the text. It is not clear, however, whether the world that cooperates and the world that is to be built up are one and the same world; it is not clear what meaning is intended by the word "world" in every instance. In any event, we can be sure that the authors, who were aware that they spoke for the Church, acted on the assumption that they themselves were not the world but its counterpart and that they had up to then had a relationship to it that was, in fact, unsatisfactory where it existed at all. To that extent, we must admit, the text represents a kind of ghetto-mentality. The Church is understood as a closed entity, but she is striving to remedy the situation. By "world", it would seem, the document understands the whole scientific and technical reality of the present and all those who are responsible for it or who are at home in its mentality.

Linked to this striking concept of a contrast between two realms, in which "world" refers to all those forces that are responsible for the present, is a second fundamental characteristic of the text: the concept of dialogue as its basic formal classification. The Council, it states, "can find no more eloquent expression of its solidarity and respectful affection for the whole human family . . . than to enter into dialogue with it. . . ."[15] The relationship between Church and world is regarded, then, as a "colloquium", as a speaking-with-one-another and as a mutual search for solutions in which the Church brings to bear her own particular contributions and hopes that with the contributions of others progress will be made.

It is surely permissible to see as the motivation behind this formal conception the Council's strong sentiment with regard to the dangers and needs that confront mankind today. This concentration on current pragmatic, economic, political and social tasks is made abundantly clear by the designation of the "building up of human society" (cf. p. 1000) as the goal of the dialogue. Anyone whose ear is still attuned to the speeches made during the last session of the Council knows how eager the Fathers were, after two years of arguing theological questions, to do something for mankind that would be concrete, visible and tangible. The feeling that now, at last, the world had to be, and could be, changed, improved and humanized—this feeling had quite obviously taken hold of them in a way that was not to be resisted. After all the surprises that had emerged in the realm of theology proper, there reigned a feeling at once of euphoria and of frustration. Euphoria, because it seemed that nothing was impossible for this Council which had the strength to break with attitudes that had been deeply rooted for centuries; frustration, because all that had thus far been done did not count for mankind and only increased the longing for freedom, for openness, for what was totally different.

With this is revealed a third characteristic of the document we are considering. The text and, even more, the deliberations from which it evolved breathe an astonishing optimism. Nothing seems impossible if humanity and Church work together. The attitude of critical reserve toward the forces that have left their imprint on the modern world is to be replaced by a resolute coming to terms with their movement. The

---

[15] *Pastoral Constitution on the Church in the Modern World (Gaudium et spes)*, in *Vatican Council II, The Conciliar and Post Conciliar Documents*, Austin Flannery, O. P., gen. ed. (Northport, N. Y.: Costello, 1975), 904. Further references to *Gaudium et spes* will be given in the text. [Trans.]

affirmation of the present that was sounded in Pope John XXIII's address at the opening of the Council is carried to its logical conclusion; solidarity with today seems to be the pledge of a new tomorrow. The basic determining factor of the whole seems to me to lie in the relationship between goal and means. The Church cooperates with the world for the building up of society. She hopes in this way "to carry on the work of Christ" (p. 905): namely, "to bear witness to the truth" (ibid.), "to serve and not to be served" (ibid.; end of preface). The social commitment evidenced in this dialogue with the world is presented here as a task directly imposed by the gospel so that its truth can exert its full influence. This will be accomplished in two ways: on the one hand, this truth will be the element that makes the dialogue fruitful; on the other hand, it will be recognized by the efficacy of what is accomplished. Its relationship with social action is thus a unique one of tension between goal and means in which social activity is to be understood predominantly as concrete action.

If it is desirable to offer a diagnosis of the text as a whole, we might say that (in conjunction with the texts on religious liberty and world religions) it is a revision of the *Syllabus* of Pius IX, a kind of countersyllabus.[16] Harnack, as we know, interpreted the *Syllabus* of Pius IX as nothing less than a declaration of war against his generation.[17] This is correct insofar as the *Syllabus* established a line of demarcation against the determining forces of the nineteenth century: against the scientific and political world view of liberalism. In the struggle against modernism this twofold delimitation was ratified and strengthened. Since then many things have changed. The new ecclesiastical policy of Pius XI produced a certain openness toward a liberal understanding of the state. In a quiet but persistent struggle, exegesis and Church history adopted more and more the postulates of liberal science, and liberalism, too, was obliged to undergo many significant changes in the great political upheavals of the twentieth century. As a result, the one-sidedness of the position adopted by the Church under Pius IX and Pius X in response to the situation created by the new phase of history inaugurated by the French Revolution

[16] *Syllabus* was the designation given to the collection of eighty statements in which Pius IX took a critical stand with regard to the spiritual and political problems caused by secularization. The *Syllabus* was sent to the bishops in 1864 and led, especially in France, to sharp disagreements. Cf. Roger Aubert, "Syllabus", in LTK 9:1202–3. The position taken in the *Syllabus* was adopted and continued in Pius X's struggle against "Modernism". For a discussion of the whole development, see H. Jedin, ed., *Handbuch der Kirchengeschichte* 6:1 and 6:2: *Die Kirche in der Gegenwart* (Freiburg: Herder, 1971 and 1973).

[17] Adolf v. Harnack, *Lehrbuch der Dogmengeschichte* 3, 5th ed. (Tübingen: Mohr, 1923), 757, n. 1: "Prepared in advance (i.e., insofar as the Vatican was concerned) by the *Syllabus* . . . , which, along with much that was bad, condemned also, in its totality, the good spirit of the nineteenth century."

was, to a large extent, corrected *via facti,* especially in Central Europe, but there was still no basic statement of the relationship that should exist between the Church and the world that had come into existence after 1789. In fact, an attitude that was largely prerevolutionary continued to exist in countries with strong Catholic majorities. Hardly anyone today will deny that the Spanish and Italian Concordats strove to preserve too much of a view of the world that no longer corresponded to the facts. Hardly anyone today will deny that, in the field of education and with respect to the historico-critical method in modern science, anachronisms existed that corresponded closely to this adherence to an obsolete Church-state relationship. Only a careful investigation of the different ways in which acceptance of the new era was accomplished in various parts of the Church could unravel the complicated network of causes that formed the background of the "Pastoral Constitution", and only thus can the dramatic history of its influence be brought to light.

Let us be content to say here that the text serves as a countersyllabus and, as such, represents, on the part of the Church, an attempt at an official reconciliation with the new era inaugurated in 1789. Only from this perspective can we understand, on the one hand, its ghetto-mentality, of which we have spoken above; only from this perspective can we understand, on the other hand, the meaning of this remarkable meeting of Church and world. Basically, the word "world" means the spirit of the modern era, in contrast to which the Church's group-consciousness saw itself as a separate subject that now, after a war that had been in turn both hot and cold, was intent on dialogue and cooperation. From this perspective, too, we can understand the different emphases with which the individual parts of the Church entered into the discussion of the text. While German theologians were satisfied that their exegetical and ecumenical concepts had been incorporated, representatives of Latin countries, in particular, felt that their concerns, too, had been addressed; topics proposed by Anglo-Saxon theologians likewise found strong expression, and representatives of Third World countries saw, in the emphasis on social questions, a consideration of their particular problems.

II. *Later developments*

1. Euphoria of the beginning

What has since happened to all of this? It is possible, I think, to distinguish three phases in the history of the influence exerted by the text in the first decade after the Council. At first, there was a period of beginning, marked by the euphoria of reform; we might designate as its high points the second general conference of Latin American bishops that was held in Medellin in 1968 and the appearance of the *Dutch Catechism* in 1966. But the founding of the periodical *Concilium* (1965) and the appearance of the lexicon *Sacramentum Mundi* (since 1967) in the same languages in which *Concilium* is published also belong here. In German-speaking countries, an important event of this era was the publication of *Publik*.

Concilium was the first clear sign of a new way. Appearing simultaneously in seven languages and supported by an editorial staff scattered throughout the world, it expressed the new *Internationale* of progress that owed its existence to the Council. The spirit of the Council was to find in this publication a permanent organ for the perpetuation of its influence. Both its title and its internal organization were to be evidence of its intention of preserving and developing the conciliarity of the church and of thus bringing to fruition the new recognition accorded to the body of theologians. It was the discovery that this universal impulse to enter into the modern age existed all over the world and that only such a worldwide association could give power to the thought of the theologians that brought the editorial staff together; they wanted to be, as it were, a permanent council of theologians that would increasingly realize the promise of this beginning in a constant exchange with all the vital forces of the present. If conciliarity as the new form of Catholicity meant to internationalize national tendencies, this automatically implied that from now on the tendencies of the varied particular churches would also have a determinative impact and that it could no longer be expected that the direction would be set by a single central source. The peak of the development was quickly transferred, on the one hand, to the Netherlands, on the other, to Latin America.

There were, of course, considerable differences between these two peaks of progressivism. In the Netherlands, liturgical and ecumenical matters were in the foreground. Liturgical reform very quickly exceeded official limits; ecumenical zeal could no longer be restrained within established bounds. It should, nevertheless, be added that the climate, as it were, of the whole process bore the decisive mark of *Gaudium et spes*. The feeling that, in reality, there were no longer any walls between Church and world, that every "dualism": body-soul, Church-world, grace-nature and, in the last analysis, even God-world, was evil—this feeling became more and more a force that gave direction to the whole. In such a rejection of all "dualism", the optimistic mood that seemed actually to have been canonized by the words *Gaudium et spes* was heightened into the certainty of attaining perfect unity with the present world and so into a transport of adaptation that had sooner or later to be followed by disenchantment.

Latin America followed a very different course. Even more directly than in the Netherlands, *Gaudium et spes* left its mark on postconciliar development. During the years of the Council, the bishops of this subcontinent had achieved organizational unity in the form of a Latin American Council of Bishops, the CELAM. The moving power of this union was, above all, the awareness of social responsibility for a continent that, even after its political liberation from the colonial domination of the Iberian powers, still lived in oppressive dependence—this time, on the Anglo Saxon economy first of England, then of the United States. The cry of the poor that made itself heard there had a direct and particularly profound impact on the Catholic bishops because there was question here of a continent that is, at least statistically, almost totally Catholic, a continent that contains most of the world's Catholics. That precisely this Catholic continent should be one of the poorest became, in the historical awakening of the Council, a challenge that could no longer remain unanswered. Consequently, the first extraordinary assembly of the Latin American Bishops' Council, in Mar del Plata in 1966, had as its central theme the social and economic problem, which, in line with the thinking of the Council, it addressed from the perspective of "reform", that is, according to the Western concept of building up by means of development.[18] The second CELAM conference, held in Medellin in 1968, found itself in a new climate. From the encyclical *Populorum progressio,* which appeared in 1967, and from the manifesto signed in 1967 by fifteen bishops of the Third World, they had received a new theme: "liberation".[19] With this was introduced a second and fateful stage in the reception of the influence of *Gaudium et spes.* The drama of Camillo Torres, the guerilla priest with the name of one of the liberators from Spanish dominion, who was killed in February 1966, acquired increasingly historical dimensions.[20] The period of optimistic agreement with the modern spirit, with its progress and with its offer of development for underdeveloped countries, came almost abruptly to an end. For A. García Rubio, the advent of the theology of liberation meant, at the same time, the crisis of the modern world. Latin America can find no promise of help for its problems in enlightened progress. On the contrary, it sees therein precisely the reason for its misery. Its goal cannot be to become "modern" but to overcome "the modern spirit and the modern dialectic, the fullest expression of which is to be found in Hegel. Marxist dialectic must also be overcome. . . ."[21] This is—

[18] Cf. A. García-Rubio, "Die lateinamerikanische Theologie der Befreiung, I", in IKZ 2/73: 400–423; quotation is on 406–7. See also, Roger Vekemans, "Die lateinamerikanische Theologie der Befreiung. Ein Literaturbericht, II", in ibid., 434–48.

[19] García-Rubio, 407ff.; Vekemans, 439–40.

[20] Emil L. Stehle provides brief and accurate information about Camillo Torres in *Indio-Latein Amerika* (Düsseldorf-Oberhausen, 1971), 133–41.

[21] García-Rubio, 422.

and from the Latin American perspective, with full right—exactly the opposite of the direction taken by *Gaudium et spes* and, especially, by its postconciliar acceptance in the Netherlands. The problem of Latin America was and is, in fact, not reconciliation with the spirit of the modern era, identification with the ideology of Western Europe and the United States. If, for the Church in Europe, such a reconciliation might appear to be a return home from the ghetto, a solution of old problems about the relationship of Church and state and, in consequence, the healing of a trauma, that was and is not true of Latin America. Granted, the French Revolution had provided the opportunity of liberation from the Iberian powers; but immediately afterward the spirit of liberalism and capitalism fostered by the Anglo Saxon powers had become an even more painful slavery, for these only apparently liberated countries, which, as a result, could certainly not find their identity in this spirit or regard it as their "return home". By a kind of inner necessity, therefore, the optimism of the countersyllabus gave way to a new cry that was far more intense and more dramatic than the former one.

Thus the intellectual cohesion of the *Concilium*-front was likewise called into question—indeed, its very foundation, namely, union in the spirit of the modern era, was shown to be flawed. In view of these circumstances, it seemed only logical that progressive Latin Americans should level sharp criticism precisely against the representatives of progressive European and North American thought. Hans Küng was accused of a shockingly reactionary political attitude and of being blind to the practical dimensions of the problem.[22] The theology of secularization was criticized for its lack of clarity and its political naiveté.[23] Rahner and Congar were accused of naiveté in the orientation of their thought;[24] even the European and American theologians who advocated revolution and violence were not spared.[25] Hugo Assmann, one of the principal spokesmen of Latin America, expressed his agreement with Père Le Guillou, who spoke of charlatanism in reference to the events in France in May 1968.[26] In view of all this, Latin America sought its own way under the slogan of "liberation", in which there appeared a new distinctive element of the influence of *Gaudium et spes*: insistence on a theology proper to Latin America—an idea that soon found resonance on the other side of the Atlantic in the call for an African theology. As we know, the Catholic University of Santiago in Chile became the center for such experiments in

[22] H. Assmann, in Vekemans, 438.
[23] Ibid.
[24] Ibid., 442.
[25] Ibid., 443ff.
[26] Ibid., 443.

a new orientation of thought; as we know also, it was precisely there that the crisis of what had thus been begun was heightened into tragic realism.[27]

2. Disenchantment and crisis

With the reference to the shift in Latin American thought as contrasted with the euphoria with which the Church in the West had greeted the modern spirit, the end of the first phase of the history of the influence of the "Pastoral Constitution on the Church in the Modern World" was likewise indicated. García Rubio expresses the change in this way: "The initial optimism quickly gave way to an increasing pessimism about the extent to which this theology was capable of shedding light on the fundamental reality of Latin America."[28] From a global perspective it must be admitted that the years of euphoria were followed by a period of disenchantment and crisis. I can recount here only a few evidences of this many-leveled process. In this connection the fate of the *Dutch Catechism* and the course of the Dutch Church as a whole must be mentioned first. The corrections introduced into the text by Rome did not succeed in lessening the certainty and unity of the conscience of the postconciliar Church in Europe with regard to progress but rather, by the resultant heightening of anti-Roman sentiment, made her even more determined. It was not the criticism from Rome that so quickly extinguished the meteoric brilliance of this book but the internal development of Church and theology in the Netherlands, which soon outstripped the stage of friendly confidence that was mirrored in the Catechism. The urge to develop led now to radicalization, in the light of which what had been considered progressive yesterday was judged today to be incredibly reactionary. The Catechism was denounced in the land of its origin as an expression of bourgeois Christianity; it was accused, for instance, of speaking not only mythologically but even mythically, that is, of not just interpreting human existence but of ascribing to faith a reality proper to it: "We cannot rid ourselves of the impression that, according to these texts, there is supposed to exist somewhere a reality proper to faith alongside the

---

[27] On this subject, cf. the report written on the eve of the Chilean revolution by M. Arias Reyero, "Theologie in Chile heute", in IKZ 2 (1973): 449–57. For an instructive discussion of the development of that time and the motives therefore, see especially Sergio Silva, *Glaube und Politik: Herausforderung Lateinamerikas. Von der christlich inspirierten Partei zur Theologie der Befreiung* (Bern: Herbert Lang, 1973). A cross section of works characteristic of the more recent Latin American theology can now be found in two volumes edited by Equipo Seladoc, *Panorama de la teología Latinoamericana* 1 and 2 (Salamanca: Ediciones Sigueme, 1975).

[28] García-Rubio, 409.

ordinary reality of daily life."[29] T. van der Berk, the author of these words, adds: "There is a 'Roman reality' and a 'Roman language'. Where the Catechism adheres to the former, it is at once apparent in the language."[30] For such a "theology", the reality of faith has become a Roman reality—what an unintended *laus Romae* in a dark hour! When progress causes faith to be regarded as but an anachronistic facet of Church policy, it has undoubtedly achieved its goal: the suppression of dualism, identification with the world; but its meeting with the modern world occurs too late to enable it to share in the relative innocence that world once possessed and in its early hopes. When the modern era is no longer seen from the unreal perspective of the ghetto but is experienced in its naked reality, it is obvious that it knows it has come to an end and is struggling in despair against its own lack of orientation.

If Latin America was the first, because of its historical unfamiliarity with the European and Anglo Saxon phenomenon of the "modern era", to break away from the concept of reform by evolution that characterized the end of the Council and the early postconciliar era, the new development was not long in making itself felt in Europe as well. The most sensitive breeding ground, and those in which the new tendency most quickly became known, were, understandably enough, the student centers in which the collapse of the liberal and conservative mentality of postwar Western Europe was brought about with elemental violence. Countercurrents were at work here which are difficult to assess; after the period of reconstruction occurred a mutual interaction of politico-economic changes, psychological changes deriving from the attainment of spiritual responsibility by a generation that had had no experience of war and radical changes in the religious consciousness of both Catholics and Protestants.[31] Characteristic of the whole situation was the fact that the turning, with a kind of rapturous fervor, to a Marxism that was at once anarchical and utopian not only bore within itself a religious pathos but was also supported primarily by student chaplains and student groups, who saw in it the dawning of a fulfillment of Christian hopes. The most outstanding event was that which occurred in France in May 1968. Dominicans and Jesuits stood on the barricades; the interdenominational communion that took place during the ecumenical Mass celebrated on the barricades was long regarded as a kind of salvation-historical event, as a revelation-event

---

[29] T. van den Berk, "Über den Sprachgebrauch des Holländischen Katechismus", in *Concilium* 6 (1970): 188–91; quotation is on 190.

[30] Ibid.

[31] I have attempted a more detailed analysis of these relationships in my book *Dogma und Verkündigung*, 439–47.

that introduced a new era of Christianity.[32] Naïve affirmation of the world
had turned into a radical battle cry not only against the modern era but
against the establishment per se. Such a militant attitude aroused new enthusiasm in young persons who thought they had found in it once again
the élan of Christianity, who perceived its revolutionary force and who, at
the same time, experienced Christianity as a promise, a potential for what
was different, what was better, and hence as a new challenge. When we
know the background, we can understand, to some extent, why the
KDSE [Katholische Deutsche Studenten Einigung: German Catholic Student Union], which was founded by the bishops after the war as an
umbrella organization of all Catholic student associations, became an
ideological center that assigned itself the brave task of becoming "the condition that would make possible a new Church" in which the Christian
concepts of liberation, service and communion would be impregnated
with new Marxist realism.

I regard as the third indication the Congress organized by the editors of
Concilium in Brussels in 1970 to mark the fifth anniversary of the founding
of their periodical. The meeting was obviously intended as an antithesis to
the congress of theologians initiated by the Pope and supported by
innumerable cardinals, archbishops and bishops that was held in Rome in
1966 and by means of which Rome had attempted to keep the newly
awakened power of theology in consonance with the hierarchy; but also
evident was a certain unmistakable antithesis to the International Ponti-
fical Commission of Theologians founded in 1969. *Concilium* sought to
establish itself, on the model of the ancient rights of the Sorbonne, as the
true center of teaching and teachers in the Church, to become the real
rallying-place of theologians from all over the world. But Brussels became, in fact, a turning point after which the authority of that union for
progress began to crack. The great scholars associated with *Concilium*—
Rahner, Congar, Schillebeeckx, Küng—were not as united as they had
thought. Participants were often offended by the manner in which they
were obliged to associate themselves with statements in the preparation of
which they had had no share. They could no longer remain oblivious of a
fact of which many of them had previously been unaware: that "progress"
no longer represented a unified concept and that, in many particulars, it
was perilously close to dissociating itself from the core of Christian tradition.

In the public consciousness of the Church in Germany, the demise of
Publik became, ultimately, the event that marked the end of these
developments. Anyone who reads the passionate comments of that time

---

[32] Cf. the critical analysis by M.-J. Le Guillou, Olivier Clement, Jean Bosc, *Évangile et
révolution. Au coeur de notre crise spirituelle* (Paris: Éditions du Centurion, 1968).

cannot help wondering why the end of a publication that had not yet made its mark could cause such a breach in the history of salvation, could be a "return to the ghetto". In fact, however, the failure of the attempt begun with such high aspirations meant the farewell to an illusion that had found there the sign of its own reality. For the leaders of postconciliar progressivism, *Publik* had become the place where Church and world united, where the trauma of the ghetto was overcome. But—the world did not accept it. *Publik* never ceased to be an unreal world created by intellectuals.

Only since that time has it become generally clear to the Church that progress no longer represents a unified force and that it is no longer possible to act in terms of the simple options offered by the Council. During the Council, the majority of bishops and theologians had shared a mutual concern to combat what was obsolete and to teach the courageous acceptance of the new as a duty for the Church of today. Since then it seems to be generally accepted that, to be in the right, one has only to affirm the new and reject the old. Anyone who objected, as Hans Urs von Balthasar was alone in doing,[33] that the program of the Council was not so easily realizable was counted among those who had not read the signs of the time. Only when the ruins of false hopes came crashing down was certainty shattered and new questions raised.

3. Present state of the question

It is perhaps too soon to say that for some time now the era of crisis has been changing into an era of consolidation. Let us ask, first, what we are to think of what has taken place thus far. The summary I have presented in a few short pages seems to suggest a negative diagnosis. Is anything left but the heaped-up ruins of unsuccessful experiments? Has *Gaudium et spes* been definitively translated into *luctus et angor*?[34] Was the Council a wrong road that we must now retrace if we are to save the Church? The voices of those who say that it was are becoming louder and their followers more numerous. Among the more obvious phenomena of the last years must be counted the increasing number of integralist groups in which the desire for piety, for the sense of the mystery, is finding satisfaction. We must be on our guard against minimizing these movements. Without a doubt, they represent a sectarian zealotry that is the antithesis of Catholicity. We can-

---

[33] Two programmatic texts published during the early postconciliar period might be mentioned here: *Wer ist ein Christ?* (Einsiedeln, 1965) and *Cordula oder der Ernstfall* (1966).

[34] In the conciliar text, "luctus et angor" (grief and anguish) are the words that immediately follow the introductory words "Gaudium et spes".

not resist them too firmly. But we must likewise ask ourselves, in all earnestness, why such contractions and distortions of faith and piety have
such an effect and are able to attract those who, by the basic conviction of
their faith as well as by personal inclination, are in no way attracted by
sectarianism. What drives them into a milieu in which they do not belong?
Why have they lost the feeling of being at home in the larger Church? Are
all their reproaches unfounded? Is it not, for example, really strange that
we have never heard bishops react as strongly against distortions in the
heart of the liturgy as they react today against the use of a Missal of the
Church that, after all, has been in existence since the time of Pius V? Let it
be said again: we should not adopt a sectarian attitude, but neither should
we omit the examination of conscience to which these facts compel us.

What shall I say? First of all, one thing seems to me to have become
abundantly clear in the course of these ten years. An interpretation of the
Council that understands its dogmatic texts as mere preludes to a still
unattained conciliar spirit, that regards the whole as just a preparation for
Gaudium et spes and that looks upon the latter text as just the beginning of
an unswerving course toward an ever greater union with what is called
progress—such an interpretation is not only contrary to what the Council
Fathers intended and meant, it has been reduced *ad absurdum* by the course
of events. Where the spirit of the Council is turned against the word of the
Council and is vaguely regarded as a distillation from the development
that evolved from the "Pastoral Constitution", this spirit becomes a
specter and leads to meaninglessness. The upheavals caused by such a
concept are so obvious that their existence cannot be seriously disputed. In
like manner, it has become clear that the world, in its modern form, is far
from being a unified entity. Let it be said once for all: the progress of the
Church cannot consist in a belated embrace of the modern world—the
theology of Latin America has made that all too clear to us and has
demonstrated thereby the rightness of its cry for liberation. If our criticism
of the events of the decade after the Council has guided us to these insights,
if it has brought us to the realization that we must interpret Vatican
Council II as a whole and that our interpretation must be oriented toward
the central theological texts, then our reflections could become fruitful for
the whole Church and could help her to unite in sensible reform. The
"Constitution on the Church" is not to be evaluated in terms of the
"Pastoral Constitution", and certainly not in terms of an isolated reading
of the intention expressed in the prefatory paragraphs, but vice versa: only
the whole in its proper orientation is truly the spirit of the Council.

Does this mean that the Council itself must be revoked? Certainly not. It
means only that the real reception of the Council has not yet even begun.
What devastated the Church in the decade after the Council was not the

Council but the refusal to accept it. This becomes clear precisely in the history of the influence of *Gaudium et spes*. What was identified with the Council was, for the most part, the expression of an attitude that did not coincide with the statements to be found in the text itself, although it is recognizable as a tendency in its development and in some of its individual formulations. The task is not, therefore, to suppress the Council but to discover the real Council and to deepen its true intention in the light of present experience. That means that there can be no return to the *Syllabus*, which may have marked the first stage in the confrontation with liberalism and a newly conceived Marxism but cannot be the last stage. In the long run, neither embrace nor ghetto can solve for Christians the problem of the modern world. The fact is, as Hans Urs von Balthasar pointed out as early as 1952, that the "demolition of the bastions" is a long-overdue task.

The Church cannot choose the times in which she will live. After Constantine, she was obliged to find a mode of coexistence with the world other than that necessitated by the persecutions of the preceding age. But it bespeaks a foolish romanticism to bemoan the change that occurred with Constantine while we ourselves fall at the feet of the world from which we profess our desire to liberate the Church. The struggle between *imperium* and *sacerdotium* in the Middle Ages, the dispute about the "enlightened" concept of state churches at the beginning of the modern age, were attempts to come to terms with the difficult problems created in its various epochs by a world that had become Christian. In an age of the secular state and of Marxist messianism, in an age of worldwide economic and social problems, in an age when the world is dominated by science, the Church, too, faces anew the question of her relationship with the world and its needs. She must relinquish many of the things that have hitherto spelled security for her and that she has taken for granted. She must demolish longstanding bastions and trust solely to the shield of faith. But the demolition of bastions cannot mean that she no longer has anything to defend or that she can live by forces other than those that brought her forth: the blood and water from the pierced side of the crucified Lord (Jn 19:31–37). "In the world you will have trouble, but be brave: I have conquered the world" (Jn 16:33). That is true today, too.

The prospect—a parable

With some hesitation, I shall attempt, by way of conclusion, to portray the drama of the first post-conciliar decade with its opening scene and its climax in a parable that, in view of the harshness of our experiences, may seem to be a highly inappropriate flight into the realm of fancy.

Nevertheless, despite the inadequacy and the questionable applicability inherent in every comparison, this parable does not seem to me to be so very far removed from our own experiences. I refer to what was, perhaps, the most perfect literary expression of the drama of the end of the Middle Ages and the beginning of the modern age—written by an author who knew himself to be more experienced in suffering than in song: Miguel de Cervantes.[35] His *Don Quixote* begins as a farce, a crude mockery that is far from being a work of the imagination or a piece of light literature. The humorous auto-da-fé in the sixth chapter, in which the pastor and the barber burn the books of the unfortunate knight, is a very authentic gesture: the world of the Middle Ages is cast out, the door is barred against its reentry; it belongs now irrevocably to the past. In the person of Don Quixote, a new age mocks the old one. The knight becomes a fool; awakened from the dreams of yesteryear, a new generation faces reality without disguise and without adornment. In the lighthearted ridicule of the first chapter, there is reflected something of the change, of the self-assurance, of a new age that has forgotten its dreams, has discovered reality and is proud of having done so. But, as the novel progresses, something strange happens to the author. He begins gradually to love his foolish knight. This cannot, certainly, be explained simply by the fact that he was offended by the mockery of a literary thief who turned his noble fool into a lowly clown, although it may well have been the figure of the false Don Quixote that first made him fully aware that his fool had a noble soul; that the foolishness of consecrating his life to the protection of the weak and the defense of truth and right had its own greatness. Behind the foolishness, Cervantes discovers the simplicity. "He can do evil to no one but rather does good to everyone, and there is no guile in him."[36] What a noble foolishness Don Quixote chooses as his vocation: "To be pure in his thoughts, modest in his words, sincere in his actions, patient in adversity, merciful toward those in need and, finally, a crusader for truth even if the defense of it should cost him his life."[37] The foolish deeds have become a lovable game behind which may be seen the purity of his heart—indeed, the center of his foolishness, as we are now aware, is identical with the strangeness of the good in a world whose realism has nothing but scorn for one who accepts truth as reality and risks his life for it. The arrogant certainty with which Cervantes burned his bridges behind him and laughed at an earlier age has become a nostalgia for what was lost. This is

[35] For the quotations from Don Quixote, I have used the German translation by Ludwig Braunfels in the edition published by the Deutsches Bücherbund (Stuttgart-Hamburg, n.d.); quotation is on 61.

[36] Ibid., 637.

[37] Ibid., 678.

not a return to the world of the romances of chivalry but a consciousness of what must not be lost and a realization of man's peril, which increases whenever, in the burning of the past, he loses the totality of himself.

Did we not also have, in the ten years after *Gaudium et spes*, experiences that, despite the differences of level, were not entirely unlike those that lie behind the metamorphosis of Don Quixote? We started out boldly and full of confidence in ourselves; there may have been, in thought and, perhaps, also in reality, many an auto-da-fé of scholarly books that seemed to us to be foolish novels of chivalry that led us only into the land of dreams and made us see dangerous giants in the beneficial effects of technology, in the vanes of its windmills. Boldly and certain of victory, we barricaded the door of a time that was past and proclaimed the abrogation and annihilation of all that lay behind it. In conciliar and postconciliar literature, there is abundant evidence of the ridicule with which, like pupils ready for graduation, we bade farewell to our outmoded schoolbooks. In the meantime, however, our ears and our souls have been pierced by a different kind of ridicule that mocks more than we had wanted or wished. Gradually we have stopped laughing; gradually we have become aware that behind the closed doors are concealed those things that we must not lose if we do not want to lose our souls as well. Certainly we cannot return to the past, nor have we any desire to do so. But we must be ready to reflect anew on that which, in the lapse of time, has remained the one constant. To seek it without distraction and to dare to accept, with joyful heart and without diminution, the foolishness of truth—this, I think, is the task for today and for tomorrow: the true nucleus of the Church's service to the world, *her* answer to "the joy and hope, the grief and anguish of the men of our time" (*Gaudium et spes,* 903).

ACKNOWLEDGMENTS

PART ONE

Chapter 1, 1A. "Was ist für den christlichen Glauben heute konstitutiv?": in H. Rossmann, J. Ratzinger, *Mysterium der Gnade. Festschrift für J. Auer* (Regensburg, 1975), 11–19.

Chapter 1, 1B. "Taufe, Glaube und Zugehörigkeit zur Kirche—die Einheit von Struktur und Gehalt": published under the title "Taufe, Glaube und Zugehörigkeit zur Kirche", in *Internationale katholische Zeitscheift Communio* 5 (1976): 218–34. French translation in *Communio* 1 (1976): 9–21. English translation (excerpts) in *Theology Digest* 25 (1977): 126–31. Spanish translation in *Selecciones de teología* 16 (1977): 237–48.

Chapter 1, 1C. "Die Kirche als Heilssakrament": in J. Reikerstorfer, *Zeit des Geistes. Zur heilsgeschichtlichen Herkunft der Kirche* (Vienna, 1977), 59–70.

Chapter 1, 2A. "Glaube als Umkehr—Metanoia": published under the title "Metanoia als Grundbefindlichkeit christlicher Existenz", in E. Chr. Suttner, *Busse und Beichte, Drittes Regensburger Ökumenisches Symposium* (Regensburg, 1972), 21–37.

Chapter 1, 2B. "Glaube als Erkenntnis und als Praxis—die Grundoption des christlichen Credo": published under the title "Ich glaube an Gott den allmächtigen Vater", in *Internationale katholische Zeitschrift Communio* 4 (1975): 10–18; also in W. Sandfuchs, *Ich glaube* (Würzburg, 1975), 13–24. Italian translation in *Strumento internazionale per un lavoro teologico: Communio* 4 (1975). Spanish translation (abridged) in *Selecciones de teología* 15 (1976, no. 59): 254–59. French translation: *Je crois. Explication du symbole des apôtres* (Paris, 1978), 7–20. Revised in W. Sandfuchs, *Brückenbau im Glauben* (Leipzig, 1979), 17–29.

Chapter 1, 2C. "Glaube als Vertrauen und Freude—Evangelium": published under the title "Ist Glaube wirklich 'frohe Botschaft'?", in H. Boelaars, R. Tremblay, eds., *In libertatem vocati estis. Miscellanea B. Häring* (Studia Moralia XV, Rome, 1977), 523–33 and in Italian translation: *Chiamati alla libertà* (Rome, 1980), 149–61.

Chapter 2, 1A. "Anthropologische Grundlegung des Begriffs Überlieferung": published under the title "Tradition und Fortschritt", in *ibw-Journal* 12 (1974): 1–7; also in A. Paus, *Freiheit des Menschen* (Graz, 1974), 9–30. Reprinted in: *Theol. Jb. 1979,* ed. Ernst, Feiereis, Hübner, Reindl (Leipzig), 189–203.

Chapter 2, 1B. "Taufe und Formulierung des Glaubens—Traditions-bildung und Liturgie": published under the title "Taufe und Formulierung des Glaubens", in *Didaskalia* 2 (1972): 23–34; also in *Ephemerides theologicae Lovanienses* 49 (1973): 76–86.

Chapter 2, 1C. "Das Credo von Nikaia und Konstantinopel: Geschichte, Struktur und Gehalt": published under the title "Das I. Konzil von Konstantinopel 381", in *Internationale katholische Zeitschrift Communio* 10 (1981).

Chapter 2, 1D. "Kurzformeln des Glaubens? Über das Verhältnis von Formel und Auslegung mit einem Anhang über Wandelbares und Unwandelbares in der Kirche": published under the title "Noch einmal: 'Kurzformeln des Glaubens' ", in *Internationale katholische Zeitschrift Communio* 2 (1973): 258–64. Appendix in: *Internationale katholische Zeitschrift Communio* 7 (1978): 182ff.

Chapter 2, 1E. "Die Bedeutung der Väter im Aufbau des Glaubens": published under the title "Die Bedeutung der Väter für die gegenwärtige Theologie", in *ThQu* 148 (1968): 257–82; reprint in Κληρονομία 1 (1969): 15–38; Spanish translation (excerpts) in *Selecciones de teología* 31 (1969): 265–72. Published with discussion in Th. Michels, *Geschichtlichkeit der Theologie* (Salzburg–Munich, 1970), 63–81; discussion, 81–95.

Chapter 2, 2A. "Heil und Geschichte": in *Wort und Wahrheit* 25 (1970): 3–14. Excerpts in *Selecciones de teología* 40 (1971): 314–22. Published under the title "Heil und Geschichte. Gesichtspunkte zur gegenwärtigen theologischen Diskussion des Problems der 'Heilsgeschichte' ", in Regensburger *Universitätszeitung* 5 (1969): Heft 11, 2–7. Extensively revised for the present work.

Chapter 2, 2B. "Heilsgeschichte, Metaphysik und Eschatologie": published under the title "Heilsgeschichte und Eschatologie. Zur Frage nach dem Ansatz des theologischen Denkens", in *Theologie im Wandel* (Festschrift zum 150-jährigen Bestehen der Katholisch-Theologischen Fakultät an der Universität Tübingen. 1817–1967), ed. J. Neumann and J. Ratzinger (Munich–Freiburg, 1967), 68–89. Reprinted in A. Dänhardt, ed., *Theologisches Jahrbuch* (Leipzig, 1970), 56–73.

PART TWO

Chapter 1A. "Die ökumenische Situation—Orthodoxie, Katholizismus und Reformation": Published under the title "Prognosen für die Zukunft des Ökumenismus", in *Bausteine für die Einheit der Christen* 17, Heft 65 (1977): 6–14. French translation in *Proche Orient Chrétien*,

Jerusalem 26 (1976): 209–19; in German, in *Ökumenisches Forum,* Grazer Hefte für konkrete Ökumene 1 (1977): 31–41. English translation (excerpts) in *Theology Digest* 25 (1977): 200–205. Reprint in German, in *Pro oriente, Ökumene—Konzil—Unfehlbarkeit* (Innsbruck, 1979), 208–15.

Chapter 1B. "Rom und die Kirchen des Ostens nach der Aufhebung der Exkommunikationen von 1054": published under the title "Das Ende der Bannflüche von 1054. Folgen für Rom und die Ostkirchen", in *Internationale katholische Zeitschrift Communio* 3 (1974): 289–303; also in *Pro oriente. Auf dem Weg zur Einheit des Glaubens* (Innsbruck–Munich, 1976), 101–13. French translation in *Istina* (1975), 87–99.

Chapter 1C. "Klarstellungen zur Frage der 'Anerkennung' der Confessio Augustana durch die katholische Kirche": published under the title "Anmerkungen zur Frage einer 'Anerkennung' der Confessio Augustana durch die katholische Kirche", in *Münchener Theologische Zeitschrift* 29 (1978): 225–37.

Chapter 1D. "Ökumene in der Sackgasse? Anmerkungen zur Erklärung 'Mysterium ecclesiae' (June 24, 1973)": published under the title "Ökumenisches Dilemma? Zur Diskussion um die Erklärung 'Mysterium Ecclesiae' ", in *Internationale katholische Zeitschrift Communio* 3 (1974): 56–63. Reprinted in *L'Osservatore Romano, Wochenausgabe in deutscher Sprache* 4: 33 (August 16, 1974), 6ff.

Chapter 2A. "Das Weihesakrament (Ordo) als sakramentaler Ausdruck des Prinzips Überlieferung": published under the title "Die kirchliche Lehre vom sacramentum ordinis", in *Pluralisme et Oecuménisme en Recherches Théologiques. Mélanges offerts au R. P. Dockx, O.P* (Bibliotheca Ephemeridum Theologicarum Lovaniensium XLIII, Paris, 1976), 155–66; also in: *Internationale katholische Zeitscheift Communio* 10 (1981): 435–45.

Chapter 2B. "Opfer, Sakrament und Priestertum in der Entwicklung der Kirche": in: *Catholica* 26 (1972): 108–25. English translation (excerpts) in *Theology Digest* 21 (1973): 100–105.

Chapter 2C. "Der Priester als Mittler und Diener Jesu Christi im Licht der neutestamentlichen Botschaft": published under the title "Der Priester als Mittler und Diener Christi", in P. Mai, *100 Jahre Priesterseminar in St. Jakob zu Regensburg 1872–1972* (Regensburg, 1972), 53–68.

Chapter 3A. "Recht der Gemeinde auf Eucharistie? Die 'Gemeinde' und die Katholizität der Kirche": not previously published.

Chapter 3B. "Ökumene am Ort": in *Catholica* 27 (1973): 152–65. Published under the title "Die Bedeutung der Ökumene am Ort", in *L'Osservatore Romano, Wochenausgabe in deutscher Sprache,* 2:49 (December 8, 1972), 8–10.

PART THREE

Chapter 1A. "Was ist Theologie?": in *Internationale katholische Zeitschrift Communio* 8 (1979): 121–28. French translation in H. Volk, *La Foi comme adhésion* (Paris–Namur, n.d. [1980]), 149–68.

Chapter 1B. "Kirche und wissenschaftliche Theologie": in W. Sandfuchs, ed., *Die Kirche* (Würzburg, 1978), 83–95. English translation in *Communio. International Catholic Review* 7 (1980): 332–42.

Chapter 2A. "Glaube und Bildung": published under the title "Bildung und Glaube in unserer Zeit. Drei Thesen zur christlichen Bildung", in *ibw-Journal* 13 (1975): 113–16.

Chapter 2B. "Glaube und Erfahrung": published under the title "Erfahrung und Glaube. Theologische Bemerkungen zur katechetischen Dimension des Themas", in *Internationale katholische Zeitschrift Communio* 9 (1980): 58–70.

Chapter 2C. "Die Gabe der Weisheit": in W. Sandfuchs, *Die Gaben des Geistes. Acht Betrachtungen* (Würzburg, 1977), 35–48.

EPILOGUE

Section A. "Bilanz der Nachkonzilszeit—Misserfolge, Aufgaben, Hoffnungen": private circulation only.

Section B. "Kirche und Welt: Zur Frage nach der Rezeption des II. Vatikanischen Konzils": published under the title "Der Weltdienst der Kirche. Auswirkungen von 'Gaudium et spes' in letzten Jahrzehnt", in *Internationale katholischen Zeitschrift Communio* 4 (1975): 439–54. Reprint in A. Bauch, A. Glässer, M. Seybold, *Zehn Jahre Vaticanum II* (Regensburg, 1976), 36–53.